BACK TO BASICS

GOD, FAMILY AND COUNTRY

By

David M. Church

The Tennessee Publishing House
496 Mountain View Drive
Mosheim, Tennessee 37818-3524

BACK TO BASICS

GOD, FAMILY AND COUNTRY

By

David M. Church

Published in the United States
By
The Tennessee Publishing House
Mosheim, Tennessee March 2011
First Edition, First Printing

Cover Design: Kellie Warren-Underwood

Disclaimer:

This document is an original work of the author. It may include reference to information commonly known or freely available to the general public. Any resemblance to other published information is purely coincidental. The author has in no way attempted to use material not of his own original unless such information has been cited, documented or given some other properly recognized written form of credit for such work The Tennessee Publishing House disclaims any association with or responsibility for the ideas, opinions or facts as expressed by the author of this book.

Any biblical scriptures used are taken from either the English Standard Version of the Holy Bible. The New International Version Study Bible. Copyright 1995 by the Zondervan Corporation,

**Printed in the Unites States of America
Cataloging-in-Publication
ISBN: 978-1-58275-250-1 Paperback
Copyright March 2011 by David M. Church**

ALL RIGHTS RESERVED

TABLE OF CONTENTS

Foreword   i

Chapter One
America's Christian Heritage   1

Chapter Two
God's Footprint in the American Culture   37

Chapter Three
Wiping Away God's Footprint   85

Chapter Four
Revaluing the Family   121

Chapter Five
Respect for Parenthood Redux   155

Chapter Six
The Nuclear Family versus the Homosexual Agenda   185

Chapter Seven
Love of Country   209

Chapter Eight
The American People Want Leadership   253

Chapter Nine
The Dangers of Political Correctness   283

Notes   332

DEDICATION

This is dedicated to all those Americans who are unseen and unheard but still believe that we are one nation under God; that the family is the brick of society; and that the United States is a blessed nation.

FOREWORD

Like many other average Americans, David Church has found himself asking, "Are America's best days over with?" With each passing day, America seems to move farther away from its fundamental building blocks that have made her great since her birth. Those rudiments revolve around the themes of God, family, and country. America's exceptionalism seems to be fading away just as the themes of God, family, and country continue to lose their prominence in American culture.

Although the United States was founded on Judeo-Christian principles, one would not think so today as there seems be a cover-up of the Christian blueprints that have made our nation great and eventually evolving her into a global superpower. David reintroduces the reader to our Christian heritage and illustrates how God's footprint was involved in the founding and establishment of the United States of America. Moreover, David illustrates how our Founding Fathers established a precedent of reverence for God for future generations of Americans to follow. Throughout our history, many of our leaders have shared this same sentiment as our Founding Fathers; however, that does not seem to have stalled the increasingly defiant anti-God forces from removing acknowledgments, images, references, or symbols of Christianity from American society.

Next to reverence for God, the institution of family has contributed to a stable America throughout our history. There was once a time when family was respected, sought after, and elevated. David points out how the institution of family is being challenged unlike never before as a result of our cultural and social degradation and self-absorbed lifestyles. David encourages the reader to look at the responsibilities of parenthood from a counter-cultural perspective and to embrace it with pride, accountability, and excitement, thus contributing to the future well-being of American society. In taking a stand for family in America, David assumes a bold position against homosexual marriage in an effort to protect the sacred and divine institution of traditional marriage. By presenting some hard truths that align with God's position on family and many other good Americans' attitude on family preservation, David yearns to see respect for family revived among a distracted generation in the United States.

David goes on to remind the reader the good of America despite her shortfalls throughout her short history. While there are many things in the United States to be grateful for and proud of, America suffers from a dearth of patriotism. America is need of an injection of love of country for the long-term. This revival injection entails revisiting the essential principles of leadership in order to encourage our leaders to stay in synch with the will of the American people. When a spirit of connectivity exists between those governing and those being governed, we can expect to see a rise in national pride and love of country. Our history has proven that when the people are empowered versus disempowered, America is at its best. Our love of country will further be energized when we eliminate the runaway political correctness from our culture. David presents two examples where political correctness can be removed in order to reignite a spirit of patriotism in America: the fight against the domestic threat of illegal immigration and the international threat of terrorism.

Despite the grim outlook of the United States as a result of being disoriented from our bedrock themes of God, family, and country, David presents hope for the American people. Just as the United States matured into a blessed and formidable country as a result of her fondness for God, family, and country, America can recover from her economic, social, and cultural depression by orienting on these same bedrock themes that have made us exceptional. America does not have to suffer from a total moral, social, and cultural implosion. As a country, are we willing to return to our faithful roots? If we are willing, America's best days are maintainable.

Lastly, I may add that David Church is one of the finest young writers I have had the privilege to read and do a Foreword for, in several decades. I can only imagine how much better he will get in the years to come. His work is wonderfully researched and documented to the extent of there being no ground left uncovered for the reader. This is a terrific book for many excellent reasons.

> Dahk Knox, Ph.D., Ed.D., D.Sc., Psy.D.
> Author, Publisher, Christian Psychologist
> and Senior Pastor CCHM

CHAPTER ONE
AMERICA'S CHRISTIAN HERITAGE

It all begins with GOD! When God is placed at the core of our daily activities we can expect to reap His divine favor and blessings. What other country in all of history besides the United States (U.S.) has progressed so expediently in such a short timeframe, while it simultaneously abounded with liberties, freedoms, natural resources, prosperity, and so much more? There isn't one.

Above all other countries, the U.S. dominates in the political, military, economic, and cultural spheres of influence. Today the U.S. has global supremacy as its democratic government is active in spreading liberty and freedom across the world especially in less developed regions; its military is recognized as the most powerful; its economic strength is sought by others across the globe; and its culture has a footprint across the international community.

In order to grasp this American dominance, take for example, our economy. The U.S. has a population that makes up approximately only four percent of the world's population, but its gross domestic product (GDP) is about 26 percent of the world's total GDP.[1] In fact, the American economy is larger than the summation of the next four largest economies: Japan, Germany, China, and the United Kingdom.[2] Whether or not America maintains this position is highly debatable in our current economic trials. Willem Buiter, chief economist at Citigroup, predicted "China should overtake the U.S. to become the largest economy in the world by 2020, then be overtaken by India by 2050."[3] Even though we are currently experiencing economic struggles, the U.S. economy has been and is still the largest in the world. The American economy is only one example to illustrate how God has blessed this great country of ours.

WE REAP WHAT WE SOW

Due to the religious drive of our earliest settlers, our Founding Fathers' submission and dependence on God, and our country's subsequent willingness to emphasize God in society, the U.S. has been blessed with divine favor. At his first inaugural address, with his hand on an open Bible, George Washington assertively declared that "every step by which [the people of the United States] have advanced to the character of an independent nation seems to have been distinguished by some token of providential agency."[4] On another occasion, John Adams proclaimed: "As the safety and prosperity of nations ultimately and essentially depend on the protection and the blessing of Almighty God, and the national acknowledgment of this truth is not only an indispensable duty which the people owe to Him..."[5] Similarly, on a separate occasion, James Madison said: "And to the same Divine Author of every good and perfect gift we are indebted for all these privileges and advantages, religious as well as civil, which are so richly enjoyed in this favored land."[6] These quotes from Godly men are much more than antiquated words from antiquated American figureheads, but they are words of wisdom that reflected the hearts and minds of our founders.

In today's society, it appears as if there is more contempt than appreciation for the tutelage of our founders. Despite our nation's remarkable growth and historic progression since its birth, today we are at the brink where we as a people need to examine and query the direction we are heading as a nation. References from our neglected Godly heritage provide a solid compass in which to do so. In order to restore America, we must know our historical truth and building blocks. Why doubt something that is grounded in truth?

Our Founding Fathers knew the role that God played in creating the U.S. and were not craven to acknowledge and promote it in public. Our nation is a great nation not as a result of our political luminaries, our military prowess, economic stability, or cultural superiority, but because we are one nation under one God. Even though our Christian heritage is being threatened each and every day and remnants of anything God-related are being attacked, we are still one nation under God.

One does not have to look far to discern the correlation between submission to God and ensuing divine favor, and at the same time, receive genuine hope for the future- the Bible. The Bible reminds us: *"Blessed is the nation whose God is the LORD, the people he chose for his inheritance."* **Psalm 33:12 (NIV)** The Bible is the trove that has withstood opposition since its infancy and is still applicable to all societies of all cultures throughout the entire world. This is no coincidence especially since books have come and gone over the years. The Bible is still capable of providing us both direction and hope for the future, if we permit it.

As a result of our progressive rebellion against God over the years, an amalgam of unfavorable circumstances continues to deluge the United States, thus diminishing our divine favor and protection. These circumstances include, but not limited to, perennial corruption, perversion, internal and extramural threats to national security, sovereignty, and identity, moral depravity, societal strife, lust, greed, and pride. Some may argue this is just the way society is today, but I contend it is something deeper. Circumstances are bound to change over time, but principles are not supposed to change. President Lincoln acknowledged this divine cause-and-effect relationship in his proclamation appointing a National Fast Day on March 30, 1863. He declared without hesitation:

> "We have been the recipients of the choicest bounties of Heaven. We have been preserved, these many years, in peace and prosperity. We have grown in numbers, wealth and power, as no other nation has ever grown. But we have forgotten God. We have forgotten the gracious hand which preserved us in peace, and multiplied and enriched and strengthened us; and we have vainly imagined, in the deceitfulness of our hearts, that all these blessings were produced by some superior wisdom and virtue of our own. Intoxicated with unbroken success, we have become too self-sufficient to feel the necessity of redeeming

and preserving grace, too proud to pray to the God that made us! It behooves us, then, to humble ourselves before the Offended Power, to confess our national sins, and to pray for clemency and forgiveness."[7]

In his book, *Words That Work,* Dr. Frank Luntz wrote "it is not what you say, it is what people hear" that catches people's attention.[8] I am not sure about you, but I glean and hear nothing but beauty, strength, and inspiration from these simple but potent words. How many of us hunger to hear something akin to President Lincoln's remarks from our leadership today? If you reflect a moment on Lincoln's genuine and poignant words, you would conclude that they are applicable 148 years later. So, why wouldn't we embrace such wisdom from one of our most respected presidents?

This cause-and-effect relationship should be no surprise since the lack of deference for God begets a void and this void must be filled with something. The absence of absolutism invokes people to act or behave in a way that is right in their own perspective, causing the void to be filled with something other than righteousness. In our society today, good is being accepted as evil and evil as good; today everything is backwards. On this earth, there will always be some presence of iniquity, but when a society espouses a supine temperament towards that iniquity, how can it expect to survive? Sooner or later, there will be divine consequences for this iniquity. We have lost our cultural orientation as truth is being ignored for false doctrine and false hope.

In order for us to gauge where we need to go as a society, we must rewind history to see what the basis of our nation is. We must begin by referencing the rudimentary tenets of our heritage. The Word of God warns us of the importance of having historical cognizance: *"For everything that was written in the past was written to teach us, so that through endurance and the encouragement of the Scriptures we might have hope."* **Romans 15:4 (NIV)** If we fail to understand the roots of our heritage, we are prone to lose the true identity of our blessed nation. Just as we desire to learn about our family roots, as a collective society, we should have the same enthusiasm when it comes to learning about our national roots and heritage. All too often we get caught up in the current moment as we delight in the present time while becoming oblivious to our past history. During his farewell address in 1989, President Reagan admonished Americans the danger in neglecting our heritage. His words could not be more fitting today as we collectively live hedonistic and self-indulgent lifestyles. According to President Reagan, "...We've got to teach history based not on what's in fashion but what's important."[9] If we adopt President Reagan's advice, we would have the wisdom and prescience to deal with future events because an appreciation of our heritage would provide a compass off of which to operate from. This philosophy would permit us to fall in line with Winston Churchill's similar perspective on history and heritage: "The farther backward you can look the farther forward you are likely to see."[10]

AMERICA'S CHRISTIAN FOOTPRINT

Unequivocally, Christian principles were the driving force in the founding and subsequent establishment of the United States; therefore, the U.S. is a Christian nation. Now that does not mean that everyone in America is of the Christian faith nor does it mean that a theocracy has been established. What it does mean is that American culture has been largely shaped and formed by Christian values and that it permits freedom of religion by tolerating other religions to be practiced in the U.S. In his book entitled, *The United States: A Christian Nation,* Associate Justice David Brewer made this clear. According to Justice Brewer, "in the case of *Holy Trinity Church vs. United States*, 143 U.S. 471, that court, after mentioning various circumstances, added, 'these and many other matters which might be noticed, add a volume of unofficial declarations to the mass of organic utterances that this is a Christian nation."[11]

Many of the Founding Fathers were Orthodox Trinitarian Christians who viewed the country as a Godly nation. They did much more than practice a religion comprised of man-made laws and go through the legalistic and trite religious rituals; they possessed a personal relationship with God. It was basic Christian principles and beliefs that guided their dependence on God and their decision-making. For example, during his Thanksgiving Proclamation in October 1789, George Washington made the piercing assertion that "Whereas it is the duty of all Nations to acknowledge the providence of Almighty God, to obey his will, to be grateful for his benefits, and humbly to implore his protection and favor..."[12] The founders believed in an Almighty God who is omnipresent and omnipotent. Moreover, they believed religion promoted social and civic order and that it was the bastion of liberty.

Americans today do not share the same sentiment and are being deluded otherwise as a result of multiculturalism and ultra-tolerance. Hence, our freedoms are being used against us as multiculturalism and ultra-tolerance are being foisted upon us, thus causing us to avert our fundamental principles as spurious doctrine propagates. As we fail to reflect on our historical past, we run the risk of sullying our national identity for future generations.

It was not until I was in my early thirties that I acquired a profound understanding and appreciation of our Christian heritage. This education and wisdom was not acquired through my public education as a child but through my self-study as an adult. I believe that all Americans need to revisit the history lessons surrounding our Christian heritage in order to acquire this same appreciation and to preclude Americans from being bamboozled by the pushing of multiculturalism and ultra-tolerance. With this historical truth, a nationalistic and patriotic fervor of what it means to be a citizen of this great land will follow. Moreover, with an appreciation and respect of our fundamental roots, we should be able to discern the course of our future footsteps as a nation. This is where it begins and what the American people should rally around. After all, our Christian heritage has delivered us to where we are today, overcoming major obstacles and challenges, leaving us as the most blessed nation.

Right from the start, God was at work in the founding of America.

Putting aside the different arguments as to who reached continental North America first, many Americans know Christopher Columbus as the explorer who was in search of the New World and desired to prove that the world was round. What most Americans do not know about is the source of the internal passion that spurred Columbus to set sail to the New World. In Columbus' own words:

> "At this time I've seen and put in study to look into all the Holy Scriptures, which our Lord opened to my understanding (I could sense His hand upon me), so that it became clear to me that it was feasible to navigate from here to the Indies; and He gave me the will to execute the idea...I have already said that for the execution of the enterprise of the Indies, neither reason nor mathematics, nor world maps were profitable to me; rather the prophecy of Isaiah was completely fulfilled."[13]

As a believer and follower of God, Columbus was an avid reader and follower of the Bible. Columbus was not solely driven by self-ambition or the English royalty's sponsorship, but more importantly by a God-given impulse. He possessed an internal desire that resonated within him which in turn gave him credible reason to believe in his voyage. I do not know about you, but I find it absolutely refreshing to know that Columbus' urge to discover the New World was not solely for self-pleasure or self-aggrandizement, but it was a direct result of a Godly influence on his conscience. God's plan for this country was at work. As a result of Columbus's voyage to the New World, further exploration followed, eventually bringing the Pilgrims to North America. Even before the days of America's founding, our heritage was instantly intertwined with divine aegis. Tell me now that God did not have a divine purpose for the U.S.

MORE THAN SIMPLY PILGRIMS

We are all familiar with the story of the Pilgrims landing at Plymouth Rock especially since it is still retold each year around the Thanksgiving holiday. But how many of us are aware the Pilgrims had an insatiable appetite to practice Christianity devoid of government infringement? As the Thanksgiving holiday becomes subject to increased commercialization each year, we no longer reflect upon the true meaning of Thanksgiving and the historical aspects of it.

Initially, the Pilgrims broke away from the Church of England to eschew religious persecution and harassment as they settled in Holland. As a result of Holland's tolerance, the Pilgrims believed they had a great opportunity to exercise their religion without external encumbrance. Although the Pilgrims encountered some economic challenges in Holland, it was the dominant Dutch culture that threatened the purity of the Pilgrim identity and culture, thus causing them to set out on a voyage to the New World. Hence, their hopes of establishing a colony in the New World were driven largely by their desire to live a life with the Bible as their guide.[14] Is it any coincidence that our earliest settlers were Bible believing Christians? If there is one thing that God has, it is a plan regardless of its rationality to the human mind.

Every Thanksgiving, we flippantly reflect back on the Pilgrims feasting on what became known as Thanksgiving Day without appreciating what the Pilgrims encountered to get to that point of celebrating that memorable feast of thanks. When examining the Pilgrims, it is important to note the various challenges and obstacles they had to overcome in order to reach the New World. Donald Trump once said that "everything in life is luck."[15] I would contest that the Pilgrims had something much more powerful and ethereal than luck; they had God's divine protection and direction. When something is ordained by God and executed with a divine purpose, luck has nothing to do with it. That specific divine act will eventually come to fruition no matter how unfavorable or incredulous the circumstances are.

Society freely talks about luck or good fortune, but what we do not realize is that these connotations suggest that we are victims of circumstance. The truth is we serve a sovereign God and everything is under His control, whether we want to admit it or comprehend it. What is meant to occur under divine providence will assuredly occur. In this particular case, it was the Pilgrims' faith that sustained them through their long and arduous seaward trek to the New World. As we all know, it is natural to focus on the circumstances that surround us, but the Pilgrims obviously had their attention focused on the omnipotence and providence of the Lord God versus the circumstances surrounding them. Their desire to settle at a location free from religious persecution and interference served as their inspiration despite the obstacles before them.

One cannot ignore the miles of endless sea the Pilgrims had ahead of them as they departed the shores of England in September of 1620 with the *Mayflower*. In today's world, boaters nonchalantly rely on modern and technological boats filled with amenities including global positioning systems and other high-tech devises to assist them in navigating the seas. Obviously, the Pilgrims did not have these comforts. Although they did not have an abundance of maps and navigational tools, they relied on the crew's sea navigation skills but, most of all, their stalwart faith and drive to confront the hardships ahead and reach the New World. They fully understood it was not what they had within themselves but what they were capable of achieving with the Spirit of God within them.

The overcrowding of the Pilgrims on the *Mayflower* was one inevitable discomfort they had to deal with. Can you imagine the lack of comfort on board the *Mayflower* as approximately one hundred Pilgrims shared limited and cramped space for over sixty days in the absence of fresh air, privacy, running water, and operational bathrooms, all of which, we take for granted today? During the transatlantic voyage, the Pilgrims encountered tumultuous storms, which caused violent waves to pound the Mayflower, and ominous winds which threatened to tear the masts from the deck. These storms created the perfect conditions to scuttle a ship, but the *Mayflower* miraculously withstood the ferocious waves and potent winds. Anyone with an appreciation of just how tempestuous the seas can get from violent and wicked weather will attest that surviving this voyage by the Pilgrims was a miracle in itself.

Of particular note, there was a moment when the crew even considered turning the *Mayflower* back to England to flee the violent seas. We also cannot ignore the fact that the Pilgrims suffered as a result of low temperatures, seasickness, and disease. In addition, they more than likely did not have a surfeit of food and water supply, thus contributing to the voyage's discomfort. It is probably safe to say these conditions came across as unbearable for the Pilgrims at the time, but the Pilgrims never lost their perspective on their divine purpose and focus. Is it any coincidence then that despite the aforementioned unfavorable circumstances the Pilgrims faced, only one passenger, by the name of William Butten, did not survive the dangerous voyage?[16] Divine providence was at work right from the earliest days of our history. God had blessed America before it was even born.

Even after the Pilgrims surpassed the challenges of the sea and approached the new land, they were still faced with uncertainty. They did not have someone on the other side of the sea expecting them and ready to receive and guide them at their arrival site. I am sure they were excited to see the land as they approached the New World, but at the same time, the Pilgrims were more than likely filled with ambiguity and angst not knowing what lied ahead. Regardless, the Pilgrims were not led by fear but walked by faith. According to Christopher Hammons, an Associate Professor of Political Science, the Pilgrims "though anxious to get to shore, they sat on the deck of the little ship and looked across at the misty virgin wilderness of North America, and were scared to death."[17] Nathaniel Morton, who became the secretary of the Plymouth colony and was a firm advocate of preserving the colony's history, made note of this. He wrote:

> "Being now passed the vast ocean, and a sea of troubles before them in expectations, they had now no friends to welcome them, no inns to entertain or refresh them, no houses, or much less towns, to repair unto to seek for succor; and for the season it was winter, and they that know the winters of the country

know them to be sharp and violent, subject to cruel and fierce storms, dangerous to travel to known places, much more to search unknown coasts.

Besides, what could they see but a hideous and desolate wilderness, full of wild beasts and wild men? and what multitudes of them there were, they then knew not: for which way so ever they turned their eyes (save upward to Heaven) they could have but little solace or content in respect of any outward object; for summer being ended, all things stand in appearance with a weather-beaten face, and the whole country, full of woods and thickets, represented a wild and savage hew.

If they looked behind them, there was a mighty ocean which they'd passed, and was now as a main bar or gulf to separate them from all the civil parts of the world."[18]

In fact, many unanswered questions arose as the *Mayflower* made its final approach, but the Pilgrims courageously dealt with the challenges of the day as they came to them with the help of their steadfast faith in God. Instead of putting their focus on the unknown, the Pilgrims directed their focus on God's omniscience, sovereignty, presence, provision and love. As a result of their inexorable faith, hope replaced fear as they faced every challenging circumstance, knowing it is was not their energy, strength, wisdom or power, but it is was that of the living God reigning in and through them. They were assured by their faith that they had an appointment with destiny and God would see them through in the days ahead.

Our fundamental roots of freedom began with the Pilgrims as they fabricated the *Mayflower Compact* on November 21, 1620. The Pilgrims showed us Christianity and freedom are both interchangeable and inseparable. Dr. Charles Wolfe, who wrote on the inability of Americans to reflect on our common heritage, said this about the *Mayflower Compact:*

"It was this religious conviction of true Christianity that stirred the Pilgrims, undergirded their otherwise inexplicable courage, strengthened their moral character, lifted them to frame the *Mayflower Compact*, and thus made them 'the spiritual ancestors of all Americans'."[19]

The Pilgrims were so focused on instantly creating stability and order under the direction of God for the new colony that even before disembarking the *Mayflower* they created this document. It not only pledged loyalty to King James, it more importantly served as the first attempt of self-government in the New World. Furthermore, it formed a government based upon the consent of the governed. The 41 signers of the *Mayflower Compact* served as the initial government and agreed they would elect men that would enact, enforce, and obey laws that stemmed from the influence of God. These men "honored God and set their founding principles by the words of the Bible."[20] This reverence for God is evidenced by the words of the *Mayflower Compact*. It firmly proclaimed:

"IN THE name of God, Amen.

We whose names are underwritten, the loyal subjects of our dread sovereign Lord, King James, by the grace of God, of Great Britain, France and Ireland king, defender of the faith, etc., having undertaken, for the glory of God, and advancement of the Christian faith, and honor of our king and country, a voyage to plant the first colony in the Northern parts of Virginia, do by these presents solemnly and mutually in the presence of God, and one of another, covenant and combine ourselves together into a civil body politic, for our better ordering and preservation and furtherance of the ends aforesaid; and by virtue hereof to enact, constitute, and frame such just and equal laws, ordinances, acts, constitutions, and offices, from time to time, as shall be thought most meet and convenient for the general good of the colony, unto which we promise all due submission and obedience.

In witness whereof we have hereunder subscribed our names at Cape-Cod the 11 of November, in the year of the reign of our sovereign lord, King James, of England, France, and Ireland the eighteenth, and of Scotland the fifty-fourth. Anno Domine 1620."[21]

As you can see, God's footprint is clearly ostensible as reverence and glory to God was dominant throughout the contract. The Pilgrims were clearly driven by a divine purpose and they did not hide their intentions or their unshakeable faith. William Bradford, the second Governor of the Plymouth Colony, confirmed this when he wrote:

> "They (the Pilgrims) had a great hope and inward zeal of laying some good foundation or at least to make some way there unto for the propagating and advancing of the gospel of the kingdom of Christ in those remote parts of the world, yea though they should be but even a stepping stone unto others for the performing of so great a work."[22]

Although not widely known today, this pithy and simple document became the bedrock for our Christian heritage and served as a reference later on for the U.S. Constitution. The *Mayflower Contract* was a model for showing how inalienable rights came from God and not from any other man, government, or religion.

It is important to recognize how the Pilgrims first and foremost exalted God for the founding of the colony as acknowledged through their actions. William Bradford validated this in his writings. He wrote:

> "Being thus arrived in a good harbor, and brought safe to land, they fell upon their knees and blessed the God of Heaven who had brought them over the vast and furious ocean, and delivered them from all

the perils and miseries thereof, again to set their feet on the firm and stable earth, their proper element."[23]

They attributed their safety and success from their voyage and subsequent settling not to their own efforts or skill but to God's faithful direction and protection. It is startling to see how the Pilgrims so easily and freely praised and thanked God for just about everything. This praise and deference for God should serve as an example for us to emulate as a blessed nation. Just as the Pilgrims revealed in their lifestyle and especially during their voyage to America, praising God is a lifestyle and not a perfunctory act performed on specific man-made holidays. Such action of praise is not so evident in today's society because other temporal things have taken priority as people fill their hearts with everything else but God.

The challenges for the Pilgrims continued once they disembarked the *Mayflower*. For one, they had to battle the harsh cold winter. This is important to note because they came to the New World with limited possessions due to the close quarters on the *Mayflower*. They basically started from scratch with no habitation and limited supplies of food, raiment, and general supplies. These unfavorable conditions made the Pilgrims susceptible to disease such as scurvy and malnutrition, and as a result, a significant amount of Pilgrims passed away. We cannot forget that the Pilgrims had some apprehension of the endemic Indian population already on the colony. One concern the Pilgrims had was the Indians would discover the noticeable number of fatalities among the Pilgrims as a result of sickness, thus inciting them to conquer the remaining Pilgrims. One can only conclude that the accumulation of all these hardships presented the Pilgrims with an overwhelming burden and spawned a despondent spirit among them at times.

Miraculously, the Pilgrims maintained their gusto through their faith and resilient countenance. By focusing on their original purpose of settling in the New World, they became energized. They made the choice to be resolute and to overcome these challenges and disappointments by not falling victims to discouragement. They chose not to be consumed by their circumstances. As adherents to Scripture, could it be that the Pilgrims turned to the Book of Leviticus for their strength?

> *"If ye walk in my statutes, and keep my commandments, and do them; Then I will give you rain in due season, and the land shall yield her increase, and the trees of the field shall yield their fruit. And your threshing shall reach unto the vintage, and the vintage shall reach unto the sowing time: and ye shall eat your bread to the full, and dwell in your land safely. And I will give peace in the land, and ye shall lie down, and none shall make you afraid: and I will rid evil beasts out of the land, neither shall the sword go through your land."*
> **Leviticus 26:3-6 (KJV)**

This simple piece of history from our heritage serves as a valuable lesson learned that is still applicable today if we allow it. It not only reveals the power behind reverence for God, but it also reveals that when we see things from God's perspective, anything is possible. As we are reminded: *"...With men this is impossible; but with God all things are possible."* **Matthew 19:26 (KJV)**

The Pilgrims' faith and dependence on God eventually paid off as two indigenous Indians came into contact with the Pilgrims and befriended them after the harsh winter. Since the dawn of time, God has always used other people as vehicles to assist in unveiling a divine plan. Samoset was the first Native American the Pilgrims were exposed to. Amazingly, he spoke limited English as a result of his interaction with English traders, allowing him to communicate with the Pilgrims. On a subsequent visit to the Pilgrims' colony, Samoset brought another Indian who most Americans are familiar with- Squanto. Like Samoset, Squanto spoke English but with much more enunciation and clarity. Squanto was once held captive and brought to England where he consequently was able to learn English. Squanto probably never imagined his captivity time in England would have had a purpose and would be applied years later at the Plymouth colony. This further proves that no matter who you are, God has a divine purpose for your life.

Squanto's ability to effectively communicate with the Pilgrims permitted him to teach them how to plant and care for crops, hunt, and fish. Squanto's guidance taught the Pilgrims not only to stay alive but also to be alive. Another important role that Squanto served was that through his diplomatic and relationship skills, he was able to forestall other Indians from attacking the Pilgrims. The advent of Samoset and Squanto and the subsequent acquisition of these survival skills could not have come at a more opportune time as the Pilgrims suffered from destitution. This blessing from God provided the Pilgrims further subsistence and kept their purpose alive.

The Pilgrims were not the only ones to benefit from the Pilgrim-Indian relationship. The Pilgrims also had an influence on Squanto. Prior to his death, Squanto told William Bradford these following words: "Pray for me, Governor, that I might go to the Englishmen's God in heaven."[24] This should be no surprise or coincidence because God works all things for the good, as specified in Romans 8:28, no matter how inauspicious and capricious the circumstances may be. Albert Einstein, prominent physicist and a fan of predictability, supported this when he said, "God does not play dice."[25]

So as you can see, the Pilgrims are connoted to more than just Thanksgiving terminology such as turkey, football, pumpkin pie, and etc. The Pilgrims established a spiritual and historical footprint that served as a compass for our Founding Fathers and for the future development of our nation. Instead of reflecting on the commercialization of Thanksgiving and the contemporary associations of the holiday, we need to reflect on the Pilgrims' original intent and how they were blessed to overcome the challenges they encountered along the way. The bedrocks of our heritage were designed to provide us direction for the present and the future. Even though we are a society rapt in the present time, we must adopt a philosophy that emphasizes the importance of our Godly heritage. Let us reflect on what Patrick Henry, an active denouncer of British tyranny, said in a speech to the Virginia House of Burgesses in May 1765:

"It cannot be emphasized too strongly or too often that this great nation was founded, not by religionists, but by Christians not on religions, but on the gospel of Jesus Christ! For this very reason, peoples of other faiths have been afforded asylum, prosperity, and freedom of worship here."[26]

AMERICA'S INDEPENDENCE INCITED BY GOD

If we really take a minute to reflect on what our founders and early Americans were up against in the fight for our independence, we would discover the escape from British tyranny and the subsequent American independence was not a coincidence just as the Pilgrims coming to America was no coincidence. According to John Adams, "The highest story of the American Revolution is this: It connected in one indissoluble bond the principles of civil government with the principles of Christianity."[27] In a letter to Thomas Jefferson, John Adams wrote:

> "The general principles, on which the Fathers achieved independence, were the only Principles in which that beautiful Assembly of young Gentlemen could Unite....And what were these general Principles? I answer, the general Principles of Christianity, in which all these Sects were United: . . . Now I will avow, that I then believe, and now believe, that those general Principles of Christianity, are as eternal and immutable, as the Existence and the Attributes of God; and that those Principles of Liberty, are as unalterable as human Nature and our terrestrial mundane System..."[28]

The odds were against us as the British Empire was a respected and feared hegemony recognized around the globe. It had a reputation of being indomitable from previous rivalries with countries such as France and Spain. The British military was well organized, disciplined, funded, supplied, equipped, and trained. In addition, the British possessed the largest and most powerful navy in the world, giving it control of the international sea lanes. The British Navy was a juggernaut and was the prime reason why Britain was internationally known. According to naval mogul Admiral Alfred Thayer Mahan, speaking on Britain's prominence, "With the growth of her colonial system her war fleets also grew, but her merchant shipping and wealth grew yet faster."[29]

The circumstances of the British-American bout have parallels to the David-Goliath bout. Just as the mighty Goliath dominated inferior David in size, military experience, and armament; on the outside looking in, the British resembled Goliath, while the Americans resembled David. Any average person would argue the British had a formidable force, which was physically favored to win the American Revolution.

Compared to the British, the Americans were far from prepared to decisively confront the British. Unlike the British, the Americans did not have the abundant resources and supplies to sustain its military forces. From basic supplies such as footwear to military supplies such as firearms and gunpowder, the Americans were constrained as a result of inadequate funding from the Continental Congress. Moreover, unlike the British, the Americans lacked the numbers, organization, and structure within its military ranks. While the British military consisted of a professional, unified front composed of Regular Army, Hessians (German soldiers loyal to King George III), and American Loyalists, the American forces were far from commensurate. American forces were composed of the Continental Army and diverse militias where professionalism and reliability were not automatic or consistent throughout the different organizations.

Success on the battlefield comes from unity of command and unity of effort, both of which the American forces did not initially have. As a result of America's initial disunity and lack of organization coupled with other disheartening factors across its forces, America's outlook did not appear promising. No matter which way one looks at it, the American forces faced daunting odds against the British.

Just as David was driven by intangible and internal fervency to defeat Goliath, so were the Americans. Despite the unfavorable odds against them, the Americans were fighting for a just cause. Their cause centered on the pursuit of personal rights and individual liberty along with national independence. They understood they were only going to be free if they were willing to fight to be free.

The Americans sought to escape the oppressive reign of the British especially as enacted legislation in the form of various acts restricted the colonists' individual rights. Acts such as the Sugar Act, Stamp Act, and the Townshend Act became British impositions on the colonists. For example, in 1766, the Townshend Act placed taxes on common items such as tea, lead, paint, paper, and glass. John Dickinson, a prominent Philadelphia lawyer, published a series of letters or essays in *Letters from a Farmer*. These letters openly denounced the exorbitant taxation by the British and consequently played a role in uniting the colonists against the different acts of taxation. In his fourth letter, Dickinson eloquently declared:

> "Here is no distinction made between internal and external taxes. It is evident from the short reasoning thrown into these resolves, that every imposition "to grant to his Majesty the property of the colonies," was thought a "tax"; and that every such imposition, if laid any other way, than "with their consent, given personally, or by their representatives," was not only "unreasonable, and inconsistent with the principles and spirit of the British Constitution," but destructive "to the freedom of a people."[30]

The colonists viewed these acts as forms of bondage which induced them to rally against British oppression. They further understood God never intended for man to live under such enslavement. It is the will of God that all people live in freedom and not in slavery of any kind. The colonists opted to live in freedom versus bondage and did not settle for the status quo of British dominance. They felt neglected and exploited by the British government as taxation without representation flourished.

One of the prerequisites of a just war is that it must lead to a just peace and the American Revolution met this criterion. The colonists were justified in standing up against the proliferation of British Parliamentary power for the just cause of living in personal liberty and freedom. Since war is a contest of will, the will of the American people during this period prevailed. Although the tangible strengths of the British appeared more threatening than that of America's, this goes to show that you should never underestimate the intangible traits. As British author and clergyman, Charles Caleb Colton, once said, "Hope sees the invisible, feels the intangible and achieves the impossible."[31] The colonists' hope centered on freedom from British domination. After all, hope assumes a change of circumstances for the better.

Most Americans today are familiar with the date of July 4, 1776- the date in which the colonists issued the Declaration of Independence. Although this date may not receive the proper attention and respect it should, it is a monumental milestone in our short history. After a year of fighting the British, the colonists were further united behind the Declaration of Independence. It served as a source of inspiration for the colonists as it represented the birth of the United States and became a national symbol of American liberty and freedom. We would be wise as a nation to adopt a renewed spirit on the importance of this powerful document instead of viewing it simply as an antediluvian document. Indeed, it is a piece of history, but more importantly, it is a living document that should be a steady guide on how we should function as a government and live as a society.

Our history should be a reference of learning, and more importantly, a method of aligning with the truth. Since the truth is universal and uncompromising, there is no getting around our history and heritage. No matter how much secular and external forces try to obscure or bastardize our Christian heritage, they cannot defile the truth of it. It is what it is, but it is up to us to keep it in the front of us. The only ideology that can sustain freedom is the one this country was founded on as outlined in the Declaration of Independence.

Some of us talk of the Declaration of Independence in casual conversation, but how many of us are fully cognizant of its verbiage and truly cherish its content? The verbiage is simple but acute. It would be appropriate for us today to reflect on the meaning of its content. It reflects the ingenuity, mindset, and priorities of our Founding Fathers. It begins:

> "When, in the course of human events, it becomes necessary for one people to dissolve the political bonds which have connected them with another, and to assume among the powers of the earth, the separate and equal station to which the laws of nature and of nature's God entitle them, a decent respect to the opinions of mankind requires that they should declare the causes which impel them to the separation.
>
> We hold these truths to be self-evident, that all men are created equal, that they are endowed by their Creator with certain unalienable rights that among these are life, liberty and the pursuit of happiness. That to secure these rights, governments are instituted among men, deriving their just powers from the consent of the governed. That whenever any form of government becomes destructive to these ends, it is the right of the people to alter or to abolish it, and to institute new government, laying its foundation on such principles and organizing its powers in such form, as to them shall seem most likely to affect their safety and happiness..."[32]

John Adams said: "The Declaration of Independence laid the cornerstone of human government upon the first precepts of Christianity."[33] God's footprint is clearly visible in it as the founders acknowledged all men are created equal and are supplied with inalienable rights which man cannot interfere with, accentuated liberty over bondage, and understood man is imperfect and susceptible to iniquity. The founders were not hesitant to mention the role of God in our nation's birth certificate. In his book, *Liberty and Tyranny,*

Mark Levin affirmed the founders were "men of varying denominations but united and emphatic in the belief that the Creator was the origin of their existence and the source of their reason."[34] If there was one sentiment shared by the founders it was a rejection of any form of absolute authority carried out by man.

The opening statements of the Declaration of Independence make it clear our individual rights come not from man but from Almighty God, and man has no business interloping with these basic rights. If our rights came from anyone other than a perfect God, then they would be vulnerable to being shaped by man's imperfection. While God is the guarantor of our inalienable rights, man or government is supposed to be protective of these rights for us. Moreover, when God serves as the guarantor of rights and not man, there is more of a proclivity towards objectivity versus subjectivity, thus leaving no room for personal interpretation of who should and should not be entitled to these basic rights. One of the most quintessential principles of this great nation is optimism coupled with hope; the stronghold of optimism took root with the signing of the Declaration of Independence.

When speaking of the favor of God upon the United States, one cannot ignore the Battle of Brooklyn. According to Rod McNair, "At the dawn of the American Revolution, God intervened in a dramatic way to save General George Washington's army from defeat."[35] The Battle of Brooklyn was one of the most grisly but least popular battles during the American Revolution. In order to prevent a British attack on New York, George Washington moved his forces to fortify the city. The British had their eyes on New York City due to its strategic importance since it represented the epicenter of the colonies. Records indicate that a plethora of British ships carrying over 32,000 soldiers arrived in the New York Harbor. Compared to the American forces of approximately 12,000, the British had an overwhelming and intimidating presence. General William Howe of the British ordered his forces to attack Washington's forces in the Brooklyn Heights area, initially killing over 1,200 of Washington's men. After this initial blow, Washington was faced with the decision of either to surrender or to be obliterated. The American forces were outnumbered and outgunned to their front, while to their rear; the mighty British navy along the East Hudson River would have balked any attempt of a retreat.

No matter what option Washington would have pursued, the colonists' hope of freedom from Britain would have come to an abrupt end in the natural. The British were bound to be victorious. Could it be that Washington reflected on the Bible and how God had granted favor to Israel from its enemies prior to embarking on defeat? Perhaps the current situation motivated Washington to recount the Book of Deuteronomy:

> *"When you go to war against your enemies and see horses and chariots and an army greater than yours, do not be afraid of them, because the LORD your God, who brought you up out of Egypt, will be with you."* ***Deuteronomy 20:1 (NIV)***

Washington was familiar with the Bible and held the Bible in high esteem and once claimed, "It is impossible to rightly govern the world without God and Bible."[36] Washington held the belief that the Bible would never direct one amiss. Washington did not entertain a spirit of fear, but instead, he stood in authority with the Word of God behind him.

In the natural, what appears impossible is just the opposite in the spiritual realm. Out of nowhere, menacing weather in the form of heavy rain, chilling temperatures, and powerful winds precluded the British from instantly performing a subsequent attack on American forces. The American forces were then greeted by a favorable wind on the Hudson River to assist them in crossing the river followed by a thick fog to cloak their movement as they retreated from Brooklyn Heights. When the fog had finally lifted, amazingly, the British forces were the only remaining forces on the battlefield.

Could it be that God answered George Washington's prayers, prior to the arrival of General Howe's men? According to William Bennett, in his book entitled *The Spirit of America*, "Washington issued the order on May 15 for prayer, fasting, and humble supplication to the Lord for His continued blessings."[37] Was this coincidence then as we so often and freely assume or was it Godly intervention in the affairs of man? I will go with Godly intervention since it was not the first time nor was it the last time that God had interfered in the progression and development of America. Moreover, it should not be a surprise because we are told:

> *"Ask, and it shall be given you; seek, and ye shall find; knock, and it shall be opened unto you: For every one that asketh receiveth; and he that seeketh findeth; and to him that knocketh it shall be opened."*
> **Matthew 7:7-8 (KJV)**

Washington whole-heartedly believed in the Word of God and in all of its promises, and he was not timid to put Scripture and prayer to use. Washington's faith in action was what made the difference at the Battle of Brooklyn. Like many other founders, Washington was a God-fearing man and believed in Godly intervention. This divine intervention in the form of weather stymied British dominance on the battlefield and salvaged Washington's forces for a future fight.

The Battle of Brooklyn was not the only time General George Washington relied on his faith and prayer during the American Revolution. Yes, he was a virtuous leader and a sound military tactician, but he realized that the strength of man alone would not grant the colonies their independence. He also did not view prayer as solely a method of submitting a wish-list of needs to God, but instead, Washington valued the purpose of prayer. He understood the reward of prayer is not that we solely acquire something in return, but that we can relate to the God who supplies our needs. Prayer is all about building intimacy and a relationship with God, and Washington routinely demonstrated it. Washington's faith permitted him to pray with expectation versus just hope.

As a result of God answering his prayers throughout the fight for our independence, his faith increased, thus giving him the boldness to ask for other miracles during battles such as Valley Forge. We have heard the adage that a picture is worth a thousand words time and time again. Well, Arnold

Friberg's famous painting of "The Prayer at Valley Forge" does just that. What was created to celebrate our nation's bicentennial in 1976, is now a powerful symbol to remind us how our country overcame dire obstacles in its beginning. Think about it for a minute- a portrait of our first president on his knees humbly praying before God for divine guidance and favor. This one historical moment of Washington on his knees humbly submitted to a sovereign God embodies our entire national heritage.

It was during the frigid winter of 1777-78 at Valley Forge where we witnessed Godly intervention once again on behalf of our young nation. Washington selected Valley Forge as a location for a winter training camp for his forces since it was a strategic location in range of Philadelphia and it was not vulnerable to a surprise attack by the British. Once again, Washington and his men encountered what seemed to be insurmountable odds. Limited financial support from the Continental Congress caused the Americans to face severe shortages of food, clothing, and general supplies. General Washington made note of this in his statement on April 21, 1778:

> "To see the men without clothes to cover their nakedness, without blankets to lie upon, without shoes…without a house or hut to cover them until those could be built, and submitting without a murmur, is a proof of patience and obedience which, in my opinion, can scarcely be paralleled."[38]

The soldiers did not have the necessary clothing or garments to keep them warm. In fact, many were without quality shoes to traverse the snowy and icy terrain. Cold weather is one thing, but cold weather without the proper gear and equipment is something all different. As a result, as many as 2,000 soldiers experienced fatal diseases such as malnutrition, small pox, typhoid, pneumonia, and dysentery. Can you imagine these miserable conditions and the burden that Washington had to carry? As a leader, Washington was faced with low morale and feelings of dejection among the troops. He not only had to ensure that the soldiers were supplied amid the natural elements but that they maintained their warrior ethos and zest in the face of an unrelenting British military and the worst physical conditions.

These hardships compelled Washington again to resort to his faith for Godly intervention. A Valley Forge resident by the name of Isaac Potts witnessed Washington in quiet and reverent prayer during the infamous winter at Valley Forge. In his "Diaries and Remembrances," Reverend Nathaniel Randolph Snowden, an ordained Presbyterian minister, acknowledged Potts' testimony of Washington in prayer:

> "...Do you see that woods, & that plain?" It was about a quarter of a mile off from the place we were riding, as it happened. "There," said he, "laid the army of Washington. It was a most distressing time of ye war, and all were for giving up the Ship but that great and good man. In that woods pointing to a close in view, I heard a plaintive sound as, of a man at prayer. I tied my horse to a sapling & went quietly into the woods & to my astonishment I saw the great George Washington on his knees alone, with his sword on one side and his cocked hat on the other. He was at Prayer to the God of the Armies, beseeching to interpose with his Divine aid, as it was ye Crisis, & the cause of the country, of humanity & of the world.
>
> Such a prayer I never heard from the lips of man. I left him alone praying. I went home & told my wife, I saw a sight and heard today what I never saw or heard before, and just related to her what I had seen & heard & observed. We never thought a man could be a soldier & a Christian, but if there is one in the world, it is Washington. She also was astonished. We thought it was the cause of God, & America could prevail."[39]

Washington's focus was not on the present circumstances but on the long-term goal of achieving freedom for the good of all future Americans. He took it to another level and understood there was purpose in their current suffering and that adversity would lead to opportunity and an established freedom. God continued to serve as the founders' and the colonists' refuge, providing them the will and strength to pursue freedom and liberty. Their love for liberty followed their reverence for God.

THE U.S. CONSTITUTION TAKES FORM UNDER GODLY DIRECTION

God's divine favor and over-watch of the colonies did not end with the termination of the American Revolution, but it was also apparent as the founders developed the U.S. Constitution. Idaho gubernatorial candidate, Rex Rammell, acknowledged this while campaigning for the 2010 gubernatorial race. He confidently proclaimed "America would not exist if it wasn't for the divine hand of providence in not only intervening to win the Revolutionary War but in writing the inspired words of the Constitution."[40] The founders knew the Constitution was not the panacea for the colonists, but they believed it would serve as viable mechanism to prevent governmental tyranny and preserve individual rights. Along with the Declaration of Independence, the U.S. Constitution became a core founding document that has brought vitality, resiliency, and stability to the U.S. to this date.

Although the Constitution is not perfect, it has been a beacon of freedom and liberty for all people and it has served as a model for other countries to emulate and adopt. Even though Americans may not have the same appreciation and respect for their own Constitution, there are others across the globe that pine for such stability in their government. Things we take for granted on a daily basis are yearned for by others.

It is safe to say that many Americans are unfamiliar with the text of our own Constitution. The fundamental fabric of our very nation is foreign when it should not be. During the course of the 2010 heated debate over healthcare, at a public event, one former Congressman told his constituents he is "not worried about the Constitution" as it relates to the new health care law.[41] Whether his words were taken out of context or not is another argument, but he still confused the U.S. Constitution with the Declaration of Independence when he said this about the U.S. Constitution: "I believe it says we have the right to life, liberty and the pursuit of happiness."[42] For a Congressman who has taken an oath to support and defend the U.S. Constitution as an elected representative of the people, such comments are not assuring.

The thing that attracts others to our Constitution is that it empowers the people. The Constitution opens with the following words:

> "We the People of the United States, in Order to form a more perfect Union, establish Justice, insure domestic Tranquility, provide for the common defense, promote the general Welfare, and secure the Blessings of Liberty to ourselves and our Posterity, do ordain and establish this Constitution for the United States of America."[43]

The founders established the framework of "we the people" to ensure government oppression was a thing of the past.

The thing that makes the Constitution a bulwark is the fact the founders were grounded in the philosophy that God is omniscient and omnipotent while man is fallible. After all, it was Aristotle who declared, "Man is by nature a political animal."[44] Understanding this fallibility of man, John Adams announced that "our Constitution was made only for a moral and religious people. It is wholly inadequate to the government of any other."[45]

We should recognize the fact that prior to the 1787 convention, the colonies were separate sovereign states and were not yet united under a centralized federal government. The *Articles of Confederation* did not bind the states, thus contributing to the division and strife among them. Under the brilliancy of the founders, through the Constitution, they reallocated power from the federal government to the state governments. It is important to note the development of the

Constitution did not occur peacefully over night without vociferous debate. In fact, the founders developed the Constitution with God and prayer as its foundation. The Constitution took its principles from the *Holy Bible*.

The 1787 Constitutional Convention was full of bickering, discordance, and rambunctious disorder as delegates were in jeopardy of experiencing a deadlock. For example, large and small states initially disagreed on how population would determine state representation. While the large states wanted representation based off of population, the small states obviously did not. To prevent a political logjam from occurring, in the middle of the active disagreement, Benjamin Franklin made a speech on July 28, 1787. Notes from James Madison accounted for what he said:

> "...I have lived, Sir, a long time, and the longer I live, the more convincing proofs I see of this truth - that God Governs in the affairs of men. And if a sparrow cannot fall to the ground without His notice, is it probable that an empire can rise without His aid?"
>
> We have been assured, Sir, in the Sacred Writings, that "except the Lord build the House, they labor in vain that build it." I firmly believe this; and I also believe that without his concurring aid we shall succeed in this political building no better than the Builders of Babel: We shall be divided by our partial local interests; our projects will be confounded, and we ourselves shall become a reproach and bye word down to future ages. And what is worse, mankind may hereafter from this unfortunate instance, despair of establishing Governments by Human wisdom and leave it to chance, war and conquest. therefore beg leave to move - that henceforth prayers imploring the assistance of Heaven, and its blessing on our deliberations, be held in this Assembly every morning before we proceed to business, and that one or more of the clergy of this city be requested to officiate in that service."[46]

How moving were these words of encouragement? Ben Franklin humbled himself as he referenced the power of God over man. He acknowledged that man's strength alone is not enough to produce an independent and stable nation where liberty and equality could flourish. Perhaps he reflected on Psalm 118, which says: *"It is better to trust in the LORD than to put confidence in man."* **Psalm 118:8 (KJV)** Amazingly, the spirit of God moved within the delegates, causing them to come to a consensus on the U.S. Constitution. This is another example to illustrate how God rewards genuine prayer and reverence toward Him. It is a proven fact since the creation of man God will bestow His blessings upon the recipient(s) who establishes a relationship with Him through prayer.

In today's society, there are individuals that believe the U.S. Constitution is archaic and no longer relevant in our affairs. Such a disposition is off kilter and clearly errs from the founders' original intention and purpose of the Constitution. I would have to refer those individuals to the beautiful words of Fredrick Douglass on March 26, 1860:

> "...What, then, is the Constitution? I will tell you. It is not even like the British Constitution, which is made up of enactments of Parliament, decisions of Courts, and the established usages of the Government. The American Constitution is a written instrument full and complete in itself. No Court in America, no Congress, no President, can add a single word thereto, or take a single word thereto. It is a great national enactment done by the people, and can only be altered, amended, or added to by the people..."[47]

The founders' brilliance was seen in their intentions of establishing the Constitution as a founding document and not an ever-expanding document that is subject to change based off the animus of society at the present time. Moreover, the founders knew the Constitution was not designed to answer all of our societal issues and problems, but its purpose is to present a legal foundation under which our society functions and blossoms. Moreover, it is important to note that even though our Constitution was designed to be a fundamental legal stronghold for our society, if changes to it were necessary, there is an amendment process in place.

One of the implied purposes of the U.S. Constitution was for it to serve as a preservation of our norms and values. The founders did not intend for the U.S. Constitution to be malleable to the latest fad of political inclinations. Founding documents are designed to provide sustenance and permanence. The values that have set America apart from others are the same values represented throughout the U.S. Constitution. Trends and temperaments of society may change over time, but beliefs, values, and morals should not. It does not help that we have had Supreme Court Justices who have moved away from a strict interpretation of the Constitution. For example, Supreme Court Justice Ruth Bader Ginsburg once declared that "boldly dynamic interpretation, departing radically from the original understanding" of the Constitution is acceptable.[48]

Yes, the Constitution is over two hundred years old, but compared to other countries, the U.S. is still a young nation. Countries that are much older than the U.S. do not even have this same framework of stability and order, not even close. In our short history, the Constitution has assisted the U.S. get to the level where it is at today, so why would we doubt the relevance and applicability of something that has served us so well? What about other documents or resources that are older than the Constitution? Does society also consider them archaic and not relevant? For example, the Koran is much older than the Constitution and I do not see or hear people venting its antiquity. The Constitution may be old in today's terms but it still is not passé. We would be wise to focus more on our founders' bedrock thoughts of the Constitution versus seasonal liberal judges. Thomas Jefferson reminded us:

> "On every question of construction, let us carry ourselves back to the time when the Constitution was adopted, recollect the spirit manifested in the debates, and instead of trying what meaning may be squeezed

out of the text, or invented against it, conform to the probable one in which it was passed."[49]

Precursors to the U.S. Constitution such as the *Magna Carta* and the *Mayflower Compact* served as examples for the founders in developing the U.S. Constitution. The Constitution is an outgrowth of the two documents. Both documents revealed deference for God and placed an emphasis on limited government for the good of the people. With the *Magna Carta*, laws restricted the power of the king of England, thus comforting those being governed. The people were safe from any threat of tyranny and inequality by liberty guaranteed by the Great Charter. The beginning of the *Magna Carta* immediately revealed the emphasis on God and liberty:

> "In the first place we have granted to God, and by this our present charter confirmed for us and our heirs forever that the English Church shall be free, and shall have her rights entire, and her liberties inviolate; and we will that it be thus observed; which is apparent from this that the freedom of elections, which is reckoned most important and very essential to the English Church, we, of our pure and unconstrained will, did grant, and did by our charter confirm and did obtain the ratification of the same from our lord, Pope Innocent III, before the quarrel arose between us and our barons: and this we will observe, and our will is that it be observed in good faith by our heirs forever. We have also granted to all freemen of our kingdom, for us and our heirs forever, all the underwritten liberties, to be had and held by them and their heirs, of us and our heirs forever."[50]

The first governing document of the Plymouth Colony, the *Mayflower Compact*, is similar in nature to the *Magna Carta* because it also underlined God and the civil body politic as mentioned earlier. The U.S. Constitution follows in the footsteps of these other two documents by alluding to the fact that God is the source of our rights, emphasizing people over government, and displaying governance by law through man and not solely by the fiat of man.

If there is one thing the founders believed in and conveyed was that man is fallible and sinful. In chapter six of the Bible, we learn how the sinful nature of man saddened God:

> *"And God saw that the wickedness of man was great in the earth, and that every imagination of the thoughts of his heart was only evil continually. And it repented the LORD that he had made man on the earth, and it grieved him at his heart."* **Genesis 6:5-6 (KJV)**

The founders understood this fact, and as a result, they did not want too much power in the hands of too few. In the *Federalist #10,* James Madison avowed:

> "As long as the reason of man continues fallible, and he is at liberty to exercise it, different opinions will be formed. As long as the connection subsists between his reason and his self-love, his opinions and his passions will have a reciprocal influence on each other; and the former will be objects to which the latter will attach themselves."[51]

Since the founders knew that society is not perfect and that man is susceptible to avarice, corruption, and malfeasance in general, they adroitly devised a government that restrained men in power. Like Lord Acton, a renowned British historian, said a century after the creation of the U.S. Constitution: "Power tends to corrupt, and absolute power corrupts absolutely."[52] When man is placed in a position of power, man is enticed by that power to obtain more power. Our founders fully comprehended this and implemented measures to counteract any sort of power grab at the expense of the people.

Through the implementation of the Bill of Rights, a system of checks and balances, and federalism within the Constitution, the founders were dedicated in creating a government with limited power and protecting individual freedom. The Bill of Rights include the first ten amendments to the Constitution and provide the individual with such freedoms as free speech, religious practice, right to assemble, right to bear arms, due process, and more. A system of checks and balances prevents any one branch of government from becoming too powerful and consequently meddling with individual freedoms. Federalism limits the federal government by guaranteeing power to state governments. With these three mechanisms in place, runaway power would be hard to come by. The founders used the past oppressive history of the colonies to guide them in preserving freedom for future generations of Americans to come. Something that appears so simple was so clever; how adept of them to cover all bases and prevent a central governing authority from infringing on inalienable rights that were given to man from God.

They understood if rights were human and government given, then humans in government can take them away at their prerogative. Patrick Henry said it nicely: "The Constitution is not an instrument for government to restrain the people; it is an instrument for the people to restrain the government-less it come to dominate our lives and interests."[53] Our founders learned from history the value of individualism and personal freedom and they did everything within their purview to establish a firm system of government to prevent government oppression from resurfacing ever again. President Ronald Reagan spoke of freedom regularly and without hesitation, while at the same time attributing it to God's unconditional grace. Some of his most piercing words on freedom surfaced on May 31, 1988 when he spoke before students at Moscow State University. In one part of his speech, he firmly stated:

> "Freedom is the recognition that no single person, no single authority of government has a monopoly on the truth, but that every individual life is infinitely

precious, that every one of us put on this world has been put there for a reason and has something to offer."[54]

NEVER FORGET OUR ROOTS

Our Christian heritage should serve as our beacon of light or as part of our national compass. It is worthy of attention, praise, and deference. As a result of our fundamental heritage, we have reached political, military, economic, and cultural stability, thus giving us a quality of life that others around the world hunger for. Why would we want to alter or neglect our national heritage that has preserved us all this time? Why do we want to ignore such simple but striking phrases by our founders that reflect our pedigree? By doing so, we would be altering our national identity.

In today's age of rampant political correctness, ultra-sensitivity, and ultra-tolerance, we must have the personal strength and vigor not to hide from our national heritage. While it is one thing to read about our Christian heritage, it is another thing to construe, embrace, and live out our Christian heritage. I am confident to say the Founding Fathers would, without a doubt, prefer for us to choose the latter. Throughout my military career, I have had the opportunity to serve with various foreign military personnel, and there was one thing that I noticed about all of them- they all displayed a convincing praise for their national heritage. As a society, we need to do the same. We need to reference our Christian heritage with humbled audacity and enthusiastic appreciation. Our heritage is not a paragon, but it is unlike any other country's heritage in which our Founding Fathers established a footprint of God within our system of government. Our national principles of freedom and liberty are entwined with the principles of Christianity.

CHAPTER TWO
GOD'S FOOTPRINT IN THE AMERICAN CULTURE

Our founders established a solid precedent for our nation when it comes to dependence on and reverence for God- a precedent that needs to be revisited and reestablished today. However, in order for this to happen today, we must have a sincere appreciation of our history and heritage. Our fundamental roots should serve as a guide for our future actions.

God's footprint in American society did not come to an abrupt end after the era of our Founding Fathers. Instead, it has been present throughout our short history. Unfortunately, it is not taught, emphasized, or promoted in today's secularized society as it once was. If we are honest with ourselves, we would recognize there is unambiguous evidence of our Christian heritage throughout our history and society. A comprehensive review of such things as presidential speeches and correspondence, court cases, historical memorabilia, and our most famous monuments exhibits God's footprint on this nation. Despite these obvious signs of our Christian heritage, it is still challenged as the truth behind our Godly heritage is suppressed.

This chapter is full of many quotes from prominent Americans centered on the importance of God and the Bible in our society. Although they are just a sample, an analysis of these quotes provides the reader with a true appreciation of just how significant of a role Christianity has had in our society.

Our sixth president, John Quincy Adams, displayed the same dependence on God just as the founders did. At the end of his inaugural address on March 4, 1825, Adams professed:

> "I shall look for whatever success may attend my public service; and knowing that 'except the Lord keep the city the watchman wake but in vain,' with

fervent supplications for His favor, to His overruling providence I commit with humble but fearless confidence my own fate and the future destinies of my country."[55]

Adams released everything over to God and valued the relationship between dependence on God and God's subsequent divine favor. Adams's reverence for God was further evidenced by his membership in the American Bible Society, in which he once served as a Vice President. In his reply to an invitation to attend one of the Society's anniversaries, Adams spoke highly of the Bible:

> "The distribution of Bibles, if the simplest, is not the least efficacious of the means of extending the blessings of the Gospel to the remotest corners of the earth; for the Comforter is in the sacred volume: and among the receivers of that million of copies distributed by the Society, who shall number the multitudes awakened thereby, with good will to man in their hearts, and with the song of the Lamb upon their lips?
>
> The hope of a Christian is inseparable from his faith. Whoever believes in the divine inspiration of the Holy Scriptures, must hope that the religion of Jesus shall prevail throughout the earth. Never since the foundation of the world have the prospects of mankind been more encouraging to that hope than they appear to be at the present time. And may the associated distribution of the Bible proceed and prosper, till the Lord shall have made "bare his holy arm in the eyes of all the nations; and all the ends of the earth shall see the salvation of our God."[56]

John Quincy Adams believed that the purpose of the Bible was not simply to provide knowledge and wisdom, but also to change lives.

Our seventh president, Andrew Jackson, known for his gallantry during the Battle of New Orleans in the War of 1812, became a national hero. Although Jackson was not initially heavy into religion, his religious orientation and tendencies increased especially during his presidency. Like the founders, Jackson understood the correlation between divine providence and our nation's blessings. In his farewell address in 1837, President Jackson claimed:

> "You have the highest of human trusts committed to your care. Providence has showered on this favored land blessings without number, and has chosen you, as the guardians of freedom, to preserve it for the benefit of the human race. May he who holds in his hands the destinies of nations make you worthy of the favors he has bestowed, and enable you, with pure hearts, and pure hands, and sleepless vigilance, to guard and defend to the end of time the great charge he has committed to your keeping."[57]

As Jackson approached his death, he drew closer to God and the *Holy Bible*, making his relationship with God public. He is noted in his own words as saying:

> "I am in the hands of a merciful God. I have full confidence in his goodness and mercy. My lamp of life is nearly out, and the last glimmer is come. I am ready to depart when called. The Bible is true. The principles and statues of that holy book have been the rule of my life, and I have tried to conform to its spirit as near as possible. Upon that sacred volume I rest my hope for eternal salvation, through the merits and blood of our blessed Lord and Savior, Jesus Christ."[58]

Following Andrew Jackson's tenure as president was Martin Van Buren. Although Van Buren did not overtly broadcast his religious sentiments, there was several times in which he recognized the need for God. For example, in his inaugural address on March 4, 1837, he concluded:

> "Beyond that I only look to the gracious protection of the Divine Being whose strengthening support I humbly solicit, and whom I fervently pray to look down upon us all. May it be among the dispensations of His providence to bless our beloved country with honors and with length of days. May her ways be ways of pleasantness and all her paths be peace!"[59]

Again, another American president referenced the need to rely on God at the start of his term as president. In addition, he recognized the need for prayer in anticipation of not only getting our needs met, but also being able to relate to the one who supplies those needs.

Our founders' precedent continued to live on as President James Polk also viewed the United States as a nation that benefited from divine providence. On March 4, 1845, at the start of his inaugural address, Polk confidently remarked:

> "In assuming responsibilities so vast I fervently invoke the aid of that Almighty Ruler of the Universe in whose hands are the destinies of nations and of men to guard this Heaven-favored land against the mischiefs which without His guidance might arise from an unwise public policy. With a firm reliance upon the wisdom of Omnipotence to sustain and direct me in the path of duty which I am appointed to pursue, I stand in the presence of this assembled multitude of my countrymen to take upon myself the solemn obligation "to the best of my ability to preserve, protect, and defend the Constitution of the United States."[60]

We witness once again a national magnate who humbled himself before God and the entire nation to seek God's direction and guidance. President Polk instantly established the need for reliance on God. In an annual message to Congress on December 2, 1845, Polk expressed the same sentiments:

> "Under the blessings of Divine Providence and the benign influence of our free institutions, it stands before the world a spectacle of national happiness.
> With our unexampled advancement in all the elements of national greatness, the affection of the people is confirmed for the Union of the States and for the doctrines of popular liberty which lie at the foundation of our Government. It becomes us in humility to make our devout acknowledgments to the Supreme Ruler of the Universe for the inestimable civil and religious blessings with which we are favored."[61]

Such a proclamation should serve as assurance for the people since it reveals humility, as a man in a powerful leadership role turns to God first and primarily rather than touting his own influence, strength and power. As with anything else in life, when we think more highly of ourselves, we become dependent on ourselves and are likely to put any divine guidance aside in our decision-making. President Polk was one of our early presidents who freely attributed America's greatness to God's favor. He forfeited pride for humility when it came to relying on God in order to prolong divine favor on our nation.

President Zachary Taylor was no different. He ended his inaugural address on March 5, 1849 with the same spirit of gratitude toward God as his predecessors. He affirmed:

> "In conclusion I congratulate you, my fellow-citizens, upon the high state of prosperity to which the goodness of Divine Providence has conducted our common country. Let us invoke a continuance of the same protecting care which has led us from small beginnings to the eminence we this day occupy, and let us seek to deserve that continuance by prudence and moderation in our councils, by well-directed attempts to assuage the bitterness which too often

marks unavoidable differences of opinion, by the promulgation and practice of just and liberal principles, and by an enlarged patriotism, which shall acknowledge no limits but those of our own widespread Republic."[62]

Since our nation's independence, president after president believed and promoted the reciprocity of dependence on and reverence for God. One of the ways in which to experience God's favor is to both declare it and expect it and this is exactly what our leadership did since our founding. Our founders understood we all have access to God's favor, but it can only be activated with our faith in and dependence on God. Faith without supporting action is faith nonexistent. It is one thing to claim faith, while it is something totally different to exercise faith. Our founders understood that faith is not activated by ritual and empty rhetoric but by supporting deeds.

President Franklin Pierce also understood that the wisdom of man is finite and rather than view things from man's perspective, it is necessary to view things from God's perspective. Toward the end of Franklin Pierce's inaugural address on March 4, 1853, the fourteenth president humbly stressed:

> "But let not the foundation of our hope rest upon man's wisdom. It will not be sufficient that sectional prejudices find no place in the public deliberations. It will not be sufficient that the rash counsels of human passion are rejected. It must be felt that there is no national security but in the nation's humble, acknowledged dependence upon God and His overruling providence."[63]

The Book of Proverbs warns us of man's limited wisdom versus God's infinite wisdom:

> *"My son, if you accept my words and store up my commands within you, turning your ear to wisdom and applying your heart to understanding, and if you*

call out for insight and cry aloud for understanding, and if you look for it as for silver and search for it as for hidden treasure, then you will understand the fear of the LORD and find the knowledge of God. For the LORD gives wisdom, and from his mouth come knowledge and understanding." **Proverbs 2:1-6 (NIV)**

From the signing of the Treaty of Paris in 1783, which ended the American Revolution, to the period leading up to the Civil War, America had blossomed with success and prosperity as a result of revering and honoring God. Some will argue America fell into a comfort zone after it received its independence from Britain, causing Americans to relish in this success and prosperity, to acquire confidence in themselves, and to stray from God. Could it be that as we developed into a stable country, free of British tyranny, we became too dependent on our own strength? All too often, when a state of bliss and ease exists, God becomes a distant phenomenon. It is only when circumstances become dire that we call out to God.

As we all know, self-reliance and pride, which are both conditions common to mankind, have a tendency of settling in when things are going well. The Book of Proverbs also tells us, *"Pride goeth before destruction and a haughty spirit before a fall."* **Proverbs 16:18 (KJV)** When mankind pushes God and His commandments away, mankind is apt to make blunders in society in which destruction follows. During this period in our history, one of those blunders was the proliferation of slavery by the southern states, leading to the succession of eleven states, the subsequent internal strife within our nation, and eventually warfare between North and South.

Fortunately, the U.S. was blessed to have a president in office at the time who was a God-fearing man. President Abraham Lincoln followed in the footsteps of our founders and realized the need to depend upon God. He emphasized dependence on God versus self-reliance in the affairs of men. Lincoln attributed our successes as a young nation to God and understood the divine tenet of we reap what we sow as a nation. If we sow dependence and reliance on God, we reap His blessings and favor. On the other hand, if we sow self-reliance, pride and repudiation of God, we reap God's consequences of disobedience. Since the birth of mankind, this divine tenet has been implacable and Lincoln exercised it. Since God does not change, His principles also do not change. Lincoln further knew that we can go right to God in prayer with boldness and confidence because of His unconditional love and grace. In a message to Congress in special session on July 4, 1861, President Lincoln asserted, "And having thus chosen our course, without guile, and with pure purpose, let us renew our trust in God, and go forward without fear, and with manly hearts."[64]

President Lincoln is renowned for having the internal fortitude to stand up to one of our country's greatest injustices- slavery. Even before he assumed the duties as president, Lincoln was vocal in speaking out against slavery. In a speech in Peoria, Illinois, on October 16, 1854, he made these piercing remarks:

> "I cannot but hate [the declared indifference for slavery's spread]. I hate it because of the monstrous injustice of slavery itself. I hate it because it deprives our republican example of its just influence in the world -- enables the enemies of free institutions, with plausibility, to taunt us as hypocrites -- causes the real friends of freedom to doubt our sincerity, and especially because it forces so many really good men amongst ourselves into an open war with the very fundamental principles of civil liberty -- criticizing [sic] the Declaration of Independence, and insisting that there is no right principle of action but self-interest."[65]

During the famous Lincoln-Douglas debates in 1858, Lincoln did not hide his sentiments on slavery. He insisted all men regardless of race are included under the Declaration of Independence. According to Lincoln:

"There is no reason in the world why the negro is not entitled to all the natural rights enumerated in the Declaration of Independence, the right to life, liberty and the pursuit of happiness. I hold that he is as much entitled to these as the white man."[66]

In a letter to Henry Pierce and others, dated April 6, 1859, Lincoln eloquently claimed: "Those who deny freedom to others, deserve it not for themselves; and, under a just God, cannot long retain it."[67] Lincoln's dynamic leadership, firm character, and untiring zeal for freedom for all of mankind stood up to the evil force of slavery.

His actions to abolish slavery defined his presidency. To this day, slavery has served as a pockmark on our Christian heritage and culture. However, as mentioned in the previous chapter, we can be assured God works all things together for the greater good. No matter how great the injustice and no matter how difficult this may be able to grasp, we need to have faith in His promise. Lincoln did. Obviously Lincoln was not favorably liked especially since half of the country indulged in slavery at the top; however, he still stood on principle and fought for the equal basic treatment of all men. Lincoln understood that it was not about race but about building relationships with all mankind. Beginning the new year of 1863, Lincoln issued the Emancipation Proclamation. It opened with:

"That on the first day of January, in the year of our Lord one thousand eight hundred and sixty-three, all persons held as slaves within any State or designated part of a State, the people whereof shall then be in rebellion against the United States, shall be then, thenceforward, and forever free; and the Executive Government of the United States, including the military and naval authority thereof, will recognize and maintain the freedom of such persons, and will do no act or acts to repress such persons, or any of them, in any efforts they may make for their actual freedom."[68]

It is said that only the one who wholeheartedly and genuinely serves is qualified to lead. This is true leadership. Lincoln demonstrated this as he fought for the freedom of all men and insisted that "a house divided against itself cannot stand."[69] Lincoln was only obeying and enforcing God's declaration that man must do onto man as he would want done to him. Despite the heavy flak he received for his adamant position against slavery, Lincoln was only acting out of obedience and commitment to God's precepts.

Perhaps, one of Lincoln's most indelible speeches came on March 30, 1863 during the Civil War when he made a proclamation appointing a national day of prayer and fasting. Recognizing the severity of the state of affairs, with a humbled spirit directed towards God, Lincoln boldly proclaimed:

> "WHEREAS, The Senate of the United States; devoutly recognizing the Supreme authority and just government of Almighty God in all the affairs of men and nations, has, by a resolution, requested the President to designate and set apart a day for National prayer and humiliation.
>
> And Whereas, it is the duty of nations, as well as of men, to owe their dependence upon the overruling power of God, to confess their sins and transgressions, in humble sorrow, yet with assured hope that genuine repentance will lead to mercy and pardon, and to recognize the sublime truth announced in the Holy Scriptures and proven by all history, that those nations only are blessed whose God is the Lord.
>
> And, inasmuch as we know that by His Divine law, nations, like individuals, are subjected to punishments and chastisements in this world, may we not justly fear that the awful calamity of civil war, which now desolates the land, may be but a punishment inflicted upon us for our presumptuous sins, to the needful end of our national reformation as a whole people?

We have been the recipients of the choicest bounties of Heaven. We have been preserved these many years in peace and prosperity. We have grown in numbers, wealth, and power as no other nation has ever grown.

BUT WE HAVE FORGOTTEN GOD.

We have forgotten the gracious hand which preserved us in peace, and multiplied and enriched and strengthened us; and have vainly imagined, in the deceitfulness of our hearts, that all these blessings were produced by some superior wisdom and virtue of our own. Intoxicated with unbroken success, we have become too self-sufficient to feel the necessity of redeeming and preserving grace, too proud to pray to the God that made us!

IT BEHOOVES US, THEN, TO HUMBLE OURSELVES BEFORE THE OFFENDED POWER, TO CONFESS OUR NATIONAL SINS, AND TO PRAY TO THE GOD THAT MADE US!

Now, therefore, in compliance with the request, and fully concurring in the views of the Senate, I do, by this my proclamation, designate and set apart Thursday, the 30th day of April, 1863, as a day of National Humiliation, Fasting, and Prayer. And I do hereby request all the people to abstain on that day from their ordinary secular pursuits, and to unite, at their several places of public worship and their respective homes, in keeping the day holy to the Lord, and devoted to the humble discharge of the religious duties proper to that solemn occasion.

All this being done, in sincerity and truth, let us then rest humbly in the hope, authorized by the Divine teachings, that the united cry of the Nation will be heard on high, and answered with blessings, no less the pardon of our national sins, and restoration of our now divided and suffering country to its former happy condition of unity and peace."[70]

  Lincoln's words were rife with humility and contrition but also expectation. Lincoln knew the U.S. needed a miracle and divine favor from God during these troubled times. How else would one have expected the U.S. to get back on track- certainly not through man's strength and erudition alone? Lincoln's aforementioned words evince his conviction that the American people could experience God's goodness once again if they were to get on God's path. Like Washington during the American Revolution, Lincoln relied on his faith because he knew in his own strength he was incapable of healing the divided nation. Despite the horrors and challenges of the Civil War, Lincoln was not deterred in seeking divine help, and as a result, the Union was preserved. Like the founders, Lincoln was confident to hear from God as He has promised: *"O taste and see that the LORD is good: blessed is the man that trusteth in him."* ***Psalm 34:8 (KJV)*** It does not get any clearer than that and this promise still exists today.

  Although President Andrew Johnson is infamous for being the first sitting American president to be impeached (but not removed from office), he did have a reverence for God. Caught in the cross-fire of Civil War politics, the House of Representatives impeached him largely as a result of violating the Tenure of Office Act. This specific act prevented the president from removing anyone from office who was appointed by a former president unless approved by the Senate. Despite this legislative stricture, Johnson removed Edwin Stanton, the Secretary of War, from office.

  During the earlier days of the Civil War when the Confederate forces threatened Nashville, Johnson vowed to burn the city rather than to surrender it. The Union forces were able to prevail and Nashville was preserved. At this time, Johnson proclaimed his faith in God. He declared: "I DO believe in ALMIGHTY GOD! And I believe also in the Bible, and I say I'll be damned if Nashville shall be surrendered!"[71] On a separate occasion, as a U.S. Senator, Johnson revealed a spirit of dependence on God. He remarked:

> "Let us look forward to the time when we can take the flag of our country and nail it below the Cross, and there let it wave as it waved in the olden times, and let us gather around it and inscribed for our motto: "Liberty and Union, one and inseparable, now and forever, and exclaim, Christ first, our country next!"[72]

In his assertion, Johnson emphasized God over country. He understood that it was God who blessed the country when God was put first.

Union Army General, Ulysses S. Grant, continued this theme of dependence on God during his tenure as president. Each Thanksgiving, President Grant openly acknowledged dependence on and reverence for God in his Thanksgiving Proclamation. For example, in 1870, he proclaimed:

> "Whereas it behooves a people sensible of their dependence on the Almighty publicly and collectively to acknowledge their gratitude for his favors and mercies and humbly to beseech for their continuance; and Whereas the people of the United States during the year now about to end have special cause to be thankful for general prosperity, abundant harvests, exemption from pestilence, foreign war, and civil strife: Now, therefore, be it known that I, Ulysses S. Grant, President of the United States, concurring in any similar recommendations from chief magistrates of States, do hereby recommend to all citizens to meet in their respective places of worship on Thursday the 24th day of November next, there to give thanks for the bounty of God during the

year about to close and to supplicate for its continuance hereafter."⁷³

President Grant made it a point to recognize the true meaning of the holiday in the midst of the holiday celebrations. As it has been stressed in the past by former political giants, Grant made it a priority to retell the American people that our blessings as a nation came directly from God's goodness. We are reminded:

> *"For the LORD God is a sun and shield; the LORD bestows favor and honor; no good thing does he withhold from those whose walk is blameless. O LORD Almighty, blessed is the man who trusts in you."* **Psalm 84:11-12 (NIV)**

Rutherford Hayes, our nineteenth president, was another figurehead who served as a Vice President of the American Bible Society. The American Bible Society is still in existence 194 years later. Today it has a global outreach as it distributes Bibles in many different languages through its 147 National Bible Societies. Over the years, the American Bible Society has been effective in transforming and impacting the lives of many. President Hayes believed not only in sharing God's Word, but he also believed the Bible served as a source of strength, hope, and inspiration during those trying times. His conviction was clearly displayed when he remarked:

> "Our County Bible Society holds its yearly meeting soon. As one of the vice-presidents of the general society of the county, as a non-church member, a non-professor of religion, I may say why men of the world, friends of their country and of their race, should support the religion of the Bible--the Christian religion. To worship -- 'the great Creator to adore' -- the wish to establish relations with the Omnipotent Power which made the universe, and which controls it, is a very deeply seated principle of human nature. It is found among all races of men. It is well-nigh

universal. All peoples have some religion. In our day men who cast off the Christian religion show the innate tendency by spending time and effort in Spiritualism. If the God of the Bible is dethroned the goddess of reason is set up. Religion always has been, always will be. Now, the best religion the world has ever had is the religion of Christ."[74]

On another occasion after his presidency, Hayes declared "What a great mistake the man makes who goes about to oppose this religion! What a crime, if we may judge of men's acts by their results! Nay, what a great mistake is made by him who does not support the religion of the Bible!"[75] There is something that has to be said of our Christian heritage in which the founders established and subsequent presidents have adopted and promoted. It is not just an out-dated trend, but it is the blueprint of our culture. Generation after generation, it has had its influence on society, but today, that influence is being obstructed by anti-Christian and secular forces.

Another example of an American president who was not unabashed to acknowledge his dependence on God was Grover Cleveland who served as the twenty-second and twenty-fourth president of the United States. In his first inaugural address on March 4, 1885, he concluded with these powerful words:

> "And let us not trust to human effort alone, but humbly acknowledging the power and goodness of Almighty God, who presides over the destiny of nations, and who has at all times been revealed in our country's history, let us invoke His aid and His blessings upon our labors."[76]

Similarly, at the end of his second inaugural address on March 4, 1893, with a spirit of humility, President Cleveland firmly stated:

> "Above all, I know there is a Supreme Being who rules the affairs of men and whose goodness and

mercy have always followed the American people, and I know He will not turn from us now if we humbly and reverently seek His powerful aid."[77]

One hundred and sixteen years after our country received its independence, our political leadership was still promoting our founders' sentiments on deference for and dependence on God. I believe the majority of American people want to hear our leadership acknowledge this because it comforts and assures them that our leaders are inferior to God and they are not likely to resort to despotic and tyrannical means. The Office of the President is a powerful position recognized throughout the entire international community and when a president references servitude to the Almighty and speaks and acts in subservience to God, it is refreshing to the people of this great land. Presidents like Grover Cleveland, believed although they were privileged to hold a powerful office, God is the sovereign ruler of the universe, who ultimately decides who does and does not rule. The Word of God leaves us this very precept: *"Everyone must submit himself to the governing authorities, for there is no authority except that which God has established. The authorities that exist have been established by God."* **Romans 13:1 (NIV)**

In a letter to Reverend Wilton Merle Smith, dated March 21, 1906, Cleveland wrote:

> "But you have written words to me that will help me to constantly appreciate the fact that God who has blessed me above all other men, and directed all my ways, deserves my service, and every good cause deserves my best endeavor, as long as my life and strength hall last. I know as no one else can know my limitations, and how fixed and inexorable they are, but I shall trust God, as I have in the past, for strength and opportunity for further usefulness."[78]

Grover exercised trust in God both in and outside of the presidency. Words alone are not influential, but when a genuine spirit backs those words, those words become everything. Cleveland's words were much more than words because they were backed by verifiable behavior. It is not vacuous rhetoric that makes a lasting impact upon others, but it is subsequent proven action to support that rhetoric that fosters a lasting impact.

Our twenty-third president, Benjamin Harrison, served as a church elder and even taught Sunday school at one time. He had a penchant towards God and valued dependence on God. In a letter to Russell Harrison dated August 8, 1887, he wrote:

> "I hope you will renew your Christian faith and duties. It is a great comfort to trust God -- even if His providence is unfavorable. Prayer steadies one when he is walking in slippery places -- even if things asked for are not given."[79]

Harrison understood prayer offers peace, assurance, and stability whether or not God grants a prayer request. Moreover, since prayer is a process, God desires to do something within us first before doing something for us. Through prayer we are better able to understand, withstand, and overcome a quandary and arrive at a resolution to a trial with a spirit of peace.

Like other presidents before him, in his inaugural address, President Harrison proudly and humbly announced:

> "Entering thus solemnly into covenant with each other, we may reverently invoke and confidently expect the favor and help of Almighty God—that He will give to me wisdom, strength, and fidelity, and to our people a spirit of fraternity and a love of righteousness and peace."[80]

At the end of his address, Harrison remarked on the correlation between God's favor and our nation's blessings- a theme that has imbued American society since its founding. Although this theme has been stressed throughout this chapter by other presidents, it cannot be stressed enough because we need it back today. Harrison concluded the address with:

"No other people have a government more worthy of their respect and love or a land so magnificent in extent, so pleasant to look upon, and so full of generous suggestion to enterprise and labor. God has placed upon our head a diadem and has laid at our feet power and wealth beyond definition or calculation. But we must not forget that we take these gifts upon the condition that justice and mercy shall hold the reins of power and that the upward avenues of hope shall be free to all the people."[81]

Likewise, William McKinley expressed the same sentiments in his inaugural address. He immediately acknowledged God's divine favor on the nation. In his opening paragraph, President McKinley announced:

"IN obedience to the will of the people, and in their presence, by the authority vested in me by this oath, I assume the arduous and responsible duties of President of the United States, relying upon the support of my countrymen and invoking the guidance of Almighty God. Our faith teaches that there is no safer reliance than upon the God of our fathers, who has so singularly favored the American people in every national trial, and who will not forsake us so long as we obey His commandments and walk humbly in His footsteps."[82]

Again, the President of the United States reminded the American people about dependence and reliance on God, God's favor, and having a spirit of humility. No matter the situation, whether it is favorable or not, trivial or major, reliance on God is the answer for all situations. McKinley carried this temperament with him up until his death as he was noted for saying, "Goodbye, all; good-bye. It is God's way. His will be done."[83]

After the unfortunate assassination of President McKinley, Theodore Roosevelt assumed duties of the presidency. Well known for his support of the Progressive Movement and his quote of "speak softly and carry a big stick" to promote peace, Roosevelt was also known to make continuous references to God and the Bible. Although it may not be widely taught today, Roosevelt was not chary in emphasizing respect for God. For example, Roosevelt wrote a book entitled Fear God and Take Your Own Part, and the opening page says it all:

> "Fear God; and take your own part! Fear God in the true sense of the word means to love God, respect God, honor God; and all of this can only be done by loving your neighbor, treating him justly and mercifully and in all ways endeavoring to protect him from injustice and cruelty, thus obeying, as far as our human frailty will permit, the great immutable law of righteousness."[84]

When it comes to a call for reverence and honor to God, it cannot be made any clearer. Roosevelt said it all. Furthermore, Roosevelt spoke of the importance of preserving the soul of America and preventing it from becoming tainted by external forces outside of God. According to Roosevelt:

> "No abounding material prosperity will avail us, if our spiritual senses atrophy. The foes of our own household, shall surely prevail against us, unless there were to be in our own people, an inner life which finds its outward expression in a morality, not very widely different from that preached by the seers and the prophet of Judea when the grandeur that was Greece and the glory that was Rome, still lay in the future."[85]

This message needs to be emphasized today as money and materialism has predominated reverence for God. The love of God has been replaced by the love of money and other things. Like other presidents before him, Roosevelt understood when God is placed as the priority and everything else is ancillary, stability befalls upon a society. As evidenced in the Bible and as witnessed throughout history, a society is sure to reap economic stability and prosperity when God is placed at the center of society.

Roosevelt displayed his support of the Word of God when he wrote a letter inside the pocket New Testaments that the New York Bible Society distributed to soldiers who were entering the World War I theater of operations in 1917-1918. Roosevelt understood the Bible was the ultimate source of strength, wisdom, and favor. In fact, he is known for saying that "a thorough knowledge of the Bible is worth more than a college education."[86] In his letter to the soldiers, Roosevelt wrote:

> "THE TEACHINGS OF THE NEW TESTAMENT ARE FORESHADOWED IN MICAH'S VERSE (MICAH VI. 8): 'WHAT MORE DOES THE LORD REQUIRE OF THEE THAN TO DO JUSTICE, AND TO LOVE MERCY, AND TO WALK HUMBLY WITH THY GOD?'
>
> DO JUSTICE; AND THEREFORE FIGHT VALIANTLY AGAINST THE ARMIES OF GERMANY AND TURKEY, FOR THESE NATIONS IN THIS CRISIS STAND FOR THE REIGN OF MOLOCH AND BEELZEBUB ON THIS EARTH.
>
> LOVE MERCY; TREAT PRISONERS WELL; SUCCOR THE WOUNDED; TREAT EVERY WOMAN AS IF SHE WERE YOUR OWN SISTER; CARE FOR THE LITTLE CHILDREN, AND

BE TENDER WITH THE OLD AND HELPLESS.

WALK HUMBLY; YOU WILL DO SO IF YOU STUDY THE LIFE AND TEACHINGS OF THE SAVIOR.

MAY THE GOD OF JUSTICE AND MERCY HAVE YOU IN HIS KEEPING."[87]

Roosevelt exhorted soldiers not only to adopt an intrepid spirit but to do so with a spirit of humility with their focus on God for His strength and favor. What greater comfort is there for a soldier in harm's way to be consoled by the Word of God? As a military officer himself during the Spanish-American War and a recipient of the Medal of Honor, Roosevelt appreciated the solace that the Word of God provides in trying times such as warfare.

Our twenty-seventh president, William Howard Taft, was another president who publicly called upon the support of God during his stint as president. He acknowledged the necessity of divine aid to assist with the heavy onus of being the president of the U.S. I am not sure about you, but every time I hear someone in a prominent leadership position genuinely acknowledge God with heart and not rhetoric, I am soothed. During his inaugural address, he concluded:

> "Having thus reviewed the questions likely to recur during my administration, and having expressed in a summary way the position which I expect to take in recommendations to Congress and in my conduct as an Executive, I invoke the considerate sympathy and support of my fellow-citizens and the aid of the Almighty God in the discharge of my responsible duties."[88]

During his presidency, each Thanksgiving, President Taft recognized the blessings that the U.S. had received from God. For example, he began his 1912 proclamation with:

> "A God-fearing nation, like ours, owes it to its inborn and sincere sense of moral duty to testify its devout gratitude to the All-giver for the countless benefits it has enjoyed. For many years it has been customary at the close of the year for the national Executive to call upon his fellow-countrymen to offer praise and thanks to God for the manifold blessings vouchsafed to them in the past and to unite in earnest suppliance for their continuance."[89]

Like others before him, President Taft was not absentminded to the fact there is a direct relationship between reverence for God and our nation's subsequent well-being. A nation is sure to reap success, stability, and prosperity when God is exulted.

President Woodrow Wilson entered the White House with a respect and appreciation for Christianity. In fact, when he was the New Jersey Governor, he delivered a speech entitled "The Bible and Progress" in which he connected Biblical guidance with civic progression. In the speech, Wilson proudly professed, "America was born a Christian nation. America was born to exemplify that devotion to the elements of righteousness which are derived from the revelations of Holy Scripture."[90] There is no room for interpretation in Wilson's declaration. In today's secular society, this message is not as lucid as it once was. As other religions are tolerated while Christianity is vilified in our multicultural atmosphere, efforts are made to conceal our bedrock of Christian heritage.

In both his inaugural addresses, Woodrow Wilson acknowledged the importance and relevance of depending on God. In his first inaugural address, he concluded:

> "This is not a day of triumph; it is a day of dedication. Here muster, not the forces of party, but the forces of humanity. Men's hearts wait upon us;

men's lives hang in the balance; men's hopes call upon us to say what we will do. Who shall live up to the great trust? Who dares fail to try? I summon all honest men, all patriotic, all forward-looking men, to my side. God helping me, I will not fail them, if they will but counsel and sustain me!"[91]

In his second inaugural address, Wilson remarked: "I pray God that I may be given the wisdom and prudence to do my duties in the true spirit of this great people."[92] Throughout his two terms as president, Wilson had a reputation of turning to God and the Bible for wisdom, strength, and favor. At one particular moment, he prayed:

> "There are a good many problems before the American people today and before me as President, but I expect to find the solution to those problems just in the proportion that I am faithful in the study of the Word of God."[93]

Wilson's trust in God could not have been more appropriate especially since at the time of his second term, Germany defied American neutrality from warfare by sinking innocent American merchant ships. Despite these complications, Wilson highlighted the importance of trusting in God especially during trying times. After all, it is adversity that truly manifests the strength of our faith. Since times of adversity are opportunities to exercise trust in God, in turn, they allow us the chance to witness the goodness and power of God.

Another one of our presidents who valued dependence on God was Warren Harding. Prior to his presidency, he was known to have said, "It is my conviction that the fundamental trouble with the people of the United States is that they have gotten too far away from Almighty God."[94] Like others before him, Harding took a bold position to promote the fact that God demands mankind to develop an intimate relationship with Him and thus rely on Him for the most frivolous matters to the most pivotal matters of life. Harding's reverence for God and appreciation for the spiritual motivation of our Founding Fathers is witnessed in the opening of his inaugural address. He declared:

> "Standing in this presence, mindful of the solemnity of this occasion, feeling the emotions which no one may know until he senses the great weight of responsibility for himself, I must utter my belief in the divine inspiration of the Founding Fathers. Surely there must have been God's intent in the making of this new-world Republic. Ours is an organic law which had but one ambiguity, and we saw that effaced in a baptism of sacrifice and blood, with union maintained, the Nation supreme, and its concord inspiring. We have seen the world rivet its hopeful gaze on the great truths on which the founders wrought."[95]

President Harding concluded the address by emphasizing the need for him to walk closely to God- a message that is worth reflecting upon and embracing in today's degenerate and anti-Christian society. Harding ended with these words:

> "I accept my part with single-mindedness of purpose and humility of spirit, and implore the favor and guidance of God in His Heaven. With these I am unafraid, and confidently face the future.
>
> I have taken the solemn oath of office on that passage of Holy Writ wherein it is asked: "What doth the Lord require of thee but to do justly, and to love mercy, and to walk humbly with thy God?" This I plight to God and country."[96]

Calvin Coolidge was another American president who spoke openly about God and Christianity. President Coolidge reminded Americans of the spiritual versus temporal aspect of America. In a nation richly blessed as America, it is wise to be reminded of eternal matters especially since we live in an ever-increasing profane culture. At the end of his inaugural address, Coolidge finished with these thoughts:

> "America seeks no earthly empire built on blood and force. No ambition, no temptation, lures her to thought of foreign dominions. The legions which she sends forth are armed, not with the sword, but with the cross. The higher state to which she seeks the allegiance of all mankind is not of human, but of divine origin. She cherishes no purpose save to merit the favor of Almighty God."[97]

At another address later on during his presidency, Coolidge spoke of this same aspect of temporal versus spiritual. At the end of his address to commemorate the 150th anniversary of the Declaration of Independence, President Coolidge reminded Americans:

> "No other theory is adequate to explain or comprehend the Declaration of Independence. It is the product of the spiritual insight of the people. We live in an age of science and of abounding accumulation of material things. These did not create our Declaration. Our Declaration created them. The things of the spirit come first. Unless we cling to that, all our material prosperity, overwhelming though it may appear, will turn to a barren scepter in our grasp. If we are to maintain the great heritage which has been bequeathed to us, we must be like-minded as the fathers who created it. We must not sink into a pagan materialism. We must cultivate the reverence which they had for the things that are holy. We must follow the spiritual and moral leadership which they showed. We must keep replenished, that they may glow with a more compelling flame, the altar fires before which they worshiped."[98]

In his remarks, Coolidge brought the American people back to our fundamental roots to remind them of the important things in life. It was our divine freedom as a result of our founders' dependence on God that spawned prosperity and not vice versa. He admonished that reverence for God is where our priority should be focused on.

He put political correctness aside and spoke of Christianity with boldness and veracity. For example, Coolidge spoke at an international convention of the Young Men's Christian Association of the United States and Canada where he punctuated the relevance of Christianity. In his address, he said this of Christianity:

> "Those who have become partakers of its inspirations and its consolations, since it first began its early march over the hostile territory of the Roman Empire, have been constantly spreading its truths among all their associates. If that faith is to maintain its vitality that work must go on. It is not enough that there should be action in the pulpits - there must be reaction in the pews. It will not be sufficient to have exalted preaching by the clergy unless there is exalted living by the laity. Your Christian Associations represent a practical effort to organize and augment in every field the lay forces and to translate the truths of religion into the life of the people."[99]

In this segment, Coolidge referred to the fact that the Church alone should not be the only vehicle used in the promotion, sustainability, and expansion of Christianity. According to Coolidge, the people should have a role to play just as much as the Church does when it comes to spreading the truth of Christianity.

President Herbert Hoover's comments during his inaugural address on depending upon God could not have been more appropriate especially since the unfortunate Wall Street Crash of 1929 had materialized in the United States within the first year of his presidency and consequently brought economic malaise throughout the nation. In his opening remarks Hoover said:

"THIS occasion is not alone the administration of the most sacred oath which can be assumed by an American citizen. It is a dedication and consecration under God to the highest office in service of our people. I assume this trust in the humility of knowledge that only through the guidance of Almighty Providence can I hope to discharge its ever-increasing burdens."[100]

This is exactly the type of disposition that leadership should adopt during periods of uncertainty and agony. The exercise of humility and dependence on God is a great starting point for any situation, whether it is during strenuous or perfunctory times. Facing the unknown is much more comforting when one's faith rests in the One with absolute power. A spirit of humility and dependence on God relieves burdens, quells anxiety, and restores faith, all of which were needed during the Great Depression.

In his book entitled *American Individualism*, Hoover wrote on the spirit of individualism and explained how every individual is guaranteed individual freedom as a divine right. In one particular chapter, Hoover called attention to the fact that the blessings we reap are not solely the result of our own personal vigor and strength. Instead, there is a spiritual element involved. Our own inspiration is temporal and finite, while divine inspiration is eternal and infinite. When our priority is first set on God we can expect some semblance of peace as things naturally fall into place:

> *"But seek ye first the kingdom of God, and his righteousness; and all these things shall be added unto you.*
>
> *Take therefore no thought for the morrow: for the morrow shall take thought for the things of itself. Sufficient unto the day is the evil thereof."* **Matthew 6:33-34 (KJV)**

In his book, Hoover similarly wrote:

"OUR social and economic system cannot march toward better days unless it is inspired by things of the spirit. It is here that the higher purposes of individualism must find their sustenance. Men do not live by bread alone."[101]

After his time as president, Herbert Hoover continued to emphasize the need to call upon God. In a nationally broadcast radio address to decry Communism and to encourage United Nations' membership be restricted to those nations who reject Communism, Hoover called for a spiritual mobilization. His words were:

"What the world needs today is a definite, spiritual mobilization of the nations who believe in God against the hideous ideas of the police state and human slavery. The world needs mobilization against this creeping Red Imperialism. The United States needs to know who are with us in the cold war against these practices, and whom we can depend on."[102]

Recognizing the severity and magnitude of the Communist threat, Hoover did not hesitate to seek the Lord since he understood that no challenge is too great for God. Despite the lurking threat of Communism, Hoover knew that God was still in control and could be moved by a spiritual mobilization.

During Hoover's presidential administration, the Star-Spangled Banner officially became the United States' national anthem. Although Francis Scott Key first introduced the words of the national anthem in a poem in which he referred to the Battle of Baltimore during the War of 1812, it took a congressional resolution in 1931 to turn his poem into our national anthem. The words of national anthems are typically emblematic of a nation's history, culture, struggles, and norms. America's national anthem references God, and rightly so, since God is engrained in our heritage. How many of us have ever actually paid attention to our anthem's lyrics?

Of particular note are the last several lines in which God is recognized:

> "OH! THUS BE IT EVER, WHEN
> FREEMEN SHALL STAND
> BETWEEN THEIR LOVED HOME AND
> THE WAR'S DESOLATION!
> BLEST WITH VICTORY AND PEACE,
> MAY THE HEAV'N RESCUED LAND
> PRAISE THE POWER THAT HATH MADE AND
> PRESERVED US A NATION.
> THEN CONQUER WE MUST, WHEN
> OUR CAUSE IT IS JUST,
> AND THIS BE OUR MOTTO:
> "IN GOD IS OUR TRUST."
> AND THE STAR-SPANGLED BANNER IN TRIUMPH
> SHALL WAVE
> O'ER THE LAND OF THE FREE AND THE HOME OF
> THE BRAVE![103]

Franklin Delano Roosevelt, our only president to be elected three terms in office, had his hands full as the United States was embroiled in the Great Depression and entered World War II after the Japanese attacks on Pearl Harbor. Roosevelt did not know what the outcome of the war would be, but he had faith and confidence that victory was attainable. The burdens of the presidency do not get any heavier than what faced President Roosevelt. Despite the incredible weight Roosevelt carried as president, he maintained a spirit of optimism. Was it any coincidence then that he often referenced God?

Roosevelt also became known for reaching out to the American people through routine radio broadcasts called "fireside chats." For example, at the end of one "fireside chat" in 1935, President Roosevelt gave praise to God for His guidance and protection. He said:

> "We have survived all of the arduous burdens and the threatening dangers of a great economic calamity.

We have in the darkest moments of our national trials retained our faith in our own ability to master our destiny. Fear is vanishing and confidence is growing on every side, renewed faith in the vast possibilities of human beings to improve their material and spiritual status through the instrumentality of the democratic form of government. That faith is receiving its just reward. For that we can be thankful to the God who watches over America."[104]

One of Roosevelt's greatest and most memorable radio addresses to the American people occurred on June 6, 1944. During this historic broadcast, Roosevelt humbly called upon God and energized the faith of the American people in support of American troops as they waded through the macabre beaches of Normandy on D-Day. The radio address is important to reflect on because once again it illustrated one of our key leaders in all of American history recognizing the need to call upon God during a dire time for favor, protection, and guidance. Roosevelt humbly and confidently prayed:

"My Fellow Americans:

Last night, when I spoke with you about the fall of Rome, I knew at that moment that troops of the United States and our Allies were crossing the Channel in another and greater operation. It has come to pass with success thus far.

And so, in this poignant hour, I ask you to join with me in prayer: Almighty God: Our sons, pride of our nation, this day have set upon a might endeavor, a struggle to preserve our Republic, our religion, and our civilization, and to set free a suffering humanity.

Lead them straight and true; give strength to their arms, stoutness to their hearts, steadfastness in their faith.

They will need Thy blessings. Their road will be long and hard. For the enemy is strong. He may hurl back our forces. Success may not come with rushing speed, but we shall return again and again; and we know that by Thy grace, and by the righteousness of our cause, our sons will triumph.

They will be sore tried, by night and by day, without rest -- until the victory is won. The darkness will be rent by noise and flame. Men's souls will be shaken with the violence of war.

For these men are lately drawn from the ways of peace. They fight not for the lust of conquest. They fight to end conquest. They fight to liberate. They fight to let justice arise, and tolerance and goodwill among all Thy people. They yearn but for the end of battle, for their return to the haven of home.

Some will never return. Embrace these, Father, and receive them, Thy heroic servants, into Thy kingdom.

And for us at home -- fathers, mothers, children, wives, sisters, and brothers of brave men overseas, whose thoughts and prayers are ever with them -- help us, Almighty God, to rededicate ourselves in renewed faith in Thee in this hour of great sacrifice.

Many people have urged that I call the nation into a single day of special prayer. But because the road is long and the desire is great, I ask that our people devote themselves in a continuance of prayer. As we rise to each new day, and again when each day is spent, let words of prayer be on our lips, invoking Thy help to our efforts.

Give us strength, too -- strength in our daily tasks, to redouble the contributions we make in the physical and the material support of our armed forces.

And let our hearts be stout, to wait out the long travail, to bear sorrows that may come, to impart our courage unto our sons wheresoever they may be.

And, O Lord, give us faith. Give us faith in Thee; faith in our sons; faith in each other; faith in our united crusade. Let not the keenness of our spirit ever be dulled. Let not the impacts of temporary events, of temporal matters of but fleeting moment -- let not these deter us in our unconquerable purpose.

With Thy blessing, we shall prevail over the unholy forces of our enemy. Help us to conquer the apostles of greed and racial arrogances. Lead us to the saving of our country, and with our sister nations into a world unity that will spell a sure peace -- a peace invulnerable to the scheming of unworthy men. And a peace that will let all of men live in freedom, reaping the just rewards of their honest toil.

Thy will be done, Almighty God. Amen."[105]

Through his national prayer, Roosevelt provided the American people hope and strength that through reliance and dependence on God, the United States military would prevail on the beaches of Normandy. Prevail it did but at a heavy price with approximately 2,500 American soldier fatalities and even more casualties. Roosevelt's relevant prayer validated the fact that God does listen to and answer righteous prayer requests. Due to the significance of D-Day, June 6, 1944 is one of those dates that every American should reflect on. No matter how much D-Day becomes a distant memory, it is one of those perpetual dates in history that cannot be forgotten for it contributed to the greatness of our nation to this day.

When Harry S. Truman assumed the duties of the presidency, he was also faced with significant domestic and foreign issues. His presidency was defined by his decision to bring World War II to an end by using nuclear weapons on Japan, his leadership in supporting the Marshall Plan to assist with the reconstruction of Europe, and his energy to stifle

Communism through the Truman Doctrine. In the midst of all this activity during his two terms in office, Truman did not neglect calling upon God. President Truman reinvigorated a spiritual campaign in hopes of vanquishing Communism through a global, united religious movement. At a speech in May 1950 at Gonzaga University in Washington, Truman concluded with:

> "In the face of aggressive tyranny, the economic, political, and military strength of free men is a necessity. But we are not increasing our strength just for strength's sake.
>
> We must be strong if we are to expand freedom. We must be strong if free men are to be able to satisfy their moral obligations.
>
> It is the moral and religious beliefs of mankind which alone give our strength meaning and purpose.
>
> The struggle for peace is a struggle for moral and ethical principles. These principles unite us with religious people in every land, who are striving, as we are striving, for brotherhood among men.
>
> In everything we do, at home and abroad, we must demonstrate our clear purpose, and our firm will, to build a world order in which men everywhere can walk upright and unafraid, and do the work of God."[106]

President Truman was one who understood the importance of and valued the significance of our spiritual roots in the founding of this great country. Using the Bible and the Constitution as his guides, Truman promoted the need for God and acknowledged man's desire to live in freedom. At the Attorney General's Conference on law enforcement problems in 1950, Truman spoke of our Godly heritage:

"The fundamental basis of this Nation's law was given to Moses on the Mount. The fundamental basis of our Bill of Rights comes from the teachings which we get from Exodus and St. Matthew, from Isaiah and St. Paul. I don't think we emphasize that enough these days."[107]

In a society that is bountiful with blessings, where it is all too common to take things for granted and become absorbed in materialism and the busyness of daily living, God easily escapes our thoughts. Such references back to our basic roots of God in our country and the freedom that follows cannot be emphasized enough especially since man gets caught up with the trends of society at the time and forgets about God.

Our next president who maintained deference for our Christian heritage and who was also known for his firm leadership and strategic decisiveness during World War II was Dwight Eisenhower. During his presidency, the words "under God" were added to the Pledge of Allegiance. Francis Bellamy, a socialist minister, created the original Pledge of Allegiance in 1892 which stated: "I pledge allegiance to my Flag and the Republic for which it stands, one nation indivisible, with liberty and justice for all."[108] As a result of Eisenhower's clout at the time, his reverence for God, and his anathema of Communism, Eisenhower pushed for the words "under God" to be added to the pledge. Since 1954 we have been pledging our flag with these simple but meaningful words:

"I PLEDGE ALLEGIANCE TO THE FLAG OF THE UNITED STATES OF AMERICA AND TO THE REPUBLIC FOR WHICH IT STANDS, ONE NATION UNDER GOD, INDIVISIBLE, WITH LIBERTY AND JUSTICE FOR ALL."

How many of us have actually reflected on these words and associated them with our Godly heritage and historical progression? More than likely, after reciting the pledge in school, day after day and year after year, the words have lost their purposeful meaning and have become insipid. This is especially true since our Christian heritage is not reflected upon and promoted as it once was. The simple words that describe our very fabric have morphed into nothing but unappreciated rote. Our pledge is something to be internalized, not just memorized. While signing the bill to input the words "under God" in the pledge, Eisenhower affectionately said:

> "In this way we are reaffirming the transcendence of religious faith in America's heritage and future; in this way we shall constantly strengthen those spiritual weapons which forever will be our country's most powerful resource in peace and war."[109]

Acknowledging the importance of depending upon God, Eisenhower spoke of the relevance of adding "under God" to the Pledge of Allegiance at a Knights of Columbus meeting. In his address, Eisenhower remarked:

> "We are particularly thankful to you for your part in the movement to have the words 'under God' added to our Pledge of Allegiance. These words will remind Americans that despite our great physical strength we must remain humble. They will help us to keep constantly in our minds and hearts the spiritual and moral principles which alone give dignity to man, and upon which our way of life is founded. For the contribution which your organization has made to this cause, we must be genuinely grateful."[110]

President Eisenhower was also instrumental in making "In God We Trust" the official motto of the United States. Although the phrase was on U.S. coins since the Civil War, Eisenhower's Secretary of Treasury, George Humphrey, recommended the phrase also be added to paper currency. "In God We Trust," four simple words, which have exhibited America's heritage since its founding, were first printed on paper currency in 1957. These four words have strengthened our identity as a Christian nation. Although we handle money on a daily basis, how many of us have actually reflected on these four simple words and thought of their meaning as it relates to our national development?

Despite Lyndon Johnson's polemical tenure as President as a result of the Vietnam War imbroglio, President Johnson did show reverence towards God throughout his presidency. For example, at the National Day of Prayer in 1965, Johnson proclaimed:

> "Few nations have been so favored by Almighty God, and it is altogether fitting that a day be set aside for this purpose.
>
> Thus it is in the same spirit of humility and conviction demonstrated by our forefathers that I urge each citizen, according to his own conscience to pause on that day to acknowledge our dependence upon God.
>
> In these days of peril and uncertainty, I urge that each of us plead for wisdom, strength and courage.
>
> I urge that we pray for God-given vision and determination to make the sacrifices demanded by our responsibilities to our fellow men in our own Nation and in other lands of this world."[111]

Johnson reminded the American people that just as the founders trusted in God and encouraged Americans to trust in God, the American people must follow in their footsteps. Johnson could not have proffered the American people any more important reminder especially since the Vietnam War divided the country.

On September 8, 1974, President Gerard Ford pardoned Richard Nixon for his actions during the Watergate scandal for the benefit of the country. Within his pardon speech, in an attempt to unite the country, Ford placed an emphasis on God and the role that God has played since our founding. Ford remarked:

"I have promised to uphold the Constitution, to do what is right as God gives me to see the right, and to do the very best that I can for America.

I have asked your help and your prayers, not only when I became President but many times since. The Constitution is the supreme law of our land and it governs our actions as citizens. Only the laws of God, which govern our consciences, are superior to it.

As we are a nation under God, so I am sworn to uphold our laws with the help of God. And I have sought such guidance and searched my own conscience with special diligence to determine the right thing for me to do with respect to my predecessor in this place, Richard Nixon, and his loyal wife and family."[112]

At a time when the nation was in need of healing, Ford granted the pardon in order to surpass the unfortunate crisis and to get on with the more important issues at the time demanding attention. At the same time, Ford referenced our nation's Godly roots to keep the American people focused on what the United States stood for. In other words, Ford did not want the defects of the Watergate scandal to adulterate America's righteous image because he did not equate America's past with its future. As long as man is present on this earth, there will always be room for fallibility. The key is to address the fallibility when it occurs; fix it; and rise above it by reverting back to our Godly heritage. President Ford did just that as he was more interested in focusing on the future of America versus being tangled in past disappointments.

Perhaps one of the most popular contemporary presidents who displayed his reverence and need for God was Ronald Reagan. Known as the "Great Communicator," Reagan possessed spiritual dexterity as he spoke with his heart and was not timorous to display his Christian values. His speeches overflowed with references to God. He deeply valued our country's fundamental Christian heritage and appreciated how our founders promoted God's blessings upon the United States. In a prayer breakfast at Dallas in 1984, Reagan persuasively said:

"WITHOUT GOD, THERE IS NO VIRTUE, BECAUSE THERE'S NO PROMPTING OF THE CONSCIENCE. WITHOUT GOD, WE'RE MIRED IN THE MATERIAL, THAT FLAT WORLD THAT TELLS US ONLY WHAT THE SENSES PERCEIVE. WITHOUT GOD, THERE IS A COARSENING OF THE SOCIETY. AND WITHOUT GOD, DEMOCRACY WILL NOT AND CANNOT LONG ENDURE. IF WE EVER FORGET THAT WE'RE ONE NATION UNDER GOD, THEN WE WILL BE A NATION GONE UNDER."[113]

Reagan further believed that reverence for God and democracy is inseparable. When God is placed first and everything else is subordinate in society, a society is destined to reap individual freedom and societal prosperity. As a result of Reagan's Christian vigor, he reviled Communism and its oppression of the people who have to live under it. He understood our democracy is not perfect, but it does not certainly oppress the people and deprive them of their divine rights like Communism does. He also believed Communism restrained any kind of reverence for God while the state dominated. In his famous "Evil Empire" speech to a meeting of the National Association of Evangelicals in Orlando, Florida, Reagan prayed for the people living under the totalitarian chains of Communism. Reagan prayed:

"YES, LET US PRAY FOR THE SALVATION OF ALL OF THOSE WHO LIVE IN THAT TOTALITARIAN DARKNESS -- PRAY THEY WILL DISCOVER THE JOY OF KNOWING GOD. BUT UNTIL THEY DO, LET US BE AWARE THAT WHILE THEY PREACH THE SUPREMACY OF THE STATE, DECLARE ITS OMNIPOTENCE OVER INDIVIDUAL MAN, AND PREDICT ITS EVENTUAL DOMINATION OF ALL PEOPLES ON THE EARTH, THEY ARE THE FOCUS OF EVIL IN THE MODERN WORLD."[114]

Reagan was consistent in honoring God on all occasions. Whether it was a joyful incident or a grief-stricken tragedy, Reagan was sure to include God in the event. In the aftermath of the Shuttle explosion on January 28, 1986, the country was in need of consolation and assurance. A week later after this horrific tragedy, Reagan continued to assure the nation as he spoke at the National Prayer Breakfast. With composure, Reagan spoke on joy:

> "I used to think it was a poem about the joy of escaping gravity, but even more, it's a poem about joy. And God gave us joy; that was His gift to us. We've all been sad the past week, and yet there was something good about the way we wept together as we said goodbye and suddenly re-remembered that we are a family. And now the time has come to remember the words of the Bible, "Weeping may endure for a night, but joy cometh in the morning (see Ps. 30:5)."[115]

Reagan understood that our circumstances are not the source of our joy, but that the presence of God living within us is the ultimate source of our joy. Reagan was telling the American people that their sadness could be uplifted through their dependence on God. The only way that we can lose our joy is by choosing to relinquish it on our own accord. Reagan's faith helped him convey comfort to the American people.

Both Presidents George H. Bush, and son, George W. Bush, firmly believed in the role God played in America's heritage and revered God during their time in office. George H. Bush acknowledged the power behind prayer in his public addresses. In his address to the National Association of Evangelicals in March 1992, President Bush said, "Prayer always has been important in our lives. And without it, I really am convinced, more and more convinced that no man or no woman who has the privilege of serving in the Presidency could carry out their duties without prayer."[116] On another occasion, the same year, at a Prayer Breakfast he spoke of prayer. He said:

> "You know, I've been President for 3 1/2 years now. More than ever, I believe with all my heart that one cannot be President of our great country without a belief in God, without the truth that comes on one's knees. For me, prayer has always been important but quite personal."[117]

President Bush understood that genuine prayer seeks to ascertain God's will in order to carry out His agenda versus one's own personal agenda. Moreover, through time in prayer, one is investing in a lifelong and intimate relationship with God. As president, Bush was convinced that prayer sustained him throughout his time in office.

President George W. Bush believed in and frequently commented on the association between God and freedom. He firmly believed it was the will of God that all people have the opportunity to live in freedom. Although his decision to invade Iraq was highly controversial, one of his main arguments for doing so was to free the Iraqi people from the tyrannical reign of Saddam Hussein. He desired for the Iraqi people to live in freedom and not oppression. In his 2004 State of the Union Address, President Bush remarked:

> "We also hear doubts that democracy is a realistic goal for the greater Middle East, where freedom is rare. Yet it is mistaken and condescending to assume that whole cultures and great religions are incompatible with liberty and self-government. I believe that God has planted in every human heart the desire to live in freedom. And even when that desire is crushed by tyranny for decades, it will rise again."[118]

President Bush was convinced that regardless of one's culture and circumstances, the human soul hungers for freedom since it is a shared human value.

GOD'S FOOTPRINT THROUGHOUT THE NATIONAL CAPITOL

Anyone who has been to Washington D.C. and has not paid close attention to the surroundings would be amazingly surprised to discover the number of references there are to God on the monuments and memorials. Reverence towards God is displayed on our most iconic monuments. If our nation's past was not reverent of God, then why are our most public buildings ornamented by biblical and Godly references? In a city otherwise known for its political gamesmanship, deference for God is on display for all Americans to absorb. If only our political leaders and the American people could put those references to practice. In 1951, President Truman gave an address to the Washington Pilgrimage of American Churchmen in which he pointed out our Godly footprint. Within the address, he remarked:

> "You will see, as you make your rounds, that this Nation was established by men who believed in God. You will see that our Founding Fathers believed that God created this Nation. And I believe it, too. They believed that God was our strength in time of peril and the source of all our blessings."[119]

In his opinion for *Van Orden v. Perry*, Chief Justice William Rehnquist mentioned something similar to reflect the footprint of God on our society. Thomas Van Orden sued the state of Texas in federal district court, in which he argued a Ten Commandments monument on the grounds of the state capitol building was unconstitutional. Rehnquist strongly commented:

"IN THIS CASE WE ARE FACED WITH A DISPLAY OF THE TEN COMMANDMENTS ON GOVERNMENT PROPERTY OUTSIDE THE TEXAS STATE CAPITOL.

SUCH ACKNOWLEDGMENTS OF THE ROLE PLAYED BY THE TEN COMMANDMENTS IN OUR NATION'S HERITAGE ARE COMMON THROUGHOUT AMERICA. WE NEED ONLY LOOK WITHIN OUR OWN COURTROOM. SINCE 1935, MOSES HAS STOOD, HOLDING TWO TABLETS THAT REVEAL PORTIONS OF THE TEN COMMANDMENTS WRITTEN IN HEBREW, AMONG OTHER LAWGIVERS IN THE SOUTH FRIEZE. REPRESENTATIONS OF THE TEN COMMANDMENTS ADORN THE METAL GATES LINING THE NORTH AND SOUTH SIDE OF THE COURTROOM AS WELL AS THE DOORS LEADING INTO THE COURTROOM. MOSES ALSO SITS ON THE EXTERIOR EAST FACADE OF THE BUILDING HOLDING THE TEN COMMANDMENTS TABLETS."[120]

On the Washington Monument, the words "*Laus Deo*" which means "Praise to be to God" are inscribed at the apex of the monument on the aluminum cap that faces the U.S. Capitol. Could it be any coincidence that these words are located at the highest point of the city over probably the most influential city in the international community? In addition, in the staircase, there are biblical verses inscribed in the blocks of the monument. For example, one verse is taken from ***Exodus 28:36*** and reads, "*Holiness unto the Lord.*" It would be great if the American tourists paid more attention to these Godly references and their connection to our heritage rather than just the physical beauty of the monument. No doubt, the Washington Monument is a sonorous site to witness, but more importantly, it symbolizes George Washington, the father of America, who possessed an intimate and personal affinity with God.

The Jefferson Memorial is no different for it contains a handful of references to God. Within the statue chamber is the inscription: "I have sworn upon the altar of God eternal hostility against every form of tyranny over the mind of man." Moreover three of the four panels reference God. One of the panels has an excerpt from the Declaration of Independence:

"We hold these truths to be self-evident that all men are created equal, that they are endowed by their Creator with certain inalienable rights, among these are life, liberty, and the pursuit of happiness, that to secure these rights governments are instituted among men..."

Another panel contains the words:

"Almighty God hath created the mind free...All attempts to influence it by temporal punishments or burthens...are a departure from the plan of the Holy Author of our religion...No man shall be compelled to frequent or support any religious worship or ministry or shall otherwise suffer on account of his religious opinions or belief, but all men shall be free to profess and by argument to maintain, their opinions in matters of religion. I know but one code of morality for men whether acting singly or collectively."

A third panel references God with these words:

"God who gave us life gave us liberty. Can the liberties of a nation be secure when we have removed a conviction that these liberties are the gift of God? Indeed I tremble for my country when I reflect that God is just, that his justice cannot sleep forever. Commerce between master and slave is despotism. Nothing is more certainly written in the book of fate than these people are to be free. Establish the law for educating the common people. This it is the business of the state to effect and on a general plan."

The Lincoln Memorial is also inscribed with references to God. On one part of the memorial is Lincoln's famous Gettysburg Address. Of particular interest is the last sentence:

"...that we here highly resolve that these dead shall not have died in vain -- that this nation, under God, shall have a new birth of freedom -- and that government of the people, by the people, for the people, shall not perish from the earth."

On another section of the memorial is Lincoln's second inaugural address in which he references God and the Bible in talking about the Civil War and slavery. For example, at the end of the address, Lincoln declared:

"With malice toward none, with charity for all, with firmness in the right as God gives us to see the right, let us strive on to finish the work we are in, to bind up the nation's wounds, to care for him who shall have borne the battle and for his widow and his orphan, to do all which may achieve and cherish a just and lasting peace among ourselves and with all nations."

It is only appropriate that the Lincoln Memorial is decorated with Godly inscriptions since President Lincoln was a God fearing man, as described earlier, who sincerely believed in God's providence upon this great country.

The U.S. Capitol, a symbol of American freedom and democracy, is embellished with Godly imagery and references. Within the rotunda of the U.S. Capitol are eight historic and picturesque paintings, four of which reference God. The "Landing of Columbus" painting features Columbus looking up and praising God while others around him are kneeling and giving thanks. As mentioned earlier, the teachings of Scripture and Columbus's personal relationship with God had inspired him to set sail to the New World. The "Baptism of Pocahontas" painting shows a minister baptizing Pocahontas as she reverently kneels on her knees with clasped hands. The painting "Embarkation of the Pilgrims" illustrates the Pilgrims praying on the deck of the ship Speedwell prior to their departure from Holland to North America in chase of religious freedom. Included within the painting is William Brewster who is holding the Bible, Governor Carver who is kneeling and bowing his head, and pastor John Robinson who is extending his arms and looking up towards the heavens.

The group is praying in earnest for God's divine protection and guidance for their voyage ahead. The "Discovery of the Mississippi" painting reveals Spanish explorer Hernando De Soto entering the Mississippi area on his horse surrounded by Native Americas, but more importantly, it reveals a monk praying as several other gentlemen raise a crucifix into the ground. Why would these historic paintings be in the U.S. Capitol if our Christian heritage was not significant to our well-being as a nation? Symbolism is everything. Instead of viewing these paintings solely as beautiful art pieces, we need to understand the meaning behind them as it relates to God and our heritage. God clearly had a role in the founding of our nation.

In addition to the paintings, there are inscriptions referencing God throughout the Capitol. Inside the Cox corridor within the House wing is the inscription: "America! God shed His grace on Thee, and crown thy good with brotherhood from sea to shining sea!" This should sound familiar since it is taken from *America the Beautiful*. The inscription *"In God We Trust"* is located both inside the House and Senate chambers. Also inside the House chamber is a marble sculpture of Moses. In the Senate chamber is the phrase *"Annuit coeptis"* which in Latin means God has favored our undertakings.

Within the Capitol chapel is a stained glass window depicting George Washington on his knees praying with **Psalm 16:1** inscribed in the background: *"Preserve me O God for in thee do I put my trust."* How powerful is this- one of the most renowned figureheads of the United States humbly on his knee praying to God? It does not get any more symbolic than this to illustrate the depth of our Christian heritage. So, then why must we turn a blind eye towards it? The purpose of the chapel is to give lawmakers a quiet place to pray and meditate before casting votes on key issues that can have serious repercussions. It provides a serene place for lawmakers to seek wisdom, strength, and guidance from God. How appropriate?

Our Library of Congress is another historic building in which our Godly heritage is on display throughout it. Inside the Main Reading Room are eight statues above the marble columns. Above the figure Religion is the Scripture ***Micah 6:8*** that reads: *"What doth the Lord require of thee, but to do justly and to love mercy, and to walk humbly with thy God?"* In the North Corridor are four circular paintings on the wall. One of those paintings is called Knowledge. Under it is a William Shakespeare quote reading: "Ignorance is the curse of God; knowledge is the wing wherewith we fly to heaven." In the East Corridor are two of the most valuable troves located within the Library of Congress. They are the Gutenberg Bible and the Giant Bible of Mainz. While the Giant Bible of Mainz was written in ink, the Gutenberg Bible signified the beginning of the printing press for it was one of the earliest books ever printed out of Europe. Within the rotunda is a phrase from Lord Tennyson, a distinct poet from the United Kingdom, which reads: "One God, one law, one element and one far-off divine event to which the whole creation moves." Also in the rotunda is a noticeable bronze statue of Moses holding firmly onto the Ten Commandments.

The U.S. Supreme Court, our bastion of law and order, shows a reverence for God in several ways. After all, the God we serve is a God of law, justice, and order. Inside the courtroom of the Supreme Court building is an engraved sculpture of Moses carrying the Ten Commandments. In the rear of the Supreme Court on the face of the building is another statue of a seated Moses holding onto a tablet in each hand. On the West exterior facade is another depiction of Moses' head. The Ten Commandments are also located on the outer bronze doors and the oak inner doors of the United States Supreme Court building. Moses and the Ten Commandments are also located at state Supreme Courts to include the New York Supreme Court.

There are those who repute that the statues do not reflect Moses and the Ten Commandments but instead reflect general statues of law, order, and justice. Is this just another attempt to cloak our Christian roots? As we all know, the Ten Commandments came directly from the voice of God and were delivered to His servant Moses. God intended Moses to use the Commandments as a guide for God's standard of morality in regulating society. How appropriate is it then for images of Moses with the Ten Commandments to garnish our highest institution of law?

Other buildings in Washington D.C. that possess Godly references include the National Archives building. On the floor of the National Archives is a seal with the Ten Commandments. Inside the White House is the Adams Prayer Mantle which reads:

> "I pray to heaven to bestow the best of blessings on this house and all that hereafter inhabit it...May none but the honest and wise men ever rule under this roof."[121]

Outside the Ronald Reagan building is a noticeable statue of "Liberty of Worship" resting on the Ten Commandments tablet. Although this is not a complete listing of signs of God throughout our nation's capital, it is a solid list to remind us of our Christian heritage.

For anyone to argue that a Godly footprint is missing from our heritage is either ignorant of AMERICAN history or purposely out to expunge our Christian heritage. The evidence is clear as sampled throughout this chapter, but will we collectively accept it and promote it as a society? All it takes is a glance back at our history and culture. Why wouldn't we want to reflect on and celebrate our historic roots? After all, these same roots have made the U.S. the greatest and most blessed nation in the world. There is a reason why others throughout our history have turned back to the instruction and mindset of our founders.

Our founders purposely wished for vestiges of God to be visible in our society for future generations. An appreciation and understanding of our roots to include our Christian heritage will only help us progress forward in the future. Without this foundation, as a society we are likely to stray in all directions. As Winston Churchill said: "The farther backward you can look the farther forward you are likely to see."[122] Instead of neglecting and denying our Godly heritage, it is time to recapture it, embrace it, and cherish it. It is who we are as a nation and it is what both identifies and distinguishes us from other countries. In a time of uncertainty on both the domestic and international fronts, reliance on our Christian heritage is the only thing that will bring us some certainty for the future.

CHAPTER THREE
WIPING AWAY GOD'S FOOTPRINT

There was once a time in this country where the truth was a virtue, but today that is not the case as our society collectively settles for relativism versus absolutism. Absolutism tells us that our country's greatness is unequivocally a corollary of God's blessings, while relativism negates the role of God in our society. Under relativism, such a bold declaration is obscure. Relativism does not associate the greatness of America with God's divine providence and grace. Instead, other humanistic conditions outside of God are attributed to America's greatness.

What we have to remember is no matter what one believes it has no bearing on the absolute truth; there is no getting around it for it is what it is. No matter how hard one works to muzzle the absolute truth, it is futile since denial of the truth does not alter the truth. When one abdicates the truth, the truth is still there. The vision of what our great country can be should be inspired by the absolute truth of our Christian foundation and not false doctrine. Vladimir Lenin, leader of the Russian Revolution of 1917, once said, "A lie told often enough becomes truth."[123] This mindset has permeated American society, infiltrating and distorting America's Christian heritage and culture.

Our founders established our foundation based on the tenets of God. Although they could not presage the future of the country, they had a relationship with a personal God who could see the future of America. They understood America's greatness would survive only if the citizen-body were educated on our Godly heritage. Comprehension of this type not only helps us keep our focus on God, but it also helps sustain individual freedom versus falling subject to oppression. Ben Franklin once said: "A nation of well-informed men who have been taught to know and prize the rights which God has given them cannot be enslaved. It is in the region of ignorance that tyranny begins."[124] In order for the U.S. to maintain its greatness, we cannot lose site of the fact America's heritage is rooted in God. Despite our verifiable Christian history and heritage, there are those who adamantly refuse to accept our Godly ancestry as they are stirred by anti-Christian forces to undermine the foundation of the United States.

DOWNPLAYING THE BIBLE

We live in a culture that has become more aggressive in rebuking Christianity. Today, anti-Christian forces are trying to direct what our society should look like without any regards to our Christian heritage. It is as if America's Christian heritage is naught. There are those who are working diligently behind the scenes to do all they can to efface God from our culture. Part of this nefarious movement includes either distorting or even eliminating the Word of God- the Bible. Although the Bible may not be revered today like it once was, what seems to be forgotten is that the living Word of God is true for any age because it comes from an unchanging and an eternal God.

Is it any surprise then the Bible is still around today, after all these generations despite the attempts to assail, burn, or ban it? How has it managed to be rewritten in many other languages throughout the globe? Since its beginning, the Bible has survived all attempts of expunction from all different societies and it is still the most read book today. The Bible is either the most revered or hated book of all times.

I once heard someone say the Bible is like a mirror for it reveals both what a person is and is not. It exposes both the good and bad of a person. The reason why many despise the Bible is because it is full of absolute truth and that truth exposes a person's true identity; and as long as one chooses to live in rebellion to God, that truth is intimidating to face. Hence, there is no other option other than to hide from the Bible to evade this truth. One thing the Bible is not is an evolving book designed to befit our behavior at the current time, thus allowing us to feel better about ourselves and absolving us from any guilt. I have personally learned to accept the Bible as life's consummate instructional manual. I have also discovered one must have knowledge of and display obedience to the Bible in order to get the most out of it. Simply knowing the Bible is not enough. It is a guide that encompasses reproof, guidance, direction, correction, and instruction, for the good of mankind. *2 Timothy 3:16-17 (NIV)* tells us:

> *"All Scripture is God-breathed and is useful for teaching, rebuking, correcting and training in righteousness, so that the man of God may be thoroughly equipped for every good work."*

Abraham Lincoln said it best after receiving a Bible from the Loyal Colored People of Baltimore:

> "In regards to this great Book (the Bible), I have but to say it is the best gift God has given to man. All the good the Savior gave to the world was communicated through this Book. But for it we could not know right from wrong. All things most desirable for man's welfare, here and hereafter, are found portrayed in it. To you I return my most sincere thanks for the very elegant copy of the great Book of God which you present."[125]

I often think to myself, what would our founders think of American society today as God is under attack in the U.S. and banishment of the Bible has increased over the years? More than likely they would be aghast especially since they were guided and encouraged by the Word of God in their historic decision-making and actions to rise above the tyrannical government of Great Britain and to seek national independence. If it weren't for the Word of God, would we be the blessed country that we are today? I doubt it. However, in today's society, the actions of such controversial groups as the American Civil Liberties Union (ACLU) defy President Jackson's declaration of referencing the Bible as society's foundation.

One such incident occurred in January 2010 in Wilson County, Tennessee. For over six decades, uninterrupted, Gideons International has handed out Bibles to school students. Its mission is simple- to spread the Word of God. Amazingly, since its beginning, Gideons International has distributed over more than 170 million Bibles at schools around the entire country.[126] As part of its operating procedures, members of Gideons do not force students to take a Bible, but the students accept Bibles on their own volition. In one particular county, one fifth grade student complained to her parents she felt forced to take a Bible due to the fear of being turned away by others. Her parents then, in turn, informed the ACLU, and the ACLU was not slow in threatening to sue the school. In the end, a lawsuit was avoided as the Wilson County School Board decided to ban the distribution of Bibles to appease the ACLU's claims that public schools should be removed from any perception of religious affiliation. The end result was that an innocuous sixty-year-old tradition of distributing Bibles ceased in Wilson County due to the complaint of parents from one student backed by the ACLU. This was not the first time the ACLU has acted against the Word of God, and it will not be the last time. We can be sure the ACLU will use this victory as support for their future endeavors in removing God from other segments of American society.

Another example of where Bible distribution was banned occurred in Collier County, Florida. The county school board stopped the group World Changers from distributing Bibles for voluntary pick-up by high school students on Religious Freedom Day. It cannot get any more oxymoronic than this. The very book that was instrumental behind our founders' decision-making in giving us our freedoms to include religious freedom was withdrawn from students. The school board claimed the Bibles were useless in student learning and violated separation of church and state. Fortunately, a federal judge in Florida, who understood our rule of law and its roots, overturned this ridiculous ban. Mathew Staver, founder and Chairman of Liberty Counsel and Dean of Liberty University School of Law, celebrated the judge's ruling: "The Collier County School District learned an unnecessarily expensive lesson: The First Amendment does not tolerate discrimination against private religious viewpoints because of a nonexistent boogeyman wall of separation between church and state. Equal access means equal access for all viewpoints, including religious viewpoints."[127] This is the type of judicial precedent we should be cheering on because precedents like this protect our Christian heritage against future challenges.

It does not help that the Supreme Court established a precedent of banning official prayer in school with the case *Engel v. Vitale* in 1962. In this case, the parents of the students at New Hyde Park, New York public schools spoke out against the voluntarily recited, trite, and nondenominational prayer: "Almighty God, we acknowledge our dependence upon Thee, and beg Thy blessings upon us, our teachers, and our country."[128] What is so harmful about the words in this prayer? They are simply words asking God to look over our teachers and country. The sentiment of reliance on God expressed in this simple prayer is the exact sentiment our founders shared and passed on to subsequent generations. Recital of the prayer was not forced upon the students, but it was open to those who believed in their hearts God had a dominant role in society and it is necessary to depend upon God.

The court ruled the schools' use of the prayer to begin the day violated the Establishment Clause of the First Amendment. The Establishment Clause states that "Congress shall make no law respecting an establishment of religion." Despite the prayer being nondenominational and its recital being completely voluntarily, it did not matter to the court. As a result of the court's ruling, similar cases have followed where volunteer prayer, use of Christian references, and Bible distribution have all been either abridged or even terminated.

Another case that followed in the footsteps of *Engel v. Vitale* was *Abington Township School District v. Schempp* in 1963. The ruling of this case declared school-officiated Bible reading in public schools to be unconstitutional. At the start of each class day, students in Pennsylvania public schools were required to read ten Bible verses with the purpose of reminding students the importance of relying on God. *Murray v. Curlett* was a similar case in Baltimore that ruled against students participating in Bible reading. The purpose of the

Bible reading was to reinforce the need for daily dependence upon God. The court ruled these Bible reading requirements violated both the Free Exercise Clause and the Establishment Clause of the First Amendment.

Believe it or not, there was once a time in American history where Bible reading was not looked down upon but was a norm in the public education system. Bible reading was customary and widely accepted as a way of life. It was the Puritans who established the Ole' Deluder Satan Act in the mid seventeenth century to encourage Bible reading in school. The Act required all townships with fifty or more households to maintain a school in which children were taught to read and write. Part of this curriculum included Bible reading and Bible study because the Puritans believed that this biblical foundation would protect the children from satanic allurements. I am positive that the teachers, administrators, and students of those former generations would be absolutely appalled at our contemporary position on Bible reading in school. This is just another example of how America has degenerated as a society, moving away from moral absolutism and embracing relativism under the misconstrued principle of separation of church and state.

Once a precedent is established it is for the most part difficult to overturn. As Thomas Jefferson once said, "One precedent in favor of power is stronger than a hundred against it."[129] Jefferson's quote reveals another example of our founders' sapience because the aforementioned court cases established a powerful precedent that has begot more political fodder for God to be removed from our society. The way things are going in our society today and with a precedent of this type, it would not be a surprise to witness more attempts to further nullify our basic freedoms of speech and religion especially when it comes to Christianity. A further diminution of our freedoms of speech and religion would be a direct affront to our founders. After all, throughout our history, many have fought and died to preserve these fundamental rights of all Americans- rights that serve as the bedrock of our democratic republic.

Today, there is increased outright opposition and hostility to the Word of God. It was no shock then to hear about a substitute teacher, in a Chicago elementary school, who banned student Rhajheem Haymon, from privately reading his Bible during the designated "reading time" in class. Fortunately, the Thomas More Law Center challenged the Chicago school on this decision. In a letter to the school, Edward White, a lawyer for the Thomas More Law Center, wrote that "the United States Supreme Court and the United States Department of Education have assured that students are free to express their religious views while at school, a freedom that includes a student's choice to read religious materials."[130] He further explained that "a public school may not suppress or exclude the speech or expression of individual students for the sole reason that the speech is religious or contains a religious perspective."[131] The end result was the school reversed its position and allowed Rhajheem to bring a Bible to school and to read it during the designated time.

This was an important battle won, but the war against God in extirpating Bible reading and any reference to God will not cease. We must use this specific incident as one example of how we are entitled to the basic freedoms of speech and religion. Despite the many and ongoing attempts to annul God from our society, this incident should serve as hope in counteracting the anti-God movement in our country. From a time when Bible reading was fully welcomed to a time where Bible reading is now trying to be totally eliminated in school, we have transitioned from one extreme to another without any regard to our Christian heritage. To prevent this continued downfall, we must adhere to William H. Seward's declaration of: "The whole hope of human progress is suspended on the ever growing influence of the Bible."[132]

On another occasion in 2008, a Wisconsin art teacher refused to accept the drawing a student drew of a cross with the biblical reference of **John 3:16**. Julie Millan, the art teacher, asked the student to remove the biblical reference because other students were talking about it and took offense to it. With conviction and courage, the student refused, and consequently, he received a zero for this specific art project. Where was the student's opportunity to exercise freedom of expression? Or even yet, where was the opportunity for the student to redo the project? The assistant principal told the student that through his religious expression, he had imposed on the rights of other students. The lawsuit against the school claimed the school tolerates other religious references outside of the student's submitted art project. For example, there were pictures representing Hinduism that are posted in a social studies classroom.

While one religion is tolerated, the other is not. If this is not hypocrisy, I do not know what is since tolerance cannot be balanced with nontolerance. Could it be that those who seek to debase the Christian religion are incapable of tolerating any Godly Christian references because they cannot stand up to the truth? The attorney with the Alliance Defense Fund, representing the student, argued: "But where is the tolerance for religious beliefs? The whole purpose of art is to reflect your own personal experience. To tell a student his religious beliefs can legally be censored sends the wrong message."[133] It is one thing to ban all religious expression, but it is another thing, totally different, to ban religious expression of one religion and not the other.

Not too long ago, in 1982, a Joint Resolution of Congress authorized 1983 to be the "Year of the Bible." In order to grasp the significance of the Bible in shaping our society, it is worthy to reflect on the wording of the Joint Resolution. The resolution stated:

> "Whereas the Bible, the Word of God, has made a unique contribution in shaping the United States as a distinctive and blessed nation and people;
>
> Whereas deeply held religious convictions springing from the Holy Scriptures led to the early settlement of our Nation;
>
> Whereas biblical teachings inspired concepts of civil government that are contained in our Declaration of Independence and the Constitution of the United States;
>
> Whereas many of our great national leaders—among them Presidents Washington, Jackson, Lincoln, and

Wilson—paid tribute to the surpassing influence of the Bible in our country's development, as the words of President Jackson that the Bible is "the rock on which our Republic rests";

Whereas the history of our Nation clearly illustrates the value of voluntarily applying the teachings of the Scriptures in the lives of individuals, families, and societies;

Whereas this Nation now faces great challenges that will test this Nation as it has never been tested before; and

Whereas that renewing our knowledge of and faith in God through Holy Scripture can strengthen us as a nation and a people: Now, therefore, be it

Resolved by the Senate and House of Representatives of the United States of America in Congress assembled, That the President is authorized and requested to designate 1983 as a national "Year of the Bible" in recognition of both the formative influence the Bible has been for our Nation, and our national need to study and apply the teachings of the Holy Scriptures."[134]

The resolution reminded the American people of how the Bible played a role in the founding of America and throughout our history. It should not take an official resolution from Congress to remind Americans of the Bible's applicability in our society, but anything to reinforce the Bible's place in America's heritage can only help prolong America's greatness. Fortunately, throughout our history, we have had presidents who discussed the importance of the Bible in America. Perhaps, today, twenty-eight years later, another Joint Resolution from Congress is due because the American people cannot be reminded enough especially during these uncertain times.

In a society filled with many distractions, there is a high propensity to lose sight of our priorities as a nation, and if there is one thing that can reset our priorities and remind us what our nation should look like, it is the Bible. I can say this with assurance because the Word of God is irrefutable, inerrant, and absolute. The Bible is foolproof and pure as affirmed in **Proverbs 30:5-6 (NIV)**: *"Every word of God is flawless; He is a shield to those who take refuge in him. Do not add to his words, or he will rebuke you and prove you a liar."* The Bible has everything we need in order to live, prosper, and succeed. It is life's additive. There is no need to add anything to it or alter it in any way because it has exactly what we need for every circumstance in life. God warns us of this in **Revelation 22:18-19 (KJV)**:

> *"For I testify unto every man that heareth the words of the prophecy of this book, If any man shall add unto these things, God shall add unto him the plagues that are written in this book: And if any man shall take away from the words of the book of this prophecy, God shall take away his part out of the book of life, and out of the holy city, and [from] the things which are written in this book."*

Mankind could not receive any better instructions on how to live life because the Bible is replete of wisdom. The question is, will we collectively adhere to the Bible in obedience to God or will we live our own lives for ourselves? Let's also not forget semi-obedience is disobedience and believing the Word of God is not the same thing as actually doing it. As we learn to trust in God, obedience becomes more of a priority and self-aggrandizement and self-indulgence fade away.

DROPPING GOD FROM SCHOOL ADDRESSES

For the longest time, prayer at school events such as graduations or other ceremonies was acceptable and never viewed as a threat of bordering on theocracy. Every year there is a new story of a university or a school warning its guest speakers to refrain from making Godly or Christian references in their addresses. It seems to get worse each year. For example, Renee Griffin, co-valedictorian for her graduating class of 2008 at Butte High School in Montana, experienced this sanction of making references to Jesus Christ in her graduation address. Part of Renee's original remarks included:

> "I learned to persevere these past four years, even through failure or discouragement, when I had to stand for my convictions. I can say that my regrets are few and far between. I didn't let fear keep me from sharing Christ and His joy with those around me. I learned to impart hope, to encourage people to treat each day as a gift. I learned not to be known for my grades or for what I did during school, but for being committed to my faith and morals and being someone who lived with a purpose from God with a passionate love for Him."[135]

School officials directed Renee to replace the word "Christ" with "my faith" and the phrase "lived with a purpose from God" with the words "lived with a purpose, a purpose derived from my faith and based on a love of mankind."[136] To her credit, Renee had the internal moxie to stand up with boldness and conviction to the school officials. Renee believed she had every right to speak the words reflecting whatever reverberated within her. Renee's words were a reflection of her own source of motivation and were not at any way reflective of the student body. Why would our society want to repress one's heartfelt and genuine feelings? As a result of Renee refusing to comply with the school officials' directive, the school officials removed Renee completely from speaking at the graduation ceremony. This unfortunate incident left the impression one's freedoms of speech and religion are inferior to the cultural intolerance of Christianity.

The outcome of *Lee v. Weisman* in 1991 does not help our cause in preserving God in our society. A middle school principal, at a Providence, Rhode Island middle school, by the name of Robert Lee, invited a Rabbi to speak at the graduation ceremony. During his address, the Rabbi recited prayers. One of the graduates' fathers (Daniel Weisman) signaled out the Rabbi and called upon the Court to bar public school officials from permitting any sort of benediction or invocation. The Supreme Court ruled this was a violation of the Establishment Clause of the First Amendment and government involvement fostered "a state-sponsored and state-directed religious exercise in a public school."[137] According to the Supreme Court, by forcing the students to respect the time of prayer, an establishment of state religion was produced. The Supreme Court created a fallacy as it equated benedictions and invocations to a form of state religion. When our founders spoke of state religion, this is not what they had in mind.

President George H. Bush impugned the Supreme Court's ruling because he favored this type of prayer in public events. His remarks could not have been more appropriate and supportive of preserving reverence for God in our society. He commented:

> "I am very disappointed by the Supreme Court's decision in *Lee v. Weisman*. The Court said that a simple nondenominational prayer thanking God for the liberty of America at a public school graduation ceremony violates the first amendment. America is a land of religious pluralism, and this is one of our Nation's greatest strengths. While we must remain neutral toward particular religions and protect freedom of conscience, we should not remain neutral toward religion itself. In this case, I believe that the Court has unnecessarily cast away the venerable and proper American tradition of nonsectarian prayer at public celebrations. I continue to believe that this type of prayer should be allowed in public schools."[138]

President Bush understood and believed in the difference between establishing a state religion and simply reflecting on God in a nondenominational manner without forcing it on others. Today, separation of church and state has been distorted and consequently abused. The whole purpose of separation of church and state was to obviate a state religion from being formed so as to preserve our freedom of religion. The purpose of it is to protect the church from the state and not the state from the church. The founders understood a tyrannical government could easily give rise to a state religion if a strong foundation embodying freedom of religion was not instituted. The founders believed people should have the freedom to worship based off their personal conscience and not government coercion. Now, separation of church and state has taken on a new meaning as it has unfortunately descended into separation of God and state. Separation of God and state is something our founders never intended because they considered religion to be the anchor of liberty; they understood our source of liberty was from God. Our country was designed off the concept of freedom of religion and not freedom from religion. As we learned earlier, our Christian foundation accents the need for God in society.

DROPPING THE TEN COMMANDMENTS FROM SOCIETY

Another example of our contemporary society attempting to remove traces of God from society is the removal of the Ten Commandments from public places. I find it amazing that as a society we would want to purge ourselves of God's moral standards of regulating society. Moreover, they represent the basis of social order. *1 Timothy 1:8-11 (KJV)* professes the good in having laws:

> *"But we know that the law [is] good, if a man use it lawfully; Knowing this, that the law is not made for a righteous man, but for the lawless and disobedient, for the ungodly and for sinners, for unholy and profane, for murderers of fathers and murderers of mothers, for manslayers, For whoremongers, for them that defile themselves with mankind, for*

menstealers, for liars, for perjured persons, and if there be any other thing that is contrary to sound doctrine; According to the glorious gospel of the blessed God, which was committed to my trust."

The Ten Commandments have been around forever for all cultures and all nations to abide by with the common purpose of keeping mankind from falling into total sordid degradation and society from degenerating into anomie. There are those who view the Ten Commandments to be obsolete and no longer relevant. If we remove God along with all promotions of righteousness from society, the only thing left is man; and, since man is fallible, adulteration and injustice are likely to swell. Hence, a standard of moral authority is necessary for all societies and this is why we must have the Ten Commandments.

Have we forgotten the Ten Commandments came directly from the voice of God to Moses? God provided the Ten Commandments in order to protect both the individual and society at-large. The Ten Commandments are not solely recommendations or suggestions, but they are absolute and irrevocable precepts that assist us in our daily decision-making by regulating our behavior. God gave society the Ten Commandments as a reminder of the weakness and frailty of mankind. Man may try to downgrade the significance of the Ten Commandments, but that does not diminish God's expectation of man's behavior. No ideology or source of reason can abate the law of God because the law of God cannot be exterminated. Regardless of what man rules the acceptable behavior of man to be, the Ten Commandments will always be God's conduct for man. Moreover, God did not offer the Commandments to mankind for debate, but as ubiquitous decrees subject to obedience. Granted, we will never be perfect and in total compliance to them 100% of the time, but they are designed to be absolutes and serve as man's parameters in life.

Although the Ten Commandments are absolutes, there are those who have settled for relativism and adhere to them only on their own conditions. Instead of heeding to them, there are those who manipulate them for their own self-assurance. No amount of massaging or camouflaging can pale God's absolute precepts; they are God's immutable standard for behavior in man.

One example where the true meaning of the Ten Commandments has been tarnished was when Father Tim Jones, parish priest of St Lawrence and St Hilda, told his congregation it was all right to steal. In December of 2009, in reference to the eighth commandment, "Thou shall not steal," he preached:

> "My advice, as a Christian priest, is to shoplift. I do not offer such advice because I think that stealing is a good thing, or because I think it is harmless, for it is neither. I would ask that they do not steal from small, family businesses, but from large national businesses, knowing that the costs are ultimately passed on to the rest of us in the form of higher prices. I would ask them not to take any more than they need, for any longer than they need."[139]

Father Jones justified his reasoning with the argument that God's love for the poor prevailed over the avarice of the rich. Indeed, God has unconditional love for the poor, but He also has the same level of love for the rich. After all, God encompasses all love and He loves all of mankind, despite its iniquitous nature, the same. What we neglect is the fact there is only one judge of man and that judge is God. So, if the rich are derelict with their blessings of wealth, God will have the ultimate say, not man, not even a religious figure. This incident of reducing the eighth commandment sets a dangerous precedent especially since someone of religious association initiated it. Such behavior of compromise only fuels anti-Christian and secular forces to erase references to the Ten Commandments throughout society. Can you imagine a society where God's oracles are totally compromised and no longer are upheld? What kind of anarchy would we have then?

We have witnessed on several occasions where there have been successful attempts to remove Ten Commandments references from public places in our society. For example,

U.S. District Judge Stewart Dalzell ordered the removal of a Ten Commandments plaque from the Chester County Courthouse in Pennsylvania in 2002. After 82 years of being displayed without any opposition, all of a sudden, it was deemed unconstitutional. According to Judge Dalzell, "The tablet's necessary effect on those who see it is to endorse or advance the unique importance of this predominantly religious text for mainline Protestantism."[140] Despite the opinion of the majority of Pennsylvania citizens supporting the display and rebuking the judge's ruling, one single atheist with ACLU backing abrogated an 82-year old tradition. There is something wrong when a minority that spurns our Christian heritage gets its way over the majority that venerates our Christian heritage. As a society, we have descended a long way from John Adams' view of and reverence for the Ten Commandments, as he spoke on the importance of protecting private property:

> "If 'Thou shalt not Covet' and 'Thou shalt not steal', were not commandments of Heaven, they must be made inviolable precepts in every society, before it can be civilized or made free."[141]

On another occasion, in 2003, U.S. District Judge Myron Thompson ruled that the monument of the Ten Commandments in the rotunda of the Alabama's state judicial building violated the U.S. Constitution's principle of separation of religion and government. Alabama Chief Justice Roy Moore, who granted the placement of the monument two years prior, strongly posited that the Ten Commandments are the fundamental foundation of our legal system and by preventing the display of the monument, we are blocking the acknowledgment of our Christian roots which is an affront to our freedom of religion as specified in the First Amendment.[142] This is just another example of how we throw our Christian heritage aside and learn to accept the current trend in a sensitized society.

Yet on another occasion, a federal appeals court ruled a monument of the Ten Commandments be removed from the lawn outside a county courthouse in Oklahoma. Once again, the court ruled the display was an endorsement of religion in violation of the First Amendment. Now do we see the dangers in the precedent of judicial recklessness? When a judicial precedent is set, especially one that is irresponsible in thought, similar rulings follow. Perhaps members of the judicial branch need to be reminded of their role in American government. In his book, *Constitution in Exile*, Judge Andrew Napolitano provided such a reminder. He stated:

> "The judicial branch of the federal government should be a vigilant watchdog that rules on cases that come before it to protect our natural rights and to preserve the division of power established in the Constitution."[143]

Part of our natural rights includes the right to acknowledge our Christian heritage via our freedoms of speech and worship. Once again, one individual with the backing of the notorious ACLU has caused the elimination of the monument. James Green "filed suit in federal court, alleging that display of the Ten Commandments on public property is an unconstitutional endorsement of religion by the county commissioners who approved the display."[144] Despite a previous 2005 ruling in Texas that permitted the display of a Ten Commandments monument on the grounds of the state capitol building, Oklahoma did not sway from its ruling. Moreover, the U.S. Supreme Court let the ruling remain. As you can see, sometimes when precedent favors the agenda of the anti-Christian or secular forces, they view that precedent as good; however, when a precedent goes against their agenda, that precedent has no bearing at all. For this reason, I have to side with George Washington when he said that "precedents are dangerous things; let the rein of government then be braced and held with a steady hand."[145] I thought the whole purpose of judicial precedent is to avoid seasonal malleability in order to rely on stability through principled rulings.

REMOVING WORDS AND PHRASES RELATING TO GOD

On top of the banishment of Bible distribution and reading, the suppression of Godly references in public addresses, and the removal of the Ten Commandments, we cannot forget about the other abominable attempts to remove God from our society. Such attempts include Michael Newdow's efforts to remove the words "under God" from the Pledge of Allegiance and "In God We Trust" from U.S. currency. Newdow, a nationally proclaimed atheist, believed these sacrosanct words violated his beliefs. In 2000, Newdow sued the Elk Grove Unified School District for forcing public school children to recite the pledge with the words "under God" in it. Over the last ten years the ruling has went back and forth in and out of Newdow's favor between the different courts. However, in March 2010, the federal appeals court in San Francisco ruled the words "under God" will remain in the Pledge of Allegiance and "In God We Trust" will stay on U.S. currency.

Accolades go to Judge Carlos Bea who rightfully averred: "The Pledge is constitutional;" and "the Pledge of Allegiance serves to unite our vast nation through the proud recitation of some of the ideals upon which our Republic was founded."[146] Judge Bea upheld the national and historical truth of this land. Judge Bea did exactly what we need more Americans of authority to do- enforce our Christian heritage on which this republic was formed and stand up to those who are out to devalue it. This ruling should serve as a source of inspiration especially since the same court ruled in Newdow's favor in 2002.

In spite of this commemorative milestone, this is not the time to rest. We cannot let our guard down because there will be other attempts and more judges with liberal ideological inclinations that will impose their personal beliefs on the rest of Americans without any regard to our heritage or to the collective voice of preserving our Christian heritage. We can no longer assume our Godly heritage is secure from extramural infringement. Moreover, if the American people do not stand up to the attacks on our freedoms, we are likely to lose them to an overpowering government and an off-kilter judiciary ruling by authoritative decree.

I honestly believe if the motto "In God We Trust" was removed from our currency a large percentage of Americans would not even notice or care for that fact. I hope to be proven wrong. This blasé sentiment has infested our culture as we are more preoccupied with temporal things than the things that have made our country great to include approbation of God. Personally, I have pulled out a dollar bill or coin and reflected on the words of "In God We Trust." I thought to myself of the purpose behind having these words on our currency. It is one minor way to help keep our focus on God and not money and material things.

Money in itself is not an evil thing, but the love of money is. When monetary avarice combines with an insatiable appetite for power, our focus on God is hindered as we become dependent on ourselves. With a focus bent away from God, prosperity produces a spirit of independence, causing us to feel adequate within ourselves. I find it refreshing to have these words on our currency since it reminds us God owns it all and it is the favor of God versus self-serving ambitions that grants us wealth.

As a society, we need to eliminate the misconception that wealth equates to success. Although wealth can be a sign of success, there are other factors that attribute to one's success. The most important one is achieving the goals God has predestined for us to accomplish. As acclaimed pastor and author Rick Warren denoted in his best seller *Purpose Driven Life*: "It is only in God that we discover our origin, our identity, our meaning, our purpose, our significance, and our destiny."[147]

Another example where a reference to God was removed occurred in New Haven, Connecticut. In 2010, for the first time in foreseeable years, "diplomas for New Haven high school students were printed without the phrase 'in the year of our Lord'."[148] After all this time, it was only one complaint that generated the removal of the phrase. Even though the phrase may not be widely used today, it used to be and it still has relevancy. It is actions like these that open the door to subsequent actions to withdraw references of God from society.

Public outcry is a necessity in battling the attacks against our Godly heritage. We have seen its effectiveness as long as the American people do not settle for apathy. Take for example the construction of the new Capitol Visiting Center in Washington, D.C. The purpose of the $600 million facility is to highlight our national heritage, but when it was first constructed, it was missing our national motto of "In God We Trust." It actually identified "E Pluribus Unum" as our national motto instead. Senator DeMint was one of the lawmakers who believed the new center distorted our national heritage as he said the center's "most prominent display proclaims faith not in God, but in government."[149] After a year later, as a result of the public outcry, "In God We Trust" was properly engraved on the center's wall.

ATTACK ON CHRISTIAN HOLIDAYS

We cannot talk about the removal of God from American society without talking about the annual attempts to subdue the spiritual aspect of Christmas. Over the years, Christmas has transformed more and more from a hallowed day into a commercial holiday. We have discarded the true meaning of Christmas as we neglect the fact God had come to man so man would be able to come to a merciful and forgiving God. We fail to acknowledge that without Jesus Christ there would have never been a reason for Christmas. Perhaps we need to revisit President Reagan's Christmas address on December 23, 1981. While a large part of the address focused on oppression in Poland at the time, at the end of his address, he commented on what Christmas is really about:

> "Once, earlier in this century, an evil influence threatened that the lights were going out all over the world. Let the light of millions of candles in American homes give notice that the light of freedom is not going to be extinguished. We are blessed with a freedom and abundance denied to so many. Let those candles remind us that these blessings bring with them a solid obligation, an obligation to the God who guides us, an obligation to the heritage of liberty

and dignity handed down to us by our forefathers and an obligation to the children of the world, whose future will be shaped by the way we live our lives today.

Christmas means so much because of one special child. But Christmas also reminds us that all children are special, that they are gifts from God, gifts beyond price that mean more than any presents money can buy. In their love and laughter, in our hopes for their future lies the true meaning of Christmas."[150]

Whether it is the ban of various Christmas displays and ornaments or the prohibition of saying "Merry Christmas" in public, such dictatorial banishments are absurd in a land founded on freedom of religion. Whatever happened to the sentiment that if you want to celebrate Christmas then so be it, and if you do not, then that is ok too. Now that is how a representative government founded on the freedom of religion should function. Each repressive act on Christmas builds on top of the former, thus contributing to the augmentation of this hostile movement against Christmas.

As a child growing up, I never once heard any family member mention any such fatuous action against Christmas. I only recall jovial recollections of Christmas being a joyful time of the year free from attack. What was once celebrated as a purposeful and divine holiday is now on the verge of becoming taboo due to profuse commercialization, political correctness, totalitarian dictum, and poltroonish leadership that fails to acknowledge our Christian heritage.

Each year as we approach the celebration of Christmas, there is always another news story of a governmental or school jurisdiction attempting to quench the real spirit of Christmas under the guise of separation of church and state. The intensity of these farcical acts seems to be picking up with each passing year. Over the last few years, I do not recall a Christmas season in which there was not at least one story attacking Christmas. This crafty obfuscation of Christmas is designed for the sole purpose of eliminating the real truth behind the origin of Christmas.

At the start of the 2009 Christmas season, the American Humanist Association launched a national advertisement campaign with the controversial message: "No God? ... No Problem!" The campaign displayed posters with this message in buses and trains in the cities of Washington D.C., New York, Los Angeles, Chicago, and San Francisco. In promoting the campaign, Roy Speckhardt, executive director of the American Humanist Association, said: "Religion does not have a monopoly on morality -- millions of people are good without believing in God."[151] Their timing could not have been more coincidental- right before the Christmas season in an attempt to put a damper on Christmas. It was just another attempt to spoil the true meaning of Christmas.

In reference to the message, what the humanists fail to appreciate is that we will experience problems in life with or without God, but with God in our lives, we can find peace in our problems. When an individual genuinely carries God in his or her heart, God not only shows up during the times of our problems, but He is in the middle of the problems with us providing comfort, peace, guidance, and direction. With this peace, one discovers his or her difficulty is not necessarily the problem itself; instead, it is the perception of one's problem that generates the unease, fear, and doubt. Hence, a more appropriate ad should display the message: "With God, Problems are Beatable!"

There are plenty of other examples supporting the attack on Christmas. In December 2009, Sonoma County officials banned the display of religious ornaments on Christmas trees in government buildings. A man by the name of Irv Sutley found the angel on top of the tree in the county recorder's office to be "extremely offensive" and part of the "cult" of Christianity.[152] Mr. Sutley referenced the 1989 court case of *Allegheny v. ACLU*, in which the ACLU challenged a public-sponsored nativity scene displayed outside a city-county building in Pittsburg, to support his disposition. In this case, the Supreme Court ruled that "by prominently displaying the words 'Glory to God for the birth of Jesus Christ,' the county sent a clear message that it supported and promoted

Christian orthodoxy."[153] This is just another example of the ramifications of bad precedent.

Such abhorrent behavior towards Christmas would disgust our former President Calvin Coolidge. In his presidential message to the American people on Christmas Day in 1927, he wrote:

> "To the American People: Christmas is not a time or a season but a state of mind. To cherish peace and good will, to be plenteous in mercy, is to have the real spirit of Christmas. If we think on these things, there will be born in us a Savior and over us will shine a star sending its gleam of hope to the world."[154]

President Coolidge understood Christmas was all about the Savior Jesus Christ whose sole purpose was to bring hope to man. The Savior was destined to save mankind from its iniquity and to shroud any reference to this monumental and historic benchmark sends the message that man is capable of going to God alone in his sinful nature.

There have been a number of occasions where nativity scenes have been chased out from public display over the years as a result of threatening legal action. For one, there was a complaint made by the Freedom from Religion Foundation forcing the removal of a nativity scene from a Charleston fire station. The group argued, "The creche is the universal symbol of Christianity" and it could not be displayed in front of a public building because it violated separation of church and state.[155] On another occasion, in Pennsylvania, the ACLU and Americans United for Separation of Church and State threatened legal action if Luzerne County did not remove the displayed creche and menorah from the courthouse lawn. Yet, on another occasion, a Massachusetts elementary school removed its nativity scene after being threatened by the ACLU. Years of Christmas tradition in these areas were thrown out the window for the sake of appeasement under the pretense of violating separation of church and state. These are just a few examples of nativity scenes being forced out of the public's eye during Christmas- another example of the demise of our Christian heritage as it is being comprised by political correctness, misconception of separation of church and state, and pure cowardice.

Let's think about the symbolism behind pushing nativity scenes out of American culture during Christmas time. By removing nativity scenes, are we sending the message we do not need Christ, our Savior, in our society? Jesus Christ did not push man aside when He was on Earth, but He embraced **ALL** of mankind with forgiveness, mercy, and unconditional love. Christ maintained His divine purpose of redeeming mankind and served as the bridge between sinful man and a Holy God in order to preserve man's relationship with God. And we show our deference for God, or better yet, lack of it, by withdrawing simple Christmas ornaments and displays representing this Holy day? Obviously, something is off here.

The American people must understand that by standing up to these attempts of altering the true meaning of Christmas, they are protecting our Christian heritage. What may seem as a hopeless cause, with all the aggressive efforts to attack Christmas, is not because the truth will forever be unaltered despite anti-Christian attempts to alter it. Yes, when we reject the truth we are left with a lie, but we cannot forget that behind the lie is the actual truth. As Winston Churchill said: "The truth is incontrovertible, malice may attack it, ignorance may deride it, but in the end; there it is."[156]

Believe it or not, the American people still have power to influence decisions in support of the truth. Take for example the annual Christmas parade held in the town of Patchogue in Long Island. In 2008, officials changed the name of the parade from the "Christmas Holiday Boat Parade" to the "Holiday Boat Parade." They removed the word "Christmas" from the name of the event. The people of Patchogue showed their opposition to this act by not attending the 2008 event. The people stood behind their convictions of the sacredness of Christmas and boycotted the event, and rightfully so. Due to poor attendance at the 2008 event, officials were forced to revert back to the original name of the event in 2009. The Patchogue Riverfront Committee noted that it included the word "Christmas" into the title of the event "to recognize that most of the participants celebrate the holiday."[157] The collective voice of the American people is still influential and is capable of forcing the government to govern at the consent of the governed.

The people of Patchogue need to be lauded for not tolerating the removal of Christmas in their local area, and their actions should be an encouragement to others. If Americans took similar action in their respective local areas, then the attacks on Christmas could be foiled on the national level as a whole. We should be reminded of Former Speaker of the House, Tip O'Neill's assertion that "all politics is local." No matter how overwhelming an issue may come across, citizen activism and involvement at the lowest level can gain momentum and sprout into an all-powerful national movement. Such citizen participation is still important and relevant in today's political correct and anti-God society, and the people must share and act on this conviction.

Moreover, the people must be reminded the greatness of America has always stemmed from the American people themselves and not any government or bureaucratic official. It is the people of America that controls the destiny of America- not the media, not any political party, not the government, not the affluent barons in America and across the international community- as the founders had intended. The people have a civic responsibility to express their concerns especially on matters where the government or society excuses what God reproaches. The power of the people is an amazing and powerful thing when it is exercised as seen with this Long Island local event.

The attacks on Christian holidays and holy days do not end with Christmas. The birthday of Jesus Christ is not the only Christian holiday being berated. Now, Good Friday which recognizes the consecrated death of Jesus Christ is being attacked. If you notice, no one is attacking the death of Buddha, Mohammed, or any other religious prophets, only Jesus Christ. Unlike the other religious icons or prophets, the only man to rise from the dead is being attacked. Anything that has an association to Jesus Christ, the hope for all mankind, is vulnerable to this anti-Christian movement.

In March 2010, the city of Davenport, Iowa had attempted to supplant Good Friday with the name of "Spring Holiday". Just like that, the riddance of a 2,000+ year old Christian custom from this local community was afoot. Is it coincidence this brash action took place right before the Easter holiday? I think not. Opponents of Christianity know that when the resurrection of Jesus Christ is covered up, Christianity is dead, thus disrupting the Easter celebration. One simple recommendation made by the city's Civil Rights Commission spurred the City Administrator to make this bold change without consulting the city council. Tim Hart, the commission's chairman opined: "Our Constitution calls for separation of church and state. Davenport touts itself as a diverse city and given all the different types of religious and ethnic backgrounds we represent, we suggested the change."[158] Again, this is another display of separation of church and state being misinterpreted and misused. Fortunately, the brave citizens of Davenport did not tolerate this shameless action. As a result of this citizen outcry and cacophony, Davenport regressed back to calling the Christian holiday Good Friday. This is just another example where select intolerance is besieging God and Christianity in America, while other religious symbols or associations are being tolerated.

For those who do not believe the U.S. is a Christian nation, knowing the meaning of the Christmas and Easter holidays, then why are these holidays so engrained in our society?

TOLERATING THE BLASPHEMY OF CHRISTIANITY

One would think that in today's pluralistic, ultra-tolerant, and multicultural society where we are encouraged to tolerate other people's cultures and religions, Christianity and reverence for God would indeed be protected. Moreover, since it is the foundation of our heritage, why wouldn't we want to tolerate it? Unfortunately, it is not that cut and dry. We are always instructed on tolerating other religions, but when it comes to tolerating Christianity in our own country, intolerance seems to be easily accepted.

I find it amazing how those who rhapsodize on tolerance do not tolerate the disparate actions, beliefs, and even opinions of others who disagree with them. This contradictory behavior goes against everything the purveyors of tolerance promote. Real tolerance means everyone is treated with the same dignity and respect, no matter our differences. Real tolerance also means there shouldn't be any impediments in promulgating the truth. After all, it is absolutely improbable for intolerance to coexist with tolerance. If we are going to preach tolerance, then there should not be robust efforts to wipe out God from our society. We cannot have it both ways! The founders set the best example of religious freedom in America; they encouraged all faiths and did not deny or hide their own.

While there are those who seem to be intolerant of references to God in our society, they do, however, seem to tolerate the debasement of Christianity in our society. There are plenty of examples to illustrate both the double standard as it relates to Christianity and the blatant disregard of Christianity. Just take for example, the word, "Jesus". It is striking to me see how the name of Jesus is so casually and easily used as compared to the names of other religious figureheads such as Buddha or Mohammed. It is kind of ironic how those who are so intolerant of the Christian faith are so free to use the word "Jesus" in conversation. Furthermore, it is also ironic how those who view Jesus Christ as a fictional character still use his name with passion in regular conversation. Even though society does not view it as a serious violation of the third commandment, God still considers it ignominy.

One does not have to look far to recognize this since Hollywood movies are filled with foul instances where the name of "Jesus" is nonchalantly used. It makes one wonder, what does the addition of these invectives add to the movies besides disrespect towards God? It is one thing to call out to Jesus in genuine and solemn prayer, but it is something totally different to call upon His name out of anguish and frustration and in frivolous chatter. Why are there such acts of sacrilege towards Jesus and not Buddha or Mohammed? I do not see or hear anyone calling out "Buddha" or "Mohammed" in the same insouciant manner. Could it be the reason people use the word "Jesus" so casually is because, subconsciously, they know there is truth and power behind His name?

The perversion of Christianity is not only witnessed in the movies but also in various television programs. Take for example the animated television sitcom called *Family Guy*. No doubt scenes in the various episodes are hilarious, but when scenes abase Christianity by using burlesques of Jesus to slander His character, that is crossing the line. I do not see the same people who want to remove God from society speaking out against such references in the episodes, thus revealing their hypocritical antics. Such people contradict their own cause by not being consistent. By picking and choosing which references of God should be wiped out, it reveals the subtle nature of this movement to remove references of God. Any reference of God that reveres and boosts God and our Christian heritage is not tolerated and attacked. On the other hand, any reference of God that maligns God and Christianity is tolerated and overlooked. If this is not characteristic of agenda-setting, I do not know what is.

On the antithetical extreme of tolerating distorted cartoons of Jesus, there were disparaging cartoons of the Muslim prophet Muhammad that did not receive the same tolerance. In 2005, the Dutch newspaper, *Jyllands-Posten*, posted twelve cartoons of Muhammad, all of which quickly spread throughout the international community. Muslim organizations in Denmark considered the cartoons incendiary and blasphemous and were quick to protest the publication of the cartoons. Protests quickly spread throughout the entire Muslim world as antipathy against the Danish newspaper intensified. What was meant for local and harmless satire metastasized into an international crisis as Danish embassies in Muslim countries were set afire. It got to the point where the cartoonists were provided security guards and had to go into hiding.[159] In a democracy where satire is permitted, Denmark found itself confronted with Muslim intolerance.

We witnessed this same type of intolerance a year earlier in 2004 but on a more severe level with the murder of

Dutch film director and producer, Theo van Gogh. This incident was not centered on an Islamic caricature, but rather on the expose of the Islamic culture. Van Gogh produced the film entitled *Submission*, in which he documented a film to educate people on the wicked treatment of Islamic women. As a result of his acute exposure of the mistreatment of Islamic women, Van Gogh became a target of radical Islamists. By exposing the truth, Van Gogh imperiled his own life.

Mohammed Bouyeri, a Dutch citizen and an Islamic extremist, killed Van Gogh in a gruesome manner. While Van Gogh was bicycling in central Amsterdam, Bouyeri repeatedly shot and stabbed Van Gogh to death. Attached to a knife in his torso was a note from Bouyeri threatening jihad against the West. The revelation of the truth in this incident incited an Islamic extremist to adopt intolerance over tolerance by performing a brutal murder.

Where one culture promotes tolerance but actually exercises intolerance peacefully, another culture is not as tolerant as demonstrated by its violent intolerance.

On another occasion to illustrate this extreme intolerance, the animated program, *South Park*, sarcastically referenced Mohammed in one of its episodes. This is nothing new with the program because it is known for using satire to deride other religions such as Christianity and Buddhism, politicians, professional athletes, politicians, and others. Comedy Central decided to bleep out all references of Mohammed as a result of threats made by a New York-based radical Muslim group called Revolution Muslim. On the group's website, revolutionmuslim.com, member Al-Amrikee addressed the creators of *South Park*: "We have to warn Matt and Trey that what they are doing is stupid and they will probably wind up like Theo Van Gogh for airing this show. This is not a threat, but a warning of the reality of what will likely happen to them."[160] Comedy Central's appeasement to this fringe Muslim group manifests the impact the Van Gogh incident has had on society.

As obscene and offensive as the material may have been, there is still freedom of speech in this country. I do not see Comedy Central taking the same steps in bleeping out defamatory references to Christianity, whether there are threats or not. Why the double standard where it is ok to disgrace Christianity but not Islam? There should be one standard. Either all references to religious symbols are off limits to avoid any backlash or religious satire of all religions is permitted based off of freedom of speech. And if one does not want to watch an episode, then so be it, he or she has the liberty not to do so.

CHRISTIANITY VERSUS RADICAL ISLAM

The Van Gogh incident is just a microcosm of radical Islam's overall spirit of intolerance. The same contention that exists today between Christianity and radical Islam is the same rift that has existed since the start of time. It is important to acknowledge that the God of Islam is not the same as the God of Christianity. In his book entitled *Is the Father of Jesus the God of Muhammad?* Timothy George wrote:

> "Christianity and Islam cannot simply embrace one another as "sister religions" on the basis of a shared monotheism without regard to questions about Jesus and His cross and resurrection- issues in turn that presuppose further questions about Jesus and His relationship to God."[161]

As a result of this stark fundamental difference, the values of radical Islam are incompatible with the values of the West and Christianity. One does not have to look hard to discern this contention and the battle of intolerance versus tolerance. Take for example the tolerance of Islam in the U.S. versus the intolerance of Christianity in Muslim countries. In the United States, there are over 1200 mosques, revealing America's tenet of freedom of religion.[162] In the greater Houston area alone, "there are more than 100 Muslim prayer spaces" and there is a demand to expand some and construct more.[163] As the number of mosques in the U.S. increases, so too does the possibility of preaching Sharia and anti-West radicalism. An undercover survey of 100 mosques and

Islamic schools in the U.S. discovered three in four Islamic centers preached anti-West extremism and antagonism.[164] America's freedom of religion is a good thing, but when our freedoms are used against us to usher in something that is contrarian, we have some serious problems.

There is not the same reception of Christianity in Muslim countries. How often do we see the warm welcoming of Christian houses of worship in Muslim nations? If Christianity is practiced, it is not done so openly and without fear of government encroachment and punitive repercussion.

Although not widely broadcasted, there are reports of Muslim converts to Christianity being castigated, tortured, and even killed for practicing Christianity in Muslim countries. In Iran, Ghorban Tori, a convert to Christianity, was kidnapped, and stabbed to death for serving as a Christian pastor.[165] Moreover, after Tori's death, the Ministry of Intelligence and Security arrested, tortured, and threatened other Christians.[166] Such intolerance of Christianity should be no surprise especially since President Ahmadinejad, the theocratic dictator, reportedly declared, "I will stop Christianity in this country."[167] He is solely interested in upholding the Islamic theocracy in Iran with the hope of spreading it throughout the volatile Middle East.

In Saudi Arabia, Emad Alaabadi, also a convert to Christianity, was arrested and imprisoned for disowning Islam and accepting Christianity.[168] *Asia News* also reported there are other Christians who are imprisoned in Saudi prisons.[169] For those Americans who are so quick to censure America, would you prefer to live in a theocracy like Iran? Perhaps we need to be reminded of how good we have it here in the U.S. even with our weaknesses as a nation. You are free to practice any religion of your choice or not to without government intimidation or coercion. While I was stationed in Riyadh, Saudi Arabia, I did not see one sign of Christianity other than the U.S. military chapels. However, I most certainly saw mosques and even heard the daily call to prayer.

The persecution and discrimination of Christians occurs also in places like Egypt. Reports reveal Christian girls in Egypt are kidnapped, raped, forced to renounce Christianity and convert to Islam, and forced to marry Muslim men.[170] I thought Islam was predicated on being the religion of peace? Rape, forceful conversion to Islam, and arranged marriages do not suggest peaceful actions. These few examples of theological intolerance illustrate how Islam freely accepts those who wish to convert to Islam, but reject those who convert to Christianity.

Intolerance of Christian converts by Muslims is starting to surface in the U.S. more and more. In 2009, the news media covered the story of a Muslim teenage girl who converted to Christianity out of her own free will. Out of fear for her life, Rifqa Bary ran away from her Muslim family in Columbus, Ohio and took refuge in the home of the Rev. Blake Lorenz of the Global Revolution Church in Orlando, Florida. Rifqa claimed her father had threatened to kill her for converting from Islam to Christianity. Rifqa's attorney, John Stemberger, considered Rifqa to be "a person who is ripe for apostate killing or mercy killing."[171] Stemberger also argued that in the past, Rifqa's father abused her for not adhering to Muslim traditions such as the wearing of the headscarf. Muslim intolerance by individual Islamic practitioners has spread from the Islamic totalitarian states to even the United States.

This brand of theology is exactly what our Founding Fathers spoke about when government uses God to force a religion on others. They were cognizant of the fact that a government-sponsored religion is prone to dominate other religions and not want to assimilate or even coexist with other competing religions. The founders were not gung-ho supporters of organized religion for this reason. In these aforementioned theological countries, radical Islam is much more than a religion; it is a form of government with the global purpose of spreading its ideology across the globe and establishing a worldwide caliphate. According to the *Military Guide to Terrorism in the Twenty-first Century*, "Theology extremism underlies much of the contemporary Islamic struggle."[172] This kind of theological command should remind us of how fortunate we are to live in a land where freedom of religion supposedly is promoted and exercised. Moreover, it should serve as a source of inspiration for us and energize us to countervail the anti-Christian forces in our society. All too often, we take things for granted and do not realize what we have until we lose it. And if we do not protect our freedoms, we are susceptible to losing those freedoms.

IT IS NOT TOO LATE

Before it is too late, have we thought about the backlashes of wiping God out of society? If we permit the anti-God forces to run wild with their repugnant agenda of removing God's footprint from our society, we should not expect God to be there for us when we call upon Him in times of trials and difficulties. How can we expect God to bless America when America is not blessing God? We use the phrase "God Bless America" with such ease that it has become a cliché. We need to modify the phrase to "America Bless God" in order for us to get back on our feet as a nation.

God has always given man free will, and so, if we as a society settle for a Godless society, God is only abiding by man's free will. Just know there will be a price to pay. God is a patient, merciful, loving, and forgiving God, but He is also a God of judgment, which most people fail to appreciate. Although these differing characteristics of God's nature are true, man has a tough time construing how they can all coexist with the same God. We can keep pushing God further and further away, but sooner or later, God will respond to this profanation. He has done so in the past and will do so again because His holiness cannot tolerate man's iniquity with impunity.

In the middle of this malicious movement to remove God from American society, there is still hope, but it is up to the people of this great country to take action. Despite the outlook, the U.S. belongs to the American people. Let's also not forget it is only a minority population that is defying our Godly roots and pushing this anti-God movement, and as the majority, we should be emboldened to stand up against it. Just as King Solomon reminded the people of Israel of their iniquities and of their opportunity to get right with God, the American people can find their hope in God's word:

"If my people, which are called by my name, shall humble themselves, and pray, and seek my face, and turn from their wicked ways; then will I hear from heaven, and will forgive their sin, and will heal their land." ***2 Chronicles 7:14 (KJV)***

Our land is in desperate need of healing in more than one way. Our land can be redeemed if we would just seek God's purpose and will for our nation. No matter what damage has been done to date, God is capable of restoration and working all things, positive and negative, for the good of our society. This type of healing begins with you and me, one person at a time. Each heart needs to be self-examined and brought in line with God's purpose. We may have a lot of churches and religions in the United States, but how many hearts are truly bent towards God? When we begin to view things from God's perspective, the chains of bondage from our previous shortfalls as a nation will deteriorate. As we begin to focus on God's purpose for our nation and on His Word, and become ablaze for Him, preservation of our Christian heritage will unfold and our image as a stout nation of freedom inspired by God will reemerge.

The U.S. does not need to be rebuilt but restored with God at the focal point of society. We have all the tools we need. We should be encouraged there is power in prayer. If we pray as a nation with authority and seek favor from God, we can expect a rebirth of righteousness in our nation. The Bible gives us ample examples of people asking for noble things in prayer and being granted their request. Take for example the story of Moses. Moses prayed to God for favor and strength in helping him free the people of Israel from Egypt. David prayed to God for favor and strength to overcome Goliath and his torments of the Israeli people. There are many other examples, but both of these examples clearly reveal the goodness of God as He delivered the requests for both men in accordance with His purpose and will. Hence, there is no reason why we cannot expect the same from God to help revitalize our nation. Whenever we earnestly ask God for something in bona fide prayer, we are communicating to God that we know He is capable of delivering our needs. God will give us anything we ask for as long as He knows it is good for us, and a revitalized nation with God in the forefront is undoubtedly good for this country.

I once saw a church billboard that read: "God wants full custody not only weekend visits." This sums everything up as it relates to the direction we must head in as a nation. I also once heard a simple but powerful prayer:

"LORD, LET ME KNOW YOU. AND IN THAT KNOWLEDGE, LET ME BE LIKE YOU. AND IN THAT LIKELIHOOD, LET ME IMPART YOU."

Perhaps, as a nation, if we adopted this mindset established in this billboard and prayer, our nation would see some amazing socio-economic and cultural developments. Let's also not forget that God works the most when we see it and feel it the least.

CHAPTER FOUR
REVALUING THE FAMILY

After we reestablish the foundation of our Godly heritage and reverence for God as a priority in this nation, we next need to press the importance of family in our society. In today's society, there is a battle in keeping the traditional family intact. Family is the building block of every society. In other words, it is the basic unit of society and serves as the base off of which everything else in society follows.

We cannot build a strong society without a solid appreciation of family. The family, and not the government, education system, or the media, is the primary institution responsible for passing strong and moral attitudes and values on to the younger generations. It is also through family in which one acquires an initial identity. What does and does not happen in the home of families will affect society in one form or the other. Winston Churchill encapsulated this point when he said: "There is no doubt that it is around the family and the home that all the greatest virtues, the most dominating virtues of human society, are created, strengthened and maintained."[173] Churchill's declaration is nothing new because Chinese thinker and philosopher, Confucius, said something similar many more centuries before Churchill's ascendency on the international stage. Confucius succinctly and brilliantly declared: "The strength of a nation derives from the integrity of the home."[174] In other words, if the institution of family disappears from a society then that society is destined to crumble; the two are interconnected.

Before the creation of any government or nation, there was the family as designed by God. Some will argue that you cannot have a family without a nation because a stable nation permits families to blossom. I believe that you cannot have a vibrant nation without a foundation of family in that nation because when the home fails so will society. Granted, there may be some nations that are so unstable, it is impossible for a family to stay together, but most nations have an environment hospitable enough to allow families to stay intact. The aggregate compilation of families contributes to the overall well-being of a nation. It is no secret then when family is valued and encouraged, a nation is apt to prosper and grow. On the other hand, when family is neglected and enfeebled, a nation is apt to stagnate and eventually decline. It is in the best interest of a nation to comprehend the relationship between the preservation of family and the sustainment of a nation.

During his time as president, George H. Bush made a proclamation for the National Family Week in 1989 and 1990. In the opening of the proclamation, President Bush accented the importance of family:

> "As individuals, we find in our families a sense of identity, purpose, and security. As a Nation, we find in our families the vision and strength we need to remain a truly free and just society.
>
> A family is more than a group of individuals related by blood, marriage, or adoption -- a family is a community of persons united by their love and their commitment to one another. It is through family life that our Nation's most cherished values and traditions are passed from one generation to the next. Through our experience as members of a family, we learn important lessons about love and faith, duty and fidelity, personal responsibility and concern for others. Because those lessons are conveyed to the community at large, and because the family gives us a model of human relationships after which all other social institutions are fashioned, the strength and integrity of the family are vital to our well-being as a Nation."[175]

We are at a point in history where the American family has never been tested like it is being today. There is a consortium of circumstances or forces that portend an attack on the family. Although they may not all be blatant, they are insidiously working to destroy the foundation of the traditional family in America. History shows us incidents where the weakening of the family is one of the first priorities on the agendas of despotic dictators and totalitarian regimes. They understand the power of family and especially that of a God-fearing family. In addition, they were aware that when the family becomes unglued, it is easier to push their radical agenda on the people.

Karl Marx, German revolutionist and communist, was well-known for his promotion of communism. Marx knew that the family weakens the autarkical state government of communism. He strongly believed the family hobbles the communist agenda because family brings integrity, civic structure, order, and affinity, all of which are a threat to communism.

The best example to illustrate this is Adolf Hitler's persecution and purging of the Jews during World War II. Prior to the Jews being sent to the shocking concentration camps, they were forcefully separated from their families. Jews were apprehended and freely tortured and killed without any regard to family structure and orientation. Although this is an extreme example of the family being attacked, it does illustrate the threat the family poses to the agenda of radical iconoclasts. We are not heading in this same direction since family in America is not under attack in this dramatic way, but family is under attack by intangible forces that fully recognize family is the linchpin of a strong, healthy nation. We are heading in a direction that does more to damage the institution of family than to build it up and ultimately preserve it.

RUNAWAY DIVORCE IN AMERICA

Divorce is one of these intangible forces. One interesting statistic that is noteworthy is in 2002, 59% of the American population was married, down from 62% in 1990 and 72% in 1970.[176] Although this decrease in the marriage population is a result of legal, cultural, and economic changes, and is not completely tied to the divorce rate, the divorce rate cannot be ignored. In today's society where divorce is abundant, defense of the traditional family seems like a useless task.

Most of us hear of the astonishing but erroneous statistic that one in two marriages end in divorce. In actuality, the Americans for Divorce Reform projects the divorce rate to fall somewhere in between forty and fifty percent.[177] Compared to other developed countries, the U.S. is one of the leading countries in divorce rates. One report estimates that 45.8% of the new marriages in the U.S. end in divorce as compared to 54.9% in Sweden and 46% in Australia.[178] Even though there are other countries that outdo the U.S. in divorce rates, America's high divorce rate cannot be overlooked especially since a 2008 report put together by the Institute for American Values, the Georgia Family Council, the Institute for Marriage and Public Policy, and Families Northwest "quantifies a minimum $112 billion annual taxpayer cost from high rates of divorce and unmarried childbearing."[179] It does say something about our society at large though especially since there are other developed countries that have a far less divorce rate. Take for example Spain and Italy, 15.2% and 10%, respectively.[180]

The general statistics on the divorce rate of subsequent marriages after being already divorced is even more alarming. The U.S. divorce rate after a second marriage ranges from 60-67%, while after a third marriage, the U.S. divorce rate is even higher and ranges from 73-74%.[181] Granted, there is plenty of data and statistics to verify this trend through the U.S. Census Bureau and the Department of Health and Human Services, but the data fails to reveal what exactly is in people's hearts that drives them to divorce.

For individuals who hastily plan on getting married again after a previous divorce, it is even more pivotal for them to understand and appreciate the nature of the opposite sex. Moreover, if one opts for marriage for the sole reason just to be with someone without addressing his or her inner ambitions and selfish tendencies then that marriage will not be treated as a holy covenant. For the individual who gets married over and over again, one must perform a self-examination and ask the hard questions: 1) "What are my weaknesses?" 2) How do I define marriage? and 3) "Why must I be married?" Yes, there are inevitable circumstances that cause people to undergo second and third marriages, but for those individuals, who fail at a former marriage, there must be an awakening to discover what the importance of marriage and family is to the overall well-being of a society. Until marriage is treated like the divine institution that it is, America's divorce rate will not subside. Neglect of the truth does not invalidate God's original meaning and purpose of marriage.

It does not help that our society seems to advertise and market divorce like it is just any other normal service. There is a modicum of advertisement showcasing the preservation of marriage. Where are the messages reflecting the theme of being committed to make marriage work? Whether it is from the entertainment industry, advertising billboards, or just from the general countenance of society, the message of tolerance for divorce is evident. One has to ruminate, what would our society be like if more time and effort were dedicated towards tolerating the preservation of marriage rather than freely tolerating divorce. A 2008 Gallup Poll revealed American tolerance for divorce has surged to 70% from 59% in 2001.[182] In a short time of seven years, acceptance of divorce has noticeably grown by 11%. On the other hand, it is refreshing to see on the same poll that only 7% consider married men and women having an affair as morally acceptable.[183]

What was considered an anomaly several generations ago is no longer so. What was once viewed as unthinkable, divorce is now another norm of society as it is viewed as the panacea to marriage problems. Some will argue that the arrival of the no-fault divorce laws, beginning in 1970, precipitated the tolerance for divorce in our society. If the ease of divorce was not bad enough, mechanisms such as the no-fault divorce laws only exacerbate the situation. Prior to the no-fault divorce laws, a spouse had to prove that his or her counterpart was guilty of an act such as adultery, felony, or other reprehensible acts. With no-fault divorce laws, either spouse can claim "irreconcilable differences"; proof of fault is no longer required. According to Stephen Baskerville, Fellow at the Howard Center for Family, Religion, and Society, these laws created "unilateral and involuntary divorce, so that one spouse may end a marriage without any agreement or fault by the other."[184] These no-fault divorce laws come across as another example illustrating how the value of marriage has been depreciated as married couples have lost their interest of investing in their marriage. As a society, we have gone from marriage being an investment to it being an encumbrance in a relatively short period of time.

THE DEFENSE OF MARRIAGE

There is a disturbing mindset today that marriage is more of an imposition than that of the joyful union between man and woman. One of the primary reasons why God developed the holy institution of marriage is for man and woman to delight in the companionship of one another. It is in the design of mankind to fellowship and build relationships with others, thus God created Eve for Adam's companionship. In reference to companionship, in her book *Jesus, CEO*, Laurie Jones wrote, "Companionship is a very precious and expensive commodity because it can be bought only with the one thing that seems to be so scarce: time."[185] Under true companionship, both parties share the same time as their attention is engrossed in one another. In spite of this need for companionship as one of marriage's basic purposes, the divorce rate endures. Marriage companionship does not mean the same thing today like it did yesterday; because in today's society, people want love without the commitment and physical love is not enough to sustain a marriage. Moreover, many mistake passion for love. While passion can survive without love, love cannot survive without passion. The two are not interchangeable.

One day while working out with a fellow Army Officer and good friend, we got into a conversation about marriage, and he said to me, "Marriage is hard." I could not agree with him more; marriage is hard. It is even more difficult when God is absent from one's marriage. The fallibility of man and woman promises that problems in marriage will follow. Hence, from the get-go, we should adopt an attitude of expectancy and expect challenging times in marriage. However, our relief is that God is with us during marriage to sustain us through its hardships. If we reflect back on our marriage vows, one enters into a Holy covenant not only with one's spouse but with God. Marriage is akin to a three-tier piece of rope because in marriage, there is husband and wife, intertwined with God. God acts as the supernatural binding element to keep husband and wife in harmony with one another and capable of working together and overcoming any marital tension and friction.

The only reason why Jacqueline and I have a strong and durable marriage is the fact that God is in the middle of it. We have both surrendered our marriage over to the Lord and He has delivered us through some challenging times. Take for example the year 2010. During that year, Jacqueline and I only saw each other 45 days out of the entire year. As a result of my assignment at the time, being two and half hours from our home of record, and Jacqueline taking care of her small business, we relied on God for His strength, wisdom, and spirit of resiliency and tenacity during periods of separation. This challenging period of time only enhanced our marriage as God was at the center of it.

Today, couples are quick to blame the institution of marriage rather than performing a self-examination to identify the true problems within a marriage. Instead of assuming responsibility, couples proffer endless rationales for divorce to mollify their self-interests. The causes of divorce are diverse, which includes financial distress, infidelity, a change in priorities, unsatisfactory expectations, and more. If these causes are scrutinized with an open heart and probity, at the center of most of these causes of divorce is selfishness. After all, we live in an individualistic and egocentric culture. We have heard it before, when we get to the end of self, we get to the beginning of God, and when we do, God can give us the strength to rise above our marital foibles. Marriage is a selfless institution, and until both individuals grasp this principle, a couple's marriage is likely to experience some obstacles. A marriage cannot be 50/50; it has to be 100/100. Through marriage, two self-wills become one joint will.

It can be argued people get married for the wrong reasons, out of convenience, or just prematurely. The Institute for American Values labeled marriage as a legal contract, a financial partnership, a sacred promise, a sexual union, a personal bond, and a family-making bond.[186] The institute's labeling of marriage as a sacred promise should be at the root of what marriage is all about, but it seldom is today.

At one time, society as a whole carried a genuine appreciation for what marriage truly entailed and what it represented. Today, some view marriage more of a contract than a covenant. Both words mean an agreement of some sort. While a covenant is a promise inspired by unconditional factors such as love, a contract is a promise motivated by conditional factors where something is expected in return. Under the covenant of marriage, you make a commitment not only to your spouse but also to God. Today that commitment is mocked and feared more than it is embraced.

Marriage is a lifelong commitment, and if one is not ready to stand by that commitment and uphold the responsibilities that come with it, then one should be sincere and abstain from marriage until the time is right for him or her. Marital commitment has a low tolerance for partial submission; it is all or nothing. Besides, why would you want to make a commitment if you are not whole-heartedly in it? Furthermore, where a covenant takes the other person into consideration, a contract is more self-serving. Instead of focusing on the long-term growth process of a couple during marriage, couples preoccupy themselves with the short-term problems of their marriage and seek the easy way out through divorce. It is worth asking, what is the foundation of your marriage? Is your marriage built on the covenant you made with God or on your circumstantial emotions and feelings at the time? When the going gets tough, the covenant of marriage all too easily transforms into a contract of marriage.

It is worth mentioning that there is a population of divorced people who entered a marriage with a genuine motive and appreciation of marriage being a sacred institution, or at least thought they did. Joseph Hopper conducted a study entitled "The Symbolic Origins of Conflict in Divorce," in which he interviewed 99 people on marriage, 40 of which underwent a divorce. According to Hopper, in reference to the sacredness of marriage, "For many this sacredness was literal: Marriage was an inviolable union consecrated through and before God."[187] They were convicted marriage would have its good times and its bad times, but it is still a lifetime commitment. Despite their conviction on the sacrament of marriage and their belief that marriage should endure forever, divorce still found its way in their marriage.

The words in a marriage oath seem to have become empty rhetoric versus purposeful assurance. Today, "for better or worse" has taken on a new meaning as couples become forgetful to the latter segment of "or worse" during times of difficulty. A fellow cohort of mine who underwent a bitter divorce after 18 years of marriage said it like this: "Today, the words of 'for better or worse' should be replaced with 'until you are tired of your partner'." There has been a development in which a flagrant disregard for wedding vows has become all too common. There just does not seem to be that same patience, unconditional love, and staunch commitment in marriage that once impregnated our society. How many times have we heard the common biblical verse at weddings: "*Love is patient, love is kind. It does not envy, it does not boast, it is not proud. It is not rude, it is not self-seeking, it is not easily angered, it keeps no record of wrongs.*" **1 Corinthians 13:4-5 (NIV)** Although these words have grown to become insipid and routine, they are still filled with relevance and power, deserving of reflection and applicability for sustaining a marriage. True love is measured by how much each spouse is willing to give in order to keep their marriage ignited. Besides, it is the act of giving and not taking that must dominate in a marriage.

During my own seven years of marriage, I have discovered the best depiction of marriage comes from a scene in the movie *Just Married*. The movie is a romantic comedy, but at the end of the movie there is powerful scene that has personally helped sustain me during my marriage. In the movie, Tom Leezak (played by Ashton Kutchner) consulted his dad on the hardships of marriage. Tom assumed his parents always had a happy marriage after noticing his parents looked happy in one specific photograph. Tom's dad told him that his marriage was not filled with all happy moments, but it took some unhappy moments to get to that one happy photograph of him and his wife. In other words, Tom's dad was conveying the simple fact that marriage is not always going to be filled with pure felicity, but there will be times when one's marriage is tested. This point in the movie provides a good example of how the words "for better or worse" must not only be recited in a wedding oath, but they must also be lived out and applied every day in every marriage. Many will uphold that marriage gets better as you get to know and appreciate your spouse over time. Marriage is a lifelong process.

I personally gathered the wisdom of appreciating the application of "for better or worse" by observing my own parents who have been married for over 37 years and my grandparents who were married for over 50 years. They understood marriage was more than a piece of paper but a promise to God in which they had to learn to become one and how to get over conflict as a team. Just like any other marriage, my parents and grandparents experienced both good and bad times as their marriage matured. Early in my childhood I witnessed some of those tough times with my parent's marriage, but despite those tough times, they were both in it for the long run as they were focused on protecting the future of their marriage versus feeding the present circumstances that tested their marriage.

In reference to wisdom, Confucius said: "By three methods we may learn wisdom: First, by reflection, which is noblest; second, by imitation, which is easiest; and third by experience, which is the bitterest."[188] We all leave home with some level of wisdom and knowledge about life. This is the importance of a solid home because attitudes are established, character and values are formed, and integrity developed. If there was one thing my parents passed on to me, through their actions, was deference for the covenant of marriage. We are cautioned: "*He that walketh with wise [men] shall be wise: but a companion of fools shall be destroyed.*" **Proverbs 13:20 (KJV)** The wisdom I acquired while growing up from my parents is invaluable for it has provided me a foundation and stayed with me to this very day, and it will continue to guide me for years to come. Over the years, I have ascertained that a wise person not only has knowledge and understanding, but he or she also knows how to apply that knowledge and understanding to the various circumstances of life. The adoration for the covenant of marriage I acquired from my parents has been and continues to be applied to my own personal marriage through both the good and the bad times. I am grateful to be ingrained with the fact that marriage is more of an obligation than it is an opportunity.

Acquiring wisdom on the opposite sex is another way to prolong a marriage. An understanding of the opposite sex should be a prerequisite before any marriage. Before any couple gets married today, it would be wise for both individuals to understand the psyche of both man and woman along with the emotional and psychological needs of each. I understand this may sound conventional and unworthy of mention, but do not assume you automatically grasp the differences between the two sexes. There are clear variances between man and woman on how they think, act, and behave, but many blur the distinctions. It is one thing to be inquisitive about these differences, but it is another thing to be appreciative of them. I did not get an appreciation of these differences between the two sexes until I was married. My sage wife enlightened me with this elucidation.

Most of us are familiar with John Gray's well-known book called *Men are from Mars and Women are from Venus*. In the opening of his book, Gray declared, "Without the awareness that we are supposed to be different, men and women are at odds with each other."[189] When a man is able to appreciate how a woman functions and vice versa, the two are better able to coexist with one another in accordance versus dissonance. A woman must understand and appreciate a man's masculinity, while a man must do the same with a woman's femininity. This prior situational awareness and appreciation that the two sexes have on one another's psychological, physical, and emotional differences will save couples from future heartache, hurt feelings, time squandered, and the threat of divorce. When a couple appreciates and accepts the fact they each have different needs and will not always share the same sentiments, they are more likely to complement one another and live in harmony. Of course this does not mean that one's marriage will be totally free from tribulation, but what it does mean is a couple will be better equipped to cope with one another, exemplifying the words of "for better or worse" from their marriage oath, and not turn to divorce as the only option for marriage woes. Such simple, precursory marital measures prevent divorce from being the sole exit strategy for marital relationship shortfalls.

THE BAGGAGE OF DIVORCE

Whether a divorce is peaceful or rancorous, it is damaging to the institution of family either way. A report by the Heritage Foundation insisted, "The divorce of parents, even if it is amicable, tears apart the fundamental unit of American society."[190] Even though divorce has become a pattern in our society today, as more and more children of divorce parents share a common bond, divorce has serious second and third-hand effects that not only perturbs the parent-child relationship but can also serve as a mental, emotional, and psychological scar for the children of divorced parents.

Although it was not the case in every scenario, the general observation that I had of my peers that came from a divorced family was their scholastic performance in high school was whimsical and they were diffident on their college and career plans after high school. On the other hand, my peers that were from a stable home came across as more scholastic as witnessed by their grade point averages and academic achievements and were confident on the career path they were going to follow after high school. Now I understand this may come across as judgmental and stereotypical and not as fact for every situation, but it was simply an observation within my sphere of influence during my high school years- an observation that was reinforced time and time again. One fact I knew for sure was that my fellow peers of divorced parents were innocent victims of divorce, and even though I could not empathize with them, I could only want to see the best for them. Although the responsibility of a divorce rests ultimately with the parents, the decision whether to rise above or remain snared over a parent's divorce ultimately rests with that child and no one else.

Along with poor scholastic performance, children of divorced parents also show patterns of aggressive behavior, thus causing disciplinary problems at home, in school, and in society. With marital dissonance, a void of discipline enforcement in the home usually follows. When that authoritative foundation is missing at the home, children are less bound by rules and edict. Paul Amato, subject matter expert on family sociology, conducted a study in which he signaled out the various unfavorable repercussions of divorce. One of those negative outcomes was the delinquent behavior of children of divorced parents. According to Amato, "An unhappy home environment marked by high levels of marital discord is less than optimal for the development of children."[191]

As a result of divorce, children are usually left with insecurity, angst, dejection, and uncertainty, all of which cause a child to redirect his or her attention on these emotional burdens instead of enjoying his or her innocent childhood years growing up. How can one expect a young child to be absorbed with having fun and enjoying playtime or an adolescent to be focused on school achievement when one is battling these emotions broiling on the inside of him or her? As with anything else in life, when one is strained with abnormal stresses, one is not at his or her best. As a young boy growing up, I recall only wanting to go outside to play with friends, and as an adolescent, I recall only focusing on school to become a military officer. I cannot imagine being bogged down with these emotional strains as a child growing up. Kim Leon, expert on human development and family studies, also argued how divorce yields to censurable behavior in children of divorced parents. She emphasized how studies reveal that divorce increases both younger and older children's risk of internalizing and externalizing behavior problems and lower cognitive performance.[192] Sooner or later, those internal emotions bottled up on the inside will be emanated and when they do, they usually show in a child's delinquent behavior.

The short-term effects of divorce on children are plenty. Whether they experience a decline in academic performance in school or in general behavioral performance, experience low self-esteem, or suffer from a lack of mentorship, all of these effects rob children of their childhood. There are also long-term effects that stay with children of divorced parents after adolescence and even follow them into their own marriages, as they themselves are likely to contemplate divorce. According to one study, children of divorced parents are 76% likely to follow in their parents' footsteps with divorce.[193] This is not a characteristic of every single divorce, but there are trends to suggest the infectious nature of divorce. Some will say that with an initiation of a parental divorce comes a precedent that runs the risk of spreading to the children of divorce parents in their own marriages- a curse for subsequent generations. Paul Amato partnered with Jacob Cheadle to study this phenomenon. From their research of three generations, they postulated this long-term cause:

> "Presumably, children with martially distressed parents are less likely than other children to observe and learn positive behaviors that facilitate long-term bonds with others. These children may reach adulthood with poorly developed relationship skills and a repertoire of interpersonal behaviors that undermine marital satisfaction and stability."[194]

As a result of a divorce, children more than likely lose the parental nourishment and socialization skills necessary for personal growth they would otherwise receive from a stable home. The children of divorced parents are not as likely to be ingrained with the tenets for providing a moral compass and a sense of respect. After all, we are impressionable and are products of what we have been inculcated with and of the environment in which we have been surrounded by. When there is no steady guidance and direction around to shape the children, the children have a propensity to grow up without a solid foundation on the principles of life. In turn, these shortcomings spill over into the next generational marriage as they stand in the way of relationship building and communication skills in marriage, thus making divorce an attractive alternative. The greatest gift parents can give their children is their time, and unfortunately, with a divorce, children lose out on this time.

YESTERDAY'S ROLE MODELS ARE NOT TODAY'S ROLE MODELS

Usually, as a result of a divorce, children are prone not to look at their parents the same as before the dissolution of the marriage. Not always, but in many cases, divorced parents do not have that same pristine image as they once did while married as a family, and consequently they are not looked upon as the best role models by their children. Just as a boy looks to his father for his manhood, a girl looks to his mother for her womanhood. However, after a divorce, that hunger for parental guidance tends to fade away as the children look to alternate sources of inspiration. As a result of this intimate figurehead vacuity in the home, they grow up not knowing who to trust. After a divorce, children do not have their parents around as much to look up to for that daily mentorship and guidance. As a result, a void in mentorship forms, causing children to look for alternative role models outside of the family and eventually contributing to the crumbling of the institution of the family.

Parents must be reminded even though children may not outright admit it; they desire to look to their parents as role models. It is therefore important for parents to understand the power they have. They have the power to either edify their children or to bring them down. It is all in their words and actions. Through encouragement, parental love, and the sharing of time, parents become automatic role models more than they can ever imagine.

My parents served as two of my role models. As role models, my parents always encouraged my siblings and me to transcend a high school education in order to obtain a college degree so we would not have to physically slog like they did. Besides honor towards God, respect for others, respect for the covenant of marriage, and many other things, my parents also demonstrated to us, day after day and year after year, what a strong work ethic is. I gained an appreciation for my parents' mettle to put out a good work performance even if they did not exactly love their jobs. They worked because they had to in order to support our family.

My mother worked and still does at Kentucky Fried Chicken, while my father worked as a custodian. Both had routine, laborious, and unappreciated jobs. I recall times when they worked different jobs at all different shifts to ensure they had enough money to cover our family expenditures. They did what they had to do in order to provide for the family without totally relying on the public dole or any other family members. No matter how toilsome and ungratifying a day's work may have been, they both came home from work to care and provide for their children.

There is one story of such a day my father experienced that still resonates with me to this day. There was a period where my father was working as a custodian at the county government office. Part of the job included cleaning the raunchy restrooms some of the public carelessly soiled. I remember my father coming home from work and telling us how he had to clean human feces that some slob had decorated the bathroom walls with. Years later, I drew parallels of this incident to the verse: "*Slaves, obey your earthly masters in everything; and do it, not only when their eye is on you and to win their favor, but with sincerity of heart and reverence for the Lord.*" **Colossians 3:22 (NIV)** I learned from my father that when one puts his heart into a job as if it is for the Lord, regardless of the task, futile or significant, the Lord will give one the peace and strength to get through the day. This simple act of servitude provided a valuable lesson learned that will stay with me for my entire life. It is those little lessons in life we acquire from our parents as children that provide the most value and wisdom later in life. For my parents' untiring gumption to provide for their family, they were my role models.

Of course, I had other exemplars besides my parents. Those role models included military personnel. As far as I could remember, I had an internal urge within me to become a military officer. One of those role models was Colonel Joseph Latt, who was my Air Force Junior Reserved Officer Training Corps (AFJROTC) instructor at Auburn High School, Auburn, New York. Colonel Latt was a Vietnam War veteran who flew F-4 combat missions. I emulated him not solely for his military stature but also because of his unwavering character.

He was also a bona fide Christian who loved the Lord and it was evident by his upbeat and glowing demeanor.

As a Christian, he not only talked the talk, but he also walked the walk, something you do not too often see in today's society; he was genuine in all that he did and stood on the principles of faith, integrity, honor, and duty. I recount the many times he would take the time and make the effort to correct students on the use of profanity in his presence. He simply did not tolerate it because he was true to his Christian beliefs and values. I would always think to myself, isn't it a useless task to enforce since the mouths of many high school students emit profane language. At the time, I understood why he took the time and effort to correct students, but I did not really appreciate it until I became a devout Christian myself. He served as a role model not only for the students but also for the faculty. We need this same spirit of tireless care and dedication from the teachers and administrators in our education system today.

Even in the area of role models, things seem to be backwards today. Today's generation magnifies the immoral of society and reprehends the quiet heroes of our society. Today, our youngsters are more consumed with those who possess social status and material stuff versus those who possess patriotism, love of country, and just a spirit of goodness. What ever happened to the day when policemen, firemen, American soldiers, pilots, and sailors, and other professionals epitomizing selfless service were openly praised as worthy role models? Instead role models have become reprobate TV reality, movie, and entertainment stars, unruly professional athletes, and mendacious politicians.

In today's media and tabloid culture, the younger generation is overwhelmed with celebrity worship and hungers for fame. It is up to the parents to monitor and regulate what children should be absorbing; however, parental divorce hinders such regulation. This is not to say there are not good people in these respective fields, but when society as a whole emulates those that are degenerate and ignores the honorable, something is wrong. Fame and celebrity seem to have taken dominion over propriety and selfless service.

Society has a significant role in shaping the culture, and in today's society, there is a total lionization of our culture. When it comes to role models it is important to keep in mind that every man is fallible and can never be perfected and that other person in the spotlight puts on a pair of pants just like you and I do. Hence, we must be careful when it comes to emulating man. Just think how much stronger our society would be today if there was a magnification of Holy God who is omniscient and infallible versus the magnification of fallible men.

Who are those quiet heroes that should be worthy of our praise? Those heroes include the diligent mother who stays at home to raise her children with Godly values, love for family, and love of country, while the father works to provide for the family. Those heroes include the mother who dedicates her time and efforts to the home schooling of her children. For those mothers who say they are only mothers and do not have a professional career, I implore you to remove those thoughts from your way of thinking because you have the most important job in all of society. Despite what society and the feminist movement suggest, motherhood is necessary for the survival of our society; we need you. Those heroes include the hardworking mother who works all day and comes home at the end of the day to love and care for her children. Those heroes include the father who works to provide for his family and then comes home after an arduous day's work and appreciates his wife for caring for their children in his absence. Those heroes include the single mother who single-handedly cares and provides for her children. In general, parents are heroes because they have one of the most challenging and underappreciated jobs in today's hedonistic and self-serving society.

Those heroes also include the mother married to a young military Sergeant, making a base pay of about $2500, left behind with her four children as her husband goes off to war. Those heroes include that young Sergeant voluntarily serving his country because he loves his country and is committed to selfless service. Our military heroes freely volunteer fully aware of the perilous circumstances.

Those heroes include our intrepid Border Patrol agents who have the huge burden of securing our porous borders in a post 9-11 era from violent drug and human smugglers and possible terrorists with limited support, resources, and fellow supporting agents. Those heroes include the courageous police officer that walks out of his home each day uncertain of what the day has in store for him but certain there is a possibility he may not make it back home to family members. Those heroes include the resilient spouse of a police officer who deals with this nerve-wracking uncertainty but supports his or her loved one in uniform anyways. Those heroes include the gallant firefighter who storms into a burning building, billowing with toxic smoke, and comes out exhausted and sweating profusely with smoke debris covering his face and with a rescued victim(s) in hand. Those heroes include the supportive spouse of a firefighter whose heart races every time he or she hears of or sees his or her firefighter battling a fire in their respective community.

Those heroes include the patient teachers who possess a sincere passion and dedication to have a positive influence on children despite being in a profession that is underpaid and underappreciated. Those heroes include those church members who volunteer their time with a church or community activity. Those heroes include the assiduous mine workers who work miles in the earth's surface to extract minerals necessary to provide us with the energy that has made the U.S. a global superpower. Those heroes include the condoling nurse whose feet aches after working eighteen hours straight because he or she has an unwavering passion to provide care to the elderly, the sick, and the injured. Those heroes include the small business owner who cherishes the free market principles and the spirit of entrepreneurship, producing a good or service sought by the American people. Those heroes include the truckers across America who keep commerce flowing.

These are some of the true role models in our society, worthy of virtue, respect, and praise. While they go unnoticed, those in the limelight that lead licentious lifestyles get all the attention. They do not seek glamour or praise, but they only have a committed drive to perform in their respective professions. The list of quiet heroes, that goes largely unnoticed by our society, is endless. Despite all these heroes' professions, they all work in unison around our national fundamentals, keeping America vibrant for the future. It is time to look up to these true heroes- after God, of course- and not those who lead shallow lives and live in turpitude.

SPIRIT OF INDIVIDUALISM CHALLENGES MARRIAGE

One of the reasons why marriage is no longer respected like it used to be is the fact that a spirit of individualism pervades our society. Marriage sometimes means meeting the need of your spouse, a need that you do not have, and a need that may not come at the most opportune time for you. Dependence has been replaced with independence as men and women do not feel as if they need one another like they used to, thus causing a meltdown of the family institution. Today, independence is valued over dependence. According to Jane Lewis, in her book entitled *The End of Marriage?* she wrote, "The atomized individual is unlikely to engage in fully with either family or community, which results in an 'emptying out' of these fundamental building blocks of society."[195] It does not help that our society promotes an atmosphere of self where looking out for number one is emphasized. At the center of this mindset is self-satisfaction.

Since marriage is a lifelong process, it requires steadfast commitment and it cannot be built solely on emotions and feelings; however, in today's culture, people lack the spiritual, mental, and emotional wherewithal necessary to sustain marriage during times of discontent and dissatisfaction. In today's culture, short-term satisfaction trumps long-term commitment. In this self-centered culture, everything else becomes subordinate to our own personal needs. The individual is more consumed with satisfying his or her self-interests versus committing the time, efforts, and energy necessary to build a long lasting relationship of husband and wife and to establish a family.

One factor contributing to this independent sentiment is men and women are less dependent on one another for economic stability in today's technological age. At one time in society, women were dependent on their husbands to work and provide for the family while they stayed at home to rear and raise their children. Today, women are more independent as they also work to provide for their family. The need for women to enter the workforce during World War II coupled with the advent of the feminist movement facilitated the transformation of women in our society. The feminist movement promoted the liberation of women and encouraged women to multi-task, balancing the duties of motherhood and of a career. Instead of women concentrating solely on motherhood, the feminist movement pressured women into having it all- motherhood and a career.

There are even reverse cases in which the mother is the sole provider while the father is the care taker of the children at home. In our career-driven society, women want to be able to have their careers also. Marriage and motherhood are not the priority like they once were. In the past, it was the norm for women to postpone any career ambitions prior to motherhood, while today; the norm has evolved into women seeking higher education and career ambitions over motherhood. Once certain accomplished benchmarks have been reached, then women seek the demanding but rewarding duties of motherhood. Either route to motherhood is laudable because the role of being a mother, no holds barred, is a demanding but rewarding experience. As a result of women no longer having to collectively rely on men for economic stability and survival, women have more latitude and influence in deciding whether or not to immediately enter motherhood or to pursue a personal career.

This independent spirit is further strengthened by the sex-crazed society we live in. Everywhere one looks, he or she is inundated with some sort of sexual reference via the media or just in plain view. Whether it is from a television commercial, a billboard, a motion picture film, or daily colloquy, we are overloaded with sexual innuendos more times than we can count; there is no escaping the increasing sexuality in America. Today's culture of endless advertisement trumpets sex as accepted practice with no linkage to marriage and the original purpose of sex. Sex is becoming more and more overt and is being forced on society to include on our children.

Although there are other countries where sexuality is more risqué, we have seen this risqué in the U.S. increase over the years. During extended family get-togethers on Sunday afternoon, I recall hearing relatives converse how sexual references in society have become more obvious over the years. In fact, there was a time when the word "sex" was not even mentioned in public. What was restricted in one generation is now acceptable in another. With each passing generation, it seems as if this sex-crazed sentiment has worsened as it has percolated in more areas throughout our society.

SEXUAL LIBERATION AND PERVERSION RUN AMOK

This sex-crazed society provides another challenge to preserving the institutions of marriage and family. It used to be the norm for an individual to find a spouse in marriage and then procreate to build a family. The norm that is unfolding today includes the forbearance of marriage in order to engage in unlimited, guiltless, and frolicsome sex with an inordinate number of partners. Now of course this does not include everyone, but collectively as a society, the option of marriage is not quickly pursued like it once was. Goals of achieving marital and family harmony are being replaced with goals of meeting libidinous desires and seeking sexual escapades outside of marriage. More and more people are falling victims to our sex-crazed society out of self-indulgence and hedonism. As long as we do not cherish what the true purpose of sex is, we will continue to adulterate sex by relishing solely in the pleasure aspect of it.

Since we have a tendency to adhere to societal fashions and trends, sex is no longer treated as a sacred gift from God to be used within marriage. God has given each of us this gift to use in marriage, but this gift has degenerated into something totally different. God's original purpose of sex to procreate the human race and to express unity between man and woman is being neglected; and instead, today it is desecrated and treated similar to a physical appetite that needs immediate fulfilling. God views sex as the basis on which all life is created and wants married couples to delight in it to its fullest. While God considers sex as an opportunity to mutually strengthen intimacy between husband and wife, society views sex as an act to fulfill one's temporal and physical needs. The original intent of sex within marriage was for husband and wife to physically fulfill one another, not for one to fulfill his or her selfish and self-centered sexual desires.

God designed sex as an intimate manner in which a couple can support the physical, spiritual, mental, and emotional needs of one another; however, today, sex is seldom displayed as a healthy manner of expressing love. Since love is a process, it will require commitment and intimate growth and not solely sex. Hence, a marriage relationship cannot be built strictly on eroticism. If it could, what happens then when a married couple naturally ages and loses their physical attractiveness to one another? There has to be something more than physical attraction to sustain a marriage and this includes the intangible treasures of joy, peace, and unconditional love- all of which come from God.

There is nothing wrong with sex; however, it is how we use it that gets people into trouble. God expects man to protect sex within the confines of marriage: "*Marriage should be honored by all, and the marriage bed kept pure, for God will judge the adulterer and all the sexually immoral.*" ***Hebrews 13:4 (NIV)*** When we protect the gift of sex and use it as God had intended we reap its benefits. One of those benefits includes a salutary lifestyle. According to Tara Parker-Pope, author of *For Better: The Science of a Good Marriage*, "Contemporary studies, for instance, have shown that married people are less likely to get pneumonia, have surgery, develop cancer or have heart attacks."[196] In another study to research the relationship between marital status and length of life, Richard Rogers validated that marital life contributes to lower mortality. He declared:

"The lower mortality of married people has been variously attributed to their superior integration into society, to the natural selection of healthier individuals for marriage, and to the psychological and lifestyle protection afforded by marriage."[197]

Here is another positive application of the divine tenet of we reap what we sow. On the other hand, when we abuse God's original intent of sex, unfavorable ramifications such as sexually transmitted diseases, unwanted children, abortion, rape, and more ensue- all of which collectively damage our society as a whole by fraying the institution of family. It should be no surprise then when we experience related health issues after abusing God's gift of sex. Sexual intimacy is both a privilege and a pleasure that God has bestowed upon man, but He expects man to adhere to His guidelines of engaging in sex in marriage only.

Today, sex is freely discussed in the media. Why not try hearing what the Bible has to say about it? For those who are not familiar with the Bible, they would be flabbergasted to hear the Bible is frank on the subject and is actually a pro-sex book- that is sex within marriage of course. God has a strong opinion of sex and actually promotes the gift of sex within the context of marriage. He desires for man and woman to delight in it within the divine parameters of marriage. The *Book of Song of Solomon* within the Bible promotes sexual intimacy and romance in marriage. *Song of Solomon* is filled with unrestrained sexual innuendos referencing physical body parts, the intimate embracement of a couple, and eroticism. For example, it uses euphemisms such as "to enter," "to lie with," or "to go into" to describe intercourse. A sample of this romanticism includes:

"HOW BEAUTIFUL YOUR SANDALED FEET, O PRINCE'S DAUGHTER. YOUR GRACEFUL LEGS ARE LIKE JEWELS, THE WORK OF A CRAFTSMAN'S HANDS. YOUR NAVEL IS A ROUNDED GOBLET THAT NEVER LACKS BLENDED WINE. YOUR WAIST IS A MOUND OF WHEAT ENCIRCLED BY LILIES. YOUR BREASTS ARE LIKE TWO FAWNS, TWINS OF A

GAZELLE. YOUR NECK IS LIKE AN IVORY TOWER. YOUR EYES ARE THE POOLS OF HESHBON BY THE GATE OF BATH RABBIM. YOUR NOSE IS LIKE THE TOWER OF LEBANON LOOKING TOWARD DAMASCUS. YOUR HEAD CROWNS YOU LIKE MOUNT CARMEL. YOUR HAIR IS LIKE ROYAL TAPESTRY; THE KING IS HELD CAPTIVE BY ITS TRESSES. HOW BEAUTIFUL YOU ARE AND HOW PLEASING, O LOVE, WITH YOUR DELIGHTS! YOUR STATURE IS LIKE THAT OF THE PALM, AND YOUR BREASTS LIKE CLUSTERS OF FRUIT I SAID, "I WILL CLIMB THE PALM TREE; I WILL TAKE HOLD OF ITS FRUIT." MAY YOUR BREASTS BE LIKE THE CLUSTERS OF THE VINE, THE FRAGRANCE OF YOUR BREATH LIKE APPLES, AND YOUR MOUTH LIKE THE BEST WINE. SONG OF SOLOMON 7:1-9 (NIV)

In today's pornographic and sexually-charged society, this vernacular will come across as alien to most people; but in actuality, this graphic and impassioned language embodies the purity of sex as intended by God. *Song of Solomon* depicts the true meaning of sexual love by equating sex with intimate relationship-building and the sexual union of man and woman in marriage.

Our lecherous society is fueled by the universal rise of pornography, proving to be an albatross to marriage. What was once considered frowned upon; pornography is becoming more and more mainstream without any regards to morality, standards of conduct, and proper decorum. Pornography has lost its stigmatization as it has acquired a global acceptance in a demoralized society. Even though pornography has been around society throughout all of time, today it is even more dominant due to increased technology. The rise of the Internet has facilitated the substantial rise of pornography. In the introduction of their book, *The Porning of America*, authors Carmine Sarracino and Kevin Scott summarized this rise of pornography:

> "Porn has so thoroughly been absorbed into every aspect of our everyday lives- language, fashion,

advertisements, movies, the Internet, our music, magazines, television, video games that it has almost ceased to exist as something separate from the mainstream culture, something 'out there'. That is, we no longer have to go to porn in order to get it. It is filtered to us, in some form, regardless of whether we want it or are even aware of it."[198]

Yesterday's generation of purity has been transformed into today's generation of pornification.

The rise of pornography in our society is supported by the growth of the porn industry. It is reported that the porn industry collects annual revenue between ten and fourteen billion dollars.[199] The porn industry includes movies, magazines, networks, sex toys, phone sex, Web sites, and more. In comparison, the total annual revenue for the U.S. professional sports industry is approximately sixteen billion dollars.[200] Within the sports industry are the primary sports organizations such as Major League Baseball, National Football League, National Basketball Association, and the National Hockey League. It is absolutely staggering to see where the porn industry is in comparison to the professional sports industry especially since the professional sports organizations are well-known for the exuberant revenue they accrue. The increase in the number of porn Web sites alone has grown at an alarming rate. In 2004, *USA Today* reported that since 1998, the number of porn sites has increased eighteen-fold to approximately 1.3 million.[201] Today, seven years later, one can only surmise that that number has increased even more as pornography has become more dominant in our society.

What some may argue is a form of harmless art, pornography is actually the very opposite. Just because there are no relationships, commitments, or consequences involved with pornography does not mean pornography is harmless. The occasional use of pornography which can lead to the eventual dependence on pornography eliminates the need for real people and real relationships. In fact, you can deduce that one who is enslaved to pornography is indolent in working on one's own conjugal relationship.

It all begins with a stilled pornographic picture. If one does not safeguard his or her mind from sexual enticing images, one's mind becomes infused with images that become visual anchors. What some argue as a harmless photograph(s) is actually the doorway to more intensive forms of pornography especially as current trends reveal a move towards more graphic imagery and videos. According to Pamela Paul, in her book *Pornified,* "While pornography has seeped into mainstream culture, the images that remain confined to the porn world have become increasingly intense."[202] If a user of pornography is unable to escape its enslavement, the photograph(s) will evolve into no longer being sufficient as the user's appetite for pornography hungers for videos involving actual movement and sound. Just as an illegal drug user experiments with a less potent drug and later develops an addiction to a stronger drug, it is the same phenomenon when a user of pornography begins with a nude photograph and later becomes addicted to more graphic pornography. Under both addictions, one is hoodwinked into thinking he or she can control it, but that is never the case.

One of the subtle, negative effects of pornography is it presents an individual with a distorted view of what sex should actually be. As a result, unrealistic expectations in love-making thrive in a marital relationship, and these unrealistic expectations eventually give rise to marital dissonance. When one becomes attached to pornography, he or she starts to believe sex has to be a replication of the same pornographic acts viewed. The viewer of pornography is likely to compare viewed acts of pornography with his or her own marital love-making and recognize distinct differences in the intensity and frequency of sex. In turn, this will create a void in sexual satisfaction for the viewer of pornography, causing one to shift one's attention away from the marriage union and on the lure of pornography. Moreover, when one who is enthralled with pornography, one is likely to compare the bodies of pornographic actresses/actors with his or her spouse's body, and again walk away disappointed since youth, beauty, and attractive bodies dominate pornographic movies.

The easy and convenient access to porn via the Internet certainly does not help. In the book *Sex and the*

Internet: A Guidebook for Clinicians by Alice Cooper, the chapter entitled "Internet Sexuality: Known Risks and Fresh Chances for Women" by Sandra Leiblum and Nicola Doring, the two talk of women being the recipient of this sexual deprivation as a result of their husband's indulgence with pornography. They claimed, "Personal inhibition levels, social controls, and the lack of willing partners and sexual scenes that may limit sexual activity in everyday contexts are obsolete in cyberspace. It is easy for latent desires to be realized in cyberspace."[203] Pornography not only robs a couple of their intimate sexuality, it also devalues one's marriage and defrauds the opposite spouse of time, attention, love, and energy, all of which lead to an unstable family.

The artificial and temporary satisfaction received from pornography hinders the physical affinity in an actual marital relationship. According to Joe Beam, founder of Love Path International, an organization designed to redeem marriages, "Every exposure to porn immerses you into a fantasy world that erodes the reality you could have together."[204] The user of pornography is likely to mentally, physically, and emotionally withdraw oneself from his or her spouse. Through pornography, sex is far from considered a special gift from God to mankind but as an entitlement to be indulged in for the purpose of self-contentment. Sex loses its connotation as a loving form of communication. As a result of pornography, an individual does not view his or her partner as a unique and intimate soul mate, but only as an object of self-pleasure and self-gratification. Instead of a partner being loved with genuine passion, the partner is objectified with selfish lust. Men or women who view pornography often "have difficulty forming and sustaining relationships and feeling sexually satisfied."[205] Through the use of pornography, one becomes desensitized to one's own marital vows, relationship, and sexual intimacy.

THE RISE OF COHABITATION

Another factor contributing to the dissolution of marriage and to unstable families is cohabitation. It appears as if cohabitation is glorified over marriage in today's fragmented society. Instead of married couples receiving the glory, it is unmarried couples living together that are receiving that glory. According to the *USA Today*, a study by the National Marriage Project revealed that the number of opposite-sex couples in the U.S. who cohabitate increased from approximately 500,000 in 1970 to over five million today.[206] In a matter of only three decades this number has escalated significantly, reflecting the liberalization of social policies in the U.S. It is striking to think how cohabitation of the opposite sex was once viewed as off limits. What was once considered out of bounds like divorce is now customary in our society and being justified by a myriad of self-serving reasons.

In their book entitled *The Good Girl's Guide to Living in Sin*, authors Joselin Linder and Elena Donovan Mauer, enumerated reasons justifying cohabitation to include: It saves time and money; it serves as a trial run before marriage; it is the next step in growing intimate; and it is the precursor prior to marriage.[207] The two wrote: "One of the most popular reasons for cohabitation is to test those proverbial waters- decide whether you and this guy could make marriage work."[208] At one time in my life, I actually agreed with the two authors as I cohabitated in the past; however, at that age, I did not have the same wisdom, appreciation of marriage, and reverence for God like I do today. The animus today is that since cohabitation is the trend or the way of society, it has to be right. In today's society, we are encouraged to behave in a way that comes across naturally without any regard to the consequences.

In the face of God's adamant position on premarital sex and cohabitation, those who cohabitate are more concerned about fulfilling their personal appetites and needs. It is important to keep in mind that iniquitous behavior causes people to become a chattel to their selfish desires and that it usually only brings temporary satisfaction. Self-indulgence does not guarantee fulfillment. This is just another example to support how our society has settled for relativism versus absolutism; the relative trends of society are concealing the absolute tenets of God. Several generations ago, the reasons for cohabitation would not have been cogent enough for our society to justify cohabitation. It is amazing what transpires over several decades. Even though the two authors offer reasons that come across as compelling and harmless in today's relative society, there is still the possibility of future imperceptible effects of cohabitation.

When an unmarried couple is contemplating whether or not to cohabitate, the aforesaid reasons for cohabitation more than likely come across as logical, acceptable, and captivating in a society where everyone else is doing it. Also, it is more than likely not too much thought goes into the negative effects of cohabitation during this decision-making process. Research and studies indicate this appealing decision to cohabitate could possibly have long-term unfavorable effects. Linda Waite, a Professor in Sociology, conducted a study called "The Negative Effects of Cohabitation," in which she brilliantly rendered:

> "The tentative, impermanent, and socially unsupported nature of cohabitation impedes the ability of this type of partnership to deliver many of the benefits of marriage, as does the relatively separate lives typically pursued by cohabiting partners."[209]

Her study further proclaimed cohabiting couples are more likely to experience domestic violence, psychological ailments, and depression, less likely to experience stable relationships, and less likely to be monogamous than married couples.[210] Similarly, another study conceded the same relationship between premarital cohabitation and marital stability. The study revealed, "The longer respondents cohabited before marriage, the greater their likelihood for depression, dependency, and perceived risk of separation. Conversely current relationship satisfaction declined as cohabitation length before marriage increased."[211] Both studies revealed what may seem harmless especially since it is commonly accepted by our society, cohabitation actually promises problems in the future, further defying the stability of marriage.

For those couples seeking cohabitation for the purpose of it being the step before marriage, and, as they propose, an opportunity to get to know the other person prior to marriage, they would be startled to learn of the relationship between premarital cohabitation and marital satisfaction as discovered in research. While they argue cohabitation allows the couple time for them to get to know one another more closely before marriage that time together does not always lead to a healthy and stable marriage. The naïve search for compatibility from cohabitation turns into unexpected incompatibility in the future. What couples label as a "marriage trial," cohabitation more than not turns into a "divorce trial." According to Waite, her research and others point out that "people who cohabitate have other characteristics that both lead them to cohabit in the first place and make them poor marriage material."[212]

RESTORING THE FAMILY AS THE UNIT OF SOCIETY

Just as there is hope for the restoration of our country as discussed in Chapter 3, there is also hope for restoration of the family. According to one study on covenant marriage and divorce which referenced the Roper Center for Public Opinion Research, "In a 1996 survey, only 1% of Americans said marital success was not very important to them, and only 8% said that marriage is an outdated institution."[213] Despite society's increased tolerance of divorce, the majority of people surveyed still believe in marriage. This restoration will take one heart at a time and then one family at a time, strengthening the institution of family. No matter how broken a family may be and no matter how horrible or calamitous things may appear on the outside, there is power in God's supernatural healing to bring back the sanctity of the home.

Just as God can heal a broken land, He can also heal a broken marriage and family. God can bless a broken marriage with His divine favor and transform it from an anemic to a vibrant relationship. This healing can only come about if God is placed back at the center of the home. The fragmentation of the family is a direct result of the lack of emphasis on God in the home. Having a house is not the same thing as having a home. If we disregard God's reverence for family, we can only expect problems at the home to follow because when we mess with the family, you are meddling with God's plan. There will always be dysfunction in marriage and in the home because we are fallible by nature; however, when we turn that dysfunction over to God, the family can be preserved. Instead of embracing society's remedy of divorce for family dysfunction, why don't we try embracing God instead? Whether we want to admit it or not, God is the panacea for all of our problems, no matter how minor or major they may be.

By establishing a renewed reverence for God in the home, we can align our thought process with God's, and thus empower ourselves to rise above the challenges of marriage and family life which will in turn keep families intact. We need a renewed emphasis on the adage: "A family that prays together stays together." It is simple but powerful when genuinely accepted into and applied to one's lifestyle.

If there is a reason to avoid divorce and rejuvenate one's marriage it is simply because God abhors divorce: *"I hate divorce," says the LORD God of Israel, "and I hate a man's covering himself with violence as well as with his garment," says the LORD Almighty. So guard yourself in your spirit, and do not break faith." **Malachi 2:16 (NIV)*** God does not like to see the holy covenant of marriage destroyed despite society's attempts to disguise divorce as harmless and commonly accepted.

It is the edification and preservation of marriage and not the nullification of marriage that God is interested in. God's goal of marriage is for the husband and wife to become one in Him. When God's goal of marriage is internally appreciated and embraced by both husband and wife, they will be better equipped to live in harmony and build a solid family- a family not free from the pressures of society but a family built on the foundation of God able to withstand society's attacks on the institution of family. Once this fundamental reliance on and reverence for God is established, then society can mobilize to implement new strategies to promote marriage and family recovery over divorce. When we strengthen our families at home, we are in turn bolstering America- our national family.

CHAPTER FIVE
RESPECT FOR PARENTHOOD REDUX

While the institution of family is under attack by exogenous forces within society, there are other internal factors within the realm of parenthood that are contributing to the meltdown of the family. Over the years, the family has been weakened because, little by little, parents have relinquished their power and control as parents over to the ways of society. Parents have abandoned their divine responsibility of parenthood in exchange for comfort and other conflicting priorities.

Parenthood, perhaps the most difficult but most rewarding job in society, plays an instrumental role in shaping the future of our society. Although the circumstances of society are beyond our control, parents still have a responsibility to raise their children in righteousness. In a society where there is a virile movement underway to unseat the traditional family, the last thing we need is parents washing their hands free of the duty of parenthood. The question remains: Will parents embrace their innate responsibility of parenting or will they cede it over to society out of apathy or busyness? It is time for parents to reestablish the integrity of the home and take back the upbringing of their children by simply assuming the duties of parenthood, monitoring their children's education, and by enforcing discipline in the home.

ASSUMING THE DUTIES OF PARENTHOOD

We have all heard the statement, "When in charge, take charge!" Well this pronouncement could not be any more appropriate for parents. Parents have a unique and dignified role in society and it is time for parents to embrace this role and carry it out with the respective purpose and appreciation. America's future will not be determined by the sagest politicians or the most intelligent strategic bureaucrats but by the principled parents who raise their children grounded in homage towards God, wisdom, and direction. It is worth mentioning it is the parents that have the primary onus of mentoring, raising, disciplining, and controlling their children, not the expanding government, not the entertainment industry, not the Church, not the babysitter, not daycare, and certainly not the unbalanced media and entertainment industry.

According to *I-Chin*, a classic Chinese text: "When a parent behaves like a parent, a child like a child, an elder like an elder, a youth like a youth, a husband like a husband, and a wife like a wife, then the conduct of the household is correct. Make the home correct, and the country will be stable."[214] Our society is in urgent need of hearing and abiding by this message today, for it suggests that when the home is in order, so too will be the nation.

Besides this message exuding from the churches of America, where else do you hear it, - certainly not from the majority of our elected leaders or from our schools? Our society is in need of a prominent and a courageous leader(s), capable of putting political correctness aside, to adopt a sense of urgency and call attention to this pressing matter. Where is he or she? Our leaders have no problem politicking and pontificating on such issues as health care, global warming, green energy, illegal immigration, and the list goes on. What about the most basic element of all civilization that has been here since the beginning of man- the family? Where is the same electric verve on the preservation of the family? Call it a wish of nirvana if you like, but be realistic and forthright and acknowledge that it is needed in our society unlike never before. The home must be reestablished.

In a society where distractions are copious, parents lose focus of their priorities. The priority of parenting becomes secondary as other activities take priority. The stability of the family is abandoned as other things such as money, career, hobbies, and addictions are eagerly chased after. As a nation, on the whole, we have grown ignorant to the orthodoxy of parenting. God did not make parenting an option but a command. Parents were designed so they could serve as representatives of God to their children. God ordained parents to raise children with exaltation towards God. This is supposed to be the sole responsibility of parents with everything else being subordinate: *"Fathers, do not exasperate your children; instead, bring them up in the training and instruction of the Lord."* **Ephesians 6:4 (NIV)**

As was mentioned earlier in the book, everything begins with God, and when parents fail to enforce this fundamental precept, the home can expect family tribulations. However, on the brighter side, when parents do practice this precept of putting God first in the home, everything else has a way of falling into place on its own through the mercy, grace, and favor of God. When our priorities are in order, the burdens of life take on a spiritual dimension and become less of an obstacle and more of a stepping stone through life. Perhaps once our priorities are in proper order, more people would align with Thomas Jefferson's sentiment on family: "The happiest moments of my life have been the few which I have passed at home in the bosom of my family."[215] Mr. Jefferson received this epiphany after accomplishing many of his acclaimed achievements. Enjoying one's family should be the ultimate goal of all parents.

THE RESTORATION OF PARENTHOOD

There seems to be a myth today that there is no glory in being a parent. Over the years, the duty of parenthood has been shamed and looked down upon as other professional occupations have been glamorized in our society. While the edification of parenthood has grown nonexistent, the edification of everything else has increased. It also does not help that our culture is not as family oriented as it once was.

When was the last time you heard someone praise the duties of a parent and the relevance that parents have in society? Although the message is heard here and there, it needs to be routinely resounded so the American people grasp the relevance of parenthood. Maybe if our society promoted parenthood then the glory of being a parent will resurface. Take for example President Theodore Roosevelt's Special

Message to Congress on February 15, 1909 where he did just that. In his remarks, he defended family by declaring: "Home life is the highest and finest product of civilization. Children should not be deprived of it except for urgent and compelling reasons."[216] Although Roosevelt spoke these penetrating words over a century ago, they have the same applicability today and could actually help revitalize the duty of parenthood and transform it from a thankless job to a divine responsibility full of respect, appreciation, and gratification.

It sounds ironic that the duty of parenthood is thought of as thankless, considering everything that goes into being a parent especially in a society that besmirches family. From my observations as a child growing up to this very day, there is nothing easy about it. Every day there is a different challenge with an opportunity to become a better parent. There is not one correct method in being a successful parent because all parents face different circumstances; however, all parenting demands love, patience, and time. In his book *Parents Isn't for Cowards*, Dr. James Dobson, a solid advocate of family and parenthood, confirmed the challenges of being a parent:

> "Being a good parent seems to have become more difficult in recent years. It never has been all that easy, of course. For one thing, babies come into the world with no instructions and you pretty much have to assemble them on your own. They are also maddeningly complex and there are no guaranteed formulas that work in every instance."[217]

Similarly, in their research on parental education, Mary Hicks and Joyce Williams reckoned: "As America's most popular career, parenting is the least prepared-for occupation, not listed in any index of occupations, but found in the vast majority of the home."[218] The absence of definitive directions on how to be a parent leaves parents on their own through trial and error. Parenthood is not a nine-to-five job with holiday reprieves, but it is a twenty-four/seven operation where there is no rest for parental leadership. Parents cannot afford to take sabbaticals from their children because any sort of sabbatical runs the risk of depriving children of the nourishment they deserve. Since parenthood does not happen overnight but is a process, parents are always learning along the way. Through this parental process, parents evolve and mature as they become better parents. With a renewed emphasis on parenthood, parenthood will equate to thankfulness.

Perhaps if our culture regained an appreciation of parenthood and grasped the power that parents have in shaping our society, the roles of parents will once again be acclaimed and not depreciated. How often do you hear, "My goal in life is to be a Godly mother or father?" Instead we hear, "I want to grow up and become a doctor, lawyer, politician, business owner, police man, etc." There is rare mention of parenthood. There is nothing wrong with declaring a career path because we all have divine purposes in life and we should reach for the stars, but where are the proclamations of wanting to be a Godly parent?

Growing up, I was solely driven to become a military officer and nothing else. That was all I could think about as my attention, efforts, and energy were all honed in on entering the career path of a military officer. It was all about me fulfilling my career goals. Being a father and raising a family was a distant and nebulous goal unlike in erstwhile generations where individuals had parenthood in the forefront of their decision-making. I always knew I wanted to be a father sometime in the future, but I did not internalize it. I did not acquire an appetite to be a Godly father until after I was married and exposed to my Godly wife.

It would be more refreshing to hear people declare their career dreams and goals in conjunction with their aspirations of becoming Godly parents. If we were to restore the image of parenthood, then just perhaps, people would develop a stronger desire to want to become a Godly father or mother, knowing they would be performing an influential part in contributing to a healthier society. It is also worth pointing out that some studies reveal a direct relationship between people wanting to be parents and the gratification received in return. For example, Candice Russell concluded in her study: "Wanting more children and placing 'father' high on a hierarchy of identities were positively associated with gratification among men. Placing 'mother' high on a hierarchy of identities was also significantly associated with women's gratification scores."[219] By spreading this positive message of the nexus between parenthood and subsequent gratification, as a society, we can revamp the image of parenthood and attract people to it, thus building a stronger society.

Just as an industry markets and advertises a specific profession to stoke interest and curiosity, our society must do the same by promoting the family and parenthood. The latest trends in society have always dictated the azimuth of our society. Well, it is time to galvanize our society through the edification of family and parenthood. When the institution of family is placed at the center of society behind reverence for God, it will only enhance the survivability and resiliency of our society.

THE EBB AND FLOW OF PARENTHOOD

When parents invest the time, effort, energy, and love in the upbringing of their children, they are more inclined to have children that are productive in society; thus, parents' contribution to the well-being of society is noteworthy. On the other hand, when parents do not make the same type of commitment to their children, the children are less likely to become positive contributors to society; thus, parents' contribution to society is minimal. Although this correlation should be discernable, the bottom line is parents have clout in directing the future of our society if they deem so, and it begins with building character within their children in the home.

Character building in children begins in the home under the leadership of their parents. Character will be formed by those things that are both implemented and neglected by parents throughout their children's lives. By the time children begin school and then grow up to enter the workforce, one's character has already been established. There is power in parenthood, but the decision to raise, mentor, and teach children for success in society ultimately rests with the respective parents. Those who wish to destabilize the institution of family seek to diminish this power in parenthood. If we do not protect this special prerogative of parenthood, our society will further falsify and erode it. Acknowledgment of the power parents have will help garner praise for parenthood and dispel the myth that parenthood is nothing special.

    Parents should not expect their children to be appreciative of their efforts as parents until later in life as they mature. By adopting this expectant mindset, parents will maintain their focus on the role of parenthood and prevent disappointment from settling in when they feel unappreciated. When parents grasp the fact that disappointments are inevitable in life and maintain their focus on the upbringing of their children, parental disappointments will be hindered from growing into discouragement. Appreciation for parenthood comes years later when children have grown up and acquired wisdom or when they become parents themselves. Children will not gain a true appreciation of what the duties and responsibilities of parenthood include especially as parents make unpopular decisions, lay down their foot, and enforce disciplinary action.

    Instead of parents being caught up in seeking adulation from their children on what they do as parents, they need to be more concerned about seeking trust, respect, and love from them. As mentioned in an earlier chapter, I was one who did not acquire this appreciation of what my parents did for my family until years later. There were many things that I did not agree with and understand why my parents did certain things until years later. I reflect back on my childhood years and appreciate how my parents instructed us on deference for God, provided for the family, enforced discipline, encouraged us to seek higher education and to chase our personal goals, demonstrated a strong work ethic, raised us to respect others, and taught us the importance of working to make a dollar. I understand now that these lessons on life were wisdom for the future. Parents should remain unyielding in their diligence of raising their children and expect to be appreciated for their actions as parents from their children in the long-term and not short-term.

Although parents should not expect to feel appreciated for their parenting by their children until later in life when the children have grown and matured, parents should expect their children to honor and respect them. It is the fifth commandment from God that demands so: Honor your father and your mother. If there is one reason alone why children should heed the fifth commandment, it is because parents gave them life. Even during times of difficulty when we oppose our parents, the fifth commandment is still applicable and must be adhered to. As hard as it may be sometimes due to instances of family strife and poor parental leadership, there are no exceptions to honoring one's parents. Parents will fail at times and this is just a fact of life since humanity cannot elude the fallible nature of man. Parents' failure does not nullify the commandment and grant children the right to err from it. God did not make respect for others an option or a choice based off of temporal circumstances of satisfaction. When one is quick to find fault with his or her parents during times of disappointment or discord, keep in mind the moments in life when one is deserving of the same condemnation for something else. Perfection and the fallibility of mankind are incompatible with one another. Parents who believe they are not being honored by their children, could it be that the dishonorable actions of those parents have influenced their children to hold back displaying respect? We must always perform self-examinations before exercising judgment on others.

Even though obedience and respect towards our parents are supposed to be treated as absolute commands from God for all of civilization, in our society today, it has become another type of bromide where its fundamental purpose has been blurred by a culture hijacked by relativism. When we revive the importance and relevance of honoring our parents and reestablish this commandment as a brick to our society, the institution of family can be strengthened, which in turn will uplift our nation on many fronts, making us both a formidable and respected nation across the globe.

PARENTAL OVERSIGHT OF THEIR CHILDREN'S EDUCATION

One area in which parents can take back the lead in parenthood is with the education of their children. For too long, parents have remained idle as the government, special interest groups, and school officials and administrators dictated what students in school should be learning. Innocent learning has been replaced with purposeful and autocratic indoctrination. Children are not being taught to reason and think judiciously, but they are being taught to think in a programmed manner that benefits an alternative agenda of some sort outside of sincere learning. As Abraham Lincoln once professed: "The philosophy of the school room in one generation will be the philosophy of government in the next."[220] Hence, it is not a shock that the education system would be exploited to support a specific agenda.

Since education is a lifelong process, parents have an influential role in ensuring their children are receiving a solid, unbiased education from the start which in turn will gear them for success in the future. It is true that education empowers success, but it is truer that education balanced with wisdom empowers an appreciation for success. From day one, parents must become proactive in monitoring the education of their children. It is essential for parents to know exactly what subjects are being taught in the respective grade and they should even probe the content of each course. Parents should ask their children what topics were covered in their classes; what are the views or opinions of the different teachers; and how did the teachers receive the comments of and feedback from the children? Take it a step further and ask children what does God say about a particular topic versus how it was taught in school? Parents must help children distinguish truth from error.

At one time in our history, parents did not have to fret so much over the education of their children because they were being positively influenced through the education system. Parents could send their children to school and know that their children were receiving a solid education on the fundamentals of life free of political correctness and agenda-setting indoctrination. During this former period, praise for God was at the focal point of the education system and there were no shenanigans supporting an alternative agenda. Moreover, the material in the Bible was considered educational, sage, and curriculum-worthy. The school system placed a primary focus on reverence for God and all other school subjects were subsidiary to it. Believe it or not, students acquired an education filled with wisdom versus indoctrination and were more focused and better behaved in and outside of school.

This may sound like a lot of work, but no one said parenting is easy. The long-term effect of doing so will only benefit the development of our children. If parents do not assume the ownership of this responsibility, children will be in the hands of the government, the education system, the media, and the special interests. Children belong to the parents and no one else, so why is there a collective spirit of stolidity when it comes to overseeing the education of our children? Since children are vulnerable to errant influences, parents have the duty to protect their children. Parents owe it to their children to ensure critical and analytical thinking along with morality are being encouraged in school. When parents intervene in their children's education, they would be upholding Martin Luther King Junior's stirring words on education: "We must remember that intelligence is not enough. Intelligence plus character--that is the goal of true education."[221]

THE DOWNFALL OF AMERICA'S PUBLIC SCHOOLS

As a result of the move away from God in school and the consequent deterioration of our education system, a powerful argument can be made that the removal of prayer and Bible reading from school yielded an array of problems in our schools. The collective intellectual level of American students has waned, while problems relating to violence, drugs, alcohol, suicides, teen pregnancies, discipline, strident rebellion, and others have multiplied. This is not to say that everything was pure when there was reverence for God in school, but these growing complications have taken on a predominant nature in our education system today and parents must have this awareness. In his book *America: To Pray or Not to Pray?* historian David Barton wrote:

> "While the removal of school prayer cannot be blamed for all declines, the presence or absence, legality or illegality, of prayer and acknowledgment of God in public arenas is the primary indicator of the philosophy under which official public policy is being conducted."[222]

One cannot ignore the relationship between the lack of reverence for God and the educational exigencies in our schools today.

No matter if it is in our schools or any other segment of society, when light is removed, a vacuum is created in which darkness settles. And as many have said, "Nature abhors a vacuum." This is just a fact of life that people are tepid to acknowledge; there is a constant battle between good and evil in every area of our lives and lightness cannot coexist with darkness. We cannot just jettison God at our leisure and expect Him to grant us His favor and protection at our calling. Since God has been removed from the classroom, His divine umbrella has also been removed, thus contributing to the chaos in schools. Granted, there is nothing stopping a student from carrying God in his or her heart and praying to Him throughout the day on his or her own accord, but it is striking to see how as a nation we once openly worshipped God with absolute conviction, while today that conviction has given way to relative excuses and intolerance of our Christian heritage.

On a separate note, it is not the school's responsibility to raise children in a Godly atmosphere; that is the primary role of parents. However, it is the school's responsibility to teach and promote an atmosphere which reflects the Godly heritage and legacy of our nation. Since our beginning, dependence on God has always been inherent to the fabric of our nation, thus it is our history that is in need of being instructed.

One does not have to look far to witness America's collective scholastic performance under the public education system versus the private education system. During the 1999-2000 school year, the National Center for Education Statistics (NCES) reported there were 27,223 schools, 5,262,849 students, and 404,066 teachers under the private education system compared to 84,735 schools, 45,366,227 students, and 2,905,658 teachers under the public education system.[223] Although the number of public schools dominates our education system, the private education system plays a dominant role in the education, development, and mentorship of our children. From the results of the National Assessment of Educational Progress (NAEP) 2000 tests, private school consistently outscored public schools in the areas of reading, math, and science in grades four, eight, and twelve.[224] Not only do students in private schools scholastically outscore students in public schools, but more teachers in private schools believe they have more influence and control over their students than those in public schools do.[225] The teachers in private schools also are more satisfied with their jobs and their respective schools than those teaching in public schools.[226] Is it any coincidence then that schools that revere God have fewer disciplinary problems, produce a better product in student performance, and have a more pleasant learning and working environment? When God is placed at the center of things, things have a way of falling into place in a copacetic manner.

    Over the years, violence has been on the rise in public schools against both teachers and other students. Violence in school consists of school shootings, gang activity, bullying, weapons possession, physical and verbal fighting, and more. Outside of the home, the school is supposed to be the next safest place for children, but that is quickly changing. Parents are becoming more concerned about the safety of their children while they attend school as violence in public schools inflates. After all, the horrific memories of the Columbine school shooting still remains fresh in people's minds especially as more children are carrying weapons to school. The 1997-1998 school year alone had a total of 40 people that were shot and killed while in school.[227] That was 40 too many since schools are supposed to be considered safe zones. The National Center for Educational Statistics reported:

> "71 percent of public elementary and secondary schools experienced at least one violent incident during the 1999–2000 school year (including rape, sexual battery other than rape, physical attacks or fights with and without a weapon, threats of physical attack with and without a weapon, and robbery with and without a weapon). In all, approximately 1,466,000 such incidents were reported in public schools."[228]

These numbers come across as quite striking, and it is hard to believe they are associated with our schools. Several decades ago, when childhood innocence seemed to dominate the atmosphere in schools, one would never imagine violence in schools could reach the level it has today. Mischief and frolic behavior have always been characteristics of children in school, but today's mischievous acts are of a whole different nature. Hostile name-calling has been replaced with scurrilous verbal assaults. Fights with fists have been replaced with fights with weapons such as guns and knives. Teachers were once feared and respected, but today they are flouted by out-of-control and disrespectful students. The National School Safety Center reported that "over the 5-year period from 1998 to 2002, teachers were the victims of approximately 234,000 total nonfatal crimes at school, including 144,000 thefts and 90,000 violent crimes (rape, sexual assault, robbery, aggravated assault, and simple assault)."[229] How much worse can it get? Without a foundation of reverence for God and a compass of morality, students will continue to become more absorbed with the distractions of society and lose focus of school priorities, thus creating a potential for this trend towards violence to increase. As students become more preoccupied with violence, they lose perspective on the purpose of school, the rule of law, and student propriety.

In addition to increased violence in schools, more school children are experimenting with alcohol and illicit drugs. Their attention has shifted from simple and pure matters such as homework and extracurricular activities to alcohol and drug experimentation. For example, according to the White House Office of National Drug Control Policy (ONDCP), from 1991 to 2001, past month drug use by eighth and tenth graders has increased.[230] ONDCP stated that "between 1992 and 1997, past month use of marijuana increased from 11.9% to 23.7% among 12th graders; 8.1% to 20.5% among 10th graders; and 3.7% to 10.2% among 8th graders."[231] Based off a survey conducted by the National Center on Addiction and Substance Abuse at Columbia University, "researchers concluded that 80% of the nation's high school students and 44% of middle-schoolers have personally seen illegal drugs used or sold and/or students drunk or high on the grounds of their schools."[232] What makes this unfortunate statistic worse is that parents either tolerate it or are completely unaware of it. Former Health Secretary for President Carter, Joseph Califano, affirmed this by saying that parents must "wake up to the reality of increasingly drug-infested schools."[233]

    Parents who are intimately involved in their children's life more than not have this situational awareness and know the direction in which their children are heading. Children's behavior in school is largely determined by the parental guidance and direction or lack of it they receive at home. Hence, the most effective way to prevent children from abusing alcohol and drugs is for parents to honor God in the home, possess and express a genuine love and interest for their children, and to exercise moral mentorship and leadership. When parents are involved in their children's education and avoid becoming absentee parents, they help build the confidence and self-worth of their children.

    Next to outbursts of violence in school and flagrant alcohol and drug usage by children, suicides among children have also increased. The American Foundation for Suicide Prevention reported suicide is the fifth leading cause of death among those 5-14 years old and the third leading cause of death among those 15-24 years old.[234] In addition, "among young people aged 10-14 years, the rate has doubled in the last two decades."[235] When you think about it, it is perplexing to think that the minds of young children are so preoccupied with dark thoughts of suicide and not innocent thoughts of play time, friendships, homework, family vacations, and school sports and activities. Personally, I do not even recall the word suicide being part of one's vocabulary during my teen years. It is worth asking, "How can life be so empty and shallow that young teens want to resort to suicide?" Why aren't they looking to the future and thinking there is so much to live for?

This is why it is so important to protect our minds from deviant and wicked thoughts because our thoughts, whether good or evil, eventually become implanted within our hearts and eventually develop into our actions if they are not properly sifted by our internal conscience. Since our conscience is conditioned by what we do, if we live an iniquitous lifestyle, our conscience runs the risk of becoming dull and unaffected by unrighteousness. As reverence for God is replaced by other superficial matters, a spiritual void supervenes, thus causing our thoughts to be centered on the pressures of life, our problems, and our shortfalls. Once these negative thoughts settle in and take form, suicide can become an attractive option. Thoughts govern our behavior since our actions are based upon what we believe. In other words, our actions are delayed results of our thoughts. Instead of controlling one's thoughts and relying on God for relief, school children become overwhelmed, feel helpless in their own strength, and mistakenly see suicide as their only way out.

Although the Center for Disease Control and Prevention has reported that there were more teenagers waiting to have sex in 2002 than there were in 1995, overall, teenagers are still cavorting and engaging in sexual activity in our salacious culture.[236] For example, 19% of never married females 15-17 years old have had at least one sexual partner in the last twelve months.[237] 13% of never married males 15-19 years old have had sexual intercourse 1-3 times within the last four weeks.[238] In our sexually motivated society, at first, these statistics may not come across as alarming, but they are noteworthy as teenagers should be more consumed by school and what career path they will be pursuing rather than sexual activity.

With this sexual activity also comes unplanned and unwanted consequences such as teenage pregnancies and sexually transmitted infections (STIs). Today's younger generation is ignorant to these serious consequences as it is more caught up with the temporary thrill of sexual activity. According to the Guttmacher Institute, for the first time since the early 1990s, overall rates of pregnancy among teenagers increased from 2005 to 2006.[239] What was once considered an extreme rarity is now commonly accepted and sometimes even encouraged. Take for example the Gloucester pregnancy plot where seven high school female students allegedly made a pact to get pregnant and raise their babies together. Giving birth to babies out of wedlock was treated as a calculated but glib game of some sort versus a divine blessing by these sophomore girls. Regardless of the girls' reasoning to become pregnant, one can reasonably assume that the girls had minimum parental supervision, lacked the full education on the ramifications of teenage pregnancy, and wallowed in society's twisted glorification of teenage pregnancy. It does not seem to help with such glorified television programs as *Teen Mom* aired on MTV. STIs do not discriminate and as teenagers irreverently engage in sexual activity, along come the unexpected consequences of STIs. The Guttmacher Institute reported that "of the 18.9 million new cases of STIs each year, 9.1 million (48%) occur among 15-24-year-olds."[240] Furthermore, what makes this statistic even more egregious is that "although 15-24-year-olds represent only one-quarter of the sexually active population, they account for nearly half of all new STIs each year."[241]

When teenagers are supposed to be occupied with school activities and homework, they are now preoccupied with sexual activity, unwanted pregnancies, and the treatment of STIs.

In an age of incessant sexual promotion and coverage, it will take much more than classroom education on sexual reproduction and safe sex to smother sexual activity among today's teenagers. It will be up to the parents and not our schools to steer our children in the right direction when it comes to sexual activity before marriage. Part of this guidance includes teaching children that there are consequences to our actions. As old-fashioned as it may sound in today's pleasure-seeking society, parents have the primary responsibility of establishing a Godly footprint and moral authority in the home. With this Godly footprint, moral tenets are established and consequently engrained in the psyche of children despite society's environment of sexual debauchery.

Even though not all of America's youth are troubled by the aforementioned societal woes in school, the collective face of today's younger generation is defined by substandard academic performance, violence, drugs, alcohol, suicides, sex, and unintended pregnancies versus scholastic excellence. This is evidenced by America's poor academic standing as compared to other developed countries in the international community. According to the Alliance for Excellent Education, America has one of the lowest graduation rates among developed nations belonging to the Organization for Economic Cooperation and Development (OECD).[242] In the four areas of reading literacy, scientific literacy, mathematics literacy, and problem solving, the U.S. ranked below the OECD average.[243] The U.S. ranked 15th of 29 OECD countries in reading literacy, 21st of 30 in scientific literacy, 25th of 30 in mathematics literacy, and 24th of 29 in problem solving.[244] These figures come across as surprising especially since the U.S. is the leading technological country in the world, currently has the leading economy in the world, and has the most powerful military in the world. How can our nation sustain such a renowned status with the decreasing cerebral level of today's youth as compared to the youth from other developed countries? What is going to happen in twenty years from now when we are short qualified workers to keep pace with the rest of the technological savvy world? This is especially frightening in a period where technology exponentially increases. The time is now for the American youth to shirk the societal embroilments of violence, drugs, alcohol, suicides, sex, teenage pregnancy, and sexual transmitted infections and to diligently seek scholastic excellence and innovative inquisition for the good of the country.

EXAMINING PUBLIC EDUCATION SPENDING

One would think with the Department of Education's gargantuan budget, the U.S. would have the majority of its students performing at the highest caliber. The 2010 budget for the Department of Education was $46.7 billion and $45.4 billion for 2009.[245] According to one article in the *USA Today*, from 2007-08, the national average cost per student for public education was $10,259, a 6.1 percent increase from the previous year as per the U.S. Census Bureau.[246] The same article noted: "New York spent $17,173 per student for public education in 2007-08, more than any other state and 67% more than the U.S. average."[247] We spend more money per student than any other country in the world, and our scholastic output is still horrendous as described earlier compared to other industrial countries. This shows us that spending more does not equate to smarter and more productive school children. It does suggest we are failing both the student and taxpayer. We are going astray somewhere.

While all this money may be appropriated to the Department of Education, the question remains, how much of this money actually gets to the right end user and finds its way into the actual classrooms? Or does it get caught up within the government bureaucracy and the administrators that are a part of the Department of Education? Perhaps if the money was properly allocated and distributed, the respective money would end up in the classroom, preventing teachers from purchasing classroom and project supplies with their own hard-earned money. Administration responsibilities within the Department of Education are absolutely needed, but at the same time, educational priorities and objectives must be established so that intellectual might finds its way back into the classroom. This in turn would prepare our students for today's technological and globalized society and increase our overall scholastic aptitude in the international community. This is needed more than ever especially since "the United States has fallen from first to 12th in the share of adults ages

25 to 34 with postsecondary degrees, according to a new report from the College Board."[248]

As the argument for increased education funding at all levels of government continually resurfaces, the scholastic improvement in education output is minimal. The documentary on the shortfalls of public education in America, *Waiting for Superman*, revealed that even though we have more than doubled our spending on education since the 1970s, we still fail to keep pace with the rest of the developed world. We can keep throwing money at and passing legislation and reform to correct our educational shortfalls, but if the mindset or philosophy at the root of the problem is not in order, then no amount of money, legislation, or reform will yield academic progression and improvement.

Take for example the state of Michigan. In February 2010, state officials were contemplating taxing some of life's basic services and directing the proceeds towards education as a result of Michigan's school aid fund for K-12 being short $422 million.[249] Some of these services to be taxed included dry cleaning, entertainment, car repair, and accounting and legal services.[250] 73% of the sales tax collections in Michigan are already deposited in the School Aid Fund for K-12 education.[251] When are enough taxes enough to cover education?

Under this proposal of taxing services, the government officials in Michigan failed to acknowledge the first thing consumers cut from their budgets during times of economic hardships is services they can temporarily get by without. Hence, the restraint from obtaining services will only backfire and create a shortfall in collecting funds for education. Consumers are fed up with the government raising taxes to fix government problems and mismanagement. There has to be wiser policy that gets to the heart of the education problem in America and not provide solely temporary band-aid solutions.

Parents must have this awareness so they can stand up for the education of their children.

PARENTS CAN BE THE GOAD IN PROMOTING ACADEMIC EXCELLENCE

  Education departments do not need increased funding as much as they need visionary restructuring and emphasis on the importance of higher learning, instruction, and wisdom. Parents can play a role in protecting their children's education by exercising their voice against increased taxes for education, enforcing honest teaching and learning versus indoctrinated learning stirred by programmatic memorization, keeping an eye-out for the revisionism of American history and other course material, and holding schools to a standard of academic excellence within their local school districts. It all begins at the lowest level and if parents do not stand up for academic proficiency for their children, then who will?
  In a society where competition is smothered and mediocrity is easily settled for, parents have a challenging task in promoting perseverance and academic excellence among their children. Parents will have a full time job in itself with counteracting society's countenance of mediocrity. Moreover, it does not help that there are now school programs being experimented with that pay students for their steady attendance and good grades. Students are now being allured by the profit motive of coming to school versus the personal drive of coming to school for the sole purpose of higher learning and personal growth. In 2008, Baltimore school dedicated $935,000 to improving their graduation test scores; each student was promised $110 each to improve their scores.[252] In New York City, another program made approximately 9000 fourth and seventh graders eligible for as much as $500 a piece for improving their math and English scores on the city's tests.[253] Money always serves as a powerful incentive, but when money and not personal perseverance is relied upon as the incentive for academic performance, what happens when that money evanesces? Are we establishing a dangerous precedent of promoting a spirit of dependence over independence?

Even though the majority of these programs are funded through private donors and not by the average taxpayer, you cannot force someone to genuinely enjoy something if he or she does not possess a true desire for it. As with anything else in life, some things will be relished while other things will be loathed; so why should it be any different with attending school? We should not have to entice students to want to attend school and perform well in school. It must be a personal choice, a choice that involves real life consequences.

If a student pursues education and does well in school, that student is awarded with open doors later in life. On the other hand, if a student opts not to pursue an education, then it should be no surprise he or she will have to grapple more through life and may not have as many opportunities offered. This is nothing new and is a fact of life. We are supposed to be rewarded for diligence and propriety. It is amazing how things have devolved for the worse over the years. I remember the day when perfect attendance was rewarded through a school certificate of achievement or a ribbon with public recognition and not monetary recompense. It was a big deal and many students vied for that recognition. It not only promoted healthy competition as students performed out of their own volition, but it also promoted personal accountability and responsibility. Students attended school to seek and gain knowledge in anticipation of a comfortable future not to acquire short-term comfort. The days of being motivated by long-term success from exemplary school performance are in jeopardy of now being replaced by short-term materialistic and monetary awards.

Whatever happened to the days when academic excellence was expected in the classroom and sought after by students? Have we lowered classroom standards to the point where we expect less from our students? If this same spirit of mediocrity and passivity dominated the U.S. since our inception, the face of the U.S. would not be what it is today. The U.S. did not achieve its greatness in the world by settling for lukewarm apathy. Our national feats of achieving independence from Great Britain, rising above slavery, vanquishing tyrannical regimes during World War II, obtaining the stature of a superpower, being the first country to send a man to the moon, developing innumerable innovations, helping those less fortunate around the world, and much more were all accomplished with a competitive spirit and the infectious ardor to be the best we could be regardless of domestic and international flak.

As academic standards slip, how can we expect this same sense of greatness in America? What happens in the classroom is a microcosm of what happens in our country. The same lack of responsibility and accountability in the classroom is the same phenomenon that lingers throughout our society today. Rekindling the flame of American greatness will not be easy, but it begins by parents weaning their children with this spirit of greatness from day one in the home and holding schools accountable. By doing so, parents are setting the foundation for an enduring education. After all, the only limits to one's education are what one settles for.

MONITORING CHILDREN'S TEXTBOOKS

One way in which parents can protect the education of their children is by monitoring the school textbooks their children are using in school. It is hard to imagine our education system would be utilizing textbooks that contravene our historical truth, but it appears more textbooks are either missing parts of our American history or containing erroneous historical information. Parts of our historical past are being revised for the sake of mollifying a particular agenda that disregards our true heritage. David Barton clearly detailed that "revisionists generally accomplish their goal of rewriting history by: Underemphasizing or ignoring the aspects of American history they deem to be politically incorrect and overemphasizing those portions they find acceptable; vilifying the historical figures who embraced a position they reject; and concocting the appearance of widespread historical approval for the social policy they are attempting to advance."[254] If parents do not take the time to peruse their children's textbooks, our children run the risk of being befuddled by propaganda and filled with misinformation. Parents have a responsibility in ensuring our children are being instructed on America's exceptionalism throughout her history and the role God has played in shaping America.

How else are our children going to be able to discern they are being taught honest and accurate information on our history if parents just assume schools are doing the right thing? We cannot rely on our schools to do this free of interference. In order to give an accurate representation of America, both the high and low points throughout our national history need to be taught in school because they have brought us to the point where we are today. Textbooks must reflect a true picture of our history and must be grounded in historical realism versus false nirvana. We should not be embarrassed or feel intimidated by our shortfalls throughout our history. As unfortunate as these moments may have been, we have learned from them and have matured as a nation. Similarly, we should not hide those positive times throughout our history where we stood above other countries. Through a spirit of humility, we can continue to serve as an example for other nations across the globe. Our children must be equipped with the unadulterated truth of our history, of the good and the bad times, and if school textbooks do not supply our children with historical veracity, parents must take an active role in raising their voices throughout their respective school districts. When their voices are heard and taken seriously, change cannot be stopped.

All we have to do is look at Texas and witness how change can occur with the help of external voices clamoring for accountability, veracity, and accuracy in our textbooks. In May 2010, the Texas Board of Education approved the use of textbooks that would emphasize American greatness and American capitalism in the world, the role that God and Christianity played in our society, and other conservative topics. This courageous action taken by the majority of the board members was the antithesis of the board members' actions taken ten years earlier. The 2010 vote "was the exact opposite outcome from ten years ago, when liberals pressed for a more diverse, progressive approach."[255] It is important to note the power behind the collective voice of the American people for we are still a nation "of the people, by the people, and for the people" in spite of the ungodly and undemocratic actions that have besmirched our country over the last few decades.

When the collective voice of the American people reach a certain level, our representatives, from our school boards to our highest levels of government committees, are forced into true representation. Parents should not limit their outcries of educational injustice to the respective school districts of their children. If the respective schools and school districts fail to address the concern of parents as it relates to misinformed textbooks and misguided curricula, the collective voice of the parents can reach a decibel capable of being heard by external players with more clout such as local, state, and federal legislators. Parents must maintain a spirit of tenacity and perseverance and demand more legislating over politicking when it comes to protecting the future of their children. The enforcement of morality and unbiased education is a fight worth fighting for because it will have long-term ramifications. Parents will have to make the decision- Will they stand up to educational sophistry or compromise the truth in order to just get along?

REINTRODUCING DISCIPLINE IN THE HOME

Many of the problems we are seeing unfold with today's younger generation are a result of discipline being vacant from the home. This also should not be a surprise since we have been forewarned since the dawn of time as noted in the *Book of Proverbs*: *"Train a child in the way he should go, and when he is old he will not turn from it."* **Proverbs 22:6** *(NIV)* The discipline children receive at home not only informs them, but it also provides them the wisdom and power to make wise choices throughout their lifetime.

Growing up as a child, I knew that my parents expected an atmosphere of discipline. I may not have savored in it as a child, but years later, I discerned that discipline breeds responsibility, accountability, and respect, all of which have been and will continue to be applied throughout my life. However, today, discipline is not treated as such but has a negative connotation to it.

Discipline in the home is an underestimated, intangible necessity that must be treated with respect by both parents and children alike. Parents must appreciate the fact they have significant influence and through the exercise of an effective tool called discipline, they can leave an inveterate impression with their children. It is the parents who are children's first-line role models in most cases. On the other side, children must appreciate the fact that discipline in the home is for their long-term good and not short-term vexation. When parents grasp the benefits of discipline and children learn to value themselves, they will both be able to accept discipline in the home, thus contributing to the coexistence of parents and children in a home built on a foundation of discipline. Children who are not raised in a disciplined home are likely to bring chagrin to their parents and devastation to themselves.

Could it be that parents refrain from discipline because they are afraid of being rejected by their children? Are parents more concerned about feeling accepted by their children rather than being disliked for enforcing discipline in the home? When parents are more preoccupied with being popular with their children versus unpopular, parents are actually forfeiting their parental duties. By forfeiting these duties of discipline enforcement, parents are actually jeopardizing the personal growth and progression of their children. Children need guidance and direction because there is a natural tendency for children to rebel. Without the discipline to control that rebellion, children are likely to live a life deviating from their God-given purpose. As recalcitrant as children may be at times, they actually do desire to be raised with discipline, love, and parental guidance. Granted, their external demeanor may not display it especially as they are distracted and confounded by the ways of society, but internally, their souls crave for attention and love as they want to be nurtured with parental nourishment.

In the circle of life, God designed children to yearn for such parental love and oversight, and the earlier the children experience this in life, the better. With parental love and oversight comes discipline in the home. After all, discipline is motivated by and administered out of love as displayed by God's love for man. Just as God disciplines man out of love to keep man focused on Him and to prevent man from straying, parents discipline their children out of love also to keep them on the path of righteousness: *"My son, despise not the chastening of the LORD; neither be weary of his correction: For whom the LORD loveth he correcteth; even as a father the son in whom he delighteth."* ***Proverbs 3:11-12 (KJV)***

We can all take a lesson from an old Chinese proverb: "Parents who are afraid to put their foot down usually have children who step on their toes."[256] If parents want the best for their children and ultimately our society, parents cannot be quiescent and timid in enforcing discipline. Parenting is far from being a spectator event. Tenuous parental control coupled with the lackluster enforcement of discipline is a total disservice to our children. When children are fed with fundamental principles of responsibility, accountability, propriety, and respect, children are equipped and protected for the adventure of life. When children are supplied with this type of quality guidance, the relationship between child and parent blossoms and you cannot put a price on that.

Besides unconditional love and time, the best gift parents can give their children is discipline - the gift that will keep on giving as it is passed on from family generation to family generation, consequently buttressing American society. More than ever, parents must take ownership of their children, and one of the first steps in doing so is establishing discipline in the home. If parents fail to do so, where will this discipline come from- certainly not from the school, peers, or society? So the next time you hear parenthood being trivialized and scoffed at, think of the impact you can have on your children and ultimately on the future of our society.

In enforcing discipline in the home, it is essential parents properly balance the implementation and enforcement of rules with relationship-building. Effective discipline in the home will not occur if one is without the other. In a home where rules flourish without relationship, it is likely children will grow up in steady rebellion. On the other hand, if a home is abundant in relationship-building and empty of rules, it is likely that children will grow up lacking the principles of accountability and responsibility in their life. Discipline in children does not occur overnight, but through the parental tools of verbal guidance, follow-through instruction, enduring mentorship, example-setting, and love, children will grow into productive citizens in our society. Through discipline enforcement, children understand there are consequences to bad behavior and disobedience. Furthermore, they witness the divine law of consequences that a person reaps what he or she sows. There is no greater lesson of accountability. With the enforcement of rules and the existence of relationship-building, both undergirded by love, discipline in the home can make better parents and can better equip children for the undertakings of life.

      One common trend prevalent in our society today is that parents are more concerned with being a friend to their children than a parent, and as a result, discipline in the home becomes ineffective. Moreover, parents want their children to like them more than respect them, thus annulling any attempts to develop discipline in the home. In fact, one can argue the adolescence of America is unfolding right before us. Due to this distorted mindset, the parental-child relationship becomes just another relationship akin to children's relationships with their friends, deteriorating God's design of authority structure. The hard truth is discipline is painful for both the child receiving it and the loving parent giving it. When a parent enforces discipline in the home, he or she does not necessarily savor in it, but he or she does internalize the fact that its long-term effects will always outweigh the short-term suffering or discomfort experienced by the child. It is also important parents follow through with their punitive actions when children commit a disciplinary offense. If parents fail to do so, they run the risk of undermining any sort of discipline structure they may have established.

      In enforcing discipline in the home, parents must take control, and they must do so with assertiveness rather than diffidence. Parents should not want to sequester their children from the world, but through discipline enforcement, parents should protect children from and prepare them for the harmful and sinister ways of the world. Part of doing so includes consistently setting the example and following through. No matter how paltry something may appear it must be treated with the same seriousness because children are always looking and will easily pick up on something out-of-the-ordinary or a moment when parents let down their guard. When they do, that event will leave an unforgettable impression with them and consequently challenge parents' authority in the future. When parents are consistent with their message and exercise discipline faithfully, parents will not have to walk on pins and needles and fret over being caught off guard.

For example, when a movie contradicts a home's practiced values; parents must remove that movie or turn the channel. When children spend their time with friends that violate their home values, parents must stand up and signal out the shortfalls of these friends. When schools teach subjects that run against a home's values and children's upbringing, parents must take an active role in stepping up to the school and the respective school district. It is the role of parents to protect their children even in times of unpopularity. When a system of discipline is implemented in a home from the get-go, there are expectations of the parents as the progenitors of discipline and of the children as the byproducts of discipline. Hence, there are no surprises when an incident does occur; with a system of discipline already in practice, parents know what is expected of them and children know what is expected from them.

In our society today, there seems to be more emphasis on child rights versus child responsibilities as parental authority is challenged. The fifth commandment of honoring one's father and mother seems to have taken the backseat to the promotion of children entitlements in today's society. Enforcing discipline in the home may sometimes call the need for spanking. Even though there are conflicting studies and reports on spanking as a form of discipline in the home, the decision to spank ultimately rests with the parent and no one else. Parents have a divine command from God to enforce discipline in the home, and they are the ones to decide on their method, as long as they are within legal, ethical, and moral parameters.

Proverbs 23:13 (KJV) confirms this: "*Withhold not correction from the child: for if thou beatest him with the rod, he shall not die.*" Keeping in mind that the Bible can be read literally, figuratively, and allegorically, it is important to note that under the guidance of this verse, parents cannot freely beat their children with a rod, but they must be proactive in establishing discipline in the home. However, what this verse does signify is that both verbal and physical reprimand is necessary in enforcing discipline in the home. It is up to the parents to wisely and effectively use physical chastisement and not abuse their authority. As with anything else, there is a skill-craft to it.

As one who was sometimes spanked as a child, I deem it effective as long as it is situational-based and adopted not as the only disciplinary tool of parents. The threat of being spanked taught me to evade disobedience and bad behavior. I was more interested in pleasing my parents than appeasing my childish antics, so I opted for the route of good behavior the majority of the time. When parents exercise a balance between verbal and physical reproof, backed by unconditional love, children more than likely will grow up with discipline.

There are compelling arguments for and against spanking. For example, one study of more than 2,500 toddlers from low-income families contributed spanking to poor behavior and problems with mental development.[257] As the study suggested, opponents of spanking declare that young children do not have the cognitive ability to reason and distinguish right from wrong, thus leading to erratic behavior in children. On the other side, studies suggested the direct opposite. For example, in another study of 2,600 people, "children spanked up to the age of 6 were likely as teenagers to perform better at school and were more likely to carry out volunteer work and to want to go to college than their peers who had never been physically disciplined."[258] Studies like this one reveal when discipline is enforced and controlled through spanking, children grow up with minimal behavioral problems.

As convincing as these arguments may be on both sides, parents must weigh those arguments and decide for themselves on how they should discipline their children. They still possess the freedom of choice to do so. While advocates of spanking argue spanking will strengthen discipline in the home and ultimately produce children who are better behaved, opponents of spanking argue spanking will increase youth violence and poor behavior. Regardless of the side of the argument, parents know the best method on how to actuate their children's behavior; no one knows their children better than their parents. Parents know the shortfalls of their children and know the best way in which to get their children's attention in order to get them on the right path of righteousness and good behavior. If that means an occasional spanking, then so be it. If that means verbal reprehension, then that is permissible also. Parents are the ones to make that decision and they should not be discouraged by society's negative perception of spanking.

Part of edifying the institution of family includes reinvigorating parenthood. Parents cannot dabble in parenthood, but they must bask in it and exercise it with authority and love. Parents not only have a demanding responsibility to uphold in our society, but they also have the most prestigious responsibility. Next to God, the most important thing in life is family, and parents must demonstrate this. Whether they want to accept it or not, parents are the shapers to the future of our nation. When parents wholeheartedly assume the duties of parenthood without being faint of heart, oversee their children's education and personal growth, and enforce discipline in the home, they are supporting the institution of family and consequently playing a grand role in uplifting our society. In turn, they will be tomorrow's unsung heroes for saving our country from total downfall. Half of being a good parent is just being present; presence alone can leave a profound impact on a child's life. With the exercise of these three measures, parental presence would be obvious as parents provide watch-care at home, in school, and everywhere else in between.

CHAPTER SIX
THE NUCLEAR FAMILY VERSUS THE HOMOSEXUAL AGENDA

In today's society, the traditional family is troubled not only by the sexualization of America, the rampant divorce rate, and the general disregard for the institution of family but also by the extreme homosexual agenda trying to redefine traditional marriage by forcing the legalization of homosexual marriage. The devaluation and fragmentation of marriage has led to the acceptance of same-sex marriage. Over the decades, the family has stood the test of time as couples entered the holy sacrament of marriage in order to procreate and raise a family; however, as our culture continues to degenerate and become more socially tolerant, the family is facing unprecedented challenges as the radical homosexual population attempts to turn traditional marriage upside down. Sociology professor and expert on the family, Andrew Cherlin, argued that the movement to legalize same-sex marriage is "the most recent development in the deinstitution of marriage".[259]

The foundation of family, which has always served as a stronghold of society, is no longer unassailable. Moreover, the pace at which homosexuality and same-sex marriage is being embraced in our culture is unprecedented. According to Sam Schulman, "The embrace of homosexuality in Western culture has come about with unbelievable speed--far more rapidly than the feminist revolution or racial equality."[260] With today's tolerance for homosexuality, it is reasonable to ask if gender norms are applicable anymore as the distinctions in sexes have become blurred.

In itself, homosexual marriage is oxymoronic because marriage by Godly design is a covenant between a man and a woman. With the lack of absolutism in today's society, the definition of marriage is even more subject to societal change and pressures. Generations ago, same-sex marriage was considered morally, culturally, and socially taboo, but as society has declined and flagrantly slighted

God's precepts, minorities such as the radical homosexual groups have become more energized and brazen. The absence of moral absolutism coupled with the quiet majority that advocates traditional marriage has helped produce this brazenness.

Unless we take a firm position against homosexual marriage, marriage between a man and a woman is in danger of being permanently subverted. Just as the proponents of same-sex marriage ardently work to spread their agenda, opponents of same-sex marriage must exercise the same passion and vigor to protect traditional marriage. The inability to rally around this worthwhile cause puts the future of our society at stake. Although advocates of same-sex marriage are in the minority, they are still having an impact in spreading their agenda especially as the majority of Americans are settling in the comfort zone of relativism. Just because our social norms have devolved to reflect current cultural and social trends, it does not mean that they are right and should be automatically accepted. As a society, we have an obligation to protect the establishment of traditional marriage, which will in turn only prolong the survival of our society. Let's keep in mind that being politically correct is not the same thing as being morally right. The battle to uphold righteous morality will only remain extant as long as we possess the courage and conviction to enforce it.

WHAT DOES GOD SAY ABOUT HOMOSEXUALITY AND MARRIAGE?

The first thing that must be acknowledged in preserving traditional marriage and standing up to same-sex marriage is that homosexuality runs afoul of God's design for man. From the beginning of time, God established a pure model for sexuality devoid of homosexuality; however, over the years, man has become perverted and transgressed the canons of God. God makes his position on homosexuality as clear as can be: *"Thou shalt not lie with mankind, as with womankind: it [is] abomination."* **Leviticus 18:22 (KJV)** Moreover: *"If a man also lie with mankind, as he lieth with a* *woman, both of them have committed an abomination: they shall surely be put to death; their blood [shall be] upon them."* **Leviticus 20:13 (KJV)** For those who say these words are austere or out-dated, keep in mind, I did not say them; you did not say them; the President did not say them; the Church did not say them; but they came directly from God. In addition, God did not just say this yesterday, but He is saying it today.

When I review these two verses, I do not see any room for negotiation, compromise, or misinterpretation. I only discern a definitive mandate for heterosexual relationships. The message is to the point; homosexual behavior is unacceptable not by man's standards but by God's standards. The reason why God made His precepts so simple and clear was so they would not be subject to moral ambiguities or misconception especially since mankind is likely to trivialize them and to look for reasons to justify its deviant lifestyle. Man may be able to placate his or her internal conscience with contemporary self-justifications, but they are negligible in God's eyes. However, in today's age of growing universalism, pluralism, and relativism, it is becoming increasingly difficult to keep God's absolute tenets free from confusion. We are faced with the decision: Do we align with God's edict on sexual behavior or do we align with the social approval of homosexuality?

Homosexuality must be called for what it is. It is sin. Anything outside God's order for sex is considered sin. Now I know that may sound draconian especially since the word "sin" is rarely used in our society today, but why must we camouflage it with euphemisms? We can becloud sin all we want to make it feel right, thus giving us a less guilty feeling, but it does not make the respective sin any less tolerable in the eyes of God. No matter what the sin may be, all sin is rooted in unrighteousness and signifies separation from God.

If there is one thing that God is, it is immutable- what was considered morally iniquitous and reprehensible yesterday is considered the same today and will be considered the same tomorrow despite man's growing tolerance and self-justification: *'For I am the LORD, I change not; therefore ye sons of Jacob are not consumed."* **Malachi 3:6 (KJV)**

Billy Graham categorized sin as "the rejection of all authority and the denial of all obligation to God."[261] Like other sins, homosexuality rejects God's guidelines as it is an act of rebellion against a perfect and Holy God. Homosexuality is characterized as sexual impurity and it deliberately goes against God. An out-of-control sexual appetite combined with confusion and ignorance of God's precepts opens the door for homosexuality. By accepting the truth about homosexuality, we are then provided the moral ammunition to stand up to same-sex marriage for the purpose of preserving marriage between man and woman.

When we think like God thinks and adopt his ways, the expectations of life should become maximized, thus giving us the spiritual wherewithal to stand up to societal and cultural woes. Moreover, a person becomes full of wisdom and understands what is expected of him or her. No matter how uncomfortable the truth may be and no matter how much it clashes with the tolerance of society, after aligning with God, one cannot argue he or she is lacking the moral expectations of mankind. When it comes to traditional marriage, we are expected to live the lifestyle God has ordained for man.

If we examine the days of Adam and Eve, we recognize that God purposely brought a woman (Eve) into Adam's life for companionship, establishing marriage as the first structure of society. While the animals did not provide the ultimate companionship for Adam, Eve did; as a member of the opposite sex, Eve fulfilled Adam. God did not provide Adam another man for companionship but a woman. Although the story of Adam and Eve comes across as obsolete and trite, Adam and Eve's heterogeneous and complementary relationship still serves as the prototype of traditional marriage for all of mankind. God tells us that man is supposed to be dependent on woman and vice versa: *"Nevertheless neither is the man without the woman, neither the woman without the man, in the Lord."* ***1 Corinthians 11:11 (KJV)***

God did not purpose man to be alone, but He also did not purpose man to be attracted to the same sex. The act of obedience to God, or the lack of it, will largely determine whether or not homosexual marriage survives in our culture. It is up to us to either embrace God's expectation of marriage or to downright ignore it. Either way, God's expectation is clear and is not transformable.

Further proof of God's promotion of traditional marriage is seen with the fifth commandment of honoring our fathers and mothers. God did not command us to honor our father and father or our mother and mother. Now this does not mean that homosexual parents should be dishonored or vilified, but the commandment does illustrate that God's designation of father and mother is indicative of a pure heterogeneous relationship, a relationship free of sexual debauchery. Moreover, God is adamant in promoting the procreation between man and woman. Since family is the fundamental building block for all civilizations, parents are charged with the divine responsibility to procreate in order to build and strengthen a society from generation to generation. For example, after the memorable and destructive flood of all times, God instructed Noah's family to procreate in order to restore society: *"And God blessed Noah and his sons, and said unto them, Be fruitful, and multiply, and replenish the earth."* **Genesis 9:1 (NIV)**

Everything that God commands there is a purpose behind it and when it comes to marriage and procreation, the purpose for the two is for our well-being. Whether that purpose is comprehended and accepted by mankind or not has no influence on God's intentions; procreation through traditional marriage will still be expected and enforced. Whether society wants to hear it or not, man's temporal authority will never trump God's ultimate and eternal authority.

PROLONGING SOCIETY THROUGH PROCREATION

Since procreation among same-sex partners is biologically impossible as it goes against the laws of nature, natural procreation between heterogeneous men and women is the most efficient way in prolonging a society. Even though supporters of same-sex marriage promote homosexual marriage for relation reasons and not procreation reasons, the need for procreation in society cannot be ignored. Simply put, procreation is important for any society because we are in need of future generations to prolong society.

There is a direct link between traditional marriage and childbearing. If procreation was ever to be disassociated from marriage, then same-sex partners would have a plausible and logical argument, but as mentioned earlier, God's principles and the character of God are perpetual and impervious. Although same-sex partners can obtain children through adoption or other alternate manners, a society cannot ultimately be sustained without procreation. Hence, same-sex marriage is not only detested by God, but it is also not the optimal method of sustaining society.

This may appear obvious, but we have a habit of making decisions today without the consideration of tomorrow's consequences or deference for what is morally right. Such behavior is detrimental to society. After all, whatever happens in the family impacts the community at-large. God's message is so clear that it is sometimes difficult to understand how we can violate it with such outright disobedience; however, when words and oracles from God have no meaning and when actions have no consequences to them, new definitions and boundaries arise, giving people a false sense of assurance. Faulty beliefs produce misguided lifestyles.

EMBRACING HOMOSEXUALS WHILE ENFORCING TRADITIONAL MARRIAGE

At the same time of being firm in enforcing the principles of God to protect marriage, we must have compassion for those individuals captured in the homosexual lifestyle. As the old cliché goes, "Hate the sin, but love the sinner." As hard as this action may be, God expects it from us since we are all fallible and have some shortfall (s) of our own. One may not be enslaved to the homosexual lifestyle, but another may be in bondage to pride, physical violence, adultery, another type of sexual immorality, corruption, alcohol, the skullduggery of lying, gossip, jealousy, and the list goes on.

We have a tendency to put sins in a hierarchical order of offenses and categorize them either as major or minor offenses. We fail to recognize God looks at all acts of unrighteousness the same; sin is sin and is in violation of God's behavioral expectation. All sin is serious to God and cannot be tampered with through man-made reasoning or justification. A person who revels in the homosexual lifestyle is not better or worse than one who has a reputation of being a deceptive liar. There is no such thing as a scale of unrighteousness. Tolerating any level of iniquity sets a dangerous precedent for it contradicts the principles of God and consequently facilitates man finding comfort in it. We all carry burdens and fall short of God's standards of conduct and have no right to judge others on their personal foibles. While we can dislike the act of homosexuality in protection of traditional marriage, we must have the courage and love to embrace homosexuals and encourage them to righteous behavior. We must be able to persuade them to adhere to the Word of God versus listening to the culture of today.

Over the years, the acceptance of homosexuality has increased. Public opinion analyst Karlyn Bowman pointed this out:

> "In 1973, when the highly regarded National Opinion Research Center at the University of Chicago asked people about sexual relations between two members of the same sex, 80% described them as 'always wrong' or 'almost always wrong.' When they last asked the question in 2006, 61% gave that response."[262]

Just as the tolerance for homosexuality has increased, so too has the tolerance for same-sex marriage. We do not have to tolerate the argument that as a result of changing times, we must accept homosexual marriage. Just because society continues to morally deteriorate from within does not mean we have to acquiesce to the radical homosexual agenda. At the same time, it does not mean we have to avoid homosexuals. While we do not have to tolerate the act, we do have to tolerate the people as our fellow brothers and sisters. One would be surprised at the influence one has when he or she genuinely exercises his or her convictions. By standing by God's precepts of traditional marriage and family building, without developing a superior, haughty, and judgmental attitude, one's light can radiate and potentially attract the attention and hearts of those trapped by the homosexual way of life. We have a better chance of persuading the homosexual population to righteous behavior when we stand up for traditional marriage with dignity and unwavering conviction and refrain from personal vituperation.

We must keep in mind that beliefs are transferable and are formed in the mind while convictions are not as transferable since they are formed in the heart. It should be the goal of promoters of traditional marriage for their convictions to outweigh the other's beliefs of homosexuality. Unfortunately, there are more temporal beliefs than there are righteous convictions in today's society; however, genuine and profound convictions steeped in righteousness and moral propriety are resilient to the hostile accusations of bigotry, intolerance, and myopia.

As much as homosexuality is despised by some Americans, we must recognize that homosexuals have the right to practice their sexual acts. They not only have the free will to do so, but they also have the freedom to do so in the United States. Even though they have the free will to do so, it still does not make it morally right; they will be held accountable, but that is not up to us to judge. Unlike other countries where homosexuals are publicly scourged for being homosexual, there is no such punishment in America. Countries in which homosexual relationships are prohibited for both men and women include Angola, Iran, Libya, Morocco, Pakistan, Saudi Arabia, Somalia, Yemen, Chechen Republic in Russia, and others.[263] Countries where homosexuals are even subject to the death penalty include Iran, Pakistan, Somalia, and Yemen to name a few.[264] These austere measures do not exist in a tolerant America. Just because homosexuals can freely practice homosexuality in the United States does not mean they also have the right to transform marriage into something that it is not. What homosexuals do in private is their business, but when they actively force same-sex marriage to the public stage, it becomes everyone's business.

PROMOTING HOMOSEXUALITY THROUGHOUT THE AMERICAN CULTURE

One would think that the homosexual subculture would be content in having the right to privately practice the sexual lifestyle of their choice in the U.S. especially since it is prohibited in other countries. Instead, the radical extreme of the homosexual subculture wants not only to publicly celebrate their lifestyle but also to mainstream their lifestyle. According to the Traditional Values Coalition, an organization that promotes traditional values in our society,

> "The homosexual movement in the United States has achieved unprecedented power during the past two decades as a result of its dedication to one single cause: The overhauling of Straight America to accept and embrace homosexuality as a normal variation of sexual expression."[265]

The homosexual population has equality in the U.S. in that they are able to practice sexual practices of their choice; so why must it attack the sacrament of traditional marriage? It is one thing to live in reclusion with one's sexuality, but it is all something different to broadcast it and expect others to freely embrace it. It appears as if the more cultural leeway the homosexual population acquires, the more it wants. It is not enough for them to keep their lifestyle to themselves, but they wish to push it on others and permit it to interfere with traditional marriage. The advent of new social lifestyles in our society does not justify the disruption of our already existing and permissible norms such as traditional marriage and the institution of family. Moreover, no amount of rationalization justifies immorality even if one's conscience is left undisturbed. God purposed traditional marriage to be permanent as He promoted the solidarity of traditional marriage.

The homosexual culture has sprouted all throughout our society, leaving its footprint in more and more places. What was once considered inglorious is now receiving increased attention and glorification. What was once rarely talked about in public is now being publicly and boldly promoted and advanced in society. The homosexual agenda has proliferated into the media, our schools, the courts, the government, and the entertainment industry.

The homosexual network is conducting a campaign to normalize homosexuality and redefine it as normal behavior. By first establishing homosexuality as normalcy throughout our society, the homosexual subculture can then more easily advance the argument for same-sex marriage. The more society accepts homosexuality, the more likely it will eventually accept same-sex marriage. By first brandishing homosexuality as a normal act, a precedent is established, thus opening the door for subsequent actions to promote the homosexual agenda. Before we know it, the cultural acceptance and tolerance of homosexuality can soon lead to the conversion of traditional marriage if traditional marriage is not uplifted and safeguarded.

The homosexual subculture has the media as one of its allies in spreading its message. This should be no surprise since the media overall has a proclivity to sanctify iniquity and ignore and downgrade the righteousness in society. When it comes to homosexuality, the media disavows the immoral and unnatural aspects associated with homosexuality. There is minimal mention of the dangers and negative consequences of partaking in the homosexual lifestyle. Anything tied to homosexuality that has a negative connotation to it, the media practices selective journalism. Where is the debate on homosexuality? When was the last time you witnessed the media dedicate the same amount of news coverage to the heterogeneous lifestyle and pro-family advocates?

The media very rarely presents the moral, biological, and scientific arguments opposing homosexuality. Furthermore, a vibrant and agenda-setting press coupled with an apathetic and ignorant populace breeds the grounds for distorted news coverage. Although the media is supposed to apprise and educate the populace on the latest developments, it has been more active in spreading propaganda in support of political and social agendas such as homosexuality. One would not think that the homosexual subculture, being a minority group in society, would be receiving this significant attention and promotion that it does in the media. While the media cloys the public with views and positions from the homosexual population, the media simultaneously quashes the majority of those views that contest homosexuality. Unless the media presents more balanced coverage on homosexuality, we can expect the homosexual population to count on the media to promote its cause despite the command of sexual righteousness as outlined by God. In the meantime, it will be up to the majority of Americans who believe in family and traditional marriage to stand up to the minority and to put pressure on the media in reversing the debate.

      The homosexual agenda has comfortably found its way into our schools as well, thus contributing to the homosexualization of America, beginning with our younger and innocent generations. Through indoctrination, homosexual advocate groups intend to influence students on that homosexuality is a perfectly fine and a wholesome lifestyle. Schools are not hesitant to promote the acceptance and tolerance of homosexual acts, but they minimize the dangers of homosexuality by not fully educating on the consequences of homosexuality. Instead of teaching that homosexuality is an anomaly from heterogeneous sexual behavior, schools are teaching that homosexuality is normal and is an option of sexual practice. Moreover, schools teach homosexuality is more of an identity versus a behavior of choice, thus dismissing the accountability factor associated with it. Without any educated material to counteract homosexuality, students are inundated with one side of the argument, and as a result, they are inclined to view homosexuality as tolerable. This is where the role of the parent is so pivotal in monitoring school curricula and ensuring righteousness, values, and truth are being passed onto their children in school. Parents should be doing this in the first place in the home, but if the schools are not doing their part to reemphasize it, then the parents must pick up the slack. Unfortunately we live in an age where parents cannot rely on schools to teach the truth, so it will be up to the parents to enforce the truth.

As a whole, society constantly encourages the embracement of diversity. The homosexual agenda is being spread in schools under the guise of diversity. For example, in February 2007, U.S. District Judge Mark L. Wolf ruled public schools need to teach students to embrace the homosexual culture. The parents who voiced their opinions against the school's promotion of homosexuality did not influence Judge Wolf as he opined:

> "Under the Constitution public schools are entitled to teach anything that is reasonably related to the goals of preparing students to become engaged and productive citizens in our democracy... Diversity is a hallmark of our nation. It is increasingly evident that our diversity includes differences in sexual orientation."[266]

There is nothing wrong with diversity if it occurs naturally and is not forced upon others through indirect methods and for duplicitous purposes. Furthermore, those calling for diversity are oxymoronically asking others to think the same in order to benefit their cause when it comes to the promotion of homosexuality. Where is their support for diversity in supporting the heterosexual lifestyle? Those calling for diversity when it comes to homosexuality are only interested in spreading the homosexual lifestyle and not giving the same courtesies when it comes to the heterogeneous lifestyle. Hence, the call for diversity may sound attractive on the outside, but when you "peel pack the onion" one will recognize the true motive. If sexual diversity is going to be part of the classroom dynamics, then we cannot be receptive of homosexuality only and totally dismissive of heterosexuality.

It also does not help that the Director of the Office of Safe and Drug Free Schools has a background of promoting homosexuality in our schools. Known as the "Safe School Czar," Kevin Jennings founded the Gay, Lesbian and Straight Education Network (GLSEN) during his tenure as a school teacher in Massachusetts. GLSEN "strives to assure that each member of every school community is valued and respected regardless of sexual orientation or gender identity/expression."[267] As harmless and acceptable as its mission statement may appear, part of GLSEN's motive is to promote the homosexual lifestyle on all students. Of course no one wants to see any student lambasted or bullied due to sexual orientation, but at the same time, not all parents desire for the homosexual agenda to be foisted upon their children in school either.

According to one FOX News report, Jennings has "written about his past drug abuse, expressed his contempt for religion and detailed an incident in which he did not report an underage student who told him he was having sex with older men."[268] Would it not be more logical and sensible to have someone who has a more neutral background in a key position as Director of the Office of Safe and Drug Free Schools? What is wrong with filling this position with someone who does not have such an obvious leaning towards spreading homosexuality in schools? Perhaps if Jennings was required to receive congressional confirmation, then there would have been a vetting process to review his controversial background. By having people, like Kevin Jennings, with controversial backgrounds and ulterior agendas, in key leadership positions within our education system, schools will more than likely operate outside of their purview and adopt misbegotten policy. It is the parents' role to inform their children on controversial issues such as homosexuality, not the schools. Since the schools cannot be counted on to promote absolute moral truth, parents must take the lead.

The homosexual agenda has even found itself sprouting in our courts. Nothing seems to be inviolable from the homosexual agenda, no matter how sacrament something may be. Just take for example the overturning of Proposition 8 in California. Otherwise named as the California Marriage Protection Act, it was a proposition on the California state ballot in November 2008 recognizing marriage only between a man and a woman. The majority of the California electorate voted in favor of the preservation of traditional marriage between one man and one woman. Even in a liberal state as California, people considered same-sex marriage to be outside the norm. 52.3% or 6,838,107 voters voted yes on Proposition 8 in 2008.[269] It was clear that more people were in favor of protecting traditional marriage rather than accepting homosexual marriage. This was a great feat in the fight to preserve the family and traditional marriage; however, on August 4, 2010, the opinion of one federal judge, in support of same-sex marriage, invalidated the votes of almost seven million Californians, just like that.

If this was not judicial fiat, I do not know what is. Moreover, if this does not ignite indignation among the American electorate, we are in trouble. How can one man negate democracy at work? Instead of upholding the rule of law, Judge Vaughn Walker exercised a political statement and consequently mocked not only our judiciary but also our constitutional democracy as a whole. This example of judicial tyranny sets a dangerous precedent because it causes voters to question why they need to vote if one politically-charged judge can overturn the outcome of a representative vote. The role of a judge is supposed to reflect the maintenance of the rule of law. Congressman Ron Paul of Texas reflected upon judicial tyranny in a 2004 address promoting traditional marriage before the House of Representatives:

> "The practice of judicial activism – legislating from the bench – is now standard procedure for many federal judges. They dismiss the doctrine of strict construction as outdated, instead treating the Constitution as fluid and malleable to create a desired outcome in any given case. For judges who see themselves as social activists, their vision of justice is more important than the letter of the law they are sworn to interpret and uphold. With the federal judiciary focused more on promoting a social agenda than on upholding the rule of law, Americans find themselves increasingly governed by judges they did not elect and cannot remove from office."[270]

Representative Paul's message indicates exactly how the courts have devolved from their traditional role. When judges start ruling out of sympathy and emotions versus constructive rule of law, our judiciary loses its fundamental purpose. Actions such as those committed by Judge Walker cause the American people to view judges as tendentious self-seekers versus impartial guardians of the rule of law. Some question whether or not the judge's personal feelings and emotions had some pull in Judge Walker's ruling. After all, he is openly gay.[271] No one knows for sure if his sexual preference contributed to a bias in his ruling Proposition 8 unconstitutional, but it is no surprise to ponder how he could personally benefit from his own ruling. Today's courts are making more policy than they are interpreting the law as was originally intended by our Founding Fathers. The policies some judges are making ironically seem to favor personal convictions rather than upholding our democratic rule of law.

If there is one place where the homosexual agenda is preponderant it is in the entertainment industry. Whether it is on television, in the magazines, in movies, or in music, the homosexual lifestyle is exhibited unlike never before. As a result of today's information age, the increase in technology has intensified the promotion of the homosexual lifestyle. The list of things that were once considered off limits to public view has downsized. Yes, we live in a society where one has the freedom to practice the sexual behavior of one's choice, but why must we glorify something that is immoral and why must we collectively push another's personal lifestyle on others? As a society, we have become glued to the media and entertainment industry, causing us to view what they promote as gospel truth. Thus, the message of sexual liberation emerging from the media and entertainment industry is that since homosexuality is commonly accepted in today's society, homosexual marriage should logically follow. They casually make this correlation without any regard to moral absolutism.

One medium in which the homosexual agenda is being pumped into homes is through television (TV). More and more television shows indifferently include references to the homosexual lifestyle in them. Whether the reference is direct or indirect, television programs are not reticent to promote homosexual relationships. From talk shows to reality shows to sitcoms, the display of or communication on homosexual relationships is overflowing compared to my days growing up. As a child, I cannot recall one reference to homosexuality on television. For example, "two decades ago there were no gay teens on TV," but since 1992 the number of gay teens on TV has risen.[272] In a society in which, on average, homes possess more than one television and watch an excessive amount of television, it is difficult to escape the homosexual agenda. It takes advantage of the fact that television serves as a source of not only entertainment but also learning especially for the younger generations.

According to the Nielsen Company, during the last quarter of 2008, data revealed the average television viewer watches more than 151 hours of television per month.[273] If you look at this statistic from an annual perspective, this is over 75 days of watching television per year. Imagine if parents spent at least one-quarter of this time communicating and interacting with their children. Instead of being indoctrinated with the homosexual agenda and other nefarious agendas through television, children would be acquiring genuine wisdom from their parents when television is regulated; however, there seems to be little hope of that happening. For example, a survey conducted in England of 1,000 British people revealed "parents are so caught up with their daily routines - including TV viewing - they are neglecting to find time to chatter to their children".[274] Television has become parents' source of companionship and children's babysitter and pseudo parent. The homosexual agenda is exploiting and reaching out to both populations. As children are neglected by their parents and become more and more attached to the television, they are more likely to be subjected to the encouragement and promotion of homosexual relationships and the portrayal of them as a norm in society.

In a society that ramrods tolerance and where homosexuality is promoted more in society, it is not alarming to see the number of homosexual characters increase in television shows. Television shows like *Will and Grace* portray homosexual relationships as harmless as they seek to destigmatize homosexuality. Episode after episode, the message that comes across is homosexuality is just as normal as the sexuality of a heterosexual individual. Indeed, homosexuality is more commonly accepted in our society today, but that does not mean we have to celebrate it, accept it, and be intrigued by such television sitcoms. Instead, why not choose to watch another television program that promotes family and traditional marriage? We should not feel helpless in a society that promotes such immorality. We still have the freedom of choice to not support something that goes against our principles and values. Again, we are to tolerate the person but not the immoral act. No matter how tempting a television show may be to watch due to its comic relief or sense of adventure, always reflect on doing the harder right versus the easier wrong and supporting traditional values in spite of current fads. Such practices may sound simple and ineffective, but when we collectively act, they will go a long way in supporting the preservation of righteousness. They not only support doing what is right, but they also set the example of standing up for morality in the home, thus leaving an impact with children for life. Children will grow up knowing just because society approves of something that does not mean it is morally right.

Just as the promotion of homosexuality has increased among television shows, it has also increased in the movie industry. This is particularly concerning since just about everyone enjoys watching movies. According to the Adams Media Research, in 2009, Americans spent an astronomical $9.87 billion at the box office.[275] What other better way is there to get a message out to the public than taking advantage of the extravagant number of Americans who head to the movie theaters? The box office serves as another influential source of advertisement for the homosexual agenda. Like television shows, movies have gone the direction in personifying homosexuality by portraying it as customary as apple pie. The theme of homosexuality has taken a new turn as the personification of it has begot the increased acceptance of it on the movie screen. Whether homosexuality is referenced in a major or minor way in a specific movie, either way, it suggests that homosexuality is mainstream. How many times have you watched a movie to come across a part of the movie referencing homosexuality and thought to yourself, "The movie would have been just fine without such a reference in the plot?" By portraying homosexuality as a normal act in movies, the homosexual agenda is paving the road for further acceptance of homosexuality and then homosexual marriage.

The increased coverage of homosexuality in our society has given courage to the same-sex activists and created an attitude of them being untouchable. At the same time that homosexuality has increasingly penetrated throughout the different parts of our society, same-sex activists use the high divorce rate in America to their advantage. They present the argument that since approximately half of traditional marriages end in divorce, then why can't same-sex marriage be permitted. This argument for same-sex marriage provides them self-fulfillment as they use the hardships of traditional marriage for justification for same-sex marriage. Furthermore, they argue that as long as two people are committed to one another in love, same-sex couples should have the same self-prerogative as heterosexuals to indulge in marriage. It is bad enough that traditional marriage in our society is plagued by a runaway divorce rate. Now same-sex activists want to compile this unfortunate plight by redefining traditional marriage. By exploiting our societal struggles with traditional marriage, they hope to further undercut the basic fabric of marriage. Pope Benedict XVI emphasized the severity of same-sex marriage when he declared it to be one of the "most insidious and dangerous threats to the common good today."[276] Pope Benedict XVI not only spoke out against same-sex marriage, but he also spoke boldly and passionately on the preservation of traditional marriage. In his 2006 Good Friday address, he proclaimed: "Surely God is deeply pained by the attack on the family. Today we seem to be witnessing a kind of anti-Genesis, a counter-plan, a diabolical pride aimed at eliminating the family."[277]

ACTING ON BEHALF OF TRADITIONAL MARRIAGE

While the homosexual activists muster support for their agenda through the aforementioned different conduits and offer an apologia for same-sex marriage, the advocates of traditional marriage should be just as energized, if not more, in promoting the preservation of the family. Instead of letting the homosexual activists control the language of the debate, proponents of traditional marriage must take the initiative in doing so to drown out the same-sex vernacular. Ask yourself, which do you hear more of- same-sex marriage or traditional family values? Opponents of same-sex marriage have every right to stand up to same-sex marriage just as advocates of same-sex marriage have every right to fight for same-sex marriage.

Opponents of same-sex marriage must have a lexicon of words to use in the verbal debate over same-sex marriage. Phrases such as 'God's design,' 'traditional values,' 'divine institution' and 'heterosexual union' provide such verbal fodder for the debate. Again, it is also important to note that the term "homosexual marriage" is contradictory to begin with since the definition of marriage includes a man and woman as per God's plan and purpose.

This basic and universal fact alone should serve as the impetus for standing up for what is right. Contemporary societal standards that exculpate impulsive behavior do not justify the altering of God's standard for marriage. In his efforts to protect traditional marriage, former Senator Frist of Tennessee professed, "Customs come and go and vary by time and place, but the institution of marriage has endured through millennia."[278] However, as the aggressive homosexual agenda continues to besmirch traditional marriage and the family and as the silent majority remains passive on this issue, the institution of marriage is in more danger of losing the endurance Senator Frist mentioned.

The movement to safeguard traditional marriage has been underway, but it cannot be taken for granted since homosexual activists show no signs of relenting. In 1996, the Defense of Marriage Act (DOMA) gave the states the authority to permit or ban same-sex marriage and, for federal purposes, defined marriage as a union between one man and one woman. With the signing of DOMA by President Clinton, the definition of marriage rested with the states.

However, in February 2011, the Obama administration "announced that the Department of Justice would no longer defend the Defense of Marriage Act in federal court and would press Congress to repeal the act altogether."[279] Congressman Jerry Sandler has already said he would reintroduce The Respect for Marriage Act to repeal DOMA. The name of the bill sounds harmless, but we must examine the contents of it. It not only repeals DOMA, but it also "restores the rights of all lawfully married couples—including same-sex couples—to receive the benefits of marriage under federal law. The bill also provides same-sex couples with certainty that federal benefits and protections would flow from a valid marriage celebrated in a state where such marriages are legal, even if a couple moves or travels to another state."[280] The Respect for Marriage Act is another attempt to divorce Godly precepts on marriage from today's growing cultural acceptance of homosexual marriage.

America's collective voice against same-sex marriage has been obvious as state after state has voted to preserve traditional marriage between one man and one woman. Out of all the 31 states in which same-sex marriage was put in the hands of the electorate, all 31 states voted against same-sex marriage. This sends a powerful and obvious message to the homosexual activists that the majority of Americans still recognizes the fundamental definition of marriage as marriage between one man and one woman and does not want it changed. Despite the current social fad, the American people have evinced they favor the tradition of marriage and not the deterioration of marriage.

Currently there are only five states in which same-sex couples can legally marry. Those states include Massachusetts, Vermont, New Hampshire, Connecticut, and Iowa. Of particular notice with these five states is that it was the state legislatures or courts and not the electorate that approved same-sex marriage. Could it be these states were intimidated by the collective voice of the American people in protecting traditional marriage? The question does remain: Will the American people's tolerance for homosexuality and same-sex marriage reach the point that it no longer appreciates the absolutism of marriage and God's original design of marriage? Without a doubt, people still have influence in matters that affect society, but will the people appreciate this fact and continue to apply it?

It is refreshing to see the collective voice of the American people resonate as electorate after electorate of the thirty-one states voted to defend the orthodoxy of marriage. Even states that are known to have liberal tendencies like New York had elected officials vote in favor of perpetuating traditional marriage. According to Jeremy Peters of *The New York Times*, "The 38-to-24 vote startled proponents of the bill and signaled that political momentum, at least right now, had shifted against same-sex marriage, even in heavily Democratic New York."[281] Similarly, New Jersey's State Senate rejected the legalization of same-sex marriage by a vote of 20 to 14. This was just another distinguished example especially since New Jersey has been known for its social tolerance: "The defeat in New Jersey, which has widely been viewed as one of the nation's most socially tolerant states, was a significant setback for advocates of gay marriage."[282] Both of these instances serve as examples reflecting the collective will and representation of the people as the people expressed their concerns in protecting the traditional family and upholding family values. In addition, they should also serve as a source of inspiration and motivation for the fight ahead in protecting marriage from the homosexual agenda and coattails of homosexual activists.

The issue of preserving traditional marriage goes far beyond liberal versus conservative; it is a right versus wrong issue. The people of these states understand when God decrees something obedience is expected from the people. In this case, God decreed that marriage is a holy covenant between man and woman and anything deviant from it is not marriage, no matter what society dictates. In today's culture, the final authority of God seems to have lost its relevancy, but we must remember that God's tenets are timeless. When society digresses from such a Godly decree, it is the responsibility of the people to reengage and stand up for what is right.

THE HEALTH BENEFITS OF TRADITIONAL MARRIAGE

Have you ever thought to yourself the reason why God designed marriage to be the sacred union of one man and one woman? The edict from God alone should be enough to establish the definition of marriage; but, if you sincerely think about God's definition, it makes sense and is logical no matter how much society tries to convolute it. However, in today's society, judgment has been clouded with rampant tolerance and uncontrolled sensationalism. God established parameters for sexual behavior for our benefit and health protection. God did not biologically design the human body for homosexual activity. Instead, God designed a man's body to complement a woman's body and vice versa.

When the human body is used for wanton and unnatural acts in which it is not designed for, there is no guarantee that it will be free from biological ailment. Instead, there will be malign medical consequences. Homosexual behavior increases the risk in which the human body is exposed to injury, sickness, or even disease. This is nothing new, but it is worth highlighting in a risk adverse society. Take for example men who have sex with men (MSM). According to the Center for Disease Control, "the rate of new HIV diagnoses among MSM in the U.S. is more than 44 times that of other men (range: 522-989 per 100,000 MSM vs. 12 per 100,000 other men)."[283] Despite these shocking and contrasting statistics, the homosexual subculture carries on with its reckless behavior and encourages others to believe diseases such as HIV or AIDS are diseases that are equally burdening the entire population at the same rate of risk. However, in all actuality, according to the Center for Disease Control, "MSM is the only risk group in the U.S. in which new HIV infections are increasing. While new infections have declined among both heterosexuals and injection drug users, the annual number of new HIV infections among MSM has been steadily increasing since the early 1990s."[284]

Despite the facts, the homosexual agenda paints another picture; it is adamant in smothering the truth and portraying homosexual relationships as safe, meaningful, and stable. What we must remember and put to practice is that no matter how slyly the homosexual subculture attempts to desensitize society with the active and on-going promotion of homosexuality, the truth does not cease being truth with the passage of time- homosexuality is an abomination to God and anything outside the lines of traditional marriage is unacceptable.

GETTING IT RIGHT

If our culture settles for a redefinition of marriage, then it will be difficult to retrograde back to the original definition of marriage- God's design uniting one man and one woman. Unlike some things in life where there is an ebb and flow, the definition of marriage should not be one of those; but instead, it should be unchangeable as God mandates it so. Once it is altered, it will be altered for good.

By redefining marriage, we would not only be revising the definition of marriage that has been around since the outset of man, but we would also be opening other doors to further desecrate what was once considered a sacred institution. Through a redefinition of marriage, an ill-fated precedent would be established. After one redefinition of marriage, what is there to prevent marriage from being further disgraced and redefined into something that it is not? What happens when society deems same-sex marriage as outdated and hackneyed? What happens when society loses its enthusiasm for same-sex marriage? What will be the new definition of marriage then?

If we lose the absolute definition of marriage as the divine union of man and woman now, then what is there to stop marriage from being defined as two women and one man; two men and one woman; one woman and an animal; one man and a woman robot; and the list goes on? The move away from absolutism and towards the debauchery and mockery of marriage invites all different forms of pseudo marriages that are not welcomed in the eyes of God. Moreover, the exclusivity of monogamy and procreation runs the risk of being replaced with reckless forms of promiscuity and unlimited sexual hedonism. In addition, authentic romance is subject to permanently devolve into sexual frolic. When we move away from traditional marriage, we move closer to the point when people would be able to marry anyone or anything under any condition.

As a society, will we believe in and fight for what marriage truly represents or will we let it deform out of apathy? Will we put earthly desires above the will of God? Although people have the free will to decide how they will live their lives, we do not have to standby with insouciance and accept their behavior as the norm for society. We also must consider that if homosexual marriage is legalized, what is there to say that society will not eventually brand traditional marriage as abnormal? Once again, the absence of absolutes opens the door for the possibility of everything else. Under relativism, there are no boundaries.

CHAPTER SEVEN
LOVE OF COUNTRY

The third measure in restoring America is to reinvigorate the love of country within our culture. Love for our country entails love for a nation that was founded under God, built on a foundation of a constitutional government, edified the family, and cherished the freedoms of religion, speech, the press, and the many individual freedoms we take for granted. There was once a time when love of country was largely automatic and evident as it infused all of our society; however, today there are only remnants of this love for our country. If there is a time where we need a wave of patriotism to flood our country, it is now, especially as we face asymmetrical threats from radical Islamists that run contrary to everything we stand for, are beholden to a maturing China as it steadily augments its economy and military, and as despotic presidents of countries such as Iran and Venezuela work in cahoots to emasculate the American hegemony. When the denizens of a nation are consumed with indifference and lack both global situational awareness and the collective appreciation and respect for its country, that country runs the risk of losing everything that it was founded on. And this is where we are at today.

America is in need of a fresh dosage of patriotism and nationalism from its people in order to resist the growing anti-American sentiment from both home and abroad. One does not have to wear a service uniform in order to be patriotic; we all have a role in uplifting our blessed country by standing behind her through the thick and thin. From the service clerk to the lawyer, from the stay-at-home parent to the service member, from the janitor to the surgeon, all of us have a responsibility in strengthening our national character through the exhibition of patriotism and nationalism.

Allegiance coupled with righteousness should be our daily fuel in standing up for America. Our allegiance to America should be grounded in our fundamental principles to include reverence for God, limited government, individual rights, liberty, private property, strong national defense, and national sovereignty. If we remain fallow and do not stand for something, then we will lose everything. Standing for nothing is actually standing for something. So, as an American, why not stand behind the U.S. for what she gained her independence for. If the American people do not exercise national pride, then the U.S. runs the risk of being redefined as both insiders and outsiders attempt to turn America into something it is not.

AMERICA IS NOT FREE FROM EVIL

The United States is not a perfect nation- far from it; but then again, which country is? A nation's government is run by man and since man is fallible, we cannot expect a nation to be totally free from misconduct, corruption, and injustice. However, we can expect a nation to adhere to righteousness as much as possible and to enforce accountability on its own especially when it gets off track. Dr. Stephen Covey, author of *The Seven Habits of Highly Effective People*, once said, "Accountability breeds response-ability."[285] Throughout our history, we have witnessed leaders fall short of exercising both accountability and responsibility, thus causing our country to undergo periods of turmoil. Like other countries, the U.S. has its national scars throughout its history, but despite them, it continues to strive to be a beacon of rectitude.

In order for us to refresh allegiance to America, we must first appreciate the simple premise that there is both good and evil in this world, and like oil and water, they do not and will never conjoin with one another. This basic tenet incorporates everything in life. It is not pessimistic to acknowledge the existence of evil in this world, but it is realistic because it does exist and it must not only be recognized but dealt with through aggressive righteousness. This sincere acknowledgment breeds optimism for the future of America. One can argue that without pessimism, there can be no optimism. While many will acknowledge the battle of good and evil in the spiritual world, many fail to concede that this same battle carries over into our physical world.

Regardless where one is on this planet, during this lifetime, there will be an endless schism between good and evil.

As previously mentioned, evil and good cannot coexist just as light cannot coexist with darkness. The best way to describe good is anything that falls in line with the absolutism of God's Word, while evil is anything that contradicts the absolutism of God's Word. If one is to examine the evil throughout the international community, one would discover the world is saturated with evil encompassing poverty, disease, war, famine, dejection, greed, murder, rape, and the list goes on. There is no escaping the evil in this world for it is a fact of life, but there is the individual free will to opt for good over evil and to defeat evil within our own sphere of influence. We are advised in the *Book of Romans* on how to handle evil: *"[Let] love be without dissimulation. Abhor that which is evil; cleave to that which is good. Be not overcome of evil, but overcome evil with good."* **Romans 12:9, 21 (JKV)** There are no ambiguities here in God's dictum when it comes to dealing with evil. Throughout history, we have witnessed the power of evil at home and abroad, the decisions to either settle for evil or to defeat it, and the consequences of those decisions. We have witnessed that although evil has existed and conjured periods of suffering in this world, those periods were not enduring since the decision was made to conquer the respective evil.

Who can forget the campaign of Nazism that Adolph Hitler ushered into Germany and Europe prior to World War II? As the impudent dictator of Germany, Hitler savagely removed Jews from German society and confined them to harsh concentration camps against their will. Hitler's brutal military massacred approximately six million Jews to include 1.5 million children.[286] These outrageous numbers revealed just how expediently and rampantly evil can spread if left unchecked or not taken seriously. Although this evil comes across as unthinkable especially as it becomes more and more part of history, it was this evil that help rallied the United States into World War II (WWII) after the bombing of Pearl Harbor. America understood the magnitude of this evil threat and made the bold decision to help the Allied Army defeat the imperialistic movement of Germany and the other Axis powers. The U.S. not only stood for good on the battlefield by defeating the Nazi regime, but it also exercised goodness at home by accepting approximately 140,000 Holocaust survivors as immigrants.[287] In spite of the initial opposition from the international society, the U.S. made the decision to overcome evil with good both on the home front and abroad. It was this historic movement for the good of mankind that should serve as an example of the importance of regulating and mitigating evil.

It is wise to ponder what would have happened if the U.S. did not stymie the aggressive Nazi campaign and instead let this evil suffuse all of Europe. How far west would have the Nazi regime depredated and dominated if the U.S. did not intervene? Would more of the West be speaking German today? Such recollection helps one appreciate the enormous achievement the American economic engine, the American military, and the American people accomplished during WWII, thus inciting a patriotic passion and love of country. No matter your age today, this amazing accomplishment should fill you with national pride and make you proud to be an American. It was incidents like this that have defined America. Thank God for His favor, the gallantry of our WWII veterans, and the untiring spirit of the American people. We can never forget the sacrifice that our fellow Americans made during the historic time no matter how much WWII becomes part of history and as others attempt to downplay the Nazi movement. Edmond Burke once proclaimed: "All that is necessary for the triumph of evil is that good men do nothing."[288] The U.S. appreciated the severity of the evil threat of Nazism at the time and acted against it, heeding Burke's precaution. America's active participation in WWII validated the fact that evil cannot triumph when good people do something to defeat it.

Although it has been six decades since the end of WWII, evil still exists, but today it is in the form of radical Islamic terrorism. According to the *National Strategy for Combating Terroris*m, "America is at war with a transnational terrorist movement fueled by a radical ideology of hatred, oppression, and murder."[289] Even though these radical Islamists slyly preach peace under the guise of Islam, their temperament of animosity and oppression categorize them as evil. Like the Nazis, radical Islamists are inflamed by a twisted totalitarian ideology that seeks and demands world domination regardless of the cost.

Like with the Nazi threat, the radical Islamic threat runs in direct confrontation with our democratic way of life and the freedoms associated with it. Radical Islam cannot survive in an area where freedom swarms. One major difference is that unlike the Nazis who feared death as a result of witnessing America's might, radical Islamists do not have this same fear because they do not fear death. Instead, their religion offers them false hope if they exchange their life for a distorted cause of spreading Islam through conquest. Moreover, they are convinced they have a warrant from God to do so. Their hope and highest honor is to die for a God they call Allah.

According to American writer and expert on religious violence, Mark Juergensmeyer, "Religion has supplied not only the ideology but also the motivation and the organizational structure for the perpetrators."[290] Radical Islamist terrorists believe they have an anointed right to kill anyone who does not conform to Islam, thus giving them an untouchable countenance. Hence, this characteristic makes this evil threat much more of a challenge in overcoming it. Once again, it will require the good of this generation to stand up to an evil threat that shows no signs of receding. The question remains though, does this generation have the patience and mental wherewithal to withstand the fight in order to subjugate this evil like former generations did?

Evil does not just come in the form of man-made disasters, but it also manifests itself through natural disasters. During the aftermath of Hurricane Katrina, we witnessed evil in the form of death and destruction throughout the city of New Orleans. In the words of President Bush: "Hurricane Katrina was one of the worst natural disasters in our Nation's history and has caused unimaginable devastation and heartbreak throughout the Gulf Coast Region. A vast coastline of towns and communities has been decimated."[291] New Orleans was overcome by loitering, civic unrest, loss of life, sanitation woes, and much more. Despite the suffering, the American people rallied to overcome the evil with good through altruism. Despite the initial impasse with the crisis response, the syncretism of all levels of government, the private sector, and the public saved lives contributed to the restoration of civic order, provided relief, and brought hope to the victims of Hurricane Katrina. According to *The Federal Response to Hurricane Katrina: Lessons Learned*, "Hurricane Katrina prompted an extraordinary national response that included all levels of government- Federal, State, and local- the private sector, faith-based and charitable organizations, foreign countries, and individual citizens."[292] From the works of first-hand responders to the open hearts of the American people as they donated money and volunteered their time and services in shelters across the nation, housing displaced Gulf Coast residents, American largesse and goodness flourished, thus turning the evil of a crisis into benevolence of a society.

The presence of evil in this world begs the question: If we serve a good and perfect God (which we do), then how can He allow evil to occur? First of all, it is important to recall we live in a fallen world that will one day be restored by God, but for now, evil will surface in this fallen world. Secondly, since God has granted everyone the gift of free will, evil will surface as a result of man's poor and foul decisions. Unfortunately such decisions affect not only the individual but others also and sometimes including society as a whole. Lastly, God allows tribulations and suffering in this world to get our attention and to get our hearts totally dependent upon Him, increase our faith, or alter our perspective on a respective issue. As ironic as it may sound, sometimes you may have to experience the bad in life in order to appreciate the good, thus bringing opportunity with adversity. God confirms this in the Bible: "*Not only so, but we also glory in our sufferings, because we know that suffering produces perseverance; perseverance, character; and character, hope.*" **Romans 5:3-4 (NIV)** We must also reflect on the tenet that God works all things for the good for those who love Him no matter if the human mind can comprehend it or not.

Regardless of the intensity of the evil in life, we will be left with the decision either to settle for evil or to overcome it with good. If we are to restore America's greatness, we must first expect evil in this world and be equipped mentally and physically to deal with it since evil must be confronted and not pacified. During the 2008 presidential campaign, Senator McCain recognized this position when he spoke of radical Islamists at the Values Voters Summit: "And we are summoned to fight them not only by our just concern for our physical security but by the responsibility we have always accepted to support and defend values we believe to be universal."[293]

As great as the U.S. has been over its 235 year short history, it has had its share of troubles as a result of evil seeping through. In spite of our shortfalls, the U.S. is still a good country and one in which many seek to inhabit. Even the poorest Americans possess a standard of living that others throughout the world would covet. We have learned from our shortfalls, causing us to make changes for the good and growing as a result. From abolishing slavery and segregation to granting women suffrage, America has progressed over the years. Perfection within a country is impossible, but when a country, as a whole, strives for goodness over evil, that country is marked with righteousness. Furthermore, when a nation adopts the mindset that it becomes stronger as a result of its weaknesses, its past does not present itself as an albatross for future growth.

OUR PAST DOES NOT EQUAL OUR FUTURE

A country is not defined by its past as it is by its actions during the present time and future. What has been done in the past should stay in the past as the focus is put on what we are now as a country and in the future that lies ahead. Just as a former alcoholic is not defined by his or her past struggles with alcoholism as he or she presently lives a pure life free of alcoholic behavior, our nation should not be defined by our past struggles. Instead, we should be better prepared and equipped as a result of our past shortcomings. Overall, we are a redemptive society and celebrate people rising above past behavioral struggles, so why should it be any different with our national past shortfalls?

Now that does not mean we totally forget our shortfalls as if they never happened or that we cannot use lessons learned from the past to make us stronger as a nation; however, we should not be married to or trapped by our past mistakes where evil once prevailed. Like any other country, we have had our problems. Besides, constantly turning back the clock is useless because it only creates frenzy. We must look to the future. When we concentrate on the past, we run the risk of disrupting our destiny. Sure, there is sorrow and regret when we look back at our past mistakes, but there should be elation that we have overcome them and are no longer entangled in them. President Reagan was an optimist who applauded our country's ability to rise above our inadequacies as a nation and look to the future. In his 1983 Evil Empire speech to the National Association of Evangelicals, President Reagan confirmed this sentiment:

> "There is sin and evil in the world, and we're enjoined by Scripture and the Lord Jesus to oppose it with all our might. Our nation, too, has a legacy of evil with which it must deal. The glory of this land has been its capacity for transcending the moral evils of our past."[294]

President Reagan's assertion should serve as a motivator that America's past can prepare it to be a better country for tomorrow. No matter our past and how much we may have strayed from our fundamental principles of righteousness during the path of our history, we are still capable of seeking and finding righteousness once again as long as the commitment is there and our hearts are yielded towards righteousness. Remember, righteousness is not tantamount to perfection, but it does mean that we are dedicated to Godly living and to carrying a virtuous ethos as a people.

One of the most controversial issues of our history that continues to revisit and plaque us was the plight of slavery. While one side desires to learn from this horrid period of time, another side is adamant in keeping it in the forefront as a constant reminder. No one can deny that slavery was deplorable, but why must factions continue to rub this in our country's face as if slavery still exists today? Booker T. Washington said it nicely: "There is a class of colored people who make a business of keeping the troubles, the wrongs, and the hardships of the Negro race before the public. Some of these people do not want the Negro to lose his grievances, because they do not want to lose their jobs. There is a certain class of race-problem solvers who don't want the patient to get well."[295] As a respected African American orator and political leader who was even born into a slave family, Washington's statement gives way to credence and should not be dealt with lightly. Washington rose up above the politics of the slavery and racism issue and represented the hard truth.

We need more leaders today who are veracious and are able to put behind the past (without forgetting the past) in order to have a better future. Our past shortfalls should serve as a tool or a compass in how we need to grow as a nation and not as a historical scar of infamy. We should be proud of the fact that as a nation we were able to rise above the bondage of slavery and the legal separation of black and white people. We cannot neglect the fact that the Civil War was fought where tens of thousands of soldiers were killed. Abraham Lincoln ushered in the Emancipation Proclamation in 1862, declaring the freedom of slaves in all Confederate states. With the passage of the 13th Amendment in 1865, the U.S. Congress abolished slavery. About eighty years later, racial segregation began to cease in the military, in public transportation, and in public schools. Slowly but surely, racial integration replaced racial segregation. This transformation should be something every American should be proud of because it reveals the ability of American society to do the right thing by exchanging evil for righteousness instead of being dominated by evil.

Albeit this period in our history is deserving of condemnation, we do not want to hide from it because it has made the U.S. the better country that it is today. I once heard that "yesterday's dung is tomorrow's fertilizer," and this is no different with the issues of slavery and segregation. Just as with an individual who undergoes trials in life, we are stronger as a nation as a result of our weaknesses. When we get fixated on the past, we lose focus of our future because by doing so we become drained of our vitality as we become weighed down with yesterday's shortfalls instead of tomorrow's progression. However, when we appreciate our shortfalls with a contrite spirit, righteousness is within our destiny. After all, being successful includes analyzing the past to create visions for our future. Moreover, through the analysis of history, we learn that the mistakes made usually lead to progression as seen with slavery.

One of the greatest but hardest acts after a period of any level of evil is the act of forgiveness. The human nature is quick to ask for clemency, but it is not as expedient in giving clemency. Forgiveness is the only remedy to get over this historical roadblock. With forgiveness, we must release any feelings of resentment and any desires to avenge our prior injustices. Without forgiveness, we are left with an emotional enslavement that preoccupies our thoughts and memories with past misgivings, thus tantalizing our emotions. This comes across as being easier said than done especially since human nature is apt to attach conditions to forgiveness and not adopt unconditional forgiveness. It is unconditional forgiveness only that will heal us from our past inadequacies such as slavery. In all actuality, we cannot justify holding anything against anybody because we serve a God who represents unconditional forgiveness for sinful man- so He expects the same from us when it comes to granting forgiveness to others.

One prime example of forgiveness relating to racism and racial segregation was when Johnny Lee Clary, a former Ku Klux Klan leader, became an ordained minister in one of the nation's largest African-American denominations at St. Stephen's Cathedral Church of God in Christ in San Diego. The church's pastor, Bishop George McKinney, embraced the renewed Clary and remarked: "We feel like it makes a huge statement that the former national imperial wizard of the Ku Klux Klan would join the Church of God in Christ and reach out with the Church of God in Christ to bring racial reconciliation to America."[296] Clary spoke of his transformation: "I know the answer to racial reconciliation, and that's Jesus Christ. They all come to me, even secular people are saying, 'What changed you?' I tell them, 'The only thing that changed me was the Word of God.' Because when I accepted Christ ... I had to get my mind renewed, and that was through God's Word."[297] Clary was willing to be transformed and to release his past, while Bishop McKinney was willing to grant Clary an opportunity to follow through on his desire to be renewed. This act of forgiveness is a microcosm of what our society needs to adopt as a whole when it comes to getting past the slavery and segregation period of our history. Reconciliation, redemption, and healing all are feasible with genuine and unconditional forgiveness. If we fail to forgive as a society and fail to move on, then we are only hurting ourselves and demoralizing our national pride and national character.

THE MEDIA'S ROLE IN EITHER UPLIFTING OR DOWNGRADING AMERICA

Yes, it is important to acknowledge our past imperfections as a nation, but we must also give fair acknowledgment to the things we did and continue to do right as a nation, as a culture, and as a society. It is these things that set us apart from other nations. Believe it or not, there seems to be a subpopulation out there that wants to keep America's shortfalls out in the fore without recognizing the good of America. And, of course, with today's 24/7 media coverage, it is even more challenging when the media heavily focuses on negative news stories with repetition. It is these stories on perversion, corruption, and immorality that fill the news programs versus stories that represent the values of what our country stands for. Instead of reporting, the media is more concerned with controlling the message. I am reminded of what one advertising notable by the name of William Bernbach said: "All of us who professionally use the mass media are the shapers of society. We can vulgarize that society. We can brutalize it. Or we can help lift it onto a higher level."[298] Will the mass media use its power and influence to control the message in elevating or attenuating America?

Although there are many examples to support the media's concentrated coverage of America's troubles, one example where the media overwhelmed its viewers with such coverage was the Abu Ghraib Iraqi prison abuse incident. Although the actual events occurred in late 2003, the media unleashed accounts of the abuse beginning in 2004. The unfortunate incident where American soldiers unconventionally abused and lampooned Iraqi detainees during *Operation Iraqi Freedom* (OIF) attracted mass, prolonged, and omnipresent media attention, painting an unfavorable image of the U.S. military in spite of its steady reputation. All sorts of media sources gravitated to the story with unrelenting coverage. In his commentary, "The Press is Good, But Not Good Enough," former Indiana congressman, Lee Hamilton, wrote that journalists "follow the pack, rather than pursue stories that no one else has covered."[299]

As unfortunate as this incident was, it does not define the U.S. military as a whole, but with the international and recurrent news coverage of it, one would have thought otherwise. The media did not focus on the fact that the unacceptable behavior of these few American soldiers was limited to a unit(s) that lacked the necessary leadership, discipline, work ethic, policies, guidelines, and standard operating procedures in dealing with interrogation techniques of prison detainees on the asymmetrical battlefield. As former Secretary of Defense, Donald Rumsfeld, affirmed, the photographs of tortured prisoners "represent deviant behavior and a failure of military leadership and discipline."[300] Hence, it was not an overall U.S. military issue as much as it was an isolated and individual unit issue, but the media did not promote it as such.

The endless and obsessed coverage of the prisoner abuse by the media cancelled out all the positive things the U.S. military was doing as a whole during OIF at the time. As our mighty military killed the enemy, protected the threatened Iraqi populations, and provided medical, logistical, engineer, and civic support, the media was still enamored with the Abu Ghraib scandal. What about the news that Saddam Hussein's brutal regime was defeated and that Saddam Hussein was personally captured? What about the fundamental freedoms that the Iraqi people were now able to enjoy? What about the number of schools that the American military and other resources helped construct? What about the enemy's beheadings it conducted around this time? The media was more concerned with the anomalous incident of Abu Ghraib than it was with the inhumanity of our enemies and the gallantry and philanthropy of our military. All the good of the U.S. military and the evil of our enemies were put on the backburner as coverage of Abu Ghraib continued to resurface.

Regardless of the consequences such as a tainted American image across the globe to include the Muslim world, the media was not dissuaded from keeping the notorious coverage alive. In an interview with Fox's Bill O'Reilly, Lieutenant General Ricardo Sanchez acknowledged the press "loses its objectivity when it begins to address the issues of Abu Ghraib and the emotion that is drawn out by those photographs. We lose; we lose and abandon the journalistic oath of fair and objective."[301] It is safe to say more people recollect the disturbed photographs of the abused prisoners versus images of American soldiers saving lives on the embattled Iraqi streets or providing humanitarian relief to the civic populations. Putting aside the polemical debate of whether or not the U.S. should have invaded Iraq or not, there is no question the American military performed extraordinarily in both combat and service support roles, but the American people never received that full story from the media. The combination of an eager press and an apathetic populace sets the conditions for the wrong message to get out to the public.

AMERICA'S GOOD WILL AND SACRIFICES THROUGHOUT THE WORLD

America has always been known for her greatness despite her shortfalls and that greatness includes the many good things the U.S. has done around the world for other nations and their people. President Clinton said it nicely: "There is nothing wrong with America that cannot be cured by what is right with America."[302] From ridding tyrannical regimes across the globe so that people can live in freedom and liberty to sending money, resources, and personnel to help ailing nations in times of natural disasters, the U.S. has been there for others. Now granted, the U.S. is not the provider and problem solver for all the exigencies abroad, for that is impossible, but the U.S. does have a steady inclination to give to, help, and support others.

Time after time, event after event, our nation has answered the call of philanthropy. The U.S. has the answered this call many times not simply due to our resource abundance but because the American people are giving people. These different acts of philanthropy have produced a favorable standing in the world for the U.S. What other country can match up to our generous acts of kindness? There is not one. Can you imagine the world without a model nation such as America? More than not, there would be more death, destitution, hardship, and suffering if the U.S. did not have an altruistic spirit. It is these acts of benevolence that should make us proud to be Americans; the blessings of being a superpower and having the necessary resources to assist others is something we take for granted, but to the bereft people across the world, it is something sublime.

From the plains of Europe during World Wars I and II, to the frozen tundra of Korea, to the dank jungles of Vietnam, to the desert of the Middle East, to the mountains of Afghanistan, and everywhere else in between, American treasure- in the form of money, resources, and more importantly, American lives- has been spent for the cause of liberty for others. If there is one thing alone to be proud of this great country for it is the fact that men and women have served this country with gallantry, honor, and selfless service, so that we can indulge in our daily liberties. We have been blessed to have service members serve on our behalf in the most remote areas of the globe, under the most daunting and abysmal conditions, away from family and friends, and in both peace and wartime conditions.

The American blood that has been spilled on behalf of others is eye-opening. Holidays such as Memorial Day and Veterans Day come and go, but how many of us have actually taken a moment to reflect on their true meaning and purpose and the statistics associated with the costs of preserving freedom? During WWI, 53,402 American soldiers were killed in action with 204,002 wounded.[303] During WWII, 291,557 soldiers were killed in combat with 671,846 wounded.[304] The Korean War brought 33,741 battle deaths with 103,284 wounded, while the Vietnam War brought 47,424 battle deaths with 153,303 wounded.[305] Although the number of battle fatalities and wounded were significantly less during *Desert Shield/Desert Storm*, 147 and 467 respectively, they still cannot go unnoticed.[306] As of April 2011, 1,176 American soldiers and Department of Defense (DOD) civilians were killed in action with 10,749 wounded during *Operation Enduring Freedom*.[307] Also, 3,502 American soldiers and civilians were killed in action with 32,044 wounded during *Operation Iraqi Freedom* and *Operation New Dawn*.[308] We also cannot forget those soldiers killed or injured in non-combat incidents during these aforementioned wars along with those during smaller conflicts or incidents such as the Battle of Mogadishu in Somalia, the bombing of Khobar Towers in Saudi Arabia, the bombing of the USS *Cole*, and many more. What other country has paid such a heavy price for the cause of liberty for foreigners? Again, there is not one. So the next time a holiday comes along commemorating our veterans and military, take a moment to gratify those service and family members who have made this ultimate sacrifice.

PRIDE IN AMERICA

Like many, I am proud to be an American for the simple fact we have people who desire to wear the uniform and make the sacrifice to protect our Constitution and democratic way of life. We are beholden to these heroes for preserving the freedoms of our nation throughout the years. We also cannot forget the family members of our service members. Just think of the grief and emotional turmoil that family members of these service members who made the ultimate sacrifice had to go through and are still going through. For them, life has changed forever. Widows are created, children are left empty-hearted, and families, in general, are sundered. No matter how much time has passed, the pain and hurt will always be there in one form or the other especially since family ties are enduring.

In order for us to maintain our humbled pride in America, I encourage everyone to put themselves in the shoes of the family members who have lost a service member in fighting for our nation. I am certain they would attest freedom is not free. I would also challenge Americans to reflect on these sacrifices throughout our history not just on those nationalistic federal holidays but to the point where it is engrained in our hearts and automatically emits from us in the form of appreciation and love of country. As bromide as it may sound, freedom is certainly not free because our fellow Americans gave and continue to give everything each and every day to keep America the beacon of freedom.

Another reason why we can be proud to be Americans is the fact that Americans are collectively generous and do more than their share of contributing money and resources to different regions of the globe either through charities or fund-raisers. In 2006, Americans doled approximately $295 billion to charity.[309] Now this is no nominal amount. The people donating this amazing amount of money are doing it out of personal choice. No other country comes close to matching the generous giving of the American people. According to Arthur Brooks, "in 1995 (the most recent year for which data are available), Americans gave, per capita, three and a half times as much to causes and charities as the French, seven times as much as the Germans, and 14 times as much as the Italians."[310] Since generosity is a quality of the heart, this spirit of giving tells a lot about Americans as a people. As a society, we must take pride in the fact we are empathetic to other people's suffering or penury. As a society, we could easily turn our backs and stay engrossed in our materialistic and pleasure-seeking lifestyles, but some do not. Some are givers instead.

Take for example the relief for the tsunami in Southeast Asia in 2004. The natural disaster affected the countries of Indonesia, Sri Lanka, Thailand, and India, killing more than 200,000 people. Like many times before for other global disasters, the U.S. was one of the first countries to provide an outpouring of humanitarian support. While the U.S. government donated approximately $900 million, the American people donated about two billion dollars.[311] Out of their own free will, Americans had donated money for the procurement of food, water, clothing, medical supplies, and many more needed items for the displaced people of Southeast Asia. Indonesia's reputation of not having the most affable relationship with the U.S. did not forestall this salvo of American charity. The American people put aside the Indonesian anti-Americanism and instead, without hesitation, turned their hearts to the suffering people of Indonesia.

In another example, the U.S. government and American people gave generously to the people of Haiti. In 2010, a devastating earthquake brought a catastrophic blow to an area outside of Haiti's capital, Port-au-Prince, killing more than 200,000 Haitians and displacing about 1.5 million of the already impoverished Haitian people.[312] Once again the American people came through with generous giving to help those suffering in another country. Donations not only came from the U.S. government and opulent American corporations, but they also came from average American citizens. Within seven short months after the disastrous earthquake, American individuals, foundations, and corporations raised a total of $959 million for Haiti.[313] For example, Verizon Wireless raised $22 million alone for the Red Cross with its text message campaign.[314]

Even though these two major natural calamities were out of site and out of mind, the American people's hearts were not as monetary donations poured into the different private fund raisers and charities. The American people proved once again there is no geographical distance that can stultify America's altruism. There are no limitations to the generosity of the American people. I am proud to live in a country whose people overall have an altruistic spirit and a desire to help others burdened by life's trials and tribulations. We understand we have an obligation to help others in need and we grasp the concept that God blesses people in order to bless others.

The things to be proud of America for are endless if you really think about it. The American footprint of greatness is seen across the globe. Take for example the incredible rescue of the 33 Chilean miners in October 2010. After 69 days of being stuck approximately 2,000 feet underground after a mine had collapsed, the miners were rescued one-by-one as the rescue capsule traveled up and down the fabricated escape shaft. What many do not realize was that America's footprint existed behind the scenes of the rescue. For 33 onerous days, an American driller by the name of Joe Hart along with his determined Colorado team from Layne Christensen Company drilled into the surface of the earth, creating an escape shaft that reached the entrapped miners. This is just another example of American citizens, equipment, and resources at work to help others in need. For 33 days, Hart and his team served as ambassadors of compassion for the U.S. as they toiled in representation of the American flag and its people to save the lives of total strangers. In the face of intimidating circumstances, Hart and his team remained steadfast in determination to reach the miners. Thank God for His providence and His favor in bringing the trapped miners to safety and for Americans, like Joe Hart and his team, who are filled with the compassionate appetite to help others regardless of race or nationality.

We should be proud of the ordinary people in America doing extraordinary things to keep our country on top. It is not the superficial title or position of someone that defines someone, but it is those things he or she does quietly that honors God, family, and country. I am proud of those Americans who volunteer their limited time to local community service. I am proud of the churches we have in America that promote the Word of God and our Godly heritage and continually serve and help others in spiritual, emotional, physical, and financial need. I am proud of those Americans that are innovative and adaptable entrepreneurs that promote America's spirit of capitalism by conjuring an idea, raising capital, and engendering a product or service that other Americans want. I am proud of those American service members who serve their country throughout the globe for the bona fide love of their country. I am proud of those Americans who work hard to raise their families in righteousness. I am proud of those Americans who fight for the preservation of our Christian heritage, democratic and capitalistic way of life, the U.S. Constitution, and everything else that separates America from other nations, making her exceptional. I am proud of those Americans who help our homeless and wounded veterans. The list of things to be proud of in the U.S. is endless, and I ask you to join me in sharing this pride.

I find it hard to believe that with all the different things to be proud of America for and all the liberties and luxuries we are blessed with, there are still those who chide the U.S. for her imperfections. J.R. Nyquist of *World Net Daily* put it this way: "Americans who hate America are real. They are all around us. Go into a bookstore. Look at the social studies section. Browse for a while. Ask yourself what purpose this hatred serves and what it promises to our country and the world."[315] In today's day in age, we do not need Americans who hate America because we have enough foreigners who already do just that as a result of their ignorance of what America is all about. We need Americans who believe in and admire their country.

AMERICA'S PROBLEMS FROM WITHIN

It is worthy to reiterate the premise made earlier: America is not a perfect nation and it will never be, along with any other nation; however, it is the only nation that is the closest to being perfect. From unappreciative celebrities to fastidious politicians, there is always something that seems to annoy them about America. Their lack of historical knowledge and appreciation coupled with their haughtiness produces a disrespectful nature against our country. Whether it is America's spiritual or capitalistic nature, there is no appreciation for what America is all about. Furthermore, whether it is something from our imperfect past or something else, for some, America is never good enough for them. What are we suppose to think when we see American celebrities embracing leaders of foreign countries who publicly criticize America? If it is not bad enough to be bogged down with a real and deadly enemy that despises America and what we stand for, we also have to cope with insolent Americans who do not respect their own country.

A country troubled by its own inhabitants is nothing lightly to deal with. As Cicero once wisely said:

> "A nation can survive its fools, and even the ambitious. But it cannot survive treason from within. An enemy at the gates is less formidable, for he is known and carries his banner openly. But the traitor moves amongst those within the gate freely, his sly whispers rustling through all the alleys, heard in the very halls of government itself. For the traitor appears not a traitor; he speaks in accents familiar to his victims, and he wears their face and their arguments, he appeals to the baseness that lies deep in the hearts of all men. He rots the soul of a nation, he works secretly and unknown in the night to undermine the pillars of the city, he infects the body politic so that it can no longer resist. A murderer is less to fear. The traitor is the plague."[316]

Similarly, at an address to the Young Men's Lyceum of Springfield, IL, entitled "The Perpetuation of our Political Institutions," President Lincoln asked: "At what point, then, is the approach of danger to be expected? I answer, if it ever reach us it must spring up amongst us; it cannot come from abroad. If destruction be our lot we must ourselves be its author and finisher. As a nation of freemen we must live through all time, or die by suicide."[317] Although we have some real and credible enemies out there who wish harm to America, unfortunately, we also have Americans who share the same type of sentiments as they verbally attack America. For those who envisage the U.S. as this awful nation, I invite you to indulge in one of our many freedoms- the freedom of choice. Feel free to choose another country to inhabit. After all, your selection is diverse with approximately 195 countries to select from. On your way out, ask yourself also, if the U.S. is so bad then why are others sneaking in the U.S. illegally and trying to get in legally?

  The best way to reinvigorate love of country and pride in America is to contrast how much better we have things in this country versus people living in other countries. It is all about getting back to the fundamentals and appreciating what we have in this country. We have heard it time and time again that the poorest of Americans have so much more than some well-off people in foreign countries. Although this comes across as a platitude, there is definitely some truth to it. Have you ever thought to yourself what things would be like for your life if you were born in another country? Although the human mind may not be able to comprehend it, God has a purpose and plan for everyone's life and so there is a reason why you were born here in the U.S. versus another country. Since you were born here in America then why wouldn't you want to enjoy your country and be proud of it? A nation that suffers from a callous psyche among its people is a dying nation.

  As an American, you live in a country that cherishes and promotes freedom. Through our Constitution, you are guaranteed life, liberty, and the pursuit of happiness. You do not have to worry about your personal belongings and property being foraged or your life being uprooted and endangered. You can live in the comfort of your home and raise a family in peace and harmony. You live in a country blessed with resources. You have access to some of the basic services in life such as electricity, food, water, etc. that people in other countries would yearn for. As an American, you have access to medical facilities and simple medications. As an American, you have plenty of stores to choose from to purchase food and other goods without worrying about shortages. You have the liberty to practice or not practice the religious faith of your choice without any interference. The list of things to be grateful for as Americans is infinite. Unfortunately, we take things for granted as we are settled in our comfort zone of self-indulgence, thus causing us to neglect the greatness of America.

Personally, every time I returned from a foreign country, I was relieved to be back home in the U.S. Although it is a great experience to be exposed to another land and culture, there is nothing like being home in America, as I am sure many can vouch. After coming home from visiting Haiti while being in the Dominican Republic, I was appreciative of the fact that we have comfortable bathrooms and running water unlike the outhouses I saw in Haiti. Moreover, after witnessing the profusion of trash that littered the streets in the Dominican Republic, I became grateful for the organized waste disposal and sanitation we have here in the U.S. Upon returning from a deployment in Saudi Arabia, I was appreciative of the fact that women in the U.S. are not mandated to sit in the back seat of a car or are required to be covered in a garment from head to toe so as to not expose any part of their body. It is something unusual to be driving down a highway and then looking over to see a car in another lane with a woman sitting in the backseat- while the front seat is open- and the only thing you see are two eyes engulfed in a black garb. It came across as uncanny. I am thankful that the U.S. does not promote the same oppressive environment for women. After returning from a deployment in Korea, I returned to the U.S. appreciative of the fact that the fertilizer we use on our farmlands near the urban areas is not as putrid as what is used in Korea. The freshness of air that I was accustomed to in America was absent in Korea. Upon returning from another deployment in the Balkans, I returned home with an appreciation of electricity, electric heat, and air conditioning, all of which some households did not have as a luxury. These little things I witnessed helped intensify my appreciation for the simple things in America and reminded me how great our country is.

    Things we view as insignificant and automatic at home become significant and treasured when we are without them. When we are home in America, we do not even think twice about them because they are habitual. As the adage goes, "You do not how good you have something until you lose it or are without it." I am proud to be part of a country where luxuries and freedoms are present. No matter the extent of our challenges, there is no other country I would rather be a citizen of. Through the examination of other countries and realizing how fortunate we are to live in America, we are likely to appreciate what we have in our own country, reenergize our appreciation for America, and consequently resuscitate our love for America. With a renewed love of country, the American people will be reminded of our roots and the fundamentals that have made us a mighty country, thus providing nationalistic subsistence to prolong this patriotic sentiment.

AMERICA'S HEGEMONY CAME ABOUT NOT BY COINCIDENCE

Remember, our roots are embedded in religious and democratic freedom, so no matter how far we may have deviated from them there is still hope because they can resurface if aroused. When the dreams of our future outweigh our past and current national uncertainty, this hope can revitalize our foundational roots. It is has been our fundamental roots that have contributed to our national pride and national character throughout our history, and it will be these roots that sustain patriotic fervency. Will we embrace or repudiate them?

Our spiritual and democratic roots can sustain us as a global superpower as long as we permit them to. During World War II, the U.S. military strengthened and the U.S. economy swelled, initiating the American hegemony and putting the U.S. on the international map as a global and dreaded but respected power. In his book, *The Grand Chessboard*, Zbigniew Brzezinzki confirmed that "America's economic dynamism provides the necessary precondition for the exercise of global primacy."[318] On top of our economic prowess, the implosion of the Soviet Union during the Cold War introduced the U.S. as the only superpower in the world, further contributing to the American hegemony. According to Norwegian historian, Geir Lundestad, in his text entitled *The American 'Empire'*, he speculated America's hegemony "rested on four main pillars: its vast economic superiority, its substantial military lead, the broad domestic base for the policy pursued, and America's strong international-ideological support."[319]   With the arrival of the U.S. as a global superpower, the U.S. had its cultural tentacles of influence in various areas throughout the international community. In one of his literary articles, Lundestad wrote: "The American expansion went so deep and affected so many different parts of the world that it can be said to have resulted in an American empire."[320]

The ascendency of America in the world was due to a combination of factors such as the perseverance and hope of the American people and a burgeoning military and economy, but we cannot ignore the role that our spiritual and democratic roots had. The people of the U.S. were mobilized as they rallied around the cause of defeating communist imperialism for the purpose of preserving reverence for God and God's inalienable rights of individual freedom. Whether it was the soldier on the battlefield or the woman working back home at the factory, nationalism drove them both to action. Our enemies at the time not only faced the power of our military and economic engines, but they were also in contention with the resilient and unflinching national pride of the American people.

In today's secular age it is no surprise that many do not talk about this ascendency because if they did, they would have to credit America's roots of righteousness which includes recognizing the movement to revere God and stand up to evil. Isn't it something to witness the correlation between righteousness and national pride? When the U.S. is collectively involved in a cause supporting righteousness and acting out of good intention, the American people, overall, radiate with national pride and evil is rolled back.

Today, there are those both at home and abroad that do not have the same passion for America's hegemony and some that even desire to see the hegemony of the U.S. crumble. For example, Science Czar, Dr. John P. Holdren said, "We can't expect to be number one in everything indefinitely."[321] It is understandable to see foreigners adopt this apathy and even enmity, but when Americans adopt the same disposition, there is some alarm raised. It is hard to imagine Americans who want to see their country subordinate to other countries. What is wrong with our country being the only superpower in the world? What is wrong with leading the world politically, economically, militarily, culturally, and morally?

If the U.S. does not do it, then who will- a country that does not enforce human rights; a country ruled by a tyrannical despot; a country that does not honor individual freedom; or a country where God is totally neglected and curbed? Despite America's historical shortcomings, there is no other country that has the same record of standing up to unrighteousness. Why would we want to exchange our global hegemony to be a vassal of another country? Why wouldn't we want to see others adopt our ways instead of vice-versa as long as the U.S. is not foisting its ways on others? Over the last several decades, we have seen the diffusion of the American culture and democratic way of life throughout the entire world at the acceptance of the respective countries. If America loses its global hegemony, other nations that have partnered with and relied on the U.S. will be troubled.

AMERICA'S CURRENT ECONOMY ENDANGERS OUR NATIONAL STATURE AND PRIDE

One area in which American hegemony is in question is with our economy. Since the end of World War II, the U.S. has been considered and respected as an economic giant throughout the world, but this perception is dwindling as the U.S. has become a debt laden society. As America's deficit and debt continue to precipitously increase, the U.S. runs the risk of losing her influence in the international community and quite possibly her sovereignty. Could it be that since we are moving away from our fundamental principles we are becoming more economically snared? After all, our wealth has historically been amassed as a result of our adherence to the fundamentals that have made this country great. Instead of being economically vibrant, we are financially beholden to foreign nations as a result of our unpaid debt and profligate government spending.

The Heritage Foundation affirmed our total debt is expected to grow from $7.5 trillion in 2009 to a distinguished amount of more than $15 trillion by 2020.[322] One would think the fact you cannot cure debt by incurring more debt is common knowledge, but our elected officials have pushed aside this practicality as our debt has skyrocketed. For example, during Congresswoman Nancy Pelosi's tenure as Speaker of the House, our debt had escalated approximately five trillion dollars.[323] The rise of the debt is no surprise especially with our carefree attitude on spending, but what is ironic is that at her inaugural address as Speaker in 2007, Pelosi publicly and seriously proclaimed there would be "no new deficit spending."[324] Over the recent years, when it has come to spending, political party has made no difference. Pelosi's predecessor, Congressman Hastert, saw the debt rise approximately 3.1 trillion dollars under his tenure as Speaker from 1999 to 2007.[325] Regardless of political party, both Republicans and Democrats have left the American people with a flaunting and shameless I.O.U. Our elected officials' lack of fiscal conservatism has defied Thomas Jefferson's assertion he had written in a letter to Samuel Kerchevel in 1816: "I place economy among the first and most important virtues, and public debt as the greatest of dangers to be feared. To preserve our independence, we must not let our rulers load us with perpetual debt."[326] Almost two centuries later Jefferson's quote could not be more appropriate as our debt poses a serious threat to our national identity, sovereignty, and security. Our founders understood that debt could be reduced through the proper management of our resources. Can you imagine what our founders must be thinking as our debt continues to climb with no inclination of backsliding? Moreover, they would be disgusted to know our elected officials are consumed more with political decisions versus economic decisions when it comes to America's economy.

If we revisit our pedigree and the teachings of our founders, we would see that our current economic struggles run converse to what our founders envisioned for our nation. On another occasion, Thomas Jefferson stated, "Though much an enemy to the system of borrowing, yet I feel strongly the necessity of preserving the power to borrow. Without this, we might be overwhelmed by another nation, merely by the force of its credit."[327] Our founders were cognizant of the unfavorable ramifications of spending and borrowing as it relates to our independence and stability as a nation. In addition, they also understood government is not an investor. They fancied Americans as producers and savers versus borrowers and spenders. They would have never imagined that taxpayers would be paying 414 billion dollars (for fiscal year 2010) on the interest alone to the holders of our national debt.[328] And as our spending continues to wax, so will the interest on the national debt, thus placing the taxpayer in a never ending vortex of spending and taxing.

Who would have thought the mighty United States would be financially enthralled to other nations? Certainly not the gentlemen who helped shape this great country. Approximately $3.3 trillion of our debt is held by foreign countries.[329] Countries like China and Japan are lending the U.S. significant amounts to sustain this colossal debt. China owns approximately $895 million, while Japan owns about $785 million.[330] Who would have thought China, a country that is primitive and oppressive, would be lenders to America? Similarly, who would have thought that Japan, a country we defeated in World War II, would be a major lender to the U.S. today? It comes across as odd and troubling that as a sophisticated and advanced country, we have to rely on other less developed countries to be purchasers of our government debt, but then again, when we lack a scintilla of fiscal conservatism and disregard budget deficits year after year, this should not be a surprise. When a country becomes dependent on another country for financial sustainment, its financial well-being becomes at risk and it becomes a servant to that country as annotated in ***Proverbs 22:7 (NIV)***: "...*the borrower is servant to the lender.*" What happens if these countries ever decide not to supply us with this money for our debt? Then what will the U.S. do?

I often wonder what thoughts run through politicians' minds when they see the national debt and national spending clocks continue to feverishly turn. Personally, when I see the numbers rise with no end in sight, I am disgusted. Sometime take a minute and just watch the clocks turn without cessation.

Then ask yourself, how can this rate of growth in debt be "sustained? It cannot! It is basic math; we are spending more than we can possibly bring in through tax revenue. Even the Chairman of the Joint Chiefs of Staff, Admiral Mike Mullen, admitted that "the most significant threat to our national security is our debt."[331] The Admiral's statement demonstrates that economic viability is tied to national security.

THE RISE OF CHINA

It is no shock that when we lose our economic edge, our economy feels the ramifications which affect everyone in one way or the other. While America is beleaguered by our debt, China not only owns some of our debt, but it is also experiencing significant economic growth and modernization. In his article, "American Hegemony and China's U.S. Policy," Professor Dr. Baohui Zhang pronounced: "China's rapid modernization has increased its global influence at an impressive pace."[332] The combination of our financial doldrums and China's economic and military developments challenges the American hegemony and begs the question: Will China become emboldened to challenge the United States in the near future? While the U.S. is bogged down by finding cures for its debt, China is aggressively looking for new global investments to spread its global reach. China reportedly lent a total of 110 billion dollars to other countries and companies in 2009 and 2010.[333] It is reasonable to argue that China could quite possibly take advantage of this geopolitical situation to displace the American hegemony. Although China is not there yet, China's influence throughout the international community is increasing while America's is being increasingly questioned.

One might ask just how the China footprint is expanding. For one, China has become one of the world's leading exporters in the world of numerous merchandise items. I witness this all the time as I drive up and down interstate-10 in Arizona and watch the trains drive parallel to the highway. I am always amazed to see the multitude of shipping containers with names of Chinese companies on them being carried by the train. There is not one American company's name on those containers. Think of the message this sends to America- thousands of miles away from its native land, Chinese containers are being carried on American trains, on American rails, and through every day U.S.A. Of course, it is permitted through today's age of free trade and economic globalization, but why must the U.S. be outdone as an exporter? Every time I see those trains full of Chinese containers, the image fills me with displeasure because we once were a manufacturing giant, and I cannot help but think, why must we settle for this mediocrity? It does not have to be this way if we are willing to make some practical and tough economic versus political decisions.

Another area that is disquieting is the increased number of automobiles that China has manufactured. According to the International Organization of Motor Vehicle Manufacturers, today known as the "Organisation Internationale des Constructeurs d'Automobiles" (OICA), in 2009, China produced 10,383,831 automobiles, while the U.S. produced only 2,246,470.[334] Just ten years earlier, China produced only 565,366 automobiles, while the U.S. produced 5,637,949 automobiles.[335] This decline in American automobile production should not be a surprise because our manufacturing base has decreased over the years due to outsourcing for cheap labor and lower overhead costs.

The loss of our manufacturing base further challenges American hegemony because manufacturing growth creates economic activity, jobs, stability, and overall security. What was the one thing that the U.S. had going for it during World War II that contributed to our economic and military power? We had the juggernaut of our automobile manufacturing base which was capable of transforming automobile plants into plants capable of producing military vehicles for war. Perhaps there will be another time in the future when we will have to do the same, but will we have the workforce, capital, and resources to do so? Independent writer Michael Payne said it firmly: "But America cannot and will not rebuild its economic foundation unless the driving force behind it is based on manufacturing and selling products made by American labor."[336]

Along with China's increasing economic role in the world is the increase in China's military capability and outreach. New Chinese submarines equipped with potent missiles are raising alarm in the Pacific sea lanes. Will China's expanding Navy restrict American freedom of access in the Pacific? In an annual Pentagon report to Congress, the *Military and Security Developments Involving the People's Republic of China*, supported this: "The pace and scope of China's military modernization have increased over the past decade, enabling China's armed forces to develop capabilities to contribute to the delivery of international public goods, as well as increase China's options for using military force to gain diplomatic advantage or resolve disputes in its favor."[337] Also as a result of China's booming economy, China no longer is required to depend on other countries for military equipment. *The Washington Times* reported China as being "nearly self-sufficient in building advanced weaponry following decades of importing aircraft, ships, submarines and missile technology, mainly from Russia, and the capability is raising new fears of Chinese military hegemony in Asia and arms exports to rogue states."[338] These are serious geopolitical concerns that most Americans are clueless on and could care less about.

As Americans, we must understand where we have been economically and the dangerous direction we are heading in. We must also grasp the ramifications associated with the direction we are heading. We must also appreciate the trends of growth that China is currently experiencing and how its growth affects us as we are financially indebted to China. Let's not forget that China has been around much longer than the U.S. and has seen powerful countries come and go, so China possesses incredible geopolitical wisdom. China does not think in terms of decades but in terms of centuries. Despite China's growing influence and its leverage over our debt, do not overlook the fact that the U.S. is a huge customer of China's exports.

During the 2010 mid-term political season, there was a powerful television advertisement by a non-partisan and non-profit organization called Citizens against Government Waste. It grabbed my attention as it showed future Chinese students in the year 2030 in Beijing, China studying the birth and demise of empires throughout history to include the ancient Greeks, the Roman Empire, the British Empire, and then, of course, the deceased American Empire. The professor opened the advertisement by asking his students, "Why do great nations fall?" He then answered, "...by turning their backs on the principles that made them great."[339] At the end of the ad, the professor remarked with a smirk on his face, "And of course we owned much of their debt, so now they work for us."[340] The students laughed with derision as they saw themselves above the U.S. in their new global superpower status. This should be no laughing matter to the American people because it serves as a harbinger especially since the conditions that can lead up to such a scenario could not be any more opportune today. The advertisement has an eerie tone to it for a reason. **Wake up America** and take pride in your country by acquiring geopolitical situational awareness, educating yourself on it, and acting on it. Never forget our economic strength is an instrumental part of our national power; there is a direct relationship between the two. Also, be reminded that when you owe someone money, there is almost always strings attached.

AN APPRECIATION OF SIMPLE ECONOMICS

America's contest with our epic debt is a reflection of our society's outlook on debt and spending in general. If we examine the root cause of debt, we would discover voracious greed and the vigorous desire for stuff. We have forgotten that in order to avoid debt, we must be engaged in diligence, practice personal savings, and invest prudently and wisely. Today, most people believe in the sentiment they will live within their desired means even if it requires them to borrow in order to do so. The days of saving up for a service or good prior to procuring it are bygone. Instead, the impulse to borrow in order to obtain that service or good is the adopted course of action. Moreover, the practice of frugality and conservative spending has been replaced with instant credit and the urge to spend in order to finance a lifestyle. Consumerism has found its place in America as Americans are entranced by materialism, fulfilling all of their desires and wants.

As a society, we have lost the distinction between needs and wants. The two have become fused as they are treated as one of the same things in today's self-gratifying culture. Wants are now treated as needs as there are no limitations in what and how much we procure. The art of parsimony has lost its place in American society. Our spending culture has done away with consumer temperance for consumer fulfillment. Our wants of tomorrow have taken on the dimension of our needs for today. Just as we get enmeshed in personal debt to fulfill our personal wants, our nation is caught in a maelstrom of debt as a result of our political leaders being consumed by wants over needs.

We must get back to the basic definitions of a need and a want. A need is something necessary for sustainment of life, while a want is something we desire for enjoyment or satisfaction. There is a children's book entitled *Needs and Wants* by Gillia Olson that clearly and simply teaches children the difference between the two. According to Olson, "Needs are the things we must have to live" and "wants are things we can live without."[341] Everything is not critical to our well-being. In order for our economy to be reignited, every part of our society must once again appreciate this most fundamental concept of economics.

Part of reviving our economy includes moving away from our culture of entitlement. We have become comfortable with entitlements outside of what we were originally entitled to as per our Constitution. Our government is only entitled to protect our access to life, liberty, and the pursuit of happiness. And oh yeah, it is the pursuit of happiness and not happiness. It has always been that our own personal endeavors, efforts, and diligence are at the source of our happiness and not the government. Government entitlement programs only encourage dependency on government and not self, eliminates personal responsibility and accountability, and it dwarfs individual ingenuity and initiative. We can never forget that American economic success has been and continues to be the result of personal toil, entrepreneurship, and of course, our democratic and free market institutions. The torrent of government involvement in our economy only foments dependency and destroys incentive, and when the incentive to earn disappears then we can expect the stagnation of work at home and the consequent stagnation of our economy, thus causing America's greatness within the global economy to falter.

It is self-reliance that we must promote and not reliance on government if we want to stay on top of the global economy. President Reagan called attention to this in his fourth State of the Union address in 1985: "Let us resolve that we will stop spreading dependency and start spreading opportunity; that we will stop spreading bondage and start spreading freedom."[342] Our democracy was built on the foundation of the American people being free from any form of government intrusion as our founders fought for our independence from British tyranny. Reliance on government only gives rise to false hope. If there is something in which we must rely on then why not rely on a God who has granted us favor and blessing after blessing? It is reliance on God that brings into existence genuine hope.

Our spending culture coupled with this entitlement culture forecasts a menacing future for the U.S. if we do not reverse course and adopt a culture of genuine fiscal circumspection. I like what Michael Tanner, a senior fellow at the Cato Institute, said: "There is simply no way to control our debt without getting serious about reforming entitlements."[343] While many are familiar with our debt owed to foreign nations, we cannot forget to associate our debt with the unfunded liabilities of government entitlement programs such as Social Security, Medicare, and Medicaid. They are the major drivers of our debt. The outlays for entitlement spending have steadily increased over the years with no signs of slowing down. In 2009, total expenditures for entitlement spending exceeded two trillion dollars with Social Security leading the entitlement programs with over 677 billion dollars.[344] According to Gallup, 77% of Americans believe the cost of the government's major entitlement programs "will create major economic problems".[345] Nobody is asking the question, who is going to rescue the federal government when it is financially bankrupt as a result of these growing entitlements? Remember, government programs may come across as appealing, but more than likely, they turn out to be costly and ineffective. Without any relief in site or a game plan to reduce government entitlements, we cannot grow as an economy while continuing to carry around this weight of debt.

Welfare is one of the government entitlement programs that have ballooned away from its original purpose. The *USA Today* reported, "Welfare rolls rose in 2009 for the first time in 15 years, but the 5% increase was dwarfed by spikes in the number of people receiving food stamps and unemployment insurance."[346] It is one thing for the welfare rolls to increase due to genuine need, but it is bane when the program is abused when it is exploited by the masses and given out with minimal oversight. One thing welfare should absolutely not be is a way of life but a method to get back on one's feet. Welfare should serve as a temporary crutch and not an interminable fulcrum, and anything more than a temporary solution serves as an impediment to our economic prosperity.

Granted there are select circumstances such as health issues that prevent a person from working, but the strongest argument discouraging reliance on welfare is clearly spelled out in the Bible: *"For even when we were with you, this we commanded you, that if any would not work, neither should he eat."* **2 *Thessalonians* 3:10 (*KJV*)** Everyone has an individual responsibility to work. Although our culture does not want to hear the hard truth, it cannot get any simpler than that and with the Bible serving as a source of absolutism, there is no room for misinterpretation. We all have been destined to work and serve a purpose in this world; however, welfare entitlements run in conflict with man's purpose to work and provide a living for his survival. Welfare has taken on a detestable reputation of rewarding laziness as those who are able to work refuse to work. Once people get a taste of an automatic entitlement, it is probable that a parasitic liking to it will follow. The American taxpayer has every right to question why the producers of society must subsidize the non-producers.

We have also seen a rise in food stamp usage across America. For fiscal year 2010, the Department of Agriculture forecasted there would be 40.5 million Americans on food stamps at a cost of about 59 billion dollars.[347] And it does not look any better for fiscal year 2011 as the Department of Agriculture predicts an increase to 43.3 million Americans using food stamps. As a child growing up, there was a period when my parents signed up for food stamps.[348] After looking back on this period, I learned a lot from my parents. Although they were not proud to be on food stamps, they were not embarrassed either because they had a genuine need for them for temporary relief while they worked several jobs to provide for our family. In today's society, where food stamps and welfare act as a disincentive to work for some, my parents looked at food stamps as an incentive to work. They saw food stamps as a temporary assistant and not a kind of guaranteed income. Furthermore, they did not view the government as a source of entitlement for their shortfalls or struggles. They were dependent on each other to provide for the family and not the government. Their actions revealed to me the respect they had for our country for they believed in self-reliance and not government dependence. This is the same respect of country that needs to be ablaze today.

Reliance on the public dole reduces individual responsibility and accountability and personal initiative. When there is love and respect of country, the American people are more inclined to avoid government reliance and dependence but trust in the values of individual responsibility and self-worth that have made our country strong.

AMERICA'S HERITAGE VERSUS INTERNATIONALISM

Internationalism is another threat that confronts the U.S. in safeguarding our hegemony, sovereignty, and identity. There are those who believe that the U.S. should be more like other countries in Europe and others around the globe. Have these people neglected our history and what we have been through in such a short period of time? Have they forgotten what we stand for and how we have served as a beacon of hope and light for others? Such people lack the appreciation of the uniqueness of America. There is no reason for the U.S. to be like any other country; we have our own identity and if we do not protect it, we will lose it.

In today's age of globalization and interconnectedness, internationalism is a palpable phenomenon especially as interdependence and networking among nations increase. Globalization can be both good and bad for the U.S. In his book, *In Defense of Globalization*, Jagdish Bhagwati wrote, "Globalization leads to prosperity and prosperity in turn leads to democratization of politics with the rise of the middle class."[349] We saw what happens when a nation resists economic integration when the Soviet Union crumbled from within during the Cold War, giving rise to the United States as the only global superpower. On another extreme, when a country gets a piece of economic independence from globalization, that country is quick to hold on to it along with the prosperity that comes with it.

In today's international economy, globalization further fortifies our own economy; however, when we let globalization strip us of the qualities that have distinguished us from others, then we are permitting others to define us as a nation. Moreover, we are turning over power and influence to others that are less like us. As a result of globalization's ability to make the world smaller, distances between countries become truncated and borders fade away. This in turn challenges our nation's sovereignty as laws of other countries try to penetrate our nation's borders and trump our inborn laws. When we idly standby and watch foreign influence tamper with our institutions and rule of law, we run the risk of losing everything that we have always stood for.

The reference and reliance on international law is a rebuff of our own Constitution, rule of law, and American culture. What is even more troubling is when our own judges promote international law. Former Supreme Court Justice Sandra Day O'Connor once told the *Atlanta Journal Constitution*, "I suspect that over time we will rely increasingly, or take notice at least increasingly, on international and foreign courts in examining domestic issues."³⁵⁰ During Justice Elena Kagan's confirmation hearings, she declared that foreign law can be helpful "for getting good ideas" when interpreting the U.S. Constitution.³⁵¹

Why are people so fascinated with international law when we have everything we need within our own rule of law? It was not international law that has made our country exceptional, but it was our very Constitution and rule of law. If we adopt international law, which country will serve as the precedent? What happens to our already established precedents under American rule of law? Where would the uniformity come into play? Love of country constitutes admiration for our own Constitution and rule of law versus international law. When international norms are adopted over our own rule of law, we are just whittling our U.S. Constitution. It is up to the American people to celebrate our Constitution and rule of law because our elected officials and appointed judges have certainly not all been aboard in doing so.

During the 2010 mid-term elections, we saw what Oklahoma citizens viewed of international interference when they voted down the intrusion of Sharia law in state courts. The law bans state judges from relying on Islamic law when deciding cases. The Oklahoma International Law Amendment, State Question 755, read:

> "This measure amends the State Constitution. It changes a section that deals with the courts of this state. It would amend Article 7, Section 1. It makes courts rely on federal and state law when deciding cases. It forbids courts from considering or using international law. It forbids courts from considering or using Sharia Law.
>
> International law is also known as the law of nations. It deals with the conduct of international organizations and independent nations, such as countries, states and tribes. It deals with their relationship with each other. It also deals with some of their relationships with persons.

The law of nations is formed by the general assent of civilized nations. Sources of international law also include international agreements, as well as treaties.

Sharia Law is Islamic law. It is based on two principal sources, the Koran and the teaching of Mohammed.

Shall the proposal be approved?

For the proposal
Yes: _____

Against the proposal
No: _____ "352

It passed conspicuously with 70.08% voting yes and 29.92% voting no.[353] I am confident that if this same question was posted on the ballots of every single state, the American people would have all voted in unison and in the majority against establishing international law as precedent on American soil. This is true love of country and national pride because most American people understand that our rule of law is cardinal to who we are as a people. Such democratic action strengthens and protects our American democracy from international institutions and their deleterious agendas.

Unfortunately, once again, we have seen the people's vote ignored as Muneer Awad, executive director of the Council on American-Islamic Relations in Oklahoma, filed a lawsuit, declaring that the ballot measure was unconstitutional. Despite the clear majority of people standing up to Sharia law, a district court in Oklahoma discredited the majority of Oklahomans. One person, with the help of the district court, abnegated the collective votes of 695,568 people.[354] Perhaps, these judges need to be reminded that the role of judges is to defend existing laws and not make new laws. This is absolutely sickening because we live in a land built on the will of the PEOPLE. How we vote is a direct reflection of our core beliefs, and the Oklahomans uplifted our own rule of law versus Sharia law. As an American citizen, it boggles my mind that we even have to debate this. It further infuriates me because people have died for our right to vote and subversive actions like this only dilute this precious right.

Those who promote Sharia law continue to use our freedoms against us in anticipation of spreading their agenda. Mr. Awad argued: "For Muslims, the Quran and the traditions (hadith) of the Prophet Muhammad are the basis of our faith. Shariah is a dynamic legal framework derived from the Quran, hadith, the ongoing consensus of Muslim scholars, and analytical reasoning."[355] As a result of unrestraint multiculturalism and tolerance, our own foundations and institutions of our constitutional republic are in jeopardy. Sharia law is incompatible with our system of law. There should only be one legal framework that dictates the rule of law within our country and that should be American jurisprudence. Anything other than that is unacceptable and if anyone wants anything different then they need to live somewhere else because America was not founded on Sharia law. Whatever happened to assimilation of our culture, rule of law, and America in general? Do you think you would be able to go to a country like Saudi Arabia and start spreading American constitutional jurisprudence? I think not. Mr. Awad should consider countries such as Somalia, Iran, Nigeria, Sudan, and Saudi Arabia if he wants Sharia law.

While the move towards multiculturalism seems to be growing in America, other countries in Europe are actually rejecting it because they have already witnessed how multiculturalism fragments a country's native culture. Under multiculturalism, assimilation into the respective culture is nonexistent. Instead, it results in nations being formed within an already existing nation as incomers desire their own culture, laws, and ideas in doing things. The top leaders in Germany, England, and France have all proscribed multiculturalism. French President Nicolas Sarkozy spoke on the failure of multiculturalism and the necessity to protect France's identity: "If you come to France, you accept to melt into a single community, which is the national community, and if you do not want to accept that, you cannot be welcome in France."[356] This is the sentiment we need in America if we want to protect our national character.

When we think of internationalism and international institutions, we cannot overlook the United Nations (UN). The UN has taken on a larger role in spreading international or the new world order. In his book entitled *A Deficit of Decency*, former Senator Zell Miller parodied the United Nations as the "Useless Nuisance" and stated that the UN's "real agenda was not pro-American in any sense of the word. It was all about establishing a world government that would not have the checks and balances of our constitutional form of government."[357] The question remains, how much of our sovereignty are we going to relinquish in order to succumb to this international order? Are we going to let unelected and obscure bureaucrats from the UN force international law and regulations on the United States for the sake of this new world order? International cooperation and partnerships are absolutely necessary in today's post 9-11 environment, but that does not mean we abandon our core principles and values for international cooperation. Regardless of how crucial the circumstances may look without UN backing, we must stand firm on those principles and values that have set us apart from other countries.

The UN has already revealed its incompetence and geopolitical coyness with various global issues. According to Kim Holmes, Director, The Kathryn and Shelby Cullom Davis Institute for International Studies, "Members of the Security Council and other international bodies such as the International Atomic Energy Agency need to gather the will to enforce existing obligations."[358] Where was the UN during the genocides of Rwanda and Darfur? If the worst humanitarian crises are not worthy of UN attention and resources, then what is? Where was the UN during the oil for food scandal? Where is the UN in stopping Iran's nuclear proliferations? Where is the UN's hard position against international terrorism? Where is the UN's public condemnation of the Hamas attacks on Israel? The UN continues to display its ineffectiveness with peacekeeping and protecting human rights as it strays from its original purpose.

Americans must analyze the failures of the United Nations and ask themselves why we should trust the UN with its world order agenda if the UN cannot even deliver results in spreading peace and safeguarding basic human rights. Moreover, Americans must energize their representatives in scrutinizing the money the United States gives the UN. After all, we are the largest donor to the UN, and as the UN attempts to spread international law and order while infringing on American sovereignty, we have a say in the matter. In 1996, Stefan Halper claimed, "An American withdrawal would almost certainly mean the collapse of the United Nations. Without the generous, if unwilling, support of U.S. taxpayers, the United Nations would face imminent financial ruin."[359] This leverage should be used to ensure the UN sticks to its fundamental purpose and mission rather than seeking to spread international order.

MEASURING ONE'S LOVE OF COUNTRY AND PRIDE IN AMERICA

How does one know if he or she is proud of their country? All one has to do is perform a self- examination and be honest with oneself. Ask yourself such a question as: What is it that you feel when you pass by the American flag? When you see an American flag waving in the wind on a flag pool, do you reflect on those individuals who have given their lives for our freedoms? Does a feeling of pride swell up on the inside of you when you see the red, white, and blue? What about when you see the American flag amid flags of other countries? Do you feel grateful to live in a country as great as the United States? The American flag is a powerful symbol of freedom and liberty that should make every American proud to be an American and part of the United States.

We should not be ashamed of or hesitant to display our flag for it is part of our identity as the United States of America. On one unfortunate incident, students from Live Oak High School in Morgan Hill, California were reprimanded for wearing American flag shirts on May 5, 2010, otherwise known as the Spanish holiday Cinco de Mayo. Vice Principal Miguel Rodriguez sent the students home because he said "the American flag shirts were a safety risk because they might upset Mexican students celebrating the holiday."³⁶⁰ Although Mexican students could wear patriotic shirts to celebrate their heritage on the Spanish holiday, American students were forbidden to wear American flag shirts on the soil of their own country. Not only were the American students deprived of displaying their patriotism, but their right of expression was also violated. Thankfully, the school district reproached the vice principal's decision to send the students home.

On another occasion, another school ordered a thirteen-year old boy to no longer display the American flag on the back of his bike as a result of other students complaining. Cody Alicea, who has aspirations to serve in the military one day, claimed that he was only displaying the American flag out of patriotism and to honor America's veterans. According to Cody's grandfather, the school was concerned that the display of the flag would provoke racial tensions and uprisings.³⁶¹ Personally, I find this absolutely mind-bending to hear that the display of the American flag in our own country would incite racial tensions and uprisings. What kind of hooey is this? What have we come to as a society that we would reprehend such an innocent act by an innocent child and think uprisings would be a result of patriotic fervor? Fortunately the school reneged on its decision and allowed Cody to display his flag on his bike.

We actually need more people to have this same patriotic fervor as Cody. Can you imagine what a tsunami of patriotism would do for this country especially at this time in our history? If you recall, a tidal wave of patriotism immersed our society after the attacks of 9-11, but it was short-lived. However, it should not take such a tragic event in the first place to stir up American patriotism. Our patriotism and love of country needs to be resolute and not subject to conditions. Moreover, it must be genuine and felt from the heart. It cannot be expressed by empty words and deeds, but it must come from within first then backed by supporting words and deeds. It does not take a flag to be patriotic, but a flag does serve as a vehicle to express that love of country. Let's also not forget that love of country is more than waving a flag- it is a lifestyle. It is in the way we talk and the way we act in our daily lives as Americans. Do you show your enthusiasm and gratitude for living in a country so blessed? If not, try it and see how infectious it can turn out to be.

What about the Pledge of Allegiance to the American flag? Most of us were exposed to the Pledge of Allegiance in grade school as it was recited daily at the start of class. Although its recital became simplistic and pedantic, the words composing it are pungent and meaningful. Take a look: "I pledge allegiance to the flag of the United States of America, and to the republic for which it stands, one nation under God, indivisible, with liberty and justice for all." This one sentence is replete of heritage and patriotism all Americans should take pride in. Although most of us do not recite it since we are out of school, it is always refreshing to revisit it and reflect on its substance.

Unfortunately, the pledge has lost its reverence in our society today. In February 2010, one congressman from California apparently disdained the suggestion from one attendee at a labor union meeting to recite the Pledge of Allegiance. In the congressman's defense, he stated:

> "On the morning of February 20th, I was invited to address some 500 people gathered to discuss the human tragedy of a broken immigration system and the need to fix it. At some point during that meeting, a political operative for a congressional campaign asked if we could recite the Pledge of Allegiance. The meeting was already under way and the question was unexpected. It took us all by surprise. When the speaker explained that he was serious and asked me specifically if we could say the pledge, I said yes and gestured to the moderator, who then led the entire gathering in reciting the pledge."[362]

Regardless of the circumstances, it should not be alien to have to recite the Pledge of Allegiance in a public forum; however, this event indicated something different. In the video and photo of the event, the reception to the request to recite the pledge comes across as scornful and foreign as others in attendance laughed at the request to say the pledge.

It is hard to believe we would treat our country- a country that guarantees us life, liberty, and the pursuit of happiness with copious blessings- with such indifference. It is our duty as nationalistic Americans to stand up to such acts of negligence and torpor. The Pledge of Allegiance has meaning and a purpose, so let's promote it.

What about at a sporting event when the *National Anthem* is sung? What do you feel in the inside? Do you feel proud to be an American? Do the words have meaning to you? Or do you stand there unaffected and uninspired?

CHAPTER EIGHT
The American People Want Leadership

In order to restore our foundations and renew our sense of purpose, America is in need of authentic leaders in all sectors of our society especially in the public sector. These include leaders who have America at heart and are guided by the principles that have made America great. We need leaders who are sensitive to our vulnerabilities and sincerely and unabashedly promote America's greatness and exceptionalism. With all the challenges confronting the United States today, America is in need of leaders who have the no-nonsense, leadership mindset of General George Patton. As Patton once said, "Lead me, follow me, or get out of my way."[363] It is that simple and the American people yearn for such leadership.

Political parties and ideologies aside, we need leaders full of integrity and not empty and fallacious promises in all aspects of society. We need leaders who understand genuine truth that is not relative but absolute. Maybe it would be helpful for our leaders to reflect on one of God's declarations on leadership in **Luke 16:10 (KJV)**: "*He that is faithful in that which is least is faithful also in much: and he that is unjust in the least is unjust also in much.*" We want leaders who behave, act, govern, decide, and lead in the same reverent fashion from the most trivial to the more complex situations. We need leaders in the political, economic, and military realms that are grounded in the heritage and traditions that have made this country great because anything less is detrimental to the well-being of our society during these crucial times of domestic and international dilemmas.

Our leaders must be filled with firm conviction, urgency, uncompromising character, and unhesitant courage. The absence of these equates to an absence of leadership. There is no substitution for leadership. When there is a void of leadership, we can expect that vacuum to quickly fill with distractions, alternate agendas, and time-wasting initiatives. One individual who understood and exhibited true leadership was Colin Powell. As a well-known military general during

Desert Storm and a highly esteemed diplomat on the world stage as Secretary of State, Powell exercised leadership with purpose and intent. In the book, *The Leadership Secrets of Colin Powell,* Oren Harari wrote: "One reason why Colin Powell is an effective leader is that he is not easily misled by superficial analyses, surface truths, or 'spin'".[364] Whether it was in the military or within the State Department, Powell knew as leader, when one is in charge, he or she must take charge. Today we need our leaders to take ownership, lead with authority, and deliver results without surrendering the privilege of leadership.

LEADING WITH A SENSE OF ACCOUNTABILITY

We want leaders in positions of authority who understand just because one has a position with a title does not qualify one as an effective leader. A position of authority does not equal leadership, but a genuine and effective leader earns that title of authority through diligence, humility, and record of achievement. Leadership is all about the action in a position of authority not the position of authority that demands action. American author and management guru, Kenneth Blanchard, had these curt but stirring words: "The key to successful leadership today is influence, not authority."[365] People in charge who make an impact with their subordinates usually do so as a result of their sincere influence versus the authority they hold. If we examine the definition of leadership, we would see that leadership is the ability to influence others to complete a common objective. Hence, leadership is not determined by what is on the outside of an individual, but instead, by what is in the inside of that individual. We want and need leaders who treat their position with a humbled reverence and appreciation and not a smug sense of entitlement.

With leadership comes accountability and responsibility; they are all interconnected. The three should work in tandem with one another, but unfortunately that is not the case today as people in authority seem to be absentminded as they dismiss these fundamental building blocks of leadership. People want the responsibility without the accountability associated with it. They want the acclaim and glory without the sweat and exertion. The Bible speaks clearly of responsibility and accountability: *"From everyone who has been given much, much will be demanded; and from the one who has been entrusted with much, much more will be asked."* **Luke 12:48 (NIV)** Accountability and responsibility go hand-in-hand; the greater the responsibility one holds, the greater the accountability follows. We must connect the two as one and promote them as such. Just as peanut butter complements jelly and salt complements pepper, accountability must complement responsibility. Until we restore this mindset, we will continue to see leaders devoid of substantial and influential leadership- empty suites. In today's age of uncertainty and risk-free world, the last thing America needs is empty suites charged with the duty of doing the people's business. And while today's society measures great leaders as those who possess power, authority, and prominence, I would measure valiant leaders as those who are accountable and responsible with or without power, authority, and prominence.

    Accountability among mankind was first comprised with Adam and Eve in the Garden of Eden. Adam and Eve both disobeyed God in eating the forbidden fruit from the tree of knowledge. When God recognized their disobedience, both were quick to blame their actions on someone else other than exercising self-accountability. Eve blamed her action on the serpent, while Adam blamed his action on Eve. The important takeaway is God did not expel them from the garden for their disobedience but for their lack of accountability. To this today, people are plagued with self-justification over self-accountability.

TELLING IT THE WAY IT IS

    Part of accepting accountability in a leadership role is being honest with your audience whether it is with one's subordinates or with the public. Now, I know what you may be thinking; this is common sense. You are right, but how many times have we seen public leaders fall to perjury or chicanery and not necessarily from the snide act itself? No matter how adverse a situation may be, it is the responsibility of a leader to be open and honest about it. The saying that "bad news does not get better with time" is still germane today. A sincere leader comprehends one reaps what one sows and is therefore willing to face what lies ahead. Moreover, he or she does not cover-up a crisis with excuses, obfuscations, or generalities, but addresses a crisis directly to the media or public with contrition, specifics, and a plan of action. Even though we live in a redemptive society, we still must hold our leaders accountable especially in matters of culpability.

The American people desire their leaders to convey a candid message through the media with boldness and truthfulness. Lieutenant General (LTG) Honore, renowned for his steady leadership during the aftermath of Hurricane Katrina, was one who used the media to his advantage to control and manage the message coming out of New Orleans which consequently created a perception that civic restoration was unfolding. Prior to his arrival, the image of New Orleans was a city besieged by nature's worst wrath and tangled in hopelessness. This catastrophic image began to taper as LTG Honore exercised his leadership. LTG Honore not only led with confidence and competence, but he also did not pull any punches. He did not paint any pretty pictures for the American people nor did he present any false hope, but he told things as they were. We could use more LTG Honores throughout our society because we have too many mealy mouth and circuitous leaders.

Under his nineteen rules for leadership during a disaster, in his book *Survival: How a Culture of Preparedness Can Save You and Your Family from Disaster*, LTG Honore proclaimed, "Must give media access- if you're not speaking, someone else will speak for you."[366] LTG Honore's candidness with the public prevented the media from pursuing prevarication and distorted journalism. Who can forget his famous and keen quote to the media: "Don't get stuck on stupid?"[367] LTG Honore controlled the message to the public as he boldly and cogently accentuated the need for the reporters not to focus on the past but on the current and future status. Where are these LTG Honores? Our society is in need of nonpolitically correct and bold leaders who tell it as it is. We need leaders who speak boldly without worrying what audience is out there to satisfy. LTG Honore was one who performed out of concern for what works and not for what pleases others.

A leader must not only be able to get comfortably in front of the media, but he or she must be able to be frank with the public. Far too many leaders underestimate the discernment of the American people. The American people are able to discern and differentiate a charlatan from one who is authentic. Americans are not looking for perfect leaders but authentic leaders who show a genuine interest in America. As Stephen Fink wrote in his book *Crisis Management: Planning for the Inevitable*: "Being dishonest or less than honest with the media will only escalate your crisis into proportions that will stagger you."[368] No matter how detrimental the truth may be to an organization in a crisis, a leader must have the internal fortitude to be frank with his or her audience in order to build symbiotic rapport. The American people do not want complaints, finger-pointing, or excuses. When it comes to accountability, there is minimum room for blame.

In rebuilding Continental airlines, Greg Brenneman, former president, strongly believed it was necessary to be forthright with its customers and employees on Continental's past and to seek their forgiveness. Brenneman stated, "Confession is good for everyone's soul, and often for the pocketbook as well."[369] The only thing the public demands is honesty, situational awareness, and accountability and responsibility where it is required. According to writer Sandi Sonnenfeld, "The sooner you present the facts clearly to the public, the sooner the issue will be resolved."[370] Let's not forget the common American is not so common for the American people are capable of discerning fake from real. When a leader reveals a genuine intent to be honest with everyone during a crisis, he or she may experience some short-term tribulations, but long-term, the recovery will be more expedient and fruitful.

LEADING WITH POISE AND GENUINE ACTION

Leadership demands assertiveness and not diffidence. One who is assigned a leadership role within society must be free from passivity and indecision especially during a crisis. If a crisis alone is not enough to worry about, a crisis without assured leadership makes a crisis even more challenging to deal with. Leadership is all about delivering results, and during a time of a crisis, results are needed and expected. Someone assigned to a leadership role must possess decisiveness and possess passion and sinew to gain the public's support. Decisiveness is absolutely necessary in containing a crisis because "a crisis simply will not wait."[371]

Many will argue the reason why Federal Emergency Management Agency (FEMA) Director Michael Brown resigned from FEMA was due to his inept and lifeless response in corralling federal assets in the Gulf after Hurricane Katrina. Many contested Mr. Brown had minimal experience with emergency management prior to assuming the duties of FEMA Director. In an interview with *Time* magazine, Claudia Deakins, head of public relations for the city of Edmond, remarked "Brown was an 'assistant to the city manager' from 1977 to 1980, not a manager himself, and had no authority over other employees."[372] As a result of Brown's poor leadership performance, the federal government did not immediately gain the collective support of the American people. Instead of public support settling in, partisan finger-pointing and societal strife settled in, adding to the magnitude of the already established crisis. It is sound leadership backed by credible action that eviscerates public uncertainty in times of difficulty because people naturally respond to leadership.

Real leadership also entails doing what one says he or she will do. Leadership is not measured by captivating, superficial rhetoric but by the distinct action to support one's rhetoric. Rhetoric may sound great and welcoming, but does the rhetoric promote the right policy? How many times through the years have we heard it is not what one says but what one does that makes the difference? No matter how many times this is proclaimed in our daily lives, politicians and public administrators have a reputation of not doing what they verbally promote. Instead, it is do as they say not as they do.

American people want more than thinkers; they demand doers especially since commands do not execute on their own. The majority of American people want to be energized by pro-God, pro-family, and pro-American rhetoric, but more importantly, they want to see genuine action supervene that aforesaid rhetoric. We do not want the rhetoric for the sake of one's political expediency or personal agenda-setting; we want the rhetoric backed by the action as a rallying cry. Republican or Democrat, liberal or conservative, both sides are guilty of being hypocrites for the sole purpose of personal promotion. Hypocrisy cannot coexist with leadership. I like what one writer said about hypocrisy as it relates to leadership: "Leaders, even good leaders, can be lots of things—ambitious, narcissistic, and perhaps even philandering—but they can't be hypocrites. Hypocrites cannot lead..."[373] The American people want our leaders to lead with conviction and who are more concerned with what the American populace think versus what the media reports and opines.

The American people know it is one's sincere behavior and action and not one's empty rhetoric that substantiates an individual's leadership ability. It is the actions of an individual and not his or her articulation that defines him or her: *"For as he thinketh in his heart, so is he."* **Proverbs 23:7 (KJV)** We are products of our thinking. Since our thoughts govern our behavior, our actions are a result of what we believe. How and what we intrinsically think affects our character, behavior, and conversation. Hence, just because a leader of influence says something does not mean it is gospel or that one truly believes in what one is verbally promoting. Instead, it is what is in the heart of a leader that matters. Everything else is menial. While some may be duped by one's appealing but superficial rhetoric, others are more discerning of the disparity between what one says and what one believes and eventually does. Those who have this discernment understand what John Locke meant when he said,

"The actions of men are the best interpreters of their thoughts."[374] No matter how attractive a leader may come across on the outside in both appearance and speech, we must do our due diligence and not let one's artificial traits distract us from what one believes and actually does. We must examine that leader's actions and behavior in relation to what he or she does. This is true in every aspect of our culture.

GROUNDED IN HUMILITY

Americans want leaders who do not come across as smug and infallible perfectionists. Instead, we desire leaders who act with assertiveness but with a spirit of humility and humanity. Perhaps our leaders can take a lesson on humility from English preacher and author Charles Spurgeon's *Pride and Humility* sermon:

> "Humility is to feel that we have no power of ourselves, but that it all cometh from God. Humility is to lean on our beloved, to believe that he has trodden the winepress alone, to lie on his bosom and slumber sweetly there, to exalt him, and think less than nothing of ourselves. It is in fact, to annihilate self, and to exalt the Lord Jesus Christ as all in all."[375]

Genuine leaders understand leadership is an evolving process and there is always room for leader improvement and development. In his book *Leadership,* America's Mayor, Rudolph Giuliani, wrote, "Leadership does not simply happen. It can be taught, learned, developed."[376] Just as one cannot be a foreign language interpreter without learning a foreign language, a leader cannot be a leader without learning and embracing the fundamentals of leadership and being open to leader development. We want leaders who lead when called upon and who are not closed off to suggestive tutelage. Part of being a humbled leader includes remaining open to outside support. Leaders run towards problems and use on-hand personnel and resources to their advantage to overcome problems. Without the necessary leadership during a crisis, the crisis is likely to exacerbate and lead to other sub-crises within the main crisis. According to Fink, "It can be a fatal mistake to think that a crisis, if left unattended, will heal by itself."[377] When a leader enters a crisis with assertive boldness, a sense of urgency, open to external guidance, and a plan of action, he or she is likely to get an organization out of a crisis.

LEADING WITH "WE THE PEOPLE" IN MIND

The American people want to have confidence and pride in their leaders because they are indicative of what the United States is all about. Unfortunately that confidence was absent with the 111th Congress as it possessed the lowest Gallup measured of any institution in Gallup's 35-year history. According to the Gallup's 2010 Confidence in Institutions poll, "Eleven percent of Americans say they have "a great deal" or "quite a lot" of confidence in Congress."[378] The statistic says it all. It is quite appalling that in our representative government only 11% of Americans have confidence in their leaders. If this does not paint a sour picture, I do not know what does; however, there is still hope. Thank God our Founding Fathers designed a system of government in which we have the opportunity to select our representatives every two years. Our confidence must not rest with the people elected to office but ultimately in our system of government under God's providence and authority.

Our elected officials must lead with ideas, principles, and values embedded in our constitutional framework and Godly heritage. It takes leadership to abide by and enforce these values especially in a political correct and secular society. Oftentimes, poor leadership is a result of being more concerned with pleasing something outside of one's values, afraid to make the tough decision where one's values are at stake, and being engrossed in the preservation of one's self-power versus standing up for the right values. The hard truth is an elected official has no business representing a constituency if he or she is not enchanted by the fundamental roots of our country and the things that have made America great. The principles and values adopted to establish our nation must be the same principles and values used to restore and sustain our nation. Our leaders must promote the greatness of America and how we can get back to it without feeling inconvenienced. We must hold our elected officials accountable to this expectation.

Americans demand our elected officials who brainstorm, engender, promote, vote on, and sign into law legislation to do it in a constitutional manner that honors our democratic process and respects the collective voice of the people. Americans expect our leaders to be transparent and adhere to the constitutional process of authorization, appropriation, and oversight when it comes to creating legislation. Anything less is bad business and harmful to our constitutional framework. My local congressman, Jeff Flake, said it best: "Process begets good policy."

The American people look for our leaders to treat every piece of legislation with care, taking into consideration the secondary and tertiary consequences of how the legislation affects the lives of the American people. This includes reading the legislation thoroughly and knowing exactly what is in it. Former Speaker of the House, Nancy Pelosi, said this in reference to the passage of the health care reform: "We have to pass the bill so that you can find out what is in it, away from the fog of the controversy."[379] Any versed American would view her statement as backwards for it totally defies logic and disaffirms our constitutional process. In addition, the American people are aware the longer a piece of legislation hangs around, the more earmarks are likely to accumulate in it. Sincere consideration for the legislation process should be one minimum prerequisite for any elected official.

I know there is no such thing as a perfect leader for we all have our frailties, but I do know there are a select handful of genuine leaders with sincere intentions to cater to the interests of the American people without becoming aloof. Communication with the people should not be forced interface, but it should be interactive and natural. Effective leaders understand and use the three components of communication: sender, message, and listener. Our public leaders must want to interact with the American people. Where are those leaders that make you say, "Wow, there is something extraordinary about him or her which resonates within me. He or she is the real deal in which I can relate to?"

I remember growing up as a child and hearing President Reagan speak. Yes, Ronald Reagan had his faults like every man, but there was something about him that was real. When he spoke, he did not just speak, but he communicated to the American people with purpose, clarity, infectious confidence, and attractive conviction. Even as a child I knew nothing about politics as my attention was caught up in simply being a kid, but I did discern there was something about this man that categorized him as a true leader of the people. It is no surprise then President Reagan is labeled as the "Great Communicator." In his book, *Governor Reagan: His Rise to Power,* Lou Cannon reminded the reader of Reagan's ability to rally people as a result of his genuine speech. According to Cannon, "Reagan was no intellectual, but he knew what he believed and why he believed it, and he wove his ideas, single-handedly and without the help of speechwriters..."[380] As a result of Reagan clearly communicating his beliefs and convictions to the people, others believed and responded to his resolve, thus portraying him as a leader.

Americans today hunger and thirst for political leaders who are consumed by a spirit of servant leadership in adherence to our Constitution. This almost seems improbable and countercultural in an age of hedonism and self-indulgence, but we still need leaders who put their self-agendas aside and are motivated with serving others above themselves first. I recommend all of our elected officials reference Jesus' words to His twelve disciples: *"Anyone who wants to be first must be the very last, and the servant of all."* **Mark 9:35 (NIV)** The attitude our elected officials must possess is: "I am here to work for the American people and I should not get comfortable in my current position because I am only here at the will of the American people." When our representatives view themselves as true servants for the people versus simply elected officials, they are less likely to feed their egos and less likely to become dependent on their own strength and other external influences.

We must get back to the concept that those who want to lead must first know how to serve. This is a valuable lesson in life because leaders and followers are dependent upon each other. They each provide the other with purpose for their existence. In order to be a good leader, one must first learn how to be a good follower. If one cannot follow, then one cannot lead effectively. As a cadet at the U.S. Military Academy at West Point, I learned this very precept from day one. I would argue it has been one of the most valuable lessons I have learned in my life. All of our U.S. Service Academies are premier leadership institutions with the prime purpose of transforming young men and women from followers to leaders. They are not only esteemed as being prestigious engineering colleges, but they are recognized for their leadership curricula. Their curricula of creating selfless leaders who typify duty, honor, and country should be the model all of our elected officials take up at every level of government. When our leaders know how to follow they would be more suitable to lead with sensitivity to the real collective needs of the people.

Our leaders need to be roused behind the concept "of the people, by the people, for the people." In his book entitled *How Congress Works and Why You Should Care*, former congressman, Lee Hamilton, stressed the uniqueness of our representative government:

> "A representative democracy is based upon the idea of citizen participation-The notion that ordinary people have both the right and the responsibility to be involved in their governance. And Congress, in particular, was set up to be the branch most connected to the American people's interests, hopes, and aspirations."[381]

We still live in a participatory government that demands our elected officials to be in-touch with the people and engaged in stewardship. They have a responsibility to stay connected to their constituents and to dodge self-serving allurements. Our leaders are supposed to be stewards of the American people. Moreover, our leaders must be reminded the strength of America stems from the American people and the people determine the direction our country heads in. Woodrow Wilson emphasized the significance of the American people in a representative democracy: "Just what is it that America stands for? If she stands for one thing more than another it is for the sovereignty of self-governing people." [382] Self-governing people demand representative leaders who are not self-serving but responsive to the will of the people and not only during election season but throughout their term.

The one thing that sets a leader apart from a great leader is how a leader views the relationship with his or her subordinates or followers. Are the followers treated as an integral part of an organization's mission and purpose? In today's society where leaders are praised and aggrandized while followers are neglected, the relationship between leader and followers seems to have become trivialized. One of the requirements of successful leadership is having an amenable group of followers or subordinates united under an organization's purpose. Of course, this is much easier said than done, but an effective leader has the capability to move or influence others. In his book entitled *On the Hunt*, retired Colonel David Hunt wrote about what makes extraordinary military leaders. He wrote "truly exceptional leaders" care "more about the mission and the men" than they do themselves.[383] Our military leaders are prime examples of leaders who cherish and understand the importance of the leader-follower relationship. They know it is their subordinates that drive the mission and make things happen. Without subordinate troops, there is no need for military leaders. Well, we need the same type of appreciation and obligation from our elected officials. They must appreciate the fact the American people is the reason why they have a job.

As stewards of the American people, our elected officials must have a sense of urgency when it comes to representing the American people and sustaining America's greatness. They must be reminded they work for the

American people and not vice-versa. I know this sounds cliché, but it is a basic tenet and work ethic that is missing from many of our elected officials today. With a renewed sense of urgency promoting the nexus between elected officials and the people, our country would be better off. It is up to our leaders to maintain this sense of urgency though. In his book, *A Sense of Urgency,* John Kotter wrote that "sustaining urgency over time requires that it not only be created, and created well, but that it be re-created again and again."[384] Our leaders would be wise to acknowledge Kotter's instruction and keep a sense of urgency always in front of them.

Our elected officials must go to work every day on Capitol Hill asking themselves, "Am I going to be a leader for the American people today as they elected me to be, or will I be an opportunist fulfilling my own agenda?" Obviously, the American people prefer the former, but unfortunately, the longer our elected officials remain in Washington D.C., the latter seems to prevail as elected terms of service have devolved into political careers.

THE POWER BEHIND "WE THE PEOPLE"

Our elected officials must understand and respect the power of the people and the influential role they play in our representative democracy. Moreover, our leaders must understand at the same time they desire votes from the American people, they must reciprocally be able to answer to the voters. Elected leaders cannot neglect the fact America is all about the people and not the government. With a representative government, our leaders need to understand the people will hold them accountable and remind them just who is in charge. In fact, the best lobbyists in enforcing representative government are the people themselves. It is the collective voice of the American people that determines the direction of our country. A wise and in-tuned elected official would not underestimate the power of the American people.

We witnessed the influence of the collective voice of the American people with the mid-term 2010 elections. Through the representative force of the Tea Party, the American people made their voices loud and clear. The American people were rallied around the movement of thwarting an expansive government. Just as colonial Americans protested the British government's lack of representation and over-taxation in 1773 with the Boston Tea Party, two hundred and thirty-seven years later, the American people protested the American government's non-responsive nature to the American people and its encroachment on individual freedom. Our elected officials seemed to have forgotten America was founded on the evident consensus that government must be small. In her article, "Why the Tea Party has staying power," Carrie Sheffield wrote: "While a few strident Tea Partiers are guilty of fanaticism, the overwhelming majority of these activists are motivated by a kernel of truth in their worries that federal spending as a share of the national economy has risen under President Obama (to the highest it has been since 1946) and would have escalated further under a Democratic Congress."[385] Americans of all ages, denominations, races, and political affiliations made their voices known at peaceful and respectful demonstrations and gatherings and at local town hall meetings leading up to the 2010 mid-term elections. The majority of the American people were jolted behind the cause of limited government and individual liberty.

The Tea Party's civic involvement leading up to the mid-term elections reminded us our democracy is based off the vote and not any other external factor(s). In addition, it also reminded us how Americans really do have the power to restrain the government through the vote. The 2010 mid-term results revealed "we the people" is much more than just a mantra, but there is power behind an active citizenry. When the people are energized behind a cause and champion a sense of urgency over apathy, "we the people" becomes a formidable lobbying force to reinforce our democratic principles. Despite what the media may portray, the American people are in the majority as long as civic lassitude does not settle in.

The 2010 mid-term elections, giving the Republicans 63 seats, was the greatest House of Representatives pickup in 72 years when the Democrats lost 71 seats.[386] It just goes to show no political seat is guaranteed to any one individual especially when the American people are mobilized. Incumbents who have been in office for the longest time saw their political careers taken away. For example, Congressman Paul Kanjorski of Pennsylvania, House Financial Services Capital Markets Subcommittee Chairman, who served 13 terms in Congress, lost his seat on November 2, 2010. Congressman John Spratt of South Carolina, Chairman of the Budget Committee, was another long timer who served in Congress since 1982 had also lost in 2010. Let's not forget what happened in Massachusetts after Democratic Senator Ted Kennedy passed away in August 2009. After his 46 years of service as a senator, in a major political upset, the people of Massachusetts elected Republican Scott Brown as their junior senator. Again, this just goes to show a political seat does not belong to one person, one family, or one political party. Senator Brown said it best during his campaign: "This isn't Ted Kennedy's seat. This is the people's seat."[387] Mr. Brown reminded Americans how we live in a participatory democracy in which the will of the governed matters and those being governed demand responsive elected officials. The year 2010 marked the year in which "of the people, by the people, for the people" was revived.

DEVIATING FROM AMERICA'S ROOTS

From 2006 to 2010, the American people gradually awakened as they watched the federal government amplify in size and power. They became alerted as the American government ran in contradiction to what our Founding Fathers envisioned with limited government and free enterprise. Regardless of the party affiliation during those last four years, the federal government has been engaged in alarming bailouts, stimulus plans, and more bailouts. In October of 2008, President Bush signed the $700 billion Troubled Asset Relief

Program (TARP) in which the federal government purchased bank assets to stabilize the financial markets. The initiation of TARP set a recent precedent of government involvement in our free enterprise as lavish government stimulus and bailouts were ushered in with the new administration in 2009. Government expansion in the form of the $787 billion stimulus or the American Recovery and Reinvestment Act, automobile bailouts, and the nationalization of student loans and our health care has not only increased the size of government, but it has also strengthened the precedent that the government is the only and complete answer to our problems. In a speech at George Mason University, President Obama suggested the necessity of government in our economy: "It is true that we cannot depend on government alone to create jobs or long-term growth, but at this particular moment, only government can provide the short-term boost necessary to lift us from a recession this deep and severe."[388] This reliance on government put a foreign face on our capitalistic system of government, causing the American people to rally against big government.

The recent increased role of government has given many Americans the image of socialism. And as we all know, socialism is the antithesis of capitalism because it impairs individual freedom and smothers the role of people in government. While capitalism is a decentralized and free enterprise economy, socialism is a centralized command and control economy. While the end result of capitalism is freedom by the individual, the end result of socialism is power and control by the government. Alex de Tocqueville explained the difference between the two the clearest: "Democracy and socialism have nothing in common but one word, equality. But notice the difference: while democracy seeks equality in liberty, socialism seeks equality in restraint and servitude."[389] There are stark differences between the two as they are mutually exclusive and when the government pendulum swings from capitalism to socialism, the American people are not going to sit back leisurely and without action.

Since socialism contradicts the very foundation of our government, it does not take much for the American people to discover something is off. The primary tenet of socialism is the state owns or controls the means of production. When the government controls the means of production, the people become dependent on government, thus running in direct conflict with our capitalistic heritage. Under capitalism, government is not responsible for bringing you happiness. Moreover, under our founders' vision for our government, government was never designed or purposed to be all things for all people. By permitting socialism to flourish, the American people run the risk of losing their personal decision-making ability and economic liberty. The American people understand when we nationalize something through government spending and subsequent ownership, we also lose personal and local accountability to the government.

We do not have to look far to see what happens when government activity thrives. Our own city of Detroit is known for its increased government policy and regulation. Over the last five decades, Detroit has been the recipient of countless government grants and federal programs. The local government of Detroit established a reputation of promising its residents it would take care of them through the public dole. Promise after promise, the local government offered the people of Detroit things such as public housing and welfare programs. Today, instead of economic vitality and affluence, Detroit is overwhelmed with runaway unemployment, poverty, and social welfare. Although Detroit's actual unemployment rate is significantly high, the unemployment rate for the Detroit-Livonia-Dearborn, Michigan metropolitan area was 14.4%, approximately 5% above the national average.[390] In 2009, 36.4% of Detroit residents lived below the poverty level.[391] In addition, over the years, Detroit has suffered from declining automobile manufacturing businesses, plummeting real estate, and the fleeing of its population. If America's current direction is left unaltered, Detroit can serve as a portent for the entire country of what happens when government ambitions outweigh government capabilities: overreliance on government suppresses personal and economic prosperity.

Even though aspects of socialism may come across as appealing and a utopia of sorts as government carries the ultimate burden, one would think Americans would know better especially since history has validated those countries that had flirted with socialism have also fizzled. But as mentioned in a former chapter, those who do not know their history are destined to repeat their history. Countries such as Yugoslavia, Poland, Germany, the Soviet Union, Hungary, Romania, and many others have experimented with socialism and look how they ended. Just think of how the people in countries such as Cuba and North Korea are deprived of the simple things in life under a government-controlled society.

On the other hand, if we look at our own country, which has been dominated by a private enterprise-managed model of government versus a pure government-managed model, we have reaped unprecedented prosperity. What other country under socialist rule has achieved greatness like the United States? So, why would we want to indulge in a failed model of government? Why try to fix something that isn't broke? It just does not make sense. Instead, let's reflect on what Winston Churchill said from his experience with socialism prior to World War II: "Socialism is a philosophy of failure, the creed of ignorance, and the gospel of envy, its inherent virtue is the equal sharing of misery."[392] Instead of being curious about socialism, why don't we strengthen and refine our already proven-free enterprise model? It is capitalism and not socialism that is the extension of personal liberty and individualism.

In appreciating our roots of limited government it is wise to reflect on the actions of our first President, George Washington. At the end of the American Revolution, George Washington took our country in the direction of a representative and participatory republic in which our leaders are elected and not a monarchy where there is a king. George Washington epitomized service as a public servant as he wished to serve the American people and not be served by the American people as in a monarchial government.

PEOPLE AGAINST BIG GOVERNMENT

The American people took a stand against the federal government's excessive spending as they demanded conservatism and circumspection with government spending. They deemed enough is enough when they headed to the voting booths in November 2010. While American families exercised fiscal discipline at home during the recessionary period, the American government continued to spend without urgent reason. While Americans were eating out and shopping less, spending less on recreational activities, and watching every dollar spent, the federal government casually spoke of money in terms of trillions of dollars. We have always been entangled in debts and deficits, but when billions are replaced with trillions, we are facing a new phenomenon. Moreover, when we reach monthly deficits of 223 billion dollars, like we did in February 2011, we have serious financial issues.[393] Yes, you heard correct; this is for one month.

Even the long-term economic outlook is depressing. In fact, in June 2010, the Congressional Budget Office forecasted that federal debt held by the public would grow from an estimated 62 percent of GDP in 2010 to about 80 percent by 2035.[394] Moreover, debt obligations do not vanish when revenue is slow and spending is unending. The American people felt detached from their representatives and they knew that during a period of economic hardship and unprecedented runaway debt, spending was not defendable. As a result, the American voter was not hesitant to exercise the power of the vote in order to find representatives who would be more receptive to the voice of the American voter and engage in priority-based spending and budgeting.

One would think our representatives learned their lesson from the 2010 midterm elections and heard what the American people were clamoring for. It was simple; Americans were screaming, "No more spending!" Instead, the 111th Congress tried to ramrod another omnibus bill weighed down with earmarks under the fiscal year 2011 spending bill prior to their exit in December 2010. It was like if nothing had transpired on November 2, 2010 and that the collective voice of the American people was irrelevant. These incumbents showed little respect for the representative-constituency relationship. The 1,924-page piece of legislation was comprised of 6,000 earmarks, totaling 1.1 trillion dollars.[395] It was another trillion dollar piece of legislation hastily put together with little regard to our current economic stagnation and the sentiment of the people. Even though it was a lame duck session of Congress and representatives were on their way out, it did not preclude them from exercising fiscal restraint. What will it take for our elected officials to obey the voice of the American people?

There is no other way to describe the exorbitant bill other than outrageous. On the Senate floor, Senator John McCain passionately proclaimed: "The American people couldn't have been more clear. They're tired of the wasteful spending, they're tired of big government, they're tired of sweetheart deals for special interest, and they're tired of business as usual in Washington."[396] Within the spending bill were such earmarks as "$349,000 for swine waste management in North Carolina; $413,000 for peanut research in Alabama; $235,000 for noxious weed management in Nevada; and $300,000 for the Polynesian Voyaging Society in Hawaii."[397] It does not end there: $500,000 for oyster safety in Florida; $165,000 for maple syrup research in Vermont; $208,000 beaver management in North Carolina; $522,000 for cranberry and blueberry disease and breeding in New Jersey; and the list goes on.[398]

Was it absolutely necessary for these projects to be funded in a time when we were and still are drowning in debt? Where would this money come from to pay for these earmarks? It is mind boggling to think that with our current economic crisis, our elected officials would subscribe to earmarks for things that are not of current financial priority. Thankfully, there were enough courageous and logical senators who blocked the wasteful spending and stopped the legislation fraught with earmarks from going any further.

The American people have to be suspicious of those who attempt to grab power; therefore, they demand our elected officials to abide by the constitutional process of enacting legislation. If it was not for the active citizenry of the American people during the 2010 midterm elections, then perhaps, another unwarranted spending bill would have slipped through at the expense of our future generations.

The end results of the 2010 midterms were one thing, but the voter replies to the exit poll questions were something even more striking. The exit polls concluded the American people of all regions and both political parties were filled with uneasiness for the future of the American economy. For example, 87% of the House of Representatives voters were worried about the direction of the economy in the next year.[399] Furthermore, 39% of the voters believed the highest priority for the next Congress is to reduce the budget deficit.[400] No surprise, 62% of the voters felt the top issue facing the country was the economy.[401] It will now be up to the 112th Congress to usher in a spirit of fiscal discipline and to concede to the American voters. There is a mandate to resurrect the economy by controlling federal spending and that mandate comes neither from a bureaucratic personality nor any other mandarin in our society. It comes directly from the American people. Their voices should serve as the incentive for the actions of the 112th Congress. Regardless of the political party leading the Congress, the American people demand leadership in concert with their mandate to redeem the economy and stop the government spending.

The Republican leadership of the 112th Congress created a conservative agenda entitled *A Pledge to America* in response to the American people's umbrage with the direction of the federal government. The purpose of the agenda was to revitalize the relationship between the American people and their elected officials. The preamble properly included reverence to the American people:

> "Like free peoples of the past, our citizens refuse to accommodate a government that believes it can replace the will of the people with its own. The American people are speaking out, demanding that we realign our country's compass with its founding principles and apply those principles to solve our common problems for the common good. The need for urgent action to repair our economy and reclaim

our government for the people cannot be overstated."[402]

The voice of the American people has been heard. This was a start as it revealed the value behind the will of those being governed; however, the words must be backed by tangible action under the new congressional leadership or else this document is an empty document and nugatory to the American people. Within the foreword, there is again emphasis on the purpose of the document and the importance of the people in government: "It's time to do away with the old politics: that much is clear. It's not enough, however, to swap out one set of leaders for another. Structure dictates behavior, so we have drafted this blueprint on a process of listening to the American people and fielding their concerns and ideas for turning things around."[403] The tenor of the pledge suggested a desire to serve the American people and not for the American people to be subservient to our elected officials.

Speaker of the House John Boehner opened the 112th Congress with appropriate words to reflect the overall attitude of the American populace and the outcome of the 2010 mid-term elections. His words reflected the role of people in society and how the new Congress must honor them:

> "The American people have humbled us. They have refreshed our memories as to just how temporary the privilege to serve is. They have reminded us that everything here is on loan from them. That includes this gavel, which I accept cheerfully and gratefully, knowing I am but its caretaker. After all, this is the people's House. This is their Congress. It's about them, not us. What they want is a government that is honest, accountable and responsive to their needs. A government that respects individual liberty, honors our heritage, and bows before the public it serves."[404]

Now it is up to the actions of the 112th Congress and future sessions to match up to Boehner's words. They are meaningless if they are not followed by concrete actions. The

112th Congress also opened the new session by having some of its members volunteer to read the U.S. Constitution on the House floor in order to emphasize the importance of the Constitution in our participatory government where the people have a voice. Again, if our elected officials do not lead by these principles and live out what they read, then they just wasted their time.

If one does not believe the people have the power to regulate government through our voting system, he or she is sadly mistaken. Compared to any other system of government across the globe, the American system of government is ingenious and superlative. The Founding Fathers were adamant in promoting the role of the government is to protect personal property, individual freedom, and the will of the governed. As such, the people play a vital role in keeping our government aligned with the founders' expectations. The voice of the American people is the engine behind our system of government. The outcome of the 2010 midterm elections is not the only example to validate the influence that ordinary Americans have in our democracy.

PEOPLE FOR BORDER SECURITY

We witnessed the power of the American people as they were energized to stand up to the dilemma of illegal immigration. The people rallied against illegal immigration on several occasions over the last several years. They did not believe the American taxpayer should have to bear the burden of those who violated our rule of law, and they were not reluctant in making sure our elected officials knew of their disgruntlement. Politics aside, the American people believe they should be taken care of above those who are not endemic to the United States and especially against those who slight our rules for citizenship. After all, this should not be too much to ask because our elected officials' primary duty is to defend the U.S. Constitution and enact policies that provide for and protect the American people. Our elected officials are obliged to the collective voice of their constituents.

The American people saw what happened when illegal immigration is dealt with in a lackluster manner with the passage of the Immigration Reform and Control Act of 1986. Albeit the verbiage of the legislation comes across as benign and directed towards border security, it actually granted legalization to undocumented aliens who had been in the United States unlawfully since 1982 and condoned employers who knowingly hired illegal immigrants. Upon signing the legislation on November 6, 1986, President Reagan announced:

> "The Immigration Reform and Control Act of 1986 is the most comprehensive reform of our immigration laws since 1952. In the past 35 years our nation has been increasingly affected by illegal immigration. This legislation takes a major step toward meeting this challenge to our sovereignty. At the same time, it preserves and enhances the Nation's heritage of legal immigration. I am pleased to sign the bill into law."[405]

Would President Reagan have the same sentiments today as illegal immigration continues to burden our society and after knowing the aftereffects of the 1986 legislation? What was meant to protect legal immigration actually mocked legal immigration while upholding illegal immigration, granting amnesty to approximately 2.7 million illegal immigrants.[406] What was meant to deter illegal immigration in the future actually set a precedent for future waves of illegal immigration. From this 1986 law, the American people understand a failure to enforce our rule of law at the time invalidated our rule of law, thus creating an unfavorable precedent to overcome. Americans understand failure to get operational control of the borders sends a message of invitation for future illegal immigrants. As such, the American people do not want a repeat of a failed policy that lessens border security and taunts American citizenship.

There is no question the American people demand border security and protection of American citizenship. In a *USA Today*/Gallup poll conducted in May 2010, 9 out of 10 Americans said it was "moderately to extremely important to them for the federal government to take steps" in 2010 to "secure the border against illegal immigration."[407] The same poll revealed "61 percent of Americans say they are very concerned that illegal immigrants are putting an unfair burden on U.S. schools, hospitals, and government services."[408] For any elected official not to comprehend what the American people desire when it comes to border security and illegal immigration, his or her service to his or her constituency needs to be questioned. It is no surprise then every time legislation dealing with border security and illegal immigration arises, the American people are there in force to ensure the right action and leadership follows from their elected officials.

The Secure America and Orderly immigration Act introduced by Senators John McCain and Edward Kennedy in 2005 was one such example. Once again, the title of the legislation sounds appealing, but as with anything else, the devil is in the details. Known as the McCain-Kennedy immigration bill, the American people did not stand behind it but were vehemently against it because it leaned in the amnesty direction. Granted this piece of legislation may have been trying to do the right thing by addressing the issue, but it would have permitted individuals who are already here unlawfully the opportunity to stay and acquire citizenship by only paying a $1,500 fine. In the American people's view this was amnesty because once again it rewarded law breakers with citizenship, this time with a nominal fine.

According to James Carafano, Janice Kephart, and Paul Rosenzweig, in discussing the demise of the McCain-Kennedy immigration bill, "Any comprehensive immigration reform program must encourage individuals to use lawful means to enter and reside in the United States. At the same time, it must effectively combat human smuggling, illegal border crossing, the use of falsified or stolen documents, and benefits fraud."[409] Anything other than this is unacceptable to the American people especially if it resembles anything close to the 1986 immigration legislation debacle.

Freelance writer Mark Landsbaum explained the differences but similarities between the two pieces of legislation: "The McCain-Kennedy bill is similar to the 1986 U.S. Immigration and Reform Act. The primary difference is the 1986 law granted amnesty to millions of illegal aliens who could prove they already had been in the country four years. The current proposal effectively would grant amnesty to those who pay a "fine" then wait six years for permanent legal status while working in the U.S. under a new classification of visa."[410] Although the bill never came up for an official vote, nearly twenty years later, our elected officials were still trying to usher in amnesty again. Where was the respect for the voice of the American people? Where was the leadership to learn from our past shortfalls?

In response to the American people's position on border security and illegal immigration, the U.S. House of Representatives passed the Border Protection, Antiterrorism, and Illegal Immigration Control Act of 2006. The bill would have made illegal immigration a felony, criminally castigated those who abet illegal immigrants, and funded approximately 700 miles of fence along the Southwest international border. Even though the bill did not ultimately become law, it did finally contain the language the American people demanded in providing strong border security and opposing illegal immigration. Even if needed legislation is not automatically and expediently passed due to the checks and balances within our legislative process, the American people still at least expect leadership on the part of their elected officials to do what is right and in accordance with their collective voice by initiating the respective legislation.

The battle for the right immigration legislation continued into 2006 as the Senate introduced the Comprehensive Immigration Reform Act. Although the bill was a revision of the 2005 McCain-Kennedy bill, it still bordered on amnesty for illegal immigrants. The bill would have granted illegal immigrants who have lived in the United States for more than five years the opportunity to apply for citizenship, only after paying fines and taxes. Those who have been in the country less than five years would have been liable to another set of restrictions. Once again, this was unacceptable to the American people because it would have been an insult to American citizenship and to all those who came to America through the legal channels. As a result of the differences between the House and the Senate, there was no comprehensive immigration reform and the battle prolonged.

In 2007, the Senate presented the Comprehensive Immigration Reform Act of 2007 or the Secure Borders, Economic Opportunity and Immigration Reform Act of 2007. Although the bill had measures to strengthen border security, more notably, the bill would have "provided legal status and a path to legal citizenship for the approximately 12-20 million (by some counts) illegal aliens currently residing in the United States, and provided them with what critics referred to as "amnesty".[41] Despite the initiatives supporting heightened border security, the American people were unyielding in their demand of elected officials to protect American citizenship from amnesty. The American people were relentless in calling their respective senators' offices to express their opposition to any sort of amnesty program. Opponents of the bill were so relentless in expressing their contempt of the Secure Borders, Economic Opportunity and Immigration Reform Act of 2007 they crashed the Senate's telephone system. This is just another example illustrating the influence the collective and mobilized voice of the American people can have in shaping national policy. Do not let the media or anyone else convince you otherwise.

As the economy began to deteriorate and grow more uncertain in 2008, the subject of illegal immigration took a backseat. It was not until December 2010, during Congress's lame duck session where the subject of illegal immigration surfaced again, this time in the form of the Development, Relief and Education for Alien Minors (DREAM) Act. Under the DREAM Act, children of illegal immigrants with a high school diploma or GED would have been able to apply for legal citizenship after completing two years of college or military service. Even though the approval rating for the 111th Congress was at an all-time low and there was just a historic election a month prior, in which elected officials were voted out of office, the Senate was not deterred in pushing the passage of the DREAM Act after it had passed the House.

Even with a significant section of the American people against the legislation, many of our elected officials were willing to see it through. Again, the biggest issue the American people had with the legislation was it not only relinquished illegal immigrants from the responsibility of legal citizenship, but it also put illegal immigrants above legalized American citizens. Such legislation would allow illegal immigrants to apply for in-state tuition and federal student loans. Senator Jeff Sessions of Alabama considered the DREAM Act to be "poorly drafted, filled with loopholes, and, by rewarding illegal behavior, will encourage future illegal immigration."[412] The sentiment expressed by the Senator is the exact same sentiment routinely and repeatedly expressed by the American people when it comes to citizenship amnesty of any sort.

The organization of Americans for Legal Immigration (ALIPAC) signaled out the inherent dangers of the DREAM Act and how amnesty was complicit within the legislation. According to ALIPAC, the waiver listed on page 5 line 21 Sec. 6 (a)(2) would have granted the Secretary of Homeland Security the authorization "to waive all of the enforcement requirements arbitrarily for any illegal aliens" he or she wants.[413] The waiver stated:

> "With respect to any benefit under this section and sections 7 through 16 of this Act, the Secretary of Homeland Security may waive the ground of inadmissibility under paragraph (1), (4),25 or (6) of section 212(a) of the Immigration and Nationality Act (8 U.S.C. 1182(a)) and the ground of deportability under paragraph (1) of section 237(a) of that Act (8 U.S.C. 1227(a)) for humanitarian purposes or family unity or when it is otherwise in the public interest."[414]

Of particular concern to the American people is since a piece of legislation with outright amnesty language would have a difficult time becoming law, there must be a look-out for legislation that indirectly promotes amnesty. Groups like ALIPAC teamed up with the American people will continue to hold our elected officials accountable in protecting American citizenship and our rule of law.

Fortunately, there was bipartisan support to prevent the DREAM Act legislation from advancing any further in the legislative process under the 111th Congress. It will be up to future congressional sessions to obey and represent the voice of the American people when it comes to blocking amnesty and protecting the American people from constitutional improprieties.

In a representative democracy, it is the people who dictate policy and not necessarily our elected officials, so acts like these, on behalf of the will of the governed, should serve as encouraging examples of how the people can influence government and policy. There is nothing wrong with divided government. In fact, it is a healthy sign of a true participatory republic. The American people realize we will never have a perfect government, but they do understand we must have a government accountable to the voice of the people and this demands unwavering leadership. Americans desire our elected officials to be more zealous in preserving our rule of law and protecting their already established constituencies versus creating new constituencies by coddling to the demands of illegal immigrants.

Although we are still in need of a remedy for our border security and illegal immigration predicaments, the American people have risen to the occasion and put a kibosh on any sort of amnesty policy for illegal immigrants from 2005 to 2010. Bold leadership by our elected officials working in tandem with the collective will of the American people is a recipe for unity of effort and symbiosis in our representative government. Our elected officials must lead in the areas in which the people deem necessary. Perhaps a quick reference to the 2010 *National Security Strategy* would remind them of this: "Our approach begins with a commitment to build a stronger foundation for American leadership, because what takes place within our borders will determine our strength and influence beyond them."[415] Once leadership is firmly established on our home front, we will be able to project our influence beyond our borders with more credibility and respect.

CHAPTER NINE
THE DANGERS OF POLITICAL CORRECTNESS

In order for our society to have a total and pure reinvigoration for love of country, we must also have a purge of political correctness that has run amok in our society. It is time to eliminate the political correctness that is distorting and covering our national heritage and identity, and simply muddling what we stand for. It is time to bring back the certainty of limited government, individual freedom, rule of law, and everything else that has set America apart and made it what it is today. We will not be able to do this if we do not bridle political correctness. Political correctness is outdoing common sense and this must be reversed. Political correctness must be removed from both our diction and actions. It is pragmatism backed by our national heritage that must dictate the way we govern and run our country. American economist and political commentator, Thomas Sowell, commented on political correctness: "In this era of political correctness, some people seem unaware that being squeamish about words can mean being blind to realities."[416] Today, we have reached the point where even our national security runs the risk of being jeopardized as a result of this runaway political correctness. Two areas in which political correctness is hindering national security are with illegal immigration and the battle against terrorism.

ILLEGAL IMMIGRATION IS MADE WORSE BY POLITICAL CORRECTNESS

One of the areas in need of drastic attention alongside our current economic morass is illegal immigration. For years, the United States seems to be snared in the domestic problem of illegal immigration with little signs of progression. Douglas Macarthur made perfect sense when he said, "I am concerned for the security of our great nation; not so much because of any threat from without, but because of the insidious forces working from within."[417] Although this statement is decades old, it could not be truer today especially now that we are living in a post 9-11 society where terrorists seek to enter our porous borders under the cover of illegal immigration. One would think that after the catastrophic effects of 9-11, it is the duty of the United States to play a more robust role against the influx of illegal immigration. The porous borders are vulnerable to the pivotal threat of terrorism and require more attention to ensure the protection and safety of the American people. Putting the controversial nature of illegal immigration aside, protecting our borders in a post 9-11 era should be a common sense thing to do. Hence, there is little room for political correctness when it comes to protecting American lives.

The events of 9-11 have brought closer scrutiny to our borders, and rightly so, but are we doing enough ten years later? The barbaric Middle East illegal aliens who were proven guilty for their participation in the 1993 World Trade Center bombing, the murders in front of the CIA headquarters in 1993, and participants in the 1998 conspiracy to bomb the subway system in New York all had one thing in common- they were all in the U.S. illegally.[418] Inclusive in that list would also be some of the 9-11 hijackers. This is no small matter, and so, illegal immigration can no longer be passively considered and dealt with especially in a post 9-11 era. Illegal immigration is a prominent issue that directly affects the American citizen and poses a grave threat to our national security, sovereignty, and culture.

The thought of knowing illegal aliens, who are potential terrorists, walking on the same soil as you and I, prompts fury, curiosity and bafflement. Even though we are killing terrorists overseas, we cannot afford to leave our back door open with unprotected borders in a post 9-11 era. After all, our terrorist enemies have designated our homeland as their battle space. Terrorists are clever and they continue to seek ways to cross our porous borders by manipulating the illegal immigration quagmire. As guardians of liberty and freedom, this should stimulate us even more to stand up against illegal immigration. As such, the fight against illegal immigration crosses all cultural, partisan, and ideological lines because it puts the lives and freedoms of legal Americans above those seeking to violate our rule of law.

PERSONALLY WORKING ALONG THE SOUTHWEST BORDER

I witnessed firsthand the porosity of our Southwest border when I worked with *Operation Jump Start* (OJS) - the partnership between the National Guard and the U.S. Customs and Border Protection from 2006 to 2008 to strengthen border security along the Southwest border. I was stunned at what I saw. I could not get over the number of illegal immigrants and the amount of illegal narcotics seized by our amazing Border Patrol? I thought to myself, "Wow, if only the American people really knew what exactly transpires along our Southwest border." At the end of the two years, I definitely walked away with a profound and sincere appreciation of the responsibilities our Border Patrol agents face each and every day in safeguarding our borders. I always knew our Border Patrol agents had a demanding job, but after seeing the complexity and unpredictability associated with the op tempo of their job in a post 9-11 era, I developed a renewed respect for them. They deserve the same respect and admiration as our law enforcement, fire protection, and military service members, for they provide the first line of defense of our homeland.

Our Border Patrol agents have done everything within their scope of work in fighting illegal immigration and keeping our borders safe from terrorism. The additional funding has brought more agents, better technology and equipment, increased infrastructure, and stable working relationships with other agencies and organizations; however, the challenge of having adequate coverage and oversight of our borders still remains. There is over 8000 miles of land and coastal borders Customs and Border Protection is responsible for and even with its current force structure and resources, it is still challenged in patrolling all of our borders. From my interaction and collaboration with border agents during OJS, I discovered the agents carried a spirit of effervescence and passion in carrying out their duties despite the demands of border security in a post 9-11 society. Former Secretary of Homeland Security Chertoff attested this sentiment about CBP agents in 2005 when he wrote, "...they are professional, they are tireless, they are dedicated, and all of them have made tremendous personal sacrifices for a cause greater than themselves."[419] Our leaders owe these noble patriots an appreciation of what they do on a daily basis and the necessary personnel, supplies, and resources to do their jobs effectively. We need leaders who put the truth of border security above political correctness and their personal agendas for career progression and self-exaltation.

The activity I witnessed along the Southwest border sticks with me to this day. As the Task Force Commander for the Tucson sector of operations, I was able to visit all the Border Patrol stations in the Tucson sector and witness their detainee cells overflowing with illegal immigrants. I was also able to witness the abundance of personal garbage left behind by illegal immigrants on our soil as they traversed our terrain. In addition, I discovered the excessive bundles of marijuana that are seized trying to cross our borders. I could not help but wonder how many bundles manage to shun detection and security? Moreover, I was able to witness the endless busloads of illegal immigrants being returned to Mexico after capture and processing. It is one thing to hear about such stories on the nightly news, but it is something all different when seen up close and personal. All of these discoveries gave me an appreciation of the magnitude of the illegal immigration complication and the challenges associated with enforcing border security in an era of international terrorism.

These were all eye-opening experiences, but there is one experience that echoes with me to this day. One day while visiting Hawaii National Guard troops in the Sasabe area of operations with two other Guardsmen, we came across a Mexican woman of about 30 years of age and her daughter of 5 years. They were wandering around in a lost and distraught manner and both were in tears and appeared mentally and physically exhausted. The area in which we found them was overflowing with thick vegetation and rugged and mountainous terrain. After speaking to the woman in Spanish, I learned the two have been lost for three days and were separated from their coyote and their group of illegal immigrants. The woman communicated their thirst and hunger and we provided them with water and granola bars. I could not help but mull if these two could get into our country just like that then professional terrorists are capable of doing the same. Although our hearts were saddened as we commiserated with the mother and child's discombobulated condition, we were not hesitant to turn them over to the Border Patrol as law breakers. We walked away satisfied because we knew we were doing the right thing enforcing our rule of law regardless of the harmless appearance of the illegal immigrants. After all, without rule of law, our rights have no meaning or value. After this enlightening day, I better understood the equation border security equals national security.

BORDER ENFORCEMENT IN TODAY'S OPERATIONAL ENVIRONMENT

According to the *National Defense Strategy of the United States of America*, "Uncertainty is the defining characteristic of today's strategic environment" as conventional threats have been replaced with asymmetrical threats.[420] In an operating environment of uncertainty where mercurial conditions of ambiguity and fluidity dominate, things are also no longer assumed and taken for granted. The dynamic nature of our terrorist adversaries prevents the U.S. from falling victim to complacency; our evolving and adaptive enemies keep the U.S. on the offensive and continuously alert. As the *National Strategy for Homeland Security* denoted:

> "We must guard against complacency and balance the sense of optimism that is fundamental to the American character with the sober recognition that despite our best efforts, future catastrophes - natural

and man-made-will occur, and thus we must always remain a prepared Nation."[421]

Part of being a prepared Nation is having secure borders and this does not mean selective enforcement. As a result of this strategic prudence, the U.S. soon realized it could not take the risk and treat border security with half-heartedness especially since border security is multi-dimensional in today's sophisticated and interdependent world. In a *Heritage Special Report*, homeland security experts James Carafano and Dave Heyman wrote: "The challenges of border security are more than just securing the border. They cut across issues of foreign policy, economic development, immigration, internal enforcement, trade, maritime commerce, air travel, rail and ground transport, and border control."[422]

Prior to 9-11, border security did not receive the same sense of urgency like it does in a post 9-11 era. According to one Border Patrol supervisor in the Yuma sector, in which I had the opportunity to work with during *Operation Jump Start*, "Border Patrol today is almost un-comparable to the past because now we do have a defined strategy with set parameters for measuring our successes and failures; where in the past, we did not have such a strategy." Shortly after 9-11, the Bush administration produced a series of national strategies pertaining to combating terrorism and protecting the homeland. As one of those strategies, the *National Border Patrol Strategy* provides the nation with focused guidance and direction on how the Border Patrol would adapt to and secure our borders from the post 9-11 threat. The act of terrorists circumventing the American immigration system and gaining entry into the U.S. to inflict havoc and mayhem was not considered far-fetched before 9-11, but it was viewed as unlikely. Some would argue the U.S. was largely viewed as impregnable prior to 9-11. On the other hand, today, it would not be a surprise if terrorist adversaries enter the U.S. under the guise of illegal immigration and settle as pseudo Americans but with the true intention of planning and executing a terrorist strike. In other words, our borders have come across more as an invitation than a physical albatross to foreign visitors to include possible terrorists.

Of particular concern has been the crossing of Arabic men over the U.S.-Mexico border. They have mingled in with the illegal population and exploited our penetrable borders. Could these Middle Eastern illegals be part of the next 9-11? A local newspaper in Tombstone, Arizona, the *Tombstone Tumbleweed*, reported that on June 13, 2004, Border Patrol (BP) agents came across about 158 illegal aliens near the foothills of Chiricahua Mountains. Border Patrol gained control of only 71 of these individuals, 53 of which were Middle Eastern males and spoke Arabic. An unnamed Border Patrol agent told the newspaper: "…We are told not to say a thing to the media, but I have to." Border Patrol spokesman Andy Adame denied that any middle-easterners were in this group. A week later, Wilcox Border Patrol station seized another group of illegals which included 24 Arabic speaking males in Cochise County. Half of this group escaped seizure and disappeared into the U.S. Andy Adame did release a statement saying that from October 2003 through June 2004, BP agents in the Tucson sector alone had seized 5,510 illegals from countries other than Mexico or other Central or South American countries.[423] As concerned and nationalistic Americans, what are we supposed to think after reading information like this? Does this activity insinuate preparation for another 9-11?

According to a hearing before the Select Committee on Intelligence, al Qaeda leaders are attracted to the porous Southwest border and believe that "illegal entry is more advantageous than legal entry for operational security reasons."[424] Our vulnerability in border security has been universally exposed and our enemies desire to take advantage of that vulnerability. The number of illegal immigrants entering the U.S. from Mexico is preposterous, but of particular concern is the increased number of Other-Than-Mexican (OTM) apprehensions that have occurred along our borders since 9-11. While the number of Mexican illegal immigrant apprehensions has remained relatively stable over the years, the number of OTM apprehensions has been on the rise. For example, the number of OTM apprehensions has more than doubled from 37,316 in FY2002 to 75,389 in FY2004.[425] Of these apprehensions, there has been a striking increase of OTM apprehensions along the Southwest border. More specifically, the stark increases of OTM apprehensions along the Texas border attract the most attention. OTM apprehensions increased by 613% in the Del Rio sector, 258% in the Laredo sector, and 429% in the McAllen sector.[426] According to Arizona Sheriff Paul Babeu for Pinal County, more than 20 percent of illegal immigrants passing through his county are OTMs with some having origins from "nations of interest" known for supporters of terrorists to include Iran, Yemen, Somalia, and Jordan.[427] These startling facts should be of concern for every American and an incentive to do away with political correctness when it comes to illegal immigration.

If these above statistics are not striking enough, they only represent apprehensions and not the OTMs that have eluded apprehension and now coexist within our society. The high numbers alone are only part of the problem; the other part of the problem is the dearth of available Border Patrol resources to house OTMs. Since DHS [Department of Homeland Security] lacks the detention facilities to accommodate every single apprehended OTM, "the majority of the OTMs that are apprehended are released on their own recognizance or on bond into the interior."[428] The concern is the accountability of these OTMs once they are released into the masses. Once the OTMs are released into American society, it is nearly impossible to track and monitor their whereabouts and actions. Border security coupled with reformed immigration policy devoid of political correctness is essential in maintaining national security, public safety, and civic order.

According to the *National Strategy for Combating Terrorism*, "A key component of any nation's sovereignty is control of its borders."[429] If this is really the case, then why is there political correctness in dealing with border security? This statement is succinct and direct, leaving no room for political correctness. The strategy makes it clear there is a link between a nation's sovereignty and its borders. A nation that loses control of its borders contracts external defiance and provocation which eventually leads to internal complications. This is particularly true in a post 9-11 society where borders do not act as an impediment to terrorists, as displayed by the shrewd and impudent actions of the 9-11 terrorist hijackers and the continued lawbreakers who cross our borders illegally.

In his letter in the *National Strategy for Homeland Security*, President Bush declared, "The U.S. government has no more important mission than protecting the homeland from future terrorist attacks."[430] With the possibility of terrorists further exploiting our feeble borders and our tolerance of multiculturalism in a globalized and an open border society, border security and national security have become one; they are inseparable and now work in tandem with one another. This point on globalization is further highlighted in the *Strategy for Homeland Defense and Civil Support*: "Transnational terrorist groups view the world, as an integrated, global battle space in which to exploit perceived U.S. vulnerabilities, wherever they may be."[431] A nation that freely embraces globalization at the same time it neglects its borders opens itself up to the terrorist threat. Although it is impossible for the U.S. to be 100% secure from all attempted attacks, border security is one way in which it can mitigate this vulnerability.

There have been reports revealing the terrorist group Hezbollah from Libya has been using our porous borders as a channel into the U.S. Writer Jane Jamison wrote: "There is ever-growing evidence that Middle East terrorists tied to the Lebanon-based Hezbollah are now working in conjunction with Mexican and Central American narco-cartels in Mexico and in the United States."[432] Congresswoman Sue Myrick of North Carolina, member of the House Permanent Select Committee on Intelligence, has been vocal on this issue, bringing awareness to our government, the general public, and our own Department of Homeland Security. According to the Congresswoman, "We know some of them have gotten across the border in the past, and now we know that there are people from Iran who are going to Venezuela. They are actually learning Spanish, and then they come up through Mexico to cross our border. So they're working in cahoots with Venezuela as well."[433] With such real and adaptable threats out there like Hezbollah, why would we want to make ourselves vulnerable for the sake of political correctness? We should not have to explain our intentions in enforcing border security in a post 9-11 era because we have the right to protect our people, individual freedoms, and system of government. We need more elected officials like Sue Myrick to question our porous borders and seek enforcement mechanisms versus being absorbed in political correctness. We must continue to ask our elected officials, "Does the political correctness of embracing illegal immigration rise above the security, identity, and sovereignty of our nation?

This very real threat of terrorists using our porous borders as a pathway into the U.S. cannot be dealt with lightly. According to Assistant Professor Paul Smith, "…in an age of international terrorism where modern terrorists must travel to multiple countries to either raise money, cultivate support, or conduct attacks," the vulnerability of U.S. border security cannot simply be dismissed as merely an immigration issue or social policy question."[434] In January 2011, Fox News reported that a Border Patrol agent in the Casa Grande sector in the Arizona desert found the book *In Memory of Our Martyrs*. The book celebrates suicide bombers and consisted of "short biographies of Islamic suicide bombers and other Islamic militants who died carrying out attacks" along with "letters from suicide attackers to their families, as well as some of their last wills and testaments."[435] The threat from our open borders goes far beyond innocent illegal immigrants. Due to the credible threat of terrorists masquerading themselves as illegal immigrants to gain entrance into our homeland, we must stay committed to enhanced border security.

Our Southwest border receives plenty of attention in the news, but we cannot overlook our long Northern border. It is just as likely to be breached by illegal immigrants, drug traffickers, and international terrorists. According to the U.S. Government Accountability Office (GAO), only "32 of the nearly 4,000 northern border miles in fiscal year 2010 had reached an acceptable level of security."[436] In reference to the GAO report, Michigan Congresswoman Candice Miller of Michigan voiced her concerns: "It is unacceptable to have such vulnerabilities along our northern border where we have only a handful of miles that are under operational control. To date, we are still waiting for the Administration to put forth a detailed program to secure the border. We need to gain operational control of the entire border, both north and south, and I intend on holding a hearing which examines how the Border Patrol measures operational control of the border and how to improve our coordination of those efforts."[437] Whether it is our northern or southern border, illegal immigrants, drug traffickers, and terrorists only care about getting across our borders. Where there is a will, there is a way by both terrorists and scofflaws, and as a result, we must have border security around the entire homeland.

According to Robert Bonner, the U.S. Customs and Border Protection Commissioner, "U.S. Customs and Border Protection are addressing the terrorist threat 24-hours a day. We have a multi-layered approach that encompasses working with our foreign counterparts, employing intelligence, technology, advanced information in the field and the most professional workforce worldwide."[438] There is no question about it, one of the most demanding challenges that the U.S. has in a post 9-11 era is to defend and protect our ample borders. The events of 9-11 sent a painful message to the American people that the U.S. is no longer an unassailable country physically secluded from our enemies by the surrounding oceans. As a result, Border Patrol assumed the top priority of preventing terrorists and terrorist weapons from crossing our borders into our homeland. In order to attain this objective, Border Patrol has and continues to undergo significant changes to its organization in an array of facets. Yes, an enhanced Border Patrol is not the complete remedy for the illegal immigration fiasco, but with the interference of political correctness, all of Border Patrol's advancements would be for nothing.

One would think with all this emphasis on border security as outlined in our different national strategies there would not be political correctness in addressing illegal immigration. As a result of this negligence all these years where the prefix "illegal" has been disconnected from "immigration", a countless number of illegal immigrants have taken American citizenship in their own hands and settled in the U.S. on their own accord. According to the U.S. Census Bureau's 2000 estimate, over seven million illegal aliens were living in the US.[439] With each passing year, the number of illegal immigrants in our country has steadily risen. This is proof when we condone and reward illegality, the only thing we get is more of it. The Urban Institute Immigration Studies Program estimated 9.3 million undocumented immigrants were in our country by 2004.[440] In January 2009, the Department of Homeland Security estimated the number of illegal immigrants in the U.S. to be about 10.8 million.[441] As far as the current illegal population today, well, I have heard reports of numbers as high as fifteen million. Yes, I said 15 million. Regardless of the number, any number is unacceptable. How can we ensure a safe ambience within our homeland with millions of undocumented aliens doing their own thing, on their terms, and plainly ignoring our nation's immigration laws? After all, in a post 9-11 society, heightened border security equates to the prevention of the next attack on our homeland.

ILLEGAL IS ILLEGAL

If we are going to adequately enforce our borders we are going to have to be honest with one another and tell it the way it is. The severity of illegal immigration has been distorted by political correct behavior. Thanks to political correctness, the demarcation of illegal versus legal has been erased. When political correct advocates use the term "immigrant" to describe an illegal immigrant, they fail to also associate the term "illegal" with it. Illegal immigrants are being categorized as simply immigrants. An illegal immigrant is not analogous to a legal immigrant for many reasons. Just ask any immigrant who has respected our rule of law and went through the legal process of becoming a legal American citizen. Where is our leadership in distinguishing the difference between the two types of immigration? Despite our nation being built on the rule of law, our very law of citizenry is shamelessly and continually abused by illegal immigration. In a post 9-11 society, it is too dangerous to ignore our rule of law by conflating "illegal" with "legal" immigration. The further we move away from 9-11, political correctness abounds as the tolerance for risk also continues to rise.

It is time to draw the line somewhere with illegal immigration. The best place to start is with the strict enforcement of our existing laws because a civil society is based off rule of law. Along with the enforcement of national security, the enforcement of our rule of law is incompatible with political correctness. The breach of our rule of law is an illegal act no matter how meager it may seem and not enforcing it as such sends disastrous signals. In fact, we are currently sending the message that it is ok to be here illegally.

Our rule of law is essential to who we are as a republic and a people, so why would we want to compromise it in any way? One of the things that have set us apart from other nations has been the establishment of our rule of law and its consequent civic order. When you enforce the law, obedience ensues. Moreover, when we enforce rule of law, objectivity is enforced over subjectivity. In an age where people do things subjectively and what is right in their own eyes, objectivity is a necessity. Indeed, our immigration policy needs to be revamped to expedite the process of making immigrants legal; however, in the meantime, that does not permit us to compromise our rule of law. Regardless of the law broken, it is still a broken law. In the case of an illegal immigrant, anyone who is in our country without the legal authorization is a lawbreaker. In an age of globalization, multiculturalism, and international terrorism, the enforcement of our rule of law is our greatest weapon and source of hope against illegal immigration. Will we adhere to it?

When we get in the business of picking and choosing which laws we do and do not enforce, based off likability, we set an awful precedent and undermine our rule of law. Instead, we must enforce our rule of law; from the simplest to the most complex laws, every law must be upheld and enforced as such. Take for example a domestic incident in Largo, Florida. A grandmother was arrested as a result of slapping her 18 year-old granddaughter across the face and her granddaughter later calling the local police on her. Florida law permits the slapping of children up to the age of seventeen. Despite the granddaughter's eventual plea for the police not to arrest her grandmother and the fact that the granddaughter just turned 18 years old, the local police did not waiver in enforcing the law and sending the grandmother to jail. According to Largo Police Lieutenant Mike Loux, "We have a mandatory arrest policy when dealing with domestic violence charges."[442] There was no picking and choosing here; local authorities adhered to Florida law. This incident revealed the line between legality and illegality is black and white. This is just a microcosm of how our rule of law should be enforced at the federal level. Perhaps, if we used this same simple treatment of enforcing our rule of law to fight illegal immigration and reneging political correctness, we would have a safer and a more secure border in a post 9-11 society.

THE AMERICAN PEOPLE PAY THE PRICE

It is not only our rule of law that is damaged when we exercise political correctness instead of protecting American citizenship and holding illegal immigrants accountable. The American people also pay the price and suffer from the political correctness associated with illegal immigration. Our own people who are legal American citizens, who pay their taxes, who desire assimilation into our culture, who love America, and who want to do what is right are carrying the burdens of illegal immigration in several ways. The onerous ramifications of ignoring illegal immigration have reached Americans living in both border and even non-border states across our country. As the illegal immigration problem spreads and worsens, Americans across the country are no longer immune from its aftereffects.

For one, in many cases throughout the nation, the effects of illegal immigration have been felt up close and personal by the American people. Whether as victims of vehicle accidents, negligent acts, or senseless crimes from illegal immigrants, the American people are the ones who suffer from our nation's political correctness. Our inaction to deal with this issue has brought harm and even death to

Americans as a result of fractious acts by illegal immigrants. When we do not enforce our rule of law, it is the American people that pay, every time.

  Although the stories of American people suffering as a result of inconsiderate actions by illegal immigrants are endless, here are a few. The Marti family from Idaho is no longer a united family due to an illegal immigrant. Sean Marti (24 years of age) and his five year old daughter, Sage, were killed by a drunk illegal immigrant who was driving in the wrong direction on Highway 84 in Idaho. As a result of the head-on collision, Natalie Marti fell into a coma, and fortunately, she awoke several weeks later but without her husband and daughter by her side. Here was a young couple who managed an apartment complex in Idaho stripped of their happiness and family from a careless act by an illegal immigrant. How about Stanley Hope who lost his wife to an illegal immigrant? Daniel Gonzalez Berumen of Mexico killed Kimberley in the process of stealing the family car. Our own neighborhoods are threatened by illegal immigrants who do not belong here. Then there is five year old Felix Leon who died from a hit and run accident. Felix was struck by two illegal immigrants in a truck while he was riding his bike near his house in Brownsville, Texas.[443] One cannot help but ask, "if we were more aggressive in standing up to illegal immigration, would these Americans still be alive?'

  Our own law enforcement officers across the country have even been victims of heinous and brutal crimes by illegal immigrants. Some of our very heroes who ensure our public safety on a daily basis have lost their lives. In 2006, Officer Rodney Johnson of the Houston Police Department lost his life for no reason when he was shot in the head by an illegal immigrant after a routine traffic stop. Joslyn Johnson, the officer's wife, who is also part of the Houston Police Department, claimed "her husband would be alive today if the city had bothered to check up on the gunman's immigration status."[444] The thing that is alarming and disturbing at the same time with this case is the illegal immigrant had been deported once and arrested at least three times prior to this fatal shooting.[445] It is reasonable to assume that if this illegal immigrant was properly screened and dealt with through our immigration channels, Joslyn Johnson would never be bemoaning her husband's death.

Officer Tony Zeppetella of the Oceanside Police Department lost his life after being shot by Adrian George Camacho, a five-time convicted felon and twice-deported illegal immigrant from Mexico.[446] Officer Zeppetella was simply doing a routine traffic stop when Camacho opened fire on him. How about Detective Donald Young of the Denver Police Department who was shot and killed by Raul Garcia-Gomez, an illegal immigrant who had been arrested three times prior to Young's execution.[447] Garcia-Gomez also shot and wounded Young's partner, Detective John Bishop. The two detectives were simply working off-duty as security guards at a private baptismal party at which the assailant was also attending. In this particular case, since the illegal immigrant fled back to Mexico, Mexico will not extradite the evildoer back to the U.S. if there is a likelihood of the death penalty. Then there is Shane Figueroa of the Phoenix Police Department who was killed when a drunken illegal immigrant crashed his truck into Figueroa's patrol car.[448] What is sad is the fact that Salvador Vivas-Diaz, the drunken illegal immigrant, had a history of driving under the influence and a record of deportation.[449] Again, more examples of families left without husbands and fathers and police departments without brave heroes due to the mindless acts of illegal immigrants. When do we say enough is enough and start standing up to illegal immigration with decisive resolution and respect for our rule of law instead of kowtowing to political correctness?

This is just a sample of American people suffering at the hands of illegal immigrants. The list of victims goes on, but as you can see, the criminal activity of illegal immigrants does not discriminate against gender, age or location. As the number of illegal immigrants crossing our borders increases, we can only infer that the number of people who will experience personal violations from illegal immigrants will also directly increase. Not everybody that comes to the United States appreciates our values, liberties, laws and our way of life. Why should our own people have to fear becoming victims of illegal immigrants' reckless and out-of-control behavior? American people have the right to feel safe and secure in their own nation especially since our constitutional government is charged with providing Americans life, liberty, and the pursuit of happiness.

This is not to label every single illegal immigrant as an evil person, but it is necessary to highlight the ramifications of what happens when we fail to properly enforce our rule of law. Time and time again we hear that illegal immigrants come to the U.S. solely and innocently to find work in order to provide for their families; however, the aforementioned examples tell otherwise. Who can blame them for wanting to come to our great country which is overflowing with employment opportunities, freedoms, and the comforts of life? Furthermore, by coming to America, they are able to escape the corruption, destitution, drug cartel violence, and the deplorable standard of living inside Mexico. Despite Mexico's challenges and our sympathies for the people of Mexico, this still does not permit us to exercise political correctness and push aside our own rule of law.

The issue is not whether or not an illegal immigrant is a nice or hard working individual, but the issue is a matter of what is right and wrong. Yes, we may be sympathetic to illegal immigrants' unfortunate condition, but that does not mean we have to tolerate their abuse of our rule of law. The one thing that gives foreign nationals who are not legal American citizens the chutzpah to direct our policies is our inaction in enforcing our rule of law. If you really and honestly think about it, when we enforce border security, we are actually taking a pro-immigration position because we are preserving national order and our immigration process.

Besides the breach of our national security and rule of law along with putting American lives in jeopardy, the American people also are burdened with excessive taxes from illegal immigration. For the average taxpayer, the cost is no laughing matter. Focusing on the state of Arizona, according to the Federation for American Immigration Reform (FAIR), the illegal immigration population is costing the Arizona taxpayer approximately $2.9 billion per year for education, medical care, social welfare, incarceration, and other expenses. FAIR believes "illegal immigrants take $1.6 billion from Arizona's education system, $694.8 million from health care services, $339.7 million in law enforcement and court costs, $85.5 million in welfare costs and $155.4 million in other general costs."[450] Illegal immigrants in Arizona have flooded Arizona's classrooms, hospitals, and prisons, all at the expense of the Arizona taxpayer due to political correctness in addressing illegal immigration. This certainly does not fall in line with American citizens being protected from the unwarranted infringement of foreign nationals on American soil as outlined in the Preamble of the U.S. Constitution: "We the People of the United States, in Order to form a more perfect Union, establish Justice, insure domestic Tranquility, provide for the common defense, promote the general Welfare, and secure the Blessings of Liberty to ourselves and our Posterity, do ordain and establish this Constitution for the United States of America."[451]

"ILLEGAL" VERSUS "LEGAL" IMMIGRATION AND "EXPLOITATION" VERSUS "ASSIMILATION"

When distinguishing illegal immigrants from legal immigrants it is important to point out the assimilation aspect of becoming a legalized American citizen. While earlier waves of immigrants came to America with the intention of going through the legal channels and with the desire to assimilate into the American culture, today's illegal immigrants come with the intention of deflecting the legal channels and with the lack of desire to assimilate. Their motive of breaking the law from the get-go suggests an avoidance of American assimilation. I cannot think of a clearer indicator of someone wanting to be an American than becoming a citizen through the legal and right channels. We must enforce the expectation that those wishing to obtain American citizenship must want to be an American and want to contribute to the culture of our country. Anything less should not be accepted nor tolerated because with American citizenship comes both responsibilities and obligations.

As an American citizen, there is an obligation to a common language, a common culture, a common national heritage, a common set of principles and values, a common rule of law, a common dream centered on life, liberty, and the pursuit of happiness, and a common purpose. Anyone wanting to come to America and lacks any of these commonalities should think twice before stepping foot on American soil. Besides, why would you want to be here if you do not possess these things? I know I would not want to reside somewhere else if I did not possess a true longing to fit in.

We have always been categorized as a melting pot of different ethnic groups and religions conforming to the American culture. The United States was built on immigrants wanting to assimilate and be American, not for them wanting to have their own ethnic groups and doing their own thing without any deference to the American culture. As a child growing up, I recall hearing my grandparents tell joyous stories of how earlier generations of our family came over to the United States and gladly embraced the American way of life. They were simply glad to be here because they knew they had it better off and desired to do what was necessary to become an American citizen. They understood that coming to America meant renouncing their home country. They further grasped the concept that citizenship means much more than simply being physically located in the country. They understood the loyalty involved to our culture and nation in general.

Personally, it is refreshing to look back on history and examine how my family's historical roots embodied the edification and not the marginalization of American citizenship. Like many Americans, I am the product of legal immigration. For example, my great grandfather, his wife, and three children immigrated to America from Germany in the 1920s. My great grandfather was conscripted in the German Army in 1914 and after his training, he soon found himself fighting the Russians in World War I. He was wounded as a bullet pierced his groin area and exited out his hip without shattering any bones. After fainting, he regained his composure and somehow dragged himself about a mile to a horse-drawn wagon where two soldiers helped him on it. As a result of his perseverance, he avoided being captured by the Russians. It was his vigor to live on the battlefield and his later move to America that has given rise to my family. Hence, I am a delighted recipient of legal immigration and an advocate of pro-immigration based off the needs of our country.

Respect for American citizenship and culture was evident among my great grandfather and his family. According to my great uncle, under my great grandfather's leadership, his children were taught to be law abiding and good citizens. He taught them the value of American citizenship; nothing was taken for granted. It is with great joy that I can review the family's documented diaspora from Germany to the United States and confirm this sentiment of respect for American citizenship. The copies of their official travel and citizenship documents clearly reveal immigrants who possessed a genuine passion to become LEGAL American citizens. Their signed Declaration of Intention form states:

> "...It is my bona fide attention to renounce forever all allegiance and fidelity to any foreign prince, potentate, state, or sovereignty, and particularly to Republic of Germany or (and) German Empire, of whom I am now a subject; ...and it is my intention in good faith to become a citizen of the United States of America and to permanently reside therein: SO HELP ME GOD."

I am proud to be associated with family members who had pride in America and desired legal American citizenship. Where is this same sentiment of respect for American citizenship today? Exploitation is replacing assimilation and acculturation when it comes to illegal immigration.

Unfortunately this same sentiment of assimilation is missing today from illegal immigrants as they hold on to the cultural and social traditions and ideologies of their country of origin. Instead of allegiance to America by illegal immigrants, we get just the opposite. At one rally in Los Angeles, in response to the Arizona SB1070 immigration law, one Hispanic gentleman carried a sign saying:

> "GIVE US FREE HEALTH CARE
> JOBS- NO TAXES
> HOUSE FOOD
> YOU <u>OWE</u> US AMERICA!
> WE WILL SHOOT MORE POLICE IN ARIZONA
> UNTIL WE GET FREE!"[452]

Such signs do not suggest American assimilation and allegiance but do hint at exploitation. We must demand that we remain a nation of Americans and not a nation of quasi-Americans. As President Theodore Roosevelt so adequately declared, "We can have no "50-50" allegiance in this country. Either a man is an American and nothing else, or he is not an American at all."[453] Wow, where is this sentiment today? By eliminating political correctness when it comes to illegal immigration, we would be emphasizing the point that all immigrants must incorporate America into their lives. Moreover, it would put an emphasis back on the importance of American citizenship.

BORDERS HAVE A PURPOSE

In addressing border security, radio commentator Dr. Michael Savage says it the best and in the most succinct manner out of all the pundits, elected officials, and administrators: "A nation is defined by its borders, language, and culture." Borders have given nations their identity, warranting them their national sovereignty. Within a nation's borders, a nation gives rise to a distinctive culture, language, value system, and general countenance, all of which are designed to provide commonality and a spirit of community among its inhabitants. When borders are not enforced, a nation's identity is potentially compromised. Samuel Huntington affirmed this in reference to the unrestraint Mexican immigration into America: "The persistent inflow of

Hispanic immigrants threatens to divide the United States into two peoples, two cultures, and two languages."[454] The everlasting flow of Mexican immigration, both illegal and legal, combined with the lack of assimilation into the American culture by today's immigrants, is a recipe for a disruption with our immigration management, thus leading to cultural strife. The unwillingness of today's immigrants to embrace the cultural ethos and etiquette of America, while maintaining loyalty to their native country, goes against the whole purpose of having an immigration system and challenges America's national identity and sovereignty. A tepid attitude on the importance and appreciation of borders and legal immigration along with the post 9-11 terrorism threat only heightens the need to wipe out political correctness as it relates to border security. Border security cannot be underestimated but must be addressed with a genuine spirit of pro-action versus reaction.

As ironic as it may sound, perhaps we can take a lesson from our southern neighbor, Mexico, in enforcing border security. Mexico curtails illegal immigration simply by the fact it does not put up with political correctness when it comes to protecting its borders. Illegal immigrants from Central and South America defy Mexican immigration laws, but unlike the United States, Mexico stands on its immigration rule of law and does not care about hurting people's feelings. Political commentator Michelle Malkin wrote an article entitled *"How Mexico Treats its Illegal Immigrants"* where she discussed Mexico's strict and intransigent enforcement of their immigration laws:

> "Illegal entry into the country is equivalent to a felony punishable by two years' imprisonment. Document fraud is subject to fine and imprisonment; so is alien marriage fraud. Evading deportation is a serious crime; illegal re-entry after deportation is punishable by ten years' imprisonment. Foreigners may be kicked out of the country without due process and the endless bites at the litigation apple that illegal aliens are afforded in our country."[455]

There is just no tolerance for anything other than border enforcement and immigration adherence in Mexico. Such assertive action contributes to Mexico not having a similar illegal immigration conundrum like in the U.S.

Under the Mexican Constitution, the *Ley General de Población*, or General Law on Population, it is clear there is a no-nonsense approach in dealing with illegal immigrants. Journalist and author, Dr. Waller, broke down Mexico's immigration law, pointing out its intransigence:

> "Foreigners with fake papers, or who enter the country under false pretenses, may be imprisoned:
>
> • Foreigners with fake immigration papers may be fined or imprisoned. (Article 116)
>
> • Foreigners who sign government documents "with a signature that is false or different from that which he normally uses" are subject to fine and imprisonment. (Article 116)
>
> Foreigners who fail to obey the rules will be fined, deported, and/or imprisoned as felons:
>
> • Foreigners who fail to obey a deportation order are to be punished. (Article 117)
>
> • Foreigners who are deported from Mexico and attempt to re-enter the country without authorization can be imprisoned for up to 10 years. (Article 118)
>
> • Foreigners who violate the terms of their visa may be sentenced to up to six years in prison (Articles 119, 120 and 121). Foreigners who misrepresent the terms of their visa while in Mexico – such as working without a permit – can also be imprisoned.
>
> Under Mexican law, illegal immigration is a felony. The General Law on Population says,

• A penalty of up to two years in prison and a fine of three hundred to five thousand pesos will be imposed on the foreigner who enters the country illegally. (Article 123)

• Foreigners with legal immigration problems may be deported from Mexico instead of being imprisoned. (Article 125)

• Foreigners who "attempt against national sovereignty or security" will be deported. (Article 126)"[456]

While there is definite criticism of the United States protecting its borders, both from within and without our borders, especially as states such as Arizona institute state immigration policies, we hear very little opposition on Mexico enforcing its own borders through its stern immigration policies. Odd enough, it appears as if Mexico is encouraging us to be casual with our immigration laws, while it has more hawkish immigration policies. Where is the outcry on Mexico's lack of political correctness and firm resolution against illegal immigration? Although we are not in the business of replicating the ways of other countries, Mexico has this one right when it comes to enforcing rule of law. It stands firm in protecting and enforcing legal immigration. And this is something to emulate because every single country has the right to protect its people, freedoms, borders, and government.

Let's not forget what Article IV Section 4 of the U.S. Constitution says: "The United States shall guarantee to every State in this Union a Republican Form of Government, and shall protect each of them against Invasion; and on Application of the Legislature, or of the Executive (when the Legislature cannot be convened) against domestic Violence."[457] Indeed, immigration is an issue for the federal government; however, once illegal immigrants set foot on a state's soil, it is the people of the respective state that are left with the burdens of illegal immigration. Illegal immigration cannot be ignored at the state level because many of the states' problems like crime, education, hospital care, and financial distress are tied to illegal immigration. Therefore, a state has no other repercussion than to act on behalf of their inhabitants; they are forced into action. As contentious as the issue of illegal immigration may be, when political correctness is left out, solutions arise as the most complex problems are dealt with and with favorable results. The state of Missouri has proven this.

THE RIGHT POLICY HAS PROVEN TO RETARD ILLEGAL IMMIGRATION

Within the last few years, Missouri has enacted a series of laws reflecting in accordance with the U.S. Constitution to derail illegal immigration in its state. The leaders of Missouri have taken an active role in looking out for the safety, security, and general well-being of its people. This is exactly what the majority of the American people are demanding on a national level. For starters, Missouri added a new section to Article 1 of its Constitution. Section 34 now reads:

> "That English shall be the language of all official proceedings in this state. Official proceedings shall be limited to any meeting of a public governmental body at which any public business is discussed, decided, or public policy formulated, whether such meeting is conducted in person or by means of communication equipment, including, but not limited to, conference call, video conference, Internet chat, or Internet message board. The term "official proceeding" shall not include an informal gathering of members of a public governmental body for ministerial or social purposes, but the term shall include a public vote of all or a majority of the members of a public governmental body, by electronic communication or any other means, conducted in lieu of holding an official proceeding

with the members of the public governmental body gathered at one location in order to conduct public business."[458]

In all actuality, this is not too much to ask because if immigrants truly want to assimilate into the American culture, they would make every effort to learn the English language as former immigrants have done. We should be concerned today because the appetite to learn English by illegal immigrants is absent. Since many illegal immigrants show tendencies of being illiterate in even their own language, it is reasonable to assume there would be a minimal sense of urgency on their part in learning English. We cannot forget that the English language is still the official language of America despite the influences of multiculturalism and globalization. We also cannot forget that the native language of a country serves as a primary binding element for that country's inhabitants.

Missouri has also implemented HB 1549 in 2008. Under this legislation, "Subject to appropriation, the superintendent of the Missouri state highway patrol shall designate that some or all members of the highway patrol be trained in accordance with a memorandum of understanding between the state of Missouri and the United States Department of Homeland Security concerning the enforcement of federal immigration laws during the course of their normal duties in the state of Missouri, in accordance with 8 U.S.C. Section 1357(g)."[459] The bill permitted law officials in Missouri the authority to verify the immigration status of those who are arrested. This is just another logical measure to enforce our rule of law, to keep American citizens safe, and to hold non-citizens accountable.

Missouri used this same legislation to keep illegal immigrants off the state's dole. Again, Missouri put its citizens first by taking a bold stand devoid of political correctness against illegal immigration. The elements of HB 1549 serve as a deterrent for illegal immigrants from exploiting public benefits. For example, under HB 1549:

"No alien unlawfully present in the United States shall receive any state or local public benefit, except for state or local public benefits that may be offered under 8 U.S.C. 1621(b). Nothing in this section shall be construed to prohibit the rendering of emergency medical care, prenatal care, services offering alternatives to abortion, emergency assistance, or legal assistance to any person.

As used in this section, "public benefit" means any grant, contract, or loan provided by an agency of state or local government; or any retirement, welfare, health, postsecondary education, state grants and scholarships, disability, housing, or food assistance benefit under which payments, assistance, credits, or reduced rates or fees are provided. The term "public benefit" shall not include unemployment benefits payable under chapter 288, RSMo. The unemployment compensation program shall verify the lawful presence of an alien for the purpose of determining eligibility for benefits in accordance with its own procedures.

In addition to providing proof of other eligibility requirements, at the time of application for any state or local public benefit, an applicant who is eighteen years of age or older shall provide affirmative proof that the applicant is a citizen or a permanent resident of the United States or is lawfully present in the United States, provided, however, that in the case of state grants and scholarships, such proof shall be provided before the applicant receives any state grant or scholarship. Such affirmative proof shall include documentary evidence recognized by the department of revenue when processing an application for a driver's license, a Missouri driver's license, as well as any document issued by the federal government that confirms an alien's lawful presence in the United States. In processing applications for public benefits, an employee of an agency of state or local government shall not inquire about the legal status of a custodial parent or guardian applying for a public benefit on behalf of his or her dependent child who is a citizen or permanent resident of the United States."[460]

For a third year in a row, in 2009, Missouri passed another piece of legislation to block illegal immigrants from coming to Missouri. This time Missouri acted to keep illegal immigrants from taking advantage of college benefits. Under HB 390, "No covered student unlawfully present in the United States shall receive a postsecondary education public benefit. Educational institutions awarding postsecondary education public benefits to covered students shall verify that these students are United States citizens, permanent residents, or lawfully present in the United States."[461] HB 390 is another successful measure which does not reward illegality and protects legal citizens.

There is nothing extreme or out-of-the-ordinary with the above parts of HB 1549. In fact, Missouri's success in dealing with illegal immigration has incited other states such as Arizona, Minnesota, Pennsylvania, Ohio, and others to stand up to illegal immigration. Missouri's immigration laws do nothing but encourage integration and assimilation which in turn discourages tolerance of political correctness. They simply promote our rule of law and protect American citizenship, which I am sure every legal immigrant is an advocate of especially since they took the pure initiative to become an American citizen the right way.

I am reminded of an episode of the *Undercover Boss,* in which a 7-11 delivery driver named Igor from Kazakhstan explained how he became an American citizen. He came to the United States with only fifty dollars but more importantly with an internal passion and humbled spirit to be a legal American citizen. What was even more respected was the fact that while he worked at nights, his wife worked during the days, giving them little time with one another. Like many legal immigrants and Americans, they were chasing the American dream by making ends meet as a family and without shortcuts. Like many Americans, I personally find it both inspiring and refreshing to hear stories of immigrants coming to our country through the legal channels with the sole purpose of being an American citizen and contributing to the good of America.

The 2010 *National Security Strategy* stated: "Our national security begins at home. What takes place within our borders has always been the source of our strength, and this is even truer in an age of interconnection."[462] Hence, there is a need for border security. If we are serious with our national strategies and adhere to what we put on paper, then there is absolutely no room for political correctness and the well-being of our country should take priority when it comes to dealing with illegal immigration. The rejection of political correctness in dealing with illegal immigration will bring about stronger border security. Tougher border security will bring about a reduction in the challenges tied to illegal immigration, a decrease in the infiltration of illegal narcotics across our borders, and a hindrance to terrorists' infringement. There is nothing abstruse here. What American would not want these pro-American initiatives to protect our homeland and its citizens in an era of unease and uncertainty?

POLITICAL CORRECTNESS AND NATIONAL SECURITY DO NOT MIX

As the adage goes, "There is a time and place for everything." Well, in a post 9-11 society, there is never a time or place for political correctness especially when it comes to defending our homeland from our enemies. Today, terrorism is not limited to a single act or event, but it is an ongoing process fueled by an unconventional ideology. The contemporary threat of terrorism has proven its effectiveness in unleashing death and destruction, altering our behavior, wielding fear and intimidation, and influencing our policies. There is no room for political correctness in the fight against terrorism because it is credible and viable as its tentacles have a global reach, endangering the national security of the United States in our interconnected society. Political correctness only causes distraction and it redirects our attention from the serious and complex challenges of today.

The starting points in addressing political correctness as it relates to national security are to first identify evil and call it for what it is. Evil exists and will always exist. In addition, no matter what we do as a country, there will always be other countries that have a strong animosity for America. Evil is evil and there is no room for misinterpretation nor compromise. Evil will always find a way to seep through and it will be up to us to reject it for morality.

Throughout our history, evil has come in many different forms: fascism, Marxism, Nazism, and communism. No matter what the "ism" may have been at the time, evil has showed its ugly face around the globe throughout history. And each time evil has surfaced and posed a threat to our national security, we were mobilized as a unified front at home and we overcame evil by righteous and assertive action minus political correctness and unnecessary sensitivity. The threat of terrorism today is no different for it rivals everything our nation stands for and challenges our national grit. This enduring and evolving threat will only be conquered if we keep political correctness separated from our terrorist enemy's true nature.

KNOW YOUR ENEMY

The basic tenet of any conflict is to know and appreciate your enemy. You cannot defeat your enemy until you define it. This basic situational awareness will set the stage and dictate the direction of any conflict. Acclaimed Chinese military strategist, Sun Tzu, made this explicit in his ancient text, *The Art of War:*

> "Hence the saying: If you know the enemy and know yourself, you need not fear the result of a hundred battles. If you know yourself but not the enemy, for every victory gained you will also suffer a defeat. If you know neither the enemy nor yourself, you will succumb in every battle."[463]

The 2002 *National Strategy for Homeland Security* emphasized this same sentiment shortly after 9-11: "In the war on terrorism, as in all wars, the more we know about our enemy, the better able we are to defeat that enemy. The more we know about our vulnerability, the better able we are to protect ourselves."[464]

In former conflicts, we trounced our enemies after we adequately defined and understood our enemies without any equivocation. Although Sun Tzu's guidance is primitive, it is relevant in the 21st-century security environment where hybrid threats flourish to include international terrorism.

Even though terrorism has been present for centuries in various regions across the globe, now that it has reached the shores of what was once thought of as our untouchable nation, terrorism has received significant and widespread attention since 9-11. According to *A Military Guide to Terrorism in the Twenty-First Century*, "...terrorism is rising from a tactical novelty to become, in many instances, a significant operational and strategic tool."[465] Now that terrorism is center stage in the United States and continues to draw attention, no longer is terrorism ignored and viewed as an innocuous and unlikely phenomenon in a far off land. The U.S. homeland has become a battle space in the asymmetrical war against terrorism.

Since our current threat of terrorism shows no signs of retracting, it is essential to keep the very nature of our terrorist enemies in front of us. We cannot be timid in calling them our enemies because they have already defined us as their enemies. It is normal behavior for our attention to shift away from a particular subject over time, so we are challenged not to lose sight of what we are up against including who our enemies are and what they want. We must be honest with ourselves on the strengths of our enemies and know what they are capable of doing. Without such a conviction on the realities behind terrorism, we will only be hurting ourselves.

Although September 11, 2001 was not the first time radical Islamic terrorists have targeted American assets, it was the first time they were successful in bringing a devastating blow on our homeland. The attacks sent a reverberating message throughout the globe that America is not invulnerable. Although the attacks of 9-11 got our attention, we have failed to understand to this day the magnitude of those attacks. The farther we move away from September 11, 2001, the more we seem to have lost the reality of what truly happened on 9-11. Ralph Peter explained this sentiment:

> "We still fail to recognize that the atrocities of September 11th, 2001, composed the most successful—and dramatic—achievement of the Islamic world against the West in centuries, greater than the Ottoman victory at Gallipoli, the establishment of Arab states, the nationalization of the Suez Canal, or the Iranian Counter-Revolution of 1979. It was a great day in Muslim history, and it will be remembered as such, no matter what tribulations we visit upon the terrorist networks and their state accomplices in retaliation."[466]

Ten years later, we still need a true assessment of the threat we face. Until we are able to reverse this sentiment, push aside political correctness, and fully comprehend the significance of the 9-11 attacks in the minds of our enemies, we run the risk of exposing ourselves to future attacks. And as former CIA operative, Henry Crumpton, who helped defeat the Taliban in Afghanistan in 2001, warned in an interview with *60 Minutes*: "There will be an attack in the homeland. And sadly I think we face that prospect in the future. I think we'll be hit again."[467] Haven't we learned enough from our past history of what happens when we are not upfront with the severity of the threats that face us?

Many would argue the absence of attacks on the homeland since 9-11 suggest our success against terrorism. This seems reasonable and logical, but if you think about it, it contradicts terrorists' historical trends and their asymmetrical nature. Over the course of the 1990s, terrorists targeted American assets both at home and abroad. There were years in between each of the attacks as each attack boosted al Qaeda for the next attack. When al Qaeda failed with their first attempt of the World Trade Center bombing in 1993, they successfully came back eight years later, bringing a devastating blow to the World Trade Center. Between 1993 and 2001, al Qaeda prepared itself for a stronger attack that would leave a lasting impact on American society. Therefore, we cannot rule out the possibility that al Qaeda is preparing for another attack on the U.S. that surmounts 9-11.

The 9-11 Commission made it clear to us that it is not a matter of if we get attacked again but when. As long as our terrorist enemies possess both the intent and the capability to attack us, absence of attacks cannot be handled lightly. So the absence of attacks is not a solid criterion to measure the success of our homeland security strategies. As far as the terrorists' asymmetrical nature, they are patient and resilient unlike most Americans. They are not on any sort of accelerated timeline as evidenced by the 1993 and 2001 attacks on the World Trade Center. It is their tactic to prolong this conflict because they understand the tenuous will of the American people and the historical infirm political will of the U.S. as witnessed during the Vietnam War and the Battle of Mogadishu in Somalia. Osama bin Laden repeatedly referred to these two events to describe the flaccid resolve of America in times of international pressure, public impatience, and political uncertainty. These references became rallying calls for fellow al Qaeda members and inspiration to new terrorist recruits. The fact that terrorists only have to be right once in order to be effective in inciting terror, fear, and chaos supports their patient countenance. It is their intention to abrade the spirit of the American people in this protracted campaign against terrorism. In one Congressional Research Service Report for Congress, one author said it this way: "The absence of violent conflict may simply mean that they are in a waiting period."[468]

Prior to the catastrophe of 9-11, the United States overlooked terrorist activity and dangerously viewed terrorism more as a criminal activity versus an act of war. The Clinton administration upheld a supine temperament despite all the terrorist attacks on American assets and military targets throughout the 1990s. According to one terrorism expert, Martha Crenshaw, "The Clinton administration was not initially inclined to regard terrorism as a major national security issue."[469] Instead of it being a top priority like it is in today's post 9-11 environment, terrorism "was one among many problems to be managed."[470] As a result, top military and political leaders, along with key bureaucrats remained fixated on conventional threats versus emerging asymmetrical threats such as terrorism. Even though the Cold War was over with, the Cold War mindset was still extant with our leaders as our terrorist adversaries evolved and craftily matured into a serious threat.

From the first World Trade Center bombing in 1993 to the bombing of the *USS Cole* in 2000, these terrorist attacks were viewed and treated as instances of criminal behavior versus acts of war. Although the destruction of symbolic and integral infrastructure and the loss of innocent lives occurred, American retaliation was kept to a minimum and was viewed as non-threatening by the terrorist groups. As a result, the terrorists were emboldened after each attack throughout the 1990s. Our terrorist enemies understood how political correctness hinders our ability to fully project our military might. While we are constrained by political correctness in our society, our enemies are not. In 1996, during one of his diatribes, Osama bin Laden said that the U.S. soldier is "a paper tiger" who crumples after "a few blows".[471] The piercing attacks of 9-11 spurred the Bush administration to adopt an antithetical disposition against terrorism. A new leaf was turned as treating terrorism as criminal behavior was overridden with treating it as an act of war. The opening sentence in the *National Strategy for Homeland Security* made this clear: "America is at war with terrorist enemies who are intent on attacking our Homeland and destroying our way of life."[472] The events of 9-11 set a mark in history on how we changed from a reactive to a proactive position against terrorism.

THE RELIGIOUS AFFILIATION OF OUR TERRORIST ENEMIES

In today's age of terrorism, the majority of terrorist attacks are driven by a religious element. In his article, "The Origins of New Terrorism," Matthew Morgan declared that "today's terrorists are ultimately more apocalyptic in their perspective and methods."[473] The theological terrorists of today are much more dangerous than non-religious terrorists because theological terrorists do not fear the backlashes. Today, radical Islamic terrorists are exploiting Islam to carry out their attacks.

In understanding our terrorist enemy, we must understand its radical ideology and this includes the jihadist movement associated with it. In order for us to understand our enemy, we must know what radical Islam requires of its followers. Every American should be required to view the film *Obsession* to gain a genuine appreciation of the nature of our terrorist adversaries. After all, as the movie rightly asserts and displays, "Jihad has come to America." When we grasp this reality and are able to define our enemy, we are at least provided with a compass on how to conquer this enemy. According to Dr. James Rinehart, "If you can't define something, it is impossible to study it scientifically."[474] This struggle will continue to be rigorous and time-consuming, but if we fail to define and clearly understand our enemy's purpose and intentions, this struggle will be even more difficult and frustrating. On the other hand, when we appreciate the vicious and deceptive nature of our enemies we would in turn appreciate the fact that this conflict will take more time, resources and patience. *Obsession* is loaded with applicable and alarming material on this global struggle with America at the epicenter of it, but the key themes that will grab the viewers' attention are the influence of the jihad culture and the use of hate propaganda and deception used by radical Islamists to promote their cause.

The movie does a great job in explaining the culture of jihad. Jihad is for real and will not be going away anytime soon. The faster American society accepts this, the better we will be in the long run. Too many Americans are apathetic and ignorant to the realistic threat of jihad and *Obsession* is one method of getting America's undivided attention. For some reason we do not want to accept or acknowledge that jihad is fueled by adherence to a radical religious ideology. Dr. Schmul Bar affirmed that a strategy against jihad "must be based on an acceptance of the fact that for the first time since the Crusades, Western civilization finds itself involved in a religious war..."[475]

Jihadists do not believe in the coexistence of radical Islam and Western civilization and no amount of political correctness will ever permit such coexistence. Radical Islamists totally reject the fundamental principles of the West. There is a conspicuous movement to promote radical Islam and the culture of jihad throughout the globe and the American people must have this situational awareness. There is no room for denial or ignorance when it comes to this threat. The *Report of the Future of Terrorism Task Force*, published in 2007, announced: "The most significant terrorist threat to the homeland today stems from a global movement, underpinned by a jihadist/Salafist ideology."[476]

Jihadists have the goal of overturning a specific group's ideology or way of life while simultaneously expanding their own ideology. They demand the sole tolerance of their religion by others; while at the same time, they resist the tolerance of other religions. They promote capitulation by others to their religion, but they themselves evade capitulation to outside religions. In a United States Senate Committee on Homeland Security and Governmental Affairs report entitled *Violent Islamist Extremism, The Internet, and the Homegrown Terrorist Threat*, this violent ideology was emphasized: "The core tenets of this violent ideology are straightforward, uncompromising, and absolute. The ideology calls for the pursuit and creation of a global Islamist state – a Caliphate – that unites all Muslims – the Ummah – and is governed by Islamic law – Sharia."[477] It is a "one way street" outpouring with bigotry and partiality. They intend to change the traditional norms, character, and identity of any region that is not in conformity with their own ideology. American historian Walter Laqueur put it this way: "Today's terrorists, in their majority, are not diplomats eager to negotiate or to find compromises."[478] As a result of radical Islamists' totalitarian ideology, we must be aware that our Christian way of life and the freedoms we relish stand in its way. The ideological component of this threat is too dangerous to be pushed aside.

With the current war against radical Islamists, it is like day and night as two different ideologies separate the West from radical Islam. While the West denounces and contests acts of terrorism, supporters of radical Islam glorify and promote it. Terrorism incites both sides to action albeit they are in two totally opposite directions, thus causing a head-on confrontation. According to the *National Strategy for Combating Terrorism*, "For the enemy, there is no peaceful coexistence with those who do not subscribe to their distorted and violent view of the world."[479] The American people need to be reminded of our terrorist enemies' religious element that is driving their intransigence and obstinate refusal to coexist with others.

THE MUSLIM CONNECTION TO RADICAL ISLAM

At the same time we point out that not every Muslim is a terrorist, we must be honest and acknowledge the link between today's modern terrorists and the radical Islamic ideology they proclaim. If we do not do this then we are not doing ourselves justice. The threat is much larger than we credit it. In his book *What in the World is Going On?* Dr. David Jeremiah pointed this out.

> "While the majority of the world's 1.5 billion Muslims want no part of this deadly violence and attempt to live in peace with their neighbors, the number of radicals who preach violence and terror is mushrooming around the world. Experts say that 15 to 20 percent of Muslims are radical enough to strap a bomb on their bodies in order to kill Christians and Jews. If this number is accurate, it means about three hundred million Muslims are willing to die in order to take you and me down."[480]

It is important to notice the increase in Muslim populations across the globe especially in the West. According to the Office of the Director of National

Intelligence, in its publication entitled *Global Trends 2025: A Transformed World,* "If current patterns of immigration and Muslim residents' above-average fertility continue, Western Europe could have 25 to 30 million Muslims by 2025."[481] America's declining birth rate is another interesting statistic to keep in mind. According to the Central Intelligence Agency, America's birth rate is 13.83 births/1,000 population.[482] Our terrorist enemies are fully aware of these population trends and intend to use them to their advantage in recruiting for and spreading jihad. They intend to exploit the West's tolerance of multiculturalism to reinforce their radical cause. We have seen in the past how trends in Europe have found their way in the United States. Will this same trend find its way in the United States?

Our Islamic terrorists are actually taking a tactic from Sun Tzu's playbook in spreading their cause. Sun Tzu stressed the power in defeating an enemy without a fight:

> "Thus one who excels at employing the military subjugates other people's armies without engaging in battle, captures other people's fortified cities without attacking them, and destroys other people's states without prolonged fighting. He must fight under Heaven with the paramount aim of preservation. Thus his weapons will not become dull and the gains can be preserved. This is the strategy for planning offensives."[483]

With an overflowing of the Muslim population, our terrorist enemies can have an effect on a population's culture. A nation's tolerant laws and policies welcome radical Islamists under the guise of ordinary Muslims who are peacefully practicing Islam. The radical Islamic culture is showing its dominance simply through regional migrations and subsequent mass recruiting and not through military invasion. Through their untiring patience and systematic and disingenuous approach, they are able to establish their footprint in the absence of force.

Islamic terrorists justify their wicked acts of terrorism as legit by pronouncing the acts to be acceptable in the eyes of their God; in their distorted belief, it is their religious duty to promote and exercise terrorism. The law of their God supersedes the rule of law in society, thus there are minimal constraints in exercising terrorism. Terrorists believe they have an anointed right to kill anyone who does not conform to Islam, thus giving them an untouchable countenance. As absurd as it may sound to us, terrorists use this justification with both audacity and confidence.

Radical Islamists also believe they have the divine obligation to fulfill their prophetic visions. Authors Christine Fair and Husain Haqqani wrote, "Radical Islamists want nothing less than the restoration of Islamic sovereignty to all lands where Muslims were once ascendant."[484] They are using jihad as a vehicle in regaining and retaining global Islamic sovereignty. Our enemies are vehement in their efforts of establishing a "worldwide caliphate – a theocracy – that equates to a religious dictatorship."[485] In their view, the world must be remade in their image. Islamic terror is stimulated by a totalitarian ideology that hungers for world domination and the conquest of all infidels. In a column in the *Washington Post,* titled "Make No Mistake: This Is War," former Secretary of Homeland Security, Michael Chertoff, wrote:

> "Today's extreme Islamist groups such as al-Qaeda do not merely seek political revolution in their own countries. They aspire to dominate all countries. Their goal is a totalitarian, theocratic empire to be achieved by waging perpetual war on soldiers and civilians alike. That includes the use of weapons of mass destruction."[486]

The severity of this global threat is nothing to dismiss with apathy, and so, we must stop disguising it with political correctness and as something else than what it really is. It is justified to take on a hawkish disposition when it comes to defending our national security and the American people.

OUR ENEMY'S GLOBAL OUTREACH

Unlike our conventional adversaries, the terrorist networks are not constrained to one center of gravity. Instead, they are decentralized and multi-cellular and operate in a nonbureaucratic fashion, thus making it more difficult for our forces to quarantine and defeat the ever-evolving terrorist threat. Although most Americans are familiar with the terrorist activity in Afghanistan and Iraq as a result of the recent wars, most Americans fail to understand that our terrorist enemies actively have their tentacles in other areas throughout the international community. If anyone believes that radical Islamic terrorism is only a contemporary craze and is isolated only to a few areas, they are sadly mistaken. In an interview with Sean Hannity, another former CIA operative, Gary Bernstein, mentioned that over 900,000 radicals have gone through terrorist training camps in the last twenty years. Berstein properly stated, "This is war." There was no political correctness in Bernstein's account of the terrorist threat as it was based off his personal experience in counterterrorism.

One of the more recent locations where al Qaeda's presence is increasing is Yemen. According to Abu Bakr al-Qir, Yemen's Foreign Minister, "Hundreds of al-Qaeda militants are planning terror attacks from Yemen."[487] Consequently, he has reached out to the international community for assistance. Most of us associate Yemen as the location of the *USS Cole* bombing, but ten years later, it has become a nest of al Qaeda terrorists. As a result of Yemen's lawlessness, poverty, remoteness, and rugged terrain, it has become a safe harbor for a growing insurgency. As a result of terrorists' association with non-state actors or disenfranchised organizations who do not answer to a sovereign government, Yemen's statelessness has attracted and reenergized al Qaeda members. John Brennan, the U.S. Deputy National Security Adviser, posited that the al Qaeda organization in Yemen is a greater threat to the United States than the al Qaeda group under Osama bin Laden in Pakistan.[488]

Yemen's footprint has already been identified in two foiled terrorist attacks in the U.S. In December 2009, Abdul Farouk Umar Abdulmutallab attempted to blow up Northwest 253, a commercial airliner, over Detroit by sewing bomb material in his underwear. Again, here is another example of the innovation and tenacity adopted by our terrorist enemies. What may seem aberrant in our minds is just another possibility in the minds of our enemies. Who would have ever thought of sewing explosives in one's underwear? Al Qaeda leaders in Yemen orchestrated and authorized this malicious plot with the clear intent of killing innocent civilians and bringing terror and distress to the American people. According to the investigators, the bomb did not explode- and thankfully so- because the detonator was inefficient or was not in "proper contact" with the explosive material.[489] We must not be afraid to acknowledge our enemies' creativity, but we must tell it the way it is and keep it in front of the American people, even when our patience is tested. In today's post 9-11 operating environment, nothing should be considered out-of-the-ordinary.

On another occasion, al Qaeda members based out of Yemen attempted to send printers with explosives hidden in the inside of their printer cartridges aboard cargo flights, flying from Yemen to Chicago. The packages were addressed to Jewish houses of worship in Chicago. Although the packages came across as every-day, harmless packages packed with other common items, the terrorist leaders' intent was deceitful and evil. They intended to have the packages explode midair somewhere over our east coast. Through Saudi Arabian intelligence, the cargo flights were interdicted in both England and Dubai. Dubai police claimed the chemical in the printer cartridge was the same chemical found in Abdulmutallab's underwear.[490] Fortunately, both of these attempts, which are believed to have originated out of Yemen, were prevented; however, they do reveal how the terrorist threat is for real and is originating from multi-locations.

As Americans, we must comprehend the evolving and resilient nature of how terrorists live and operate. When we sincerely understand their intentions, capabilities, and purpose and are honest with ourselves, we will be prepared mentally, psychologically, and physically. Such awareness will prevent false expectations and keep us engaged in the fight. It is up to our leaders to forsake political correctness and to constantly define and redefine and convince the American people of the evolving nature of the terrorist threats.

If our leaders believe it is worth the fight, they must continually convey how the battle is worth fighting.

HOMEGROWN TERRORISM WITHIN OUR OWN BORDERS

Our enemies are always looking for new ways to project death and terror upon us. In defining the terrorist threat, we must be knowledgeable of the home-grown aspect associated with it and how they will use the civil rights and victim-argument to carry out their actions. Terrorists have not only turned our homeland into battle space, they are hard at work in drawing American residents into their cause of militant Islam. Today, they have stepped up their recruiting efforts to obtain members who speak English and are familiar with the American culture. They want members who are engrossed in the radical Islamic ideology but who can also pass for Americans. They are brazen to the point where they are reaching out to our own population. This tactic has now intensified the fight and should alarm every single American. An article in *Newsweek* addressing the Federally Administered Tribal Areas (FATA) of Pakistan educates us on this new trend:

> "The threat from al Qaeda to the U.S. homeland is arguably more acute now than at any time since September 11. This is not because al Qaeda has become a stronger foe. (On the contrary, Osama bin Laden's terrorist network has actually been weakened in the last two years by intensified U.S. missile strikes against its leadership in FATA and a sharp backlash among Muslims worldwide against its violent excesses.) It is because a growing number of Americans have gone to FATA, the global hub of al Qaeda's terrorist operations, to join the jihad in Afghanistan—something which was very rare until recently—and al Qaeda, opportunistically, has recruited them for attacks on their country."[491]

If we turn a blind eye to their bold recruiting tactic and remain ignorant of our enemy's creative zest, we are only hurting ourselves. We must also keep in mind terrorist recruiting will increase whenever our enemy perceives American weakness and American entanglement in political correctness. Despite the frequency of changes in tactics and the home-hitting occurrence of our enemy's tactics, the American people are deserving of accurate situational awareness.

Anwar al Awlaki, a radical Muslim cleric, is one example of an American-born citizen who has gravitated to the radical Islamic ideology, promoting violence and terrorism against American citizens. Born in New Mexico, Awlaki is now an active member of an al Qaeda branch in Yemen. Due to his English-speaking ability and his upbringing in the Western culture, Awlaki is instrumental in attracting Westerners to the jihad movement- exactly what al Qaeda seeks. In fact, it is believed Awlaki was linked to Abdulmutallab's failed attempt to bring down Flight 253 and the failed attempt to explode FedEx and UPS cargo flights as mentioned above.

Just how much of a threat is Awlaki? A New York Police Department counterterrorism official labeled Awlaki as the "most dangerous man in the world."[492] As Americans, we must not be naïve in thinking Americans would not pursue such seditious behavior. It is also important for Americans to realize and reflect on how Awlaki once lived in the U.S. and traveled to different mosques to preach his radical and vehement vitriol against America. If he acted in such a manner, then there are others just as capable in the future especially as Awlaki's global influence increases and others want to follow in his footsteps.

In addition to these blown terrorist attempts, Awlaki supported the murderous terrorist, Major Nidal Hasan who massacred 13 personnel on Fort Hood. On his blog, Alwaki posted:

> "Nidal Hasan [sic] is a hero. He is a man of conscience who could not bear the contradiction of

being a Muslim and fighting against his own people. No scholar with a grain of Islamic knowledge can deny the clear cut proofs that Muslims today have the Many will argue right — rather the duty — to fight against American tyranny."[493]

There is no mincing of words here by Awlaki; it is clear that he has strong and obdurate hatred against America despite being born in the United States, offering little hope for reconciliation or compromise.

Many will argue political correctness surrounded the aftermath of the despicable Fort Hood massacre. Despite the incontestable facts of the ghastly incident and the already existing definitions of terrorism, there was extreme prudence in labeling the massacre as a terrorist attack.

What are the facts of the Fort Hood massacre? We do know 12 soldiers and one civilian security guard were killed, while 31 more soldiers were wounded after Hasan entered a military clinic and opened fire on military personnel inside the clinic.[494] Hasan's past was filled with signposts reflecting his propensity of favoring the radical Islamic ideology. For example, Hasan was known to voice and post anti-American jargon in both public and private. Hasan entered the clinic yelling out *"Allahu Akbar!"* ("God is great!") - the common phrase jihadists recite prior to committing their terrorist act.[495] Moreover, business cards of Hasan were discovered in his apartment labeling him as a "soldier of Allah".[496] All of the above indicators suggested an act of terrorism. FOX news labeled it as "the largest single terror act in America since 9/11."[497] As hard-hitting and truthful as this title may be, our society in general refrained from using it. Even though Hasan's behavioral patterns were abnormal and indicative of one who sympathized with the culture of our terrorist enemies, it appeared as if there was hesitancy in connecting Hasan to terrorism.

If we were to examine the definitions of terrorism as defined by some of our most prestigious institutions, we would conclude the Fort Hood massacre was indeed an evil act of terrorism. The Department of Defense (DOD) defines terrorism as:

"The calculated use of unlawful violence or threat of unlawful violence to inculcate fear and intended to coerce or to intimidate governments or societies in the pursuit of goals that are generally political, religious, or ideological."[498]

The Federal Bureau of Investigation (FBI) adopts the definition of terrorism as defined in the Code of Federal Regulations:

"The unlawful use of force and violence against persons or property to intimidate or coerce a government, the civilian population, or any segment thereof, in furtherance of political or social objectives."[499]

The Department of State uses the definition of terrorism contained in Title 22 of the United States Code, Section 2656f(d):

"Premeditated, politically motivated violence perpetrated against noncombatant targets by subnational groups or clandestine agents, usually intended to influence an audience."[500]

As you notice, all three organizations have different verbiage in their definitions of terrorism, but they all share the same themes as it relates to terrorism. These themes were seen with the Fort Hood tragedy. Hasan used brutal, calculated violence by shooting his innocent victims without any regard to human life. Hasan created angst and terror among the local military community, friends and family members of the victims, and Americans in general. Hasan pursued this repugnant act as a result of his antipathy of American foreign policy in the Middle East and in support of the jihad cause. With all these disturbing occurrences, why wouldn't we link the Fort Hood massacre with terrorism? I am certain the family members of those who- for no reason- lost loved ones or had loved ones wounded as a result of

Hasan's senseless act would not have any problems connecting the two. As they continue to suffer emotional distress, they do not deserve to have political correctness reduce the tragedy for what it actually was.

Several weeks after the Fort Hood massacre, the Tiger Woods' adulterous drama soon dominated the news cycle, drawing the public's attention away from the Foot Hood incident and the true nature of the radical Islamic ideology. The general public became more absorbed in the sexual escapades of Tiger Woods than the homegrown terrorist threat we face. Our terrorist enemies use our short attention span against us. Our terrorist enemies also know they do not need to physically take and hold territory in order to claim victory against us; they only need to claim innocent lives and inflict terror among our population. Our enemies are fully aware of our frailties, but do we truly have the same awareness of our own weaknesses? Or is there reluctance to accept the resurgent terrorist threat in the face of our tolerance?

If we examine would-be Times Square bomber, Faisal Shahzad of Connecticut, we will discover again how our enemies are strong-willed, committed, patient, and undeterred in bringing death, destruction, and terror to the American people. Shahzad's plan of parking a Pathfinder laden with explosives on the side of the street in a busy Times Square may have fell through, but it was clear that his intent of spreading terrorism and mass murder was unquestionable. The sole purpose of terrorism is to petrify people and this was exactly Shahzad's purpose. Why else would he want to kill and injure innocent New Yorkers? There were no military targets or objectives on this day in May 2010; it was only this terrorist's ambition to bring about public acts of death and chaos. As New York City Police Commissioner Raymond Kelly reminded Americans this was "a sober reminder that New York is a target for people who want to come here and do us harm."[501]

It was an alert street vendor and Vietnam veteran by the name of Duane Jackson who became alarmed and alerted the police. His circumstantial awareness caused him to notice smoke emitting from the Vehicle Born Improvised Explosive Device. It was an average American citizen without apathy who took the decisive action to do something. This is the reason why it is important for all of us to understand the fundamental nature of our terrorist enemies. Since innocent Americans are targets, it is essential we know exactly what we are up against and what is at stake. We are the targets of militant Islamic jihadists. We are all vulnerable to their sadistic attacks and without this basic awareness or concern, we are even more vulnerable. Although our law enforcement officials, military personnel, and first responders are all heroes, every American has a role to play in this global struggle against radical Islamic terrorists. No matter how much security we may have, if there is a lack of education on whom our enemies are then all that security is for nothing. Ignoring an active enemy does more damage than harm. Active citizenry as exhibited by Mr. Jackson is exactly what we need from our society to contend an enemy who largely views the American populace as desensitized.

In reviewing the failed bombing attempt by Faisal Shahzad, it is important to recognize the culture of deception practiced by our terrorist enemies. This is another trait of our enemies that goes largely unnoticed by most people. They will freely say or do anything to promote their radical agenda of spreading terrorism and jihad. While they may announce allegiance under apocryphal pretenses in order to gain favor, they are misleading Americans as they advance their ideology.

For example, Shahzad became a naturalized U.S. citizen on April 17, 2009 after he married an American citizen by the name of Huma Asif Mian on October 20, 2008.[502] Shahzad may have become a naturalized American citizen over time, but did he ever have a true allegiance to the United States? His actions in Time Squares revealed that his oath of citizenship in which he swore to "support and defend the Constitution and laws of the United States of America against all enemies," was null and void. Shahzad seemed to have hoodwinked even his neighbor who called him "a nice guy."[503] If there is one take-away from this incident it is that we must focus on the ideology at work that is driving radical Islamists and not their semblance of outer personality or attitude. Of course terrorists can pretend to be nice people. Terrorists are capable of carrying a pleasant but beguiling personality through the tactic of deception on the short term for the long term satisfaction of accomplishing their pernicious objective(s). We must not only understand the duplicitous nature of our enemies, but we must also repeatedly expose their duplicity. There is no room for us to be naïve in thinking otherwise; a terrorist is a terrorist.

THE WAY AHEAD

Since our current threat is rooted in ideology, we can expect it to hang around for some time. Before the Committee on Appropriations Subcommittee on Homeland Security, Brian Jenkins, the senior advisor to the president of the RAND Corporation claimed:

> "The terrorist threat is changing. We have degraded the global operational capabilities of al Qaeda, removed some of its key planners, and kept its leadership on the run. But we have not prevented jihadist leaders from communicating, blunted their message, or effectively countered their ability to radicalize and recruit angry young men."[504]

If we are going to prevail in this protracted war against terrorism, we have to at least call terrorism for what it is. In her article "Jihad by any other name," radio and television commentator Monica Crowley mentioned this: "Unless and until we see the threat clearly, call the enemy what it is and identify what motivates it, and assign blame to its proper place, we will not gain the edge we need to defeat it."[505] This is the starting point and when we do this, everything else will fall into place. We need to think like they think without adopting their ways and construe what motivates them to extreme acrimony. Just as we used bold, realistic, and truthful language backed by bold action during World War II to defeat Nazism, we need the same thing today against terrorism.

Euphemisms as they relate to terrorism are unacceptable because our enemies see right through them. When we do this, we are just hurting ourselves because our terrorist enemies look at it as if their actions are rewarded, thus causing them to increase their recruiting efforts and their operational pace. To them the political correct language means nothing.

It does not matter what political party is in power; our enemies still despise America and what she stands for. The threat is still there as our enemies remain undeterred in their efforts in spreading jihad and terror. Our enemies understand they will never be able to defeat America in a head-on conventional fight so they do everything to neutralize our military power and this includes using our political correctness against us. Congressman Peter King of New York has it right when he spoke about the radicalization of the Muslim community in America: "I will do all I can to break down the wall of political correctness and drive the public debate on Islamic radicalization."[506] This is the direction we need to head in as a nation in order to protect our national identity, sovereignty, and security. It is time we think in terms of sovereignty and nationalism. Anything else in dealing with this treacherous enemy only jeopardizes the safety and security of the American people.

NOTES

Chapter 1

[1] George Friedman, *The Next 100 Years* (New York: Doubleday, 2009), 16.
[2] Ibid.
[3] Patrick Allen, "U.S. will be the world's third largest economy, Citi says," *USA Today,* February 26, 2011, http://www.usatoday.com/money/economy/2011-02-26-cnbc-us-will-be-worlds-third-largest-economy_N.htm.
[4] Washington's Earnest Prayer, April, 30, 1789, http://www.ushistory.org/valleyforge/washington/earnestprayer.html.
[5] American History Quotes about God and the Bible, http://www.praydailyamerica.com/americanhistory.html.
[6] Presidential Thanksgiving Proclamations, http://www.pilgrimhall.org/ThanxProc1789.htm.
[7] Elder Ezra Taft Benson, "The Constitution: A Glorious Standard," http://www.zionsbest.com/glorious.html.
[8] Dr. Frank Luntz, *Words That Work* (New York: Hyperion Books, 2007), xiii.
[9] Ronald Reagan's Farewell Address to the Nation, http://www.ronaldreagan.com/sp_21.html.
[10] Available at http://www.quotesdaddy.com/quote/280806/Winston+Churchill/the-farther-back-you-can-look-the-farther-forward.
[11] David J. Brewer, *The United States: A Christian Nation* (Philadelphia: The John C. Winston Company, 1905), 11.
[12] The Thanksgiving Proclamation, October 3, 1789, http://gwpapers.virginia.edu/documents/thanksgiving/transcript.html.
[13] Kay Brigham, *Christopher Columbus: His Life and Discovery in the Light of his Prophecies* (Terrassa, Barcelona: CLIE Publishers, 1990), 53.

[14] Ron Collins, "A Brief History of the Pilgrims," http://www.mayflowerfamilies.com/colonial_life/pilgrims.htm

[15] Available athttp://thinkexist.com/quotation/everything_in_life_is_luck/202881.html.

[16] What Happened on the Voyage, http://www.mayflowerhistory.com/History/voyage5.php.

[17] Christopher W. Hammons, "Why the Pilgrims Matter," http://www.texasmayflower.com/articles/WhyThePilgrimsMatter.pdf.

[18] "The Desolate Wilderness: A chronicle of the Pilgrims' arrival at Plymouth as recorded by Nathaniel Morton," November 24, 2010, http://online.wsj.com/article/SB10001424052970204482304574216002146998902.html.

[19] Dr. Charles Wolfe, "A Crisis of National Amnesia," http://www.plymrock.org/Brochure.pdf.

[20] Mayflower Compact- The Common Anchor, http://www.allabouthistory.org/mayflower-compact.htm.

[21] The Mayflower Compact, http://www.nationalcenter.org/MayflowerCompact.html.

[22] Writings of America's Founding Fathers, http://livingsounds.org/americanhistory/fathers.html.

[23] J. James Estrada, "Thankful to God for America," November 22, 2007, Americanthinker.com, http://www.americanthinker.com/2007/11/thankful_to_god_for_america_1.html.

[24] Dr. Ralph F. Wilson, "Squanto- God's Special Indian a Thanksgiving Story," http://www.joyfulheart.com/thanksgiving/squanto.htm.

[25] Available at http://en.wikiquote.org/wiki/Albert_Einstein.

[26] Revolutionary War and Beyond, http://www.revolutionary-war-and-beyond.com/patrick-henry-quotes.html.

[27] Available at http://www.americanchristianhistory.com/ChristianHistory26.html.

[28] John Adams to Thomas Jefferson, June 28, 1813, *The Adams-Jefferson Letters: The Complete Correspondence*

Between Thomas Jefferson and Abigail and John Adams, Lester J. Cappon, ed., (Chapel Hill, NC: University of North Carolina Press, 1988), 338-340.

[29] Alfred Thayer Mahan, *The Influence of Sea Power upon History, 1660-1783,* http://www.scribd.com/doc/222011/The-Influence-of-Sea-Power-Upon-History-by-Alfred-Thayer-Mahan.

[30] John Dickinson, *Letters from a Farmer, Letter IV,* 39. http://deila.dickinson.edu/cdm4/document.php?CISOROOT=/ownwords&CISOPTR=409.

[31] Available at http://en.wikiquote.org/wiki/Talk:Hope.

[32] Declaration of Independence, http://www.ushistory.org/declaration/document/index.htm.

[33] "American History Quotes about God and the Bible," http://www.praydailyamerica.com/americanhistory.html.

[34] Mark R. Levin, *Liberty and Tyranny* (New York: Threshold Editions, 2009), 26.

[35] Rod McNair, "Brooklyn Heights: Dunkirk of the American Revolution," July/August 2006, Volume 8, Issue 4, http://www.tomorrowsworld.org/cgi-bin/tw/tw-mag.cgi?category=Magazine43&item=1153024441.

[36] Available at http://americasfoundingfathers.wordpress.com/2010/01/18/it-is-impossible-to-rightly-govern-the-world-without-god-and-bible/.

[37] William J. Bennett, *The Spirit of America* (New York: Touchstone, 1997), 393.

[38] Valley Forge Encampment: A winter of Suffering, http://www.nps.gov/history/logcabin/html/vf.html.

[39] Washington's Prayer at Valley Forge, http://www.partyof1776.net/p1776/fathers/Washington%20George/articles/PrayerVF.htm.

[40] Dan Popkey, "Idaho GOP gubernatorial candidate Rammell expands on controversial prophecy in YouTube video," January 4, 2010, http://www.idahostatesman.com/idahopolitics/story/1029316.html.

[41] "Congressman Defends His 'Constitution' Comments on Health Care Law," FOXNews.com, April 3, 2010,

http://www.foxnews.com/politics/2010/04/03/congressman-defends-constitution-comments-health-care/.
[42] Ibid.
[43] U.S. Constitution, Preamble.
[44] Available at http://www.quotationspage.com/quote/24240.html.
[45] Message from John Adams to the Officers of the First Brigade of the Third Division of the Militia of Massachusetts, http://www.beliefnet.com/resourcelib/.
[46] Speech to the Constitutional Convention on State Representation, http://www.cooperativeindividualism.org/franklin_benjamin_state_representation.html.
[47] "The Constitution of the United States: Is It Pro-Slavery or Anti-Slavery?" http://teachingamericanhistory.org/library/index.asp?document=1128.
[48] Thomas Shipping, "Intimidated judges judge well," *WorldNet Daily,* February 15, 2001, http://70.85.195.205/news/article.asp?ARTICLE_ID=21728.
[49] Common Sense Republic, http://www.commonsenserepublic.net/index.php?p=1_6_NOTABLE-QUOTES.
[50] The Magna Carta, http://www.constitution.org/eng/magnacar.htm.
[51] The Federalist No. 10: The Utility of the Union as a Safeguard against Domestic Faction and Insurrection (continued), *Daily Advertiser,* November 22, 1787, http://www.constitution.org/fed/federa10.htm.
[52] Available at http://www.phrases.org.uk/meanings/absolute-power-corrupts-absolutely.html.
[53] Available at http://www.goodreads.com/author/quotes/361839.Patrick_Henry.
[54] Address at Moscow State University (May 31, 1988), http://millercenter.org/scripps/archive/speeches/detail/3416.

Chapter 2

[55] John Quincy Adams Inaugural Address, March 4, 1825, http://www.bartelby.com/124/pres22.html.

[56] William H. Seward, *Life and Public Services of John Quincy Adams* (Auburn: Derby, Miller, & Company, 1849), 248-49.

[57] Andrew Jackson Farewell Address, 1837, http://www.nationalcenter.org/Jackson%27sFarewell.html.

[58] John Frost, *Life of Andrew Jackson: Embracing Anecdotes Illustrative of his Character; with Illustrations* (Philadelphia: Lindsay & Blakiston, 1876), 170.

[59] Martin Van Buren Inaugural Address, March 4, 1837, http://www.bartelby.com/124/pres25.html.

[60] James Polk Inaugural Address, March 4, 1845, http://bartelby.org/124/pres27.html.

[61] John T. Woolley and Gerhard Peters, The American Presidency Project [online], Santa Barbara, CA, http://www.presidency.ucsb.edu/ws/?pid=29486.

[62] Zachary Taylor Inaugural Address, March 5, 1849, http://www.bartelby.com/124/pres28.html.

[63] Franklin Pierce Inaugural Address, March 4, 1853, http://www3.bartelby.com/124/pres29.html.

[64] Collected Works of Abraham Lincoln, Volume 4, http://quod.lib.umich.edu/cgi/t/text/text-idx?c=lincoln;idno=lincoln4;rgn=div1;view=text;cc=lincoln;node=lincoln4%3A741.

[65] "Lincoln on Slavery," http://www.nps.gov/liho/historyculture/slavery.htm.

[66] R.D. Monroe, Ph.D., "Debating Douglas on the National Stage, 1857-1858," http://lincoln.lib.niu.edu/biography7text.html.

[67] "Abraham Lincoln on Preserving Liberty," *The Collected Works of Abraham Lincoln,* Roy P. Basler (ed.), http://showcase.netins.net/web/creative/lincoln/speeches/liberty.htm.

[68] The Emancipation Proclamation, http://www.archives.gov/exhibits/featured_documents/emancipation_proclamation/.
[69] "A House Divided against Itself Cannot Stand," http://www.nationalcenter.org/HouseDivided.html.
[70] National Day of Prayer - An Historical Perspective, http://chccfamily.org/NDP/prayerhistory.htm.
[71] John Savage, *The Life and Public Services of Andrew Johnson* (New York: Derby & Miller, Publishers, 1866), 274.
[72] John Savage, 247.
[73] Presidential Thanksgiving Proclamations 1870-1879: Ulysses S. Grant, Rutherford B. Hayes, http://www.pilgrimhall.org/ThanxProc1870.htm.
[74] The Religious Affiliation of 19th U.S. President, Rutherford B. Hayes, http://www.adherents.com/people/ph/Rutherford_B_Hayes.html.
[75] Ibid.
[76] Grover Cleveland First Inaugural Address, March 4, 1885, http://www.bartelby.com/124/pres37.html.
[77] Grover Cleveland Second Inaugural Address, March 4, 1893, http://www.bartelby.com/124/pres39.html.
[78] Robert Mcelroy, *Grover Cleveland: The Man and the Statesman- Volume II* (New York: Harpers & Brothers Publishers, 1923), 372.
[79] The Religious Affiliation of Benjamin Harrison, 23rd U.S. President, http://www.adherents.com/people/ph/Benjamin_Harrison_pres.html.
[80] Benjamin Harrison Inaugural Address, March 4, 1889, http://www.bartleby.com/124/pres38.html.
[81] Ibid.
[82] William McKinley Inaugural Address, March 4, 1897, http://www.bartleby.com/124/pres40.html.
[83] The Death of William McKinley, http://www.buffalohistoryworks.com/panamex/assassination/mcdeath.htm.
[84] Theodore Roosevelt, *Fear God and Take Your Own Part* (New York: Cosimo, Inc., 2005), 15.

[85] Buddy Dano, "Theodore Roosevelt, A Doer of the Word," http://www.divineviewpoint.com/TR_Doer_of_Word.pdf.
[86] Available at http://thinkexist.com/quotation/a_thorough_knowledge_of_the_bible_is_worth_more/164715.html.
[87] Article from the Ladies Home Journal, December 1917, http://www.pocketpower.org/museum/museumpix/decade1910s/leadersigs.html.
[88] William Howard Taft Inaugural Address, March 4, 1909, http://bartleby.com/124/pres43.html.
[89] Presidential Thanksgiving Proclamations 1910-1919: William H. Taft, Woodrow Wilson, http://www.pilgrimhall.org/ThanxProc1910.htm.
[90] Woodrow Wilson speech "The Bible and Progress," May 7, 1911, *Woodrow Wilson: Essential Writings & Speeches of the Scholar-President,* Mario R. Dinunzio, ed., (New York: New York University Press, 2006), 59.
[91] Woodrow Wilson First Inaugural Address, March 4, 1913, http://www.bartleby.com/124/pres44.html.
[92] Woodrow Wilson Second Inaugural Address, March 5, 1917, http://bartleby.com/124/pres45.html.
[93] Available at http://usaheritage.org/presquotes.html.
[94] Available at http://www.juntosociety.com/uspresidents/wghardng.html.
[95] Warren Harding Inaugural Address, March 4, 1921, http://www.bartleby.com/124/pres46.html.
[96] Ibid.
[97] Calvin Coolidge Inaugural Address, March 4, 1925, http://bartleby.com/124/pres47.html.
[98] John T. Woolley and Gerhard Peters, The American Presidency Project [online], Santa Barbara, CA, http://www.presidency.ucsb.edu/ws/?pid=408.
[99] John T. Woolley and Gerhard Peters, The American Presidency Project [online], Santa Barbara, CA, http://www.presidency.ucsb.edu/ws/?pid=476.
[100] Herbert Hoover Inaugural Address, March 4, 1929, http://bartleby.com/124/pres48.html.
[101] Herbert Hoover, *American Individualism* (Garden City, NY: Doubleday, Page & Company, 1922), 26.

[102] Words that Men Live By: President Herbert Hoover (1950)," The Federal Observer, April 27, 1950, http://www.federalobserver.com/words.php?words=7425.
[103] The Star Spangled Banner Lyrics By Francis Scott Key 1814, http://www.usa-flag-site.org/song-lyrics/star-spangled-banner.shtml.
[104] Address of the President Delivered by Radio from the White House, April 28, 1935, http://www.mhric.org/fdr/chat7.html.
[105] Franklin Delano Roosevelt D-Day Prayer, http://www.historyplace.com/speeches/fdr-prayer.htm.
[106] John T. Woolley and Gerhard Peters, The American Presidency Project [online], Santa Barbara, CA, http://www.presidency.ucsb.edu/ws/?pid=13486.
[107] John T. Woolley and Gerhard Peters, The American Presidency Project [online], Santa Barbara, CA, http://www.presidency.ucsb.edu/ws/?pid=13707.
[108] The Pledge of Allegiance, http://www.ushistory.org/documents/pledge.htm.
[109] The Story of the Pledge of Allegiance, http://www.americanflagfoundation.org/content/educationalresources_pledgestory.cfm.
[110] "How the words "UNDER GOD" came to be added to the Pledge of Allegiance to the Flag," http://www.kofc4504.org/undergod.html.
[111] John T. Woolley and Gerhard Peters, The American Presidency Project [online], Santa Barbara, CA, http://www.presidency.ucsb.edu/ws/?pid=27304.
[112] Gerard Ford, Pardoning Richard Nixon, September 8, 1974, http://www.historyplace.com/speeches/ford.htm.
[113] Remarks at an Ecumenical Prayer Breakfast in Dallas, Texas, August 23, 1984, http://www.reagan.utexas.edu/archives/speeches/1984/82384a.htm.
[114] Ronald Reagan, Evil Empire Speech, March 8, 1983, http://www.nationalcenter.org/ReaganEvilEmpire1983.html.
[115] Tom Freiling, *Reagan's God and Country* (Ventura, CA: Regal Books, 2000), 180.

[116] John T. Woolley and Gerhard Peters, The American Presidency Project [online], Santa Barbara, CA, http://www.presidency.ucsb.edu/ws/?pid=20677.
[117] John T. Woolley and Gerhard Peters, The American Presidency Project [online], Santa Barbara, CA, http://www.presidency.ucsb.edu/ws/?pid=21350.
[118] John T. Woolley and Gerhard Peters, The American Presidency Project [online], Santa Barbara, CA, http://www.presidency.ucsb.edu/ws/?pid=29646.
[119] Harry S. Truman, Address to the Washington Pilgrimage of American Churchmen, September 28, 1951, http://teachingamericanhistory.org/library/index.asp?document=1457.
[120] *Van Orden v. Perry*. 545 U.S. 677. U.S.Sup. Ct. **2005**, http://caselaw.lp.findlaw.com/scripts/getcase.pl?court=US&vol=000&invol=03-1500.
[121] Carrie Devorah, "God in the Temples of Government-Photo Essay," November 24, 2003, http://www.freerepublic.com/focus/f-news/1028864/posts.
[122] Available at http://www.quotesdaddy.com/quote/280806/Winston+Churchill/the-farther-back-you-can-look-the-farther-forward.

Chapter 3

[123] Available at http://thinkexist.com/quotation/a_lie_told_often_enough_becomes/195640.html.
[124] Available at http://quotes.liberty-tree.ca/quote/benjamin_franklin_quote_72bd.
[125] The Collected Works of Abraham Lincoln, Vol. 7 (New York: Wolfe Book Manufacturing Company, 1953), 542.
[126] Bob Smietana, "Wilson schools agree to ban handout of Bibles," The Tennessean, January 6, 2010, http://www.tennessean.com/article/20100106/NEWS01/1060377/1001/NEWS.
[127] "Bible Ban Overturned by School Board for Religious Freedom Day," Christianlawjournal.com, November 4, 2010,

http://www.christianlawjournal.com/news/bible-ban-overturned-by-school-board-for-religious-freedom-day/.
[128] The Oyez Project, Engel v. Vitale, 370 U.S. 421 (1962), http://oyez.org/cases/1960-1969/1961/1961_468.
[129] John C. Rives, Abridgment of the Debates of Congress from 1789 to 1856 (New York: D. Appleton & Company, 1857), 148.
[130] "Thomas More Law Center Ensures Right Of Third-Grade Student To Read Bible In Public School," July 23, 2007, http://www.thomasmore.org/qry/page.taf?id=19&_function=detail&sbtblct_uid1=3.
[131] Ibid.
[132] William J. Federer, America's God and Country: Encyclopedia of Quotations (St. Louis: Amerisearch, Inc., 2000), 551.
[133] "Student Sues Wisconsin School after Getting a Zero for Religious Drawing," FOXNews.com, April 1, 2008, http://www.foxnews.com/story/0,2933,344350,00.html.
[134] Congress Declares Bible "The Word of God," Pub. L. no. 97-280, 96 Stat 1211 (1982), http://www.usavsus.info/USAvsUS-BIBLE.htm.
[135] "Valedictorian Barred from Giving Speech Because of References to 'God' Files Suit," May 5, 2009, http://www.lifesitenews.com/ldn/2009/may/09050507.html.
[136] Ibid.
[137] The Oyez Project, *Lee v. Weisman*, 505 U.S. 577 (1992), http://oyez.org/cases/1990-1999/1991/1991_90_1014.
[138] John T. Woolley and Gerhard Peters, The American Presidency Project [online]. Santa Barbara, CA, http://www.presidency.ucsb.edu/ws/?pid=21139.
[139] Aitchison, Gavin, "It's okay to shoplift' says Father Tim Jones, parish priest of St Lawrence and St Hilda," December 21, 2009, http://www.yorkpress.co.uk/news/4813836._It___s_okay_to_shoplift__says_York_priest/.
[140] The Associated Press, "Ten Commandments plaque ordered out of Pennsylvania courthouse," March 7, 2002, http://www.mediastudies.org/templates/document.asp?documentID=15834&printerfriendly=1.

[141] John Adams, The Political Writings of John Adams, Ed. George A. Peek Jr., (Indianapolis, IN: Hackett Publishing Company, Inc., 2003), 148.
[142] "Ten Commandments monument moved," Cnn.com, November 14, 2003, http://www.cnn.com/2003/LAW/08/27/ten.commandments/.
[143] Judge Andrew Napolitano, Constitution in Exile (Nashville, TN: Thomas Nelson, Inc., 2006), 28.
[144] Warren Richey, "Supreme Court lets stand order to remove Ten Commandments monument," The Christian Science Monitor, March 1, 2010, http://www.csmonitor.com/USA/Justice/2010/0301/Supreme-Court-lets-stand-order-to-remove-Ten-Commandments-monument.
[145] Available at http://teachingamericanhistory.org/library/index.asp?document=323.
[146] The Associated Press, "'Under God' stays in pledge, 'In God We Trust' on currency," March 11, 2010, http://www.gosanangelo.com/news/2010/mar/11/under-god-stays-in-pledge-in-god-we-trust-on/.
[147] Rick Warren, Purpose Driven Life (Grand Rapids, MI: Zondervan, 2002), 18.
[148] Abbe Smith, "New Haven high school diplomas drop phrase 'in the year of our Lord'," New Haven Register, June 23, 2010, http://www.nhregister.com/articles/2010/06/23/news/new_haven/aa1_nediploma062310.txt?viewmode=fullstory.
[149] "GOP Senator: Not Enough God In Capitol Visitors Center First," The Huffington Post, January 4, 2009, http://www.huffingtonpost.com/2008/12/04/gop-senator-not-enough-go_n_148384.html.
[150] John T. Woolley and Gerhard Peters, The American Presidency Project [online], Santa Barbara, CA, http://www.presidency.ucsb.edu/ws/?pid=43384.
[151] Leslie Miller, "'No God? No problem!' say humanist group's new holiday ads," USA Today, November 23, 2009, http://content.usatoday.com/communities/Religion/post/2009/

11/no-god-no-problem-say-humanist-groups-new-holiday-ads/1.
[152] Joshua Rhett Miller, "California Official Orders Removal of Christmas Angel After Complaint," FOXNews.com, December 23, 2009, http://www.foxnews.com/us/2009/12/23/california-official-orders-removal-christmas-angel-complaint/.
[153] The Oyez Project, *Allegheny v. ACLU*, 492 U.S. 573 (1989), http://oyez.org/cases/1980-1989/1988/1988_87_2050.
[154] Charles Johnson, "A Calvin Coolidge Christmas Message," Claremont Conservative, December 25, 2009, http://www.claremontconservative.com/2009/12/calvin-coolidge-christmas-message.html.
[155] Adam Parker, "Group Requests Removal of Nativity," The Post and Courier, December 21, 2009, http://www.postandcourier.com/news/2009/dec/21/group-requests-removal-of-nativity/.
[156] Available at http://thinkexist.com/quotation/the_truth_is_incontrovertible-malice_may_attack/220093.html.
[157] The Associated Press, "Patchogue Decides to Re-Christmas its Holiday Parade," November 19, 2009, http://www.longislandpress.com/2009/11/19/patchogue-puts-christmas-back-in-celebration/.
[158] Russell Goldman, "Iowa Town Renames Good Friday to 'Spring Holiday'," ABCNews.com, March 29, 2010, http://abcnews.go.com/US/iowa-town-renames-good-friday/story?id=10233061.
[159] Paul Belien, "Jihad Against Danish Newspaper," The Brussels Journal, October 22, 2005, http://www.brusselsjournal.com/node/382.
[160] Radical Muslim Group Warns 'South Park' Creators," CBS News.com, April 21, 2010, http://www.cbsnews.com/stories/2010/04/21/entertainment/main6419829.shtml.
[161] Timothy George, *Is the Father of Jesus the God of Muhammad?* (Grand Rapids, MI: Zondervan, 2002), 75.
[162] Allied Media Corp., Muslims American Demographic Facts, http://www.allied-media.com/AM/.

[163] Associated Press, "More mosques being built in Houston area," Khou.com, November 16, 2010, http://www.khou.com/news/More-mosques-being-built-in-Houston-area-108441614.html.
[164] "Study: 3 in 4 U.S. mosques preach anti-West extremism." WorldNetDaily. February 23, 2008. http://www.wnd.com/index.php?fa=PAGE.view&pageId=57141.
[165] Iran: Convert Stabbed to Death, Compass Direct, November 28, 2005, http://www.adme.ws/Press-Reports/compass-11-28-05.pdf.
[166] Ibid.
[167] Ibid.
[168] Saudi Christian Convert Arrested and Jailed," Asia News, December 17, 2004, http://www.asianews.it/news-en/Saudi-Christian-convert-arrested-and-jailed-2134.html.
[169] Ibid.
[170] Mounir Bishay, "The Copts: Persecuted Christians of Egypt," May 6, 2009, http://www.catholic.org/international/international_story.php?id=33483.
[171] John Couwels, "Muslim teen fears for life after changing religion," Cnn.com, September 3, 2009, http://www.cnn.com/2009/CRIME/09/03/muslim.convert/.
[172] U.S. Army Training and Doctrine Command, A Military Guide to Terrorism in the Twenty-first Century (Ft. Leavenworth, Kansas, 2007), 5-4.

Chapter 4

[173] Available at http://thinkexist.com/quotation/there_is_no_doubt_that_it_is_around_the_family/161333.html.
[174] Available at http://thinkexist.com/quotation/the_strength_of_a_nation_derives_from_the/147461.html.

[175] John T. Woolley and Gerhard Peters, The American Presidency Project [online], Santa Barbara, CA., http://www.presidency.ucsb.edu/ws/?pid=1792.
[176] U.S. Divorce Statistics, DivorceMagazine.com, http://divorcemag.com/statistics/statsUS2002.shtml.
[177] Americans for Divorce Reform, "Divorce statistics collection: Summary of findings so far," http://www.divorcereform.org/.
[178] World Divorce Statistics, DivorceMagazine.com, http://www.divorcemag.com/statistics/statsWorld.shtml.
[179] "Marriage Breakdown Costs Taxpayers at Least $112 Billion a Year," http://americanvalues.org/coff/pressrelease.pdf.
[180] Ibid.
[181] Divorce Rate- U.S.A., AboutDivorce.org, http://www.aboutdivorce.org/us_divorce_rates.html.
[182] Lydia Saad, "Cultural Tolerance for Divorce Grows to 70%," Gallup.com, May 19, 2008, http://www.gallup.com/poll/107380/cultural-tolerance-divorce-grows-70.aspx.
[183] Ibid.
[184] Stephen Baskerville, "The No-Blame Game: Why No-fault Divorce is Our Most Dangerous Social Experiment," Crisismagazine.com, March 2005, http://www.crisismagazine.com/march2005/baskerville.htm.
[185] Laurie Beth Jones, *Jesus, CEO* (New York: Hyperion, 1992), 219.
[186] Institute for American Values, The Marriage Movement: A Statement of Principles, (2000), 8.
[187] Joseph Hopper, "The Symbolic Origins of Conflict in Divorce," Journal of Marriage and Family, Vol. 63, No. 2, (May 2001), 433.
[188] Available at http://www.quotedb.com/quotes/1482.
[189] John Gray, *Men are from Mars and Women are from Venus* (New York: HarperCollins Publishers, Inc., 1992), 2.
[190] Patrick Fagan and Robert Rector, "The Effects of Divorce on America," The Heritage Foundation, June 5, 2000, http://www.heritage.org/Research/Reports/2000/06/The-Effects-of-Divorce-on-America.

[191] Paul R. Amato, "Children's Adjustment to Divorce: Theories, Hypotheses, and Empirical Support," Journal of Marriage and Family, Vol. 55, No. 1, (Feb. 1993), 30.
[192] Kim Leon, "Risk and Protective Factors in Young Children's Adjustment to Parental Divorce: A Review of the Research," Family Relations, Vol. 52, No. 3, (Jul. 2003), 264.
[193] Paul R. Amato and Alan Booth, *A Generation at Risk: Growing Up in an Era of Family Upheaval* (Cambridge, MA: Harvard University Press, 1997), 115.
[194] Paul R. Amato and Jacob Cheadle, "The Long Reach of Divorce and Child Well-Being across three generations," Journal of Marriage and Family, Vol. 67, No. 1, (Feb. 2005), 193.
[195] Jane Lewis, *The End of Marriage? Individualism and Intimate Relations* (Northampton, MA: Edward Edgar Publishing, Inc., 2001), 13.
[196] Tara Parker-Pope, "Is Marriage Good for Your Health?" *The New York Times*, April 12, 2010, http://www.nytimes.com/2010/04/18/magazine/18marriage-t.html?pagewanted=all.
[197] Richard Rogers, "Marriage, Sex, and Mortality," Journal of Marriage and Family, Vol. 57, No. 2, (May 1995), 515.
[198] Carmine Sarracino and Kevin M. Scott, *The Porning of America: The Rise of Porn Culture, What it Means, and Where We Go from Here* (Boston, MA; Beacon Press Books, 2008), x.
[199] Frank Rich, "Naked Capitalists: There's No Business Like Porn Business," New York Times, May 20, 2001, http://www.nytimes.com/2001/05/20/magazine/20PORN.html.
[200] Industry Overview: Professional Sports Teams and Organizations, http://www.hoovers.com/professional-sports-teams-and-organizations/--ID__315--/free-ind-fr-profile-basic.xhtml.
[201] Jon Schwartz, "Online porn often leads high-tech way," USA Today, March 9, 2004, http://www.usatoday.com/money/industries/technology/2004-03-09-onlineporn_x.htm.

[202] Pamela Paul, *Pornified: How Pornography is Transforming Our Lives, Our Relationships, and Our Families* (New York: Henry Holt and Company, LLC, 2005), 8.
[203] Sandra Leiblum and Nicola Doring, "Internet Sexuality: Known Risks and Fresh Chances for Women," Ed. Alice Cooper, Sex & the Internet: A Guide Book for Clinicians (New York: Brunner-Routledge, 2002), 29.
[204] Joe Beam, "Pornography's Devastating Effects on Marriage," Crosswalk.com, http://www.crosswalk.com/marriage/11608263/.
[205] Pamela Paul, "The Porn Factor," Time Online, January 19, 2004, http://www.time.com/time/2004/sex/article/the_porn_factor_in_the_01a.html.
[206] Sharon Jayson, "More view cohabitation as acceptable choice," *USA Today*, June 9, 2008, http://www.usatoday.com/news/nation/2008-06-08-cohabitation-study_N.htm.
[207] Joselin Linder and Elena Donovan Mauer, *Good Girl's Guide to Living in Sin: The New Rules for Moving In with Your Man* (Avon, MA: Adams Media, 2008), 4.
[208] Ibid.
[209] Linda J. Waite, "The Negative Effects of Cohabitation," The Responsive Community, Vol. 10, No. 1, (Winter 1999/2000), 32.
[210] Ibid.
[211] John R. Hill, Ph.d. and Sharon G Evans, "Effects of Cohabitation Length on Personal and Relational Well Being," August 3, 2006, Alabama Policy Institute.
[212] Linda J. Waite, 37.
[213] Alan J. Hawkins, Steven L. Nock, Julia C. Wilson, Laura Sanchez, and James D. Wright, "Attitudes about Covenant Marriage and Divorce: Policy Implications from a Three-State Comparison," Family Relations, Vol. 51, No. 2, (Apr. 2002), 166.

Chapter 5

[214] Confucianism - Confucian Family Teaching, http://family.jrank.org/pages/319/Confucianism-Confucian-Family-Teaching.html.
[215] Thomas Jefferson Quotes and Quotations, http://www.famousquotesandauthors.com/authors/thomas_jefferson_quotes.html.
[216] John T. Woolley and Gerhard Peters, The American Presidency Project [online]. Santa Barbara, CA, http://www.presidency.ucsb.edu/ws/?pid=69681.
[217] Dr. James C. Dobson, *Parenting Isn't for Cowards* (Dallas: Word Publishing, 1987), 1.
[218] Mary W. Hicks and Joyce W. Williams, "Current Challenges in Educating for Parenthood," *Family Relations,* Vol. 30, No. 4, (Oct. 1981), 580.
[219] Candyce Smith Russell, "Transition to Parenthood: Problems and Gratifications," *Journal of Marriage and Family,* Vol. 36, No. 2, (May 1974), 298.
[220] Available at http://www.brainyquote.com/quotes/quotes/a/abrahamlin133687.html.
[221] Available at http://www.drmartinlutherkingjr.com/thepurposeofeducation.htm.
[222] David Barton, *America: To Pray or Not to Pray? (*Aledo, TX: Wall Builder Press, 1988), 6.
[223] U.S. Department of Education, National Center for Education Statistics, *A Brief Profile of America's Private Schools*, NCES 2003–417, Project Officer: Barbara Holton, Washington, DC: 2003.
[224] Council for American Private Education, "New Government Report on Private Schools," http://www.capenet.org/Outlook/Out6-02.html.
[225] Ibid.
[226] Ibid.
[227] Elizabeth Donohue, Vincent Schiraldi, and Jason Ziedenberg, (1998), "School House Hype: School shootings

and the real risks kids face in America," Washington DC: The Justice Policy Institute.

[228] Miller, A.M. (2003). Violence in U.S. Public Schools: 2000 School Survey on Crime and Safety, NCES 2004–314 REVISED, U.S. Department of Education, National Center for Education Statistics, Washington, DC: U.S. Government Printing Office.

[229] National School Safety Center, *School Safety Statistics*, (December 2006), http://www.schoolsafety.us/pubfiles/school_crime_and_violence_statistics.pdf.

[230] Office of National Drug Control Policy, (2002, October), "Fact Sheet: Drug Use Trends," http://www.whitehousedrugpolicy.gov/publications/factsht/druguse/drugusetrends.pdf.

[231] Ibid.

[232] Salynn Boyles, (2007, April 16), "Parents Blind to Rising School Drug Use," http://www.webmd.com/parenting/news/20070816/parents-blind-to-rising-school-drug-use.

[233] Ibid.

[234] American Foundation for Suicide Prevention, Facts and Figures, http://www.afsp.org/index.cfm?fuseaction=home.viewpage&page_id=050FEA9F-B064-4092-B1135C3A70DE1FDA.

[235] Ibid.

[236] Abma JC, Martinez, GM, Mosher, WD., Dawson, BS. *Teenagers in the United States: Sexual activity, contraceptive use, and childbearing*, 2002. National Center for Health Statistics. Vital Health Stat 23(24). 2004.

[237] Ibid.

[238] Ibid.

[239] Guttmacher Institute, *U.S. Teenage Pregnancies, Births and Abortions: National and State Trends and Trends by Race and Ethnicity*, January 2010.

[240] Guttmacher Institute, Facts on American Teens' Sexual and Reproductive Health Inbrief, January 2010, http://www.guttmacher.org/pubs/FB-ATSRH.pdf.

[241] Ibid.

[242] Alliance for Excellent Education, Fact Sheet: How does the United States Stack Up? International Comparisons of Academic Achievement, March 2008, http://www.all4ed.org/files/IntlComp_FactSheet.pdf.
[243] Ibid.
[244] Ibid.
[245] Office of Budget and Management, http://www.whitehouse.gov/omb/fy2010_department_education/.
[246] Cara Matthews, "New York public schools top nation in per-student spending," *USA Today,* June 29, 2010, http://www.usatoday.com/news/education/2010-06-29-school-spending_N.htm.
[247] Ibid.
[248] Daniel de Vise, "U.S. goes from leading to lagging in young college graduates," *Washington Post,* July 22, 2010, http://www.washingtonpost.com/wp-dyn/content/article/2010/07/22/AR2010072201250.html.
[249] Peter Luke, "Gov. Jennifer Granholm endorses new services tax, cutting sales tax to support businesses, schools," February 11, 2010, http://www.mlive.com/politics/index.ssf/2010/02/gov_jennifer_granholm_endorses.html.
[250] Ibid.
[251] Michigan In-Brief: Taxes on Consumers, http://www.michiganinbrief.org/edition07/Chapter5/TaxesonCons.htm.
[252] Greg Toppo, "Good grades pay off literally," *USA Today,* August 1, 2008, http://www.usatoday.com/news/education/2008-01-27-grades_N.htm.
[253] Ibid.
[254] David Barton, "Revisionism: How to Identify it in Your Children's Textbooks," January 2005, http://www.wallbuilders.com/libissuesarticles.asp?id=112.
[255] David Scott, "Conservatives win textbook battle," May 19, 2010, http://www.kxan.com/dpp/news/education/Conservatives-win-textbook-battle.

[256] Chinese Proverbs, http://oaks.nvg.org/chinese-proverbs.html.
[257] Elizabeth Landau, "Spanking detrimental to children, study says," September 16, 2009, http://www.cnn.com/2009/HEALTH/09/16/spanking.children.parenting/index.html.
[258] Study: Spanked Children May Grow Up to Be Happier, More Successful," January 4, 2010, http://www.foxnews.com/story/0,2933,581882,00.html.

Chapter 6

[259] Andrew Cherlin, "The Deinstitution of American Marriage," *Journal of Marriage and Family*, Vol. 66, No. 4, (Nov., 2004), 850.
[260] Sam Schulman, "The Worst Thing About Gay Marriage," *Weekly Standard,* Vol. 14, No. 35, June 1, 2009, http://www.weeklystandard.com/Content/Public/Articles/000/000/016/533narty.asp.
[260] International Gay and Lesbian Association, (2006, November), *LGBT World Legal Wrap Up Survey*, http://typo3.lsvd.de/fileadmin/pics/Dokumente/Homosexualitaet/World_legal_wrap_up_survey._November2006.pdf.
[260] Ibid.
[260] Traditional Values Coalition, "Homosexuality 101: A Primer," http://www.traditionalvalues.org/pdf_files/Homosexuality101.pdf.
[261] Billy Graham, *Peace with God* (W. Publishing Group, 1984), 140.
[262] Karlyn Bowman, "Gay Marriage and Public Opinion," April 27, 2009, http://www.forbes.com/2009/04/24/gay-marriage-civil-union-homosexuality-opinions-columnists-legal.html.
[263] International Gay and Lesbian Association, (2006, November), LGBT World Legal Wrap Up Survey, http://typo3.lsvd.de/fileadmin/pics/Dokumente/Homosexualitaet/World_legal_wrap_up_survey._November2006.pdf

[264] Ibid.
[265] Traditional Values Coalition, "Homosexuality 101: A Primer," http://www.traditionalvalues.org/pdf_files/Homosexuality101.pdf.
[266] Bob Unruh, "Judge orders 'gay' agenda taught to Christian children," February 24, 2007, http://www.wnd.com/?pageId=40339.
[267] Available at http://www.glsen.org/cgi-bin/iowa/all/about/history/index.html.
[268] Maxim Lott, "Critics Assail Obama's 'Safe Schools' Czar, Say He's Wrong Man for the Job," FOXNews.com, September 23, 2009, http://www.foxnews.com/politics/2009/09/23/critics-assail-obamas-safe-schools-czar-say-hes-wrong-man-job/.
[269] California Proposition 8 (2008), http://ballotpedia.org/wiki/index.php/California_Proposition_8_(2008).
[270] Ron Paul, "Protecting Marriage from Judicial Tyranny," July 22, 2004, http://www.lewrockwell.com/paul/paul197.html.
[271] Phillip Matier and Andrew Ross, "Judge being gay a nonissue during Prop. 8 trial," February 7, 2010, http://articles.sfgate.com/2010-02-07/bay-area/17848482_1_same-sex-marriage-sexual-orientation-judge-walker.
[272] Aubry D'Arminio, "Gay Teens on TV: A Timeline," EW.com, http://www.ew.com/ew/gallery/0,,20460138,00.html.
[273] Nielsen Company, Television, Internet and Mobile Usage in the U.S., (4th Quarter 2008), http://i.cdn.turner.com/cnn/2009/images/02/24/screen.press.b.pdf.
[274] "Parents spend more time watching TV than talking to their children," February 9, 2007, http://www.dailymail.co.uk/news/article-435201/Parents-spend-time-watching-TV-talking-children.html.
[275] Sarah McBride, "Cinema Surpassed DVD Sales in 2009," January 4, 2010,

http://online.wsj.com/article/NA_WSJ_PUB:SB10001424052
748704789404574636531903626624.html.

[276] Nicole Winfield, "Pope Declares Abortion and Same-Sex Marriage Most 'Insidious and Dangerous' Threats Facing the World," May 13, 2010, http://www.cnsnews.com/news/article/65872.

[277] Malcolm Moore, "Decadent world is in the grip of Satan, says Pope," April 15, 2006, http://www.telegraph.co.uk/news/worldnews/europe/italy/1515841/Decadent-world-is-in-the-grip-of-Satan-says-Pope.html.

[278] Sen. Bill Frist, "We Must Preserve Traditional Marriage," June 2, 2006, http://www.humanevents.com/article.php?id=15312.

[279] David Freelander, "Nader to Reintroduce DOMA Repeal," *The New York Observer*, February 24, 2011, http://www.observer.com/2011/politics/nadler-reintroduce-doma-repeal.

[280] Respect for Marriage Act, http://www.hrc.org/13530.htm.

[281] Jeremy W. Peters, "New York State Senate Votes Down Gay Marriage Bill," The New York Times, December 2, 2009, http://www.nytimes.com/2009/12/03/nyregion/03marriage.html.

[282] David Kocieniewski, "New Jersey Senate Defeats Gay Marriage Bill," The New York Times, January 7, 2010, http://www.nytimes.com/2010/01/08/nyregion/08trenton.html.

[283] Center for Disease Control, CDC Fact Sheet: HIV and AIDS among Gay and Bisexual Men, http://www.cdc.gov/nchhstp/newsroom/docs/FastFacts-MSM-FINAL508COMP.pdf.

[284] Ibid.

Chapter 7

[285] Available at http://en.thinkexist.com/quotation/accountability_breeds_response-ability/297755.html.

[286] Holocaust Survivors, Holocuastsurvivors.org, http://www.holocaustsurvivors.org/survivors.php.

[287] Lawrence N. Powell, "The Holocaust and History: Introduction to the Survivor's Stories," Holocuastsurvivors.org, http://www.holocaustsurvivors.org/data.show.php?di=record&da=texts&ke=6.
[288] Available at http://www.quotationspage.com/quotes/Edmund_Burke/.
[289] White House, National Strategy for Combating Terrorism (Washington, DC: Government Printing Office) September 2006, 1.
[290] Mark Juergensmeyer, *Terror in the Mind of God: The Global Rise of Religious Violence* (Los Angeles: University of California Press, 2000), 5.
[291] White House, *The Federal Response to Hurricane Katrina: Lessons Learned* (Washington, DC: Government Printing Office), September 2006, 5.
[292] Ibid, 3.
[293] "John McCain on Confronting Evil at the Values Voters Summit," http://berkleycenter.georgetown.edu/resources/show?c=Quote&r=john-mccain-on-confronting-evil-at-the-values-voters-summit.
[294] Available at http://www.youtube.com/watch?v=FcSm-KAEFFA.
[295] Available at http://quotes.liberty-tree.ca/quote/booker_t._washington_quote_4050.
[296] Andrienne S. Gaines, "Former KKK Leader Ordained in Black Pentecostal Denomination," Charismamag.com, December 3, 2009, http://elev8.com/daily-offerings/news/elev8-staff/former-kkk-leader-ordained-in-black-denomination/.
[297] Ibid.
[298] Available at http://thinkexist.com/quotation/all_of_us_who_professionally_use_the_mass_media/226984.html.
[299] Lee Hamilton, "The Press is Good, But Not Good Enough," http://www.centeroncongress.org/radio_commentaries/the_press_is_good_but_not_good_enough.php.

[300] "Donald Rumsfeld on Abu Ghraib Reports," http://www.ontheissues.org/Cabinet/Donald_Rumsfeld_Homeland_Security.htm#Abu_Ghraib_Reports.
[301] Brad Wilmouth, "Lt. General Sanchez Slams Media's Iraq Coverage on FNC," NewsBusters.org, MY 21, 2008, http://newsbusters.org/blogs/brad-wilmouth/2008/05/21/ricardo-sanchez-slams-medias-iraq-coverage-fnc.
[302] Paul F. Horvitz, "Clinton Takes Office, Calling for Renewal.'There is nothing wrong with America that cannot be cured by what is right with America.'" *The New York Times,* January 21, 1993, http://www.nytimes.com/1993/01/21/news/21iht-prez.html.
[303] U.S. Department of Veteran Affairs, "How Many American Troops Have Died in War?" July 7, 2007, http://hnn.us/roundup/comments/44965.html.
[304] Ibid.
[305] Ibid.
[306] Ibid.
[307] Available at http://www.defense.gov/news/casualty.pdf.
[308] Ibid.
[309] Arthur C. Brooks, "A Nation of Givers," American.com, March/April 2008, http://www.american.com/archive/2008/march-april-magazine-contents/a-nation-of-givers.
[310] Ibid.
[311] John Stossel, "Are Americans Cheap?" Capitalismmagazine.com, November 29, 2006, http://www.capitalismmagazine.com/politics/welfare/4854-Are-Americans-Cheap.html.
[312] "Haiti Earthquake of 2010," *The New York Times,* October 16, 2010, http://www.nytimes.com/info/haiti-earthquake-2010/.
[313] InterAction, *Haiti Accountability Report: InterAction Members' Use of Private Funds in Response to the Earthquake in Haiti,* July 13, 2010, http://www.reliefweb.int/rw/RWFiles2010.nsf/FilesByRWDocUnidFilename/KHII-87C5MM-full_report.pdf/$File/full_report.pdf

[314] Thomas Heath, "U.S. cellphone users donate $22 million to Haiti earthquake relief via text," *The Washington Post*, January 19, 2010, http://www.washingtonpost.com/wpdyn/content/article/2010/01/18/AR2010011803792.html.
[315] J.R. Nyquist, "Americans who hate America," WorldDailyNet.com, April 10, 2000, http://www.wnd.com/index.php?pageId=6435.

[316] Available at http://quotes.liberty-tree.ca/quote_blog/Marcus.Tullius.Cicero.Quote.B6EA.
[317] Address before the Young Men's Lyceum of Springfield, Illinois, by Abraham Lincoln, January 27, 1838, http://www.constitution.org/lincoln/lyceum.htm.
[318] Zbigniew Brzezinski, *The Grand Chessboard* (New York: Basic Books, 1997), 23.
[319] Robert E. Keohane, "The United States and the Postwar Order: Empire or Hegemony?" *Journal of Peace Research*, Vol. 28, No. 4, November 1991, 435-439.
[320] Geir Lundestad, "Empire by Invitation? The United States and Western Europe, 1945-1952," *Journal of Peace Research*, Vol. 23, No. 3, September 1986, 263-277.
[321] Available at http://www.redstate.com/snarkandboobs/2010/04/14/obama-and-his-administration-lament-americas-superpower-status/.
[322] William Beach & Robert Bluey, "Will Growing Government Debt Undermine the American Dream? The Implications of Mounting Federal Debt and Spending for the Debt-Paying Generation," Heritage.org, September 28, 2010, http://www.heritage.org/research/reports/2010/09/will-growing-government-debt-undermine-the-american-dream.
[323] Terence P. Jeffrey, "Debt Has Increased $5 Trillion since Speaker Pelosi Vowed, 'No New Deficit Spending'," CBSNews.com, October 25, 2010, http://www.cnsnews.com/news/article/debt-has-increased-5-trillion-speaker-pe.
[324] Ibid.
[325] Ibid.

[326] Thomas Jefferson on Politics & Government, http://etext.virginia.edu/jefferson/quotations/jeff1340.htm.
[327] Ibid.
[328] Available at http://www.federalbudget.com/.
[329] Don C. Brunell, "The National Debt: Do You Know How Much You Now Owe?" Olympia Business Watch/Association of Washington Businesses, February 7, 2010, http://www.olympiabusinesswatch.com/2010/02/the-national-debt-do-you-know-how-much-you-now-owe.html.
[330] Kimberly Amadeo, "The U.S. National Debt and How It Got So Big," About.com, June 3, 2010, http://useconomy.about.com/od/fiscalpolicy/p/US_Debt.htm.
[331] "Mullen: Debt is top national security threat," Cnn.com, August 27, 2010, http://articles.cnn.com/2010-08-27/us/debt.security.mullen_1_pentagon-budget-national-debt-michael-mullen?_s=PM:US.
[332] Baohui Zhang, "American Hegemony and China's U.S. Policy," *Asian Perspective,* Vol. 28, No. 3, 2004, 87-113.
[333] Geoff Dyer, Jamil Anderlini and Henny Sender, "China's Lending Hits New Heights," Cnbc.com, January 18, 2011, http://www.cnbc.com/id/41127737/China_s_Lending_Hits_New_Heights.
[334] 2009 Production Statistics, http://www.oica.net/category/production-statistics/.
[335] 1999 Production Statistics, http://oica.net/category/production-statistics/1999-statistics/. Reuben F. Johnson, "China builds its own high-tech military," *The Washington Times,* September 21, 2010, http://www.washingtontimes.com/news/2010/sep/21/china-builds-its-own-high-tech-military/.
[336] Michael Payne, "Unless we rebuild our manufacturing base, America cannot restore prosperity," Online Journal, February 6, 2009, http://onlinejournal.com/artman/publish/article_4327.shtml.
[337] Office of the Secretary of Defense, *Military and Security Developments Involving the People's Republic of China* (Washington, DC: Government Printing Office, 2010), I.
[338] Michael Payne, "Unless we rebuild our manufacturing base, America cannot restore prosperity," Online Journal,

February 6, 2009,
http://onlinejournal.com/artman/publish/article_4327.shtml.
[339] Available at
http://www.youtube.com/watch?v=CC8jAd84VyQ. \
[340] Ibid.
[341] Gillia M. Olson, *Needs and Wants* (Mankato, Minnesota: Capstone Press, 2009), 5-6.
[342] John T. Woolley and Gerhard Peters, The American Presidency Project [online]. Santa Barbara, CA, http://www.presidency.ucsb.edu/ws/?pid=38069.
[343] Michael Tanner, "Three little pigs: How entitlements will destroy us," *The Cyclist Economist,* July 19, 2010, http://thecynicaleconomist.com/?p=15520.
[344] Congressional Budget Office, Office of Management and Budget, http://www.cbo.gov/ftpdocs/108xx/doc10871/AppendixF.shtml.
[345] Lymari Morales, "Americans Disagree on How to Fix Entitlement Programs," Gallup.com, October 15, 2010, http://www.gallup.com/poll/143705/americans-disagree-fix-entitlement-programs.aspx.

[346] Richard Wolf, "Welfare rolls up in '09; more enroll in assistance programs," *USA Today,* January 26, 2010, http://www.usatoday.com/news/nation/2010-01-25-welfare-rolls_N.htm.
[347] "Food-stamp tally nears 40 million, sets record," May 7, 2010, http://news.yahoo.com/s/nm/20100507/ts_nm/us_food_usa_stamps.
[348] Ibid.
[349] Jagdish Bhagwati, *In Defense of Globalization* (New York: Oxford University Press, 2004), 22.
[350] "O'Connor: U.S. must rely on foreign law," WorldNetDaily.com, October 31, 2003, http://www.wnd.com/?pageId=21551.
[351] Associated Press, "Elena Kagan says she reveres military, discusses role of foreign law," Cleveland.com, June 29, 2010, http://www.cleveland.com/nation/index.ssf/2010/06/challenged_by_gop_on_blocking.html.

[352] "Oklahoma "Sharia Law Amendment", State Question 755 (2010)," Ballotpedia.org, http://www.ballotpedia.org/wiki/index.php/Oklahoma_%22Sharia_Law_Amendment%22,_State_Question_755_(2010).
[353] Ibid.
[354] Ibid.
[355] Nihad Awad, "What banning 'Shariah law' means for Oklahoma Muslims," *The Washington Post,* November 6, 2010, http://newsweek.washingtonpost.com/onfaith/guestvoices/2010/11/what_banning_shariah_means_for_oklahoma_muslims.html.
[356] "Multiculturalism has failed, says French president," February 10, 2010, http://news.yahoo.com/s/afp/20110210/wl_afp/francepoliticsimmigrationsociety_20110210231042.
[357] Zell Miller, *A Deficit of Decency* (Macon, GA: Stroud & Hall Publishers, 2005), 149.
[358] Kim R. Holmes, "The Challenges Facing the United Nations Today: An American View," Cfr.org, October 21, 2003, http://www.cfr.org/publication/6451/challenges_facing_the_united_nations_today.html?id=6451.
[359] Stefan Halper, "A Miasma of Corruption: The United Nations at 50," Cato.org, April 30, 1996, http://www.cato.org/pubs/pas/pa-253.html.
[360] "American Flag Shirts Spark Uproar at CA School," CBN.com, May 8, 2010, http://www.cbn.com/cbnnews/us/2010/May/American-Flag-Shirts-Spark-Uproar-at-CA-School/.
[361] Elissa Harrington, "School Makes Boy Take American Flag off Bike," November 12, 2010, http://www.fox40.com/news/headlines/ktxl-americanflagbike11122010,0,3045879.htmlstory.
[362] Joshua Rhett Miller, "Congressman Derided for Laughing at Suggestion to Recite the Pledge of Allegiance," FoxNews.com, February 23, 2010, http://www.foxnews.com/politics/2010/02/23/gc-congressman-laughs-pledge-allegiance-suggestion/.

Chapter 8

[363] General George S. Patton Quotes, http://www.military-quotes.com/Patton.htm.

[364] Oren Harari, *The Leadership Secrets of Colin Powell* (New York: McGraw-Hill, 2002), 79.

[365] Available at http://www.quotesstar.com/quotes/t/the-key-to-successful-leadership-139078.html.

[366] Russel Honore, *Survival: How a Culture of Preparedness Can Save You and Your Family from Disaster* (New York: Simon & Schuster, Inc., 2009), 235.

[367] Available at http://www.youtube.com/watch?v=QVBY_SqzJtI.

[368] Stephen Fink, *Crisis Management: Planning for the Inevitable* (Lincoln: iUniverse, Inc., 2002), 112.

[369] Greg Brenneman, Right Away and All at Once: How We Saved Continental, In *Harvard Business Review on Crisis Management* (pp. 87-118), 2000, (Boston: Harvard Business School Publishing).

[370] Sandi Sonnefeld, Media Policy- What media policy? In *Harvard Business Review on Crisis Management* (pp. 119-142), 2000, (Boston: Harvard Business School Publishing).

[371] Norman R. Augustine, Managing the Crisis You Tried to Prevent, In *Harvard Business Review on Crisis Management* (pp. 1-32), 2000, (Boston: Harvard Business School Publishing).

[372] Daren Fonda & Rita Healy, "How Reliable is Brown's Resume?" *Time*, September 8, 2005, http://www.time.com/time/nation/article/0,8599,1103003,00.html.

[373] Michael O'Loughlin, "Newt Gingrich, Hypocrite," Americamagazine.org, August 13, 2010, http://www.americamagazine.org/blog/entry.cfm?entry_id=3179.

[374] Available at http://thinkexist.com/quotation/the_actions_of_men_are_the_best_interpreters_of/11241.html.

[375] Aaron Sauer, "Charles Spurgeon on Humility," February 3, 2009, http://beforefoundation.com/2009/02/charles-spurgeon-on-humilty/.
[376] Rudolph W. Giuliani, *Leadership* (New York: Miramax Books, 2002), xii.
[377] Stephen Fink, *Crisis Management: Planning for the Inevitable* (Lincoln: iUniverse, Inc., 2002), 80.
[378] "Congress Approval Rating at lowest since the 70s at 11%," http://politisite.com/2010/07/22/congress-approval-rating-at-lowest-since-the-70s-at-11/.
[379] Peter Roff, "Pelosi: Pass Health Reform So You Can Find Out What's In It," *U.S. News,* March 9, 2010, http://politics.usnews.com/opinion/blogs/peter-roff/2010/03/09/pelosi-pass-health-reform-so-you-can-find-out-whats-in-it.html.
[380] Lou Cannon, *Governor Reagan: His Rise to Power* (Cambridge: Perseus Books Group, 2003), 114.
[381] Lee H. Hamilton, *How Congress Works and Why You Should Care,* 2004, (Bloomington: Indiana University Press).
[382] Available at http://thinkexist.com/quotes/woodrow_t._wilson/2.html.
[383] David Hunt, *On the Hunt* (New York: Three Rivers Press, 2007), 128.
[384] John Kotter, *A Sense of Urgency* (Boston: Harvard Business Press, 2008), 169.
[385] Carrie Sheffield, "Why Tea Party has staying power," *USA Today,* November 24, 2010, http://www.usatoday.com/news/opinion/forum/2010-11-24-column24_ST1_N.htm.
[386] Chris Cillizza, "Election 2010: Republicans net 60 House seats, 6 Senate seats and 7 governorships," *The Washington Post,* November 3, 2010, http://voices.washingtonpost.com/thefix/morning-fix/2010-election-republican-score.html.
[387] Claire Suddath, "Senator- Elect Scott Brown," *Time,* January 19, 2010, http://www.time.com/time/nation/article/0,8599,1954918,00.html.

[388] Frank Ahrens, "Capitalism In Question: Can 'Only Government' Save the Economy, As Obama Says?" *National Review,* January 12, 2009, http://www.nationalreview.com/articles/226659/how-big-government-i-i-obama/larry-kudlow

[389] Available at http://www.brainyquote.com/quotes/authors/a/alexis_de_tocqueville.html.

[390] Metropolitan Area Employment and Unemployment Summary, December 7, 2010, http://www.bls.gov/news.release/metro.nr0.htm.

[391] Detroit, Michigan (MI) Poverty Rate Data - Information about poor and low income residents, http://www.city-data.com/poverty/poverty-Detroit-Michigan.html.

[392] Available at http://thinkexist.com/quotation/socialism_is_a_philosophy_of_failure-the_creed_of/220380.html.

[393] Stephen Dinan, "U.S. sets $223B deficit record," *The Washington Times,* March 7, 2011, http://www.washingtontimes.com/news/2011/mar/7/government-posts-biggest-monthly-deficit-ever/.

[394] Congressional Budget Office, Long-Term Budget Outlook, June 2010, http://www.cbo.gov/ftpdocs/115xx/doc11579/06-30-LTBO.pdf (July 22, 2010).

[395] David A. Patten, "GOP Slams 6,000 Earmarks in Trillion-Dollar Omnibus Spending Bill," Newsmax.com, December 15, 2010, http://www.newsmax.com/Headline/gop-omnibus-spending-earmarks/2010/12/15/id/380064.

[396] Patrick Goodenough, "From Peanut Research to Pig Waste, Pork-Laden Spending Bill Called a 'Monstrosity'," December 15, 2010, http://www.cnsnews.com/news/article/peanut-research-pig-waste-pork-laden-spe.

[397] Ibid.

[398] Senator McCain Rails against Earmarks on Senate Floor, Praises TAE, December 16, 2010, http://endingspending.com/blog/2010/12/16/senator-mccain-rails-against-earmarks-on-senate-floor-praises-tae/.

[399] 2010 Exit Polls: What happened Election Night, http://www.npr.org/templates/story/story.php?storyId=131065423.
[400] Ibid.
[401] Ibid.
[402] *A Pledge to America* (Washington, DC: Government Printing Office, 2010), 3.
[403] Ibid.
[404] Available at http://www.johnboehner.house.gov/News/DocumentSingle.aspx?DocumentID=218986.
[405] "Statement on Signing the Immigration Reform and Control Act of 1986," http://www.reagan.utexas.edu/archives/speeches/1986/110686b.htm.
[406] Edwin Meese III, "An Amnesty by Any Other Name ...," *The New York Times,* May 24, 2006, http://www.nytimes.com/2006/05/24/opinion/24meese.html.
[407] Terrence P. Jeffrey, "Gallup Poll: 9 Out of 10 Americans Say Secure the Border This Year," May 5, 2010, http://www.cnsnews.com/node/65293.
[408] Ibid.
[409] James Carafano, Janice Kephart, & Paul Rosenzweig, "The McCain-Kennedy Immigration Reform Bill Falls Short," July 26, 2005, http://www.heritage.org/research/reports/2005/07/the-mccain-kennedy-immigration-reform-bill-falls-short.
[410] Mark Landsbaum, "Amnesty by Any Other Name," FrontPageMagazine.com, June 21, 2005, http://archive.frontpagemag.com/readArticle.aspx?ARTID=8203.
[411] Comprehensive Immigration Reform Act of 2007, http://www.american-immigration-help.com/comprehensive-immigration-reform-act-of-2007.html.
[412] Scott Wong, "Jeff Sessions: DREAM Act needs vetting," Politico. com, December 2, 2010, http://www.politico.com/news/stories/1210/45878.html.

[413] William Gheen, "Dream Act Amnesty Equals the Destruction of America," Alipac.com, December 16, 2010, http://www.alipac.us/article-5946-thread-1-0.html.
[414] Development, Relief and Education for Alien Minors of 2010, H.R. 5281, 111th Cong. (2010).
[415] White House, *National Security Strategy,* May 2010, (Washington: Government Printing Office).

Chapter 9

[416] Available at http://thinkexist.com/quotation/in-this-era-of-political-correctness-some-people/411398.html.
[417] Available at http://www.brainyquote.com/quotes/quotes/d/douglasmac142436.html.
[418] "The Threat of Terrorism Is from Illegal Aliens," *Phyllis Schlafly Report,* 35 (3), October 2001, http://www.eagleforum.org/psr/2001/oct01/psroct01.shtml.
[419] U.S. Customs and Border Protection, Securing America's borders: A salute to America's frontline, April 2005, (Washington: Government Printing Office), http://www.cbp.gov/linkhandler/cgov/newsroom/publications/mission/cbp_securing_borders.ctt/cbp_securing_borders.pdf.
[420] Department of Defense, *National Defense Strategy of the United States of America* (Washington: Government Printing Office, 2005), 2.
[421] Homeland Security Council, *National Strategy for Homeland Security* (Washington: Government Printing Office, 2007), 6.
[422] James Carafano & David Heyman, "DHS 2.0: Rethinking the Department of Homeland Security," The Heritage Foundation, December 13, 2004, http://www.heritage.org/Research/Reports/2004/12/DHS-20-Rethinking-the-Department-of-Homeland-Security.
[423] David Meir-Levi, "Connecting the South American Terror Dots," FrontPageMagazine.com, August 9, 2004, http://archive.frontpagemag.com/readArticle.aspx?ARTID=11889.

[424] United States. Congress. Senate. Current and projected national security threat to the United States: Hearing before the Select Committee on Intelligence, United States Senate, One Hundred Ninth Congress, first session, February 16, 2005, Washington: Government Printing Office, (S. HRG. 109-61), http://intelligence.senate.gov/threats.pdf.
[425] Lisa M. Seghetti, Jennifer Lake, Blas Nunez-Neto, Alison Siskin, K. Larry Storrs, Nathan Brooks, and Stephen Vina, Border security and the Southwest border: Background, legislation, and issues, September 28, 2005, *CRS Report for Congress*. Washington: Congressional Research Service.
[426] Blas Nunez-Neto, Alison Siskin, and Stephen Vina, Border security: Apprehensions of "Other than Mexican Aliens," *CRS Report for Congress*, September 22, 2005, Washington: Congressional Research Review, http://trac.syr.edu/immigration/library/P1.pdf.
[427] David A. Patten, "Arizona Sheriff: Obama 'Undermining' Law on the Border," Newsmax.com, September 16, 2010, http://www.newsmax.com/Headline/babeu-arizona-drug-smuggling/2010/09/16/id/370593.
[428] Blas Nunez-Neto, Alison Siskin, & Stephen Vina.
[429] White House, *National Strategy for Combating Terrorism*, February 2003, (Washington: Government Printing Office).
[430] Office of Homeland Security, *National Strategy for Homeland Security*, July 2002, (Washington: Government Printing Office).
[431] Department of Defense, *Strategy for Homeland Defense and Civil Support* (Washington: Government Printing Office, 2005), 7.
[432] Jane Jamison, "Hezbollah Infiltrating U.S. through Mexico," Uncoverage.net, July 13, 2010, http://www.uncoverage.net/2010/07/hezbollah-infiltrating-u-s-through-mexico/.
[433] Jim Meyers, " Rep. Myrick: Hezbollah Major Threat on Mexican Border," Newsmax.com, July 15, 2010, http://www.newsmax.com/InsideCover/myrick-hezbollah-mexico-border-terrorism/2010/07/15/id/364796.
[434] Paul J. Smith, "Transnational Terrorism and the al Qaeda Model: Confronting New Realities," *Parameters,* Summer

2002, http://public.gettysburg.edu/~dborock/courses/Spring/intsec/docs/smith-transnational-terror.pdf.

[435] William La Jeunesse, "Iranian Book Celebrating Suicide Bombers Found in Arizona Desert," FOXNews.com, January 27, 2011, http://www.foxnews.com/us/2011/01/27/iranian-book-celebrating-suicide-bombers-arizona-desert/.

[436] Government Accountability Office, Border Security: Enhanced DHS Oversight and Assessment of Interagency Coordination Is Needed for the Northern Border, December 2010, GAO 11-097.

[437] Available at http://candicemiller.house.gov/2011/02/miller-statement-on-challenges-northern-border-security-faces.shtml.

[438] U.S. Customs and Border Protection, Fact sheet: U.S. Customs and Border Protection- Protecting our Southern Border against the Terrorist Threat, August 20, 2004, http://www.america.gov/st/washfileenglish/2004/August/20040823170937GLnesnoM0.2022669.html.

[439] US Census Bureau, *Population Division Working Paper #61, Evaluating Components of International Migration: The Residual Foreign Born*, June 2002, http://immigration.procon.org/sourcefiles/immidoc3.pdf.

[440] Urban Institute, Undocumented Immigrants: Facts and Figures, January 12, 2004, http://immigration.procon.org/sourcefiles/immidoc10.pdf.

[441] Michael Hoefner, Nancy Rytina, and Bryan Baker, "Estimates of the Unauthorized Immigrant Population Residing in the United States: January 2009," Department of Homeland Security, January 2010, http://immigration.procon.org/sourcefiles/Estimates-of-the-Unauthorized-Immigrant-Population-Residing-in-the-United-States-January-2009-Department-of-Homeland-Security.pdf.

[442] Cleopatra Andreadis, "Florida Grandmother, 73, Arrested after Slapping the 18-Year-Old Granddaughter Who Cursed at Her," Abcnews.com, May 13, 2010, http://abcnews.go.com/TheLaw/florida-woman-arrested-slapping-granddaughter-face/story?id=10539757.

[443] Crime Victims of Illegal Aliens, http://www.immigrationshumancost.org/text/crimevictims_2.html

[444] "Widow of Houston Officer Killed by Illegal Immigrant 'Shocked' at ICE Appointment," FoxNews.com, June 25, 2010, http://www.foxnews.com/politics/2010/06/25/widow-houston-officer-killed-illegal-immigrant-shocked-ice-appointment/.

[445] Ibid.

[446] David Sterrett, "Oceanside police arrest second suspect in fatal shooting of officer," December 23, 2006, http://www.freerepublic.com/focus/f-news/1757679/posts.

[447] "Stopping Illegal Immigrant Crime," FOXNews.com, May 12, 2005, http://www.foxnews.com/story/0,2933,156319,00.html.

[448] Dave Gibson, "For these officers killed by illegal aliens, there will never be another Father's Day," June 21, 2009, http://www.examiner.com/crime-in-norfolk/for-these-officers-killed-by-illegal-aliens-there-will-never-be-another-father-s-day.

[449] Ibid.

[450] Ed Barnes, "Cost of Illegal Immigration Rising Rapidly in Arizona, Study Finds," FOXNews.com, May 17, 2010, http://www.foxnews.com/us/2010/05/17/immigration-costs-rising-rapidlty-new-study-says/.

[451] U. S. Constitution, Preamble.

[452] Available at http://www.ihatethemedia.com/los-angeles-immigration-rally-protest-sign.

[453] Available at http://thinkexist.com/quotation/we_can_have_no-allegiance_in_this_country-either/12098.html.

[454] Samuel Huntington, "The Hispanic challenge," *Foreign Policy*, March/April 2004, 30-45.

[455] Michelle Malkin, "How Mexico treats its illegal immigrants," Washingtonexaminer.com, April 29, 2010, http://washingtonexaminer.com/node/93416.

[456] J. Michael Waller, "Mexico's Immigration Law: Let's Try It Here at Home," May 8, 2006, http://www.humanevents.com/article.php?id=14632.

[457] U.S. Constitution, Art. IV, Sec. 4.
[458] Available at http://www.house.mo.gov/content.aspx?info=/bills071/biltxt/truly/HJR0007T.HTM.
[459] Available at http://www.house.mo.gov/billtracking/bills081/biltxt/truly/HB1549T.HTM.
[460] Ibid.
[461] Available at http://www.house.mo.gov/billtracking/bills091/biltxt/truly/HB0390T.HTM.
[462] White House, *National Security Strategy* (Washington, DC: Government Printing Office, 2010), 9.
[463] Lionel Giles, *Sun Tzu on The Art of War: The Oldest Military Treatise in the World,* http://www.chinapage.com/sunzi-e.html#03.
[464] Office of Homeland Security, *National Strategy for Homeland Security* (Washington, DC: Government Printing Office, 2002), 7.
[465] U.S. Army Training and Doctrine Command, *A Military Guide to Terrorism in the Twenty-first Century* (Ft. Leavenworth, Kansas, 2007), 5-2.
[466] Ralph Peters, *Beyond Terror* (Mechanicsburg, PA: Stackpole Books, 2002), 35.
[467] "Ex-CIA Operative Comes Out of the Shadows," CBSNews.com, December 27, 2009, http://www.cbsnews.com/stories/2009/12/23/60minutes/main6014887_page4.shtml?tag=contentMain;contentBody.
[468] Raphael Perl, "Combating Terrorism: The Challenge of Measuring Effectiveness," *CRS Report for Congress,* March 12, 2007.
[469] Martha Crenshaw, "Terrorism, Strategies, and Grand Strategies," *Attacking Terrorism: Elements of a Grand Strategy* (Washington, DC: Georgetown University Press, 2004), 81.
[470] Martha Crenshaw, "Terrorism, Security, and Power," Paper presented at the annual meeting of the American Political Science Association, Boston Marriott Copley Place, Sheraton

Boston & Hynes Convention Center, Boston, Massachusetts, August 28, 2002.
[471] David Plotz, "What Does Osama bin Laden Want?" September 14, 2001, http://www.slate.com/id/115404/.
[472] Homeland Security Council, *National Strategy for Homeland Security* (Washington: Government Printing Office, 2007), 1.
[473] Matthew J. Morgan, "The Origins of the New Terrorism," Parameters, Spring 2004, V. 34, p. 29-43.
[474] James F. Rinehart, *Apocalyptic Faith and Political Violence* (New York: Palgrave MacMillan, 2006), 12.
[475] Shmuel Bar. "The Religious Sources of Islamic Terrorism," *Policy Review*, Vol. 125, p. 27-38.
[476] Department of Homeland Security, Homeland Security Advisory Council, Report of the Future of Terrorism Task Force, January 2007, (Washington, DC: Department of Homeland Security).
[477] U.S. Senate Committee on Homeland Security and Governmental Affairs, Violent Islamist Extremism, The Internet, and the Homegrown Terrorist Threat, May 8, 2008, (Washington DC: Government Printing Office).
[478] Walter Lacquer, "The Terrorism to Come," *Policy Review*, August/September 2004, No. 126, p. 49-65.
[479] White House, *National Strategy for Combating Terrorism* (Washington DC: Government Printing Office, 2006), 6.
[480] David Jeremiah, *What in the World is Going On?* (Nashville: Thomas Nelson, Inc., 2008), 80.
[481] Office of the Director of National Intelligence, *Global Trends 2025: A Transformed World* (Washington DC: Government Printing Office, 2008), 25.
[482] The World Fact Book. Cia.gov. March 23, 2011. https://www.cia.gov/library/publications/the-world-factbook/geos/us.html.
[483] Sun Tzu, *The Art of War,* New Translation by Ralph Sawyer, 1994, (New York: Fall River Press).
[484] Christine Fair & Husain Haqqani, "Think Again: Islamic Terrorism," *Foreign Policy Web Exclusive,* January 2006.

[485] U.S. Army Training and Doctrine Command, *A Military Guide to Terrorism in the Twenty-first Century* (Ft. Leavenworth, Kansas, 2007), 5-4.

[486] Michael Chertoff, "Make No Mistake: This Is War," *The Washington Post,* April 22, 2007, http://www.washingtonpost.com/wp-dyn/content/article/2007/04/20/AR2007042001940.html.

[487] Joanna Sugden, "'Hundreds of al-Qaeda militants planning attacks from Yemen'," Times Online, December 29, 2009, http://www.timesonline.co.uk/tol/news/world/article6970574.ece.

[488] Larry Shaughnessy, "U.S. official: Al Qaeda in Yemen bigger threat than in Pakistan," Cnn.com, December 17, 2010, http://articles.cnn.com/2010-12-17/us/al.qaeda.yemen_1_aqap-al-qaeda-yemen?_s=PM:US.

[489] Richard Esposito and Brian Ross, "Investigators: Northwest Bomb Plot Planned by al Qaeda in Yemen," December 26, 2009, http://abcnews.go.com/Blotter/al-qaeda-yemen-planned-northwest-flight-253-bomb-plot/story?id=9426085.

[490] David Gardner, "Al Qaeda ink cartridge bomb found on Chicago-bound jet linked to mobile phone SIM card, October 30, 2010, http://www.dailymail.co.uk/news/article-1325099/FedEx-UPS-plane-terror-Al-Qaeda-bomb-linked-mobile-phone-SIM-card.html

[491] "Homecoming," *Newsweek,* September 29, 2009, http://www.newsweek.com/2009/09/29/homecoming.html.

[492] "Awlaki: 'The Most Dangerous Man in the World'," November 10, 2010, http://abcnewsradioonline.com/world-news/2010/11/10/awlaki-the-most-dangerous-man-in-the-world.html.

[493] Judith Evans, "Anwar al-Awlaki's online support for Fort Hood gunman Major Hasan," *The Times,* November 10, 2009, http://www.timesonline.co.uk/tol/news/world/us_and_americas/article6910276.ece.

[494] Ralph Peters, "Fort Hood's 9/11," *New York Post,* November 6, 2009, http://www.nypost.com/p/news/opinion/opedcolumnists/item_xjP9yGrJN7gl7zdsJ31vnJ.

[495] Bridget Johnson, "Lieberman wants probe into 'terrorist attack' by major on Fort Hood," TheHill.com, November 8, 2009, http://thehill.com/homenews/senate/66859-lieberman-wants-probe-into-terrorist-attack-on-fort-hood.

[496] "Hasan Called Himself 'Soldier of Allah' on Business Cards," FOXNews.com, November 12, 2009, http://www.foxnews.com/us/2009/11/12/hasan-called-soldier-allah-business-cards/.

[497] Walid Phares, "Ft. Hood: The Largest 'Terror Act' Since 9/11?" FOXNews.com, November 6, 2009, http://www.foxnews.com/opinion/2009/11/06/walid-phares-ft-hood-murder-terror-attack/.

[498] Under Secretary of Defense, DoD Antiterrorism (AT) Program (DoD Directive 2000.12), August 18, 2003, Washington, DC.

[499] Federal Bureau of Investigation, *Terrorism 2002-2005*, (Washington: Government Printing Office), http://www.fbi.gov/stats-services/publications/terrorism-2002-2005/terror02_05.pdf.

[500] Available at http://www.state.gov/s/ct/rls/crt/2000/2419.htm.

[501] Scott Wilson and Spencer S. Hsu, "Video from Times Square may show would-be bomber," *The Washington Post*, May 3, 2010, http://www.washingtonpost.com/wp-dyn/content/article/2010/05/02/AR2010050200470.html.

[502] "Faisal Shahzad's Life in America and Path to Citizenship," WSJ Blogs, May 4, 2010, http://blogs.wsj.com/dispatch/2010/05/04/faisal-shahzads-life-in-america-and-path-to-citizenship/.

[503] Robert Smith, "Faisal Shahzad: 'Nice Guy' Turned Terrorism Suspect," May 5, 2010, Wbur.com, http://www.wbur.org/npr/126522908/faisal-shahzad-nice-guy-turned-terrorism-suspect.

[504] Brian Jenkins, "Basic Principles for Homeland Security," Before the Committee on Appropriations Subcommittee on Homeland Security, RAND Corporation, January 30, 2007.

[505] Monica Crowley, "Jihad by any other name," *The Washington Times*, January 6, 2010,

http://www.washingtontimes.com/news/2010/jan/6/jihad-by-any-other-name/?page=1.
[506] Jennifer Epstein, "Peter King promises hearings on Muslim 'radicalization'," Politico.com, December 20, 2010, http://www.politico.com/news/stories/1210/46612.html.

Author Biography: David Church lives in Arizona with his wife of seven years, Jacqueline Church. As Christians, David and Jacqueline are advocates of God, family, and country.

A native of Auburn, New York and a graduate of the U.S. Military Academy at West Point, David Church has served in the active Army as a Tactical Control Officer with the PATRIOT missile system and he currently serves in the Army National Guard as a military intelligence officer. To complement his professional experience, from both home and abroad, David has earned separate master degrees in the areas of International Relations, Public Administration and Policy, and Homeland Security.

This book was written for the greater glory of God and dedicated to Him.

"Commit to the Lord whatever you do, and your plans will succeed." **Proverbs 16:3** *(NIV)*.

www.ingramcontent.com/pod-product-compliance
Lightning Source LLC
Chambersburg PA
CBHW030300080526
44584CB00012B/387